Introducing Radical Orthodoxy

Introducing Radical Orthodoxy

Mapping a Post-secular Theology

James K. A. Smith

Foreword by John Milbank

Baker Academic
Grand Rapids, Michigan

PATERNOSTER PRESS

© 2004 by James K. A. Smith

Published by Baker Academic
a division of Baker Publishing Group
P.O. Box 6287, Grand Rapids, MI 49516-6287
www.bakeracademic.com

and

Paternoster Press
an imprint of Authentic Media
9 Holdom Avenue, Bletchley, Milton Keyes, MK1 1QR, UK
www.authenticmedia.co.uk/paternoster

Printed in the United States of America

Library of Congress Cataloging-in-Publication Data
Smith, James K. A., 1970–
    Introducing radical orthodoxy : mapping a post-secular theology / James K. A. Smith.
       p.   cm.
    Includes bibliographical references and index.
    ISBN 0-8010-2735-7 (pbk.)
    1. Philosophical theology I. Title.
BT40.S65 2004
230'.046—dc22   2004009029

British Library Cataloguing in Publication Data
A catalogue record for this book is available from the British Library
ISBN 1-84227-350-7

Unless otherwise indicated, Scripture quotations are author's translation.

Scripture quotations identified NASB are from the NEW AMERICAN STANDARD BIBLE ®. Copyright © The Lockman Foundation 1960, 1962, 1963, 1968, 1971, 1972, 1973, 1975, 1977, 1995. Used by permission.

To
Grayson,
whose joy and exuberance invite me
to laugh out loud and sing along

Contents

Foreword

Authors frequently claim that they have been misread—and the world is right to react to this claim with a measure of skepticism. But in the present case, those authors associated with Radical Orthodoxy will surely not be able to register any such protest. Jamie Smith has done us all an immense service by presenting in clear, direct terms the central ideas, diagnoses, and projects associated with this movement.

To my mind this exercise has proved invaluable for four main reasons. First of all, Smith has effectively dispelled the notion that serious ruptures exist within the movement by showing how all the main authors move within the same horizon and operate within the same ethos, which certainly does not spring from the thoughts of one person alone or even three people alone. A certain shared core now emerges more clearly to view, although this is fortunately compatible with many diverging emphases and differences of opinion.

Second, Smith corrects many common caricatures of RO positions—especially regarding the ontology of peace, nihilism, Scotism, the role of philosophy, and the attitude toward modernity. Those wanting fast access to a sense of what RO is all about can safely turn to this volume. This is not to say that there are not some areas where Smith's account could be improved—for example, concerning RO's attitude toward analogy, theology, Platonism, and the doctrine of the fall—but such reservations are inevitable in the face of this sort of exercise. It remains the case that Smith has done a remarkably good job of providing an accessible synthesis.

Third, by simplifying without excessive distortion, Smith helps considerably in moving the debate forward. One might suppose that "a [relatively] popular guide" is mainly about communication and education. To the contrary, the exercise of trying to convey complex ideas in simple terms often helps one to see just what is really being claimed and what is really at stake. In the present case, Smith's synthesis of many different writers articulates a collective RO position in a way not so directly defined hitherto.

In the fourth place, Smith's evangelical-Dooyeweerdian reception of RO tends to bear out RO's claim that it is, indeed, an ecumenical theology that can speak to several different Christian communities. Smith is refreshingly prepared to let the RO perspective correct the one he has inherited, even though of course and quite validly he wishes to put forward his own Reformed correctives to the more generally Catholic perspectives of the main RO authors.

Perhaps what emerges most strongly from this book is the sense of a new theological mood at the outset of the twenty-first century, a mood that includes but extends beyond RO. Smith appropriately describes this as a refusal of dualisms, especially those of nature and grace and of matter and spirit. In the case of the first pair, it seems as if, in retrospect, much twentieth-century theology showed a bias to one pole or the other. A stress on the primacy of nature, the universal, and a neutral philosophy characterized the world of "correlationist" theologies, which to most young scholars today appears now like a bizarre academic twilight zone inhabited by the intellectually craven and impotent. Yet conversely, over-fidesitic theologies, tending to see theology as having its own special, positive domain of concern with belief and salvation, appear now to leave the Christian with too little guidance in other domains and to hand these over to secular authority. This seems especially unsatisfactory in a world in which science, politics, the arts, and social behavior are taking increasingly novel and sometimes bizarre directions. In this situation, the thinking Christian requires a response that is not simply pure (supposed) biblicist condemnation on the one hand nor flaccid accommodation on the other.

What we are seeing, then, is the stepping back of theology into the public domain and a consideration of its relation to the whole of human thought and action. This new mood is not easily characterized as either "liberal" or "neo-orthodox." It rather occupies the domain of what Balthasar called "the suspended middle" between grace-imbued faith and natural understanding. This domain for him and for Henri de Lubac was that of the paradoxical "natural desire for the supernatural." If such a desire affects all human existence, then all human knowledge is subject, under grace, to theological modification and qualification. But equally, if we can only, in this life, weakly understand our orientation to beatitude in terms of its fulfillment of our natures beyond their immediate givenness, then theological exploration never is done with natural, finite human understanding. To put this double point briefly: Our knowledge of things of this world can always be qualified by knowledge of God as he is in himself (given by revelation), but equally, our knowledge of God, since it is analogically mediated, is *always and only* given through a shift in our understanding of the things of this world.

Such an approach implies a synthesis—but always an uneasy and possibly aporetic synthesis—between theology and philosophy (understood as the coordination of all merely natural enquiries). The *nouvelle théologie* nurtured such an approach, which is equally and perhaps more dramatically exhibited in the Russian sophianic tradition, especially Florensky and Bulgakov. It is striking how the representatives of both approaches are now far more widely attended to by the significant younger theologians of today than all the once famous voices of twentieth-century Protestant theology.

Yet here Smith is right to say that the Dutch Calvinist tradition from Kuyper to Dooyeweerd constitutes something of an exception. As he points out, the latter expressed his strong affinities both with Maritain's project of an "integral humanism" (linking nature with grace) and with the *nouvelle théologie*, which he explicitly preferred to Barthianism. This tradition in many ways accentuated the latent catholicity of the Reformed tradition—even though (as Smith sometimes indicates) a full recovery of this catholicity would have to draw also on other resources in the Reformed legacy.

Though this would perhaps come as a surprise to many in Britain, this tradition remains quite powerfully alive in the United States (for example, in the influential "Reformed epistemology" movement associated with Plantinga and Wolterstorff), and it has of course always constituted the main background ideology of InterVarsity Fellowship, a movement that has shown increasing sophistication in recent years.

This tradition has always stressed that every fundamental aspect of human life should be celebrated by Christians, while conversely it should be subject to a transformation under the impact of grace. Clearly, this attitude exhibits much common ground with RO. Smith nonetheless indicates some ways in which the RO perspective might qualify the Kuyperian one, and I would like—beyond Smith—briefly to add to this list.

First of all, RO would not subscribe to the rather ahistoricist and static division of human life into distinct "spheres." For RO, they are more shifting and contingent, and the question of their validity and their boundaries is more uncertain. Kuyper actually far too easily accepted a cordoning-off of certain domains—for example, the economic—which is in fact a modern achievement, with dubious secular presuppositions.

Second, as Smith more than half concedes, Kuyper's understanding of theology was bizarre and inadequate. Theology for RO, as for the best Catholic tradition, is not, as for Kuyper and Dooyeweerd, a specialism. If it were, it would be idolatrous, for theology concerns not one area, not one ontic item among others, but *esse* as such, the ground of all beings, and all in relation to this ground and source. It follows (and this is one point that Smith fails to grasp) that if the Christian contribution to, say, economics, is always a theological contribution, then this is precisely because even the articulation of faith has, in part, to do with the economic realm and the difference faith makes to our consideration of this realm (think of many of the sayings of Jesus). One does not here need overcomplex divisions among types of theology. For Catholic tradition, every Christian is a theologian, because faith is always *somewhat* reflective, albeit in the mode of symbol, ritual, and narrative. There is no such thing as a "pure first order discourse," as the Yale school's somewhat barbaric deployment of Wittgenstein would have us suppose. Conversely, the "second order discourse" of the theologian is no tidily circumscribed exercise (on the Yale school model) but rather more consciously elaborates the existential quest and the perplexity of belief as such. If the former seeks its orientation between God and everything, then so does reflective theology, and in such a manner that it dynamically acts back upon, informs, and qualifies first order belief and practice.

Third, this tradition still cannot quite bring itself to subscribe to the *analogia entis*, with its accompanying ontology of participation. This is shown in Smith's fear that a stress on participation (or an overstress?), while properly insisting on the dependence of creation, will not do justice to its integrity and autonomy on its own level. But to the contrary, it is the case that, so long as Christian theology retained a somewhat Neoplatonic approach to causality, in which every higher level until that of Godhead not only caused but also "gave to be" the lower levels, it was possible to combine the idea that God is "the total cause" of everything, including the free decisions of spiritual beings, with the equal stress that finite causes are also "total" at their own level. Within this outlook, the higher cause is not "one factor" at the lower level; rather, it "gives" in its integrity the entire lower level with its own self-sufficient (in one sense) modes of operation. This Proclean understanding of cause reaches its apogee within Aquinas's Christian translation, for which what is participated is being as such. Hence that which most belongs to a thing—its very existence—is yet that which is most received as a gift. All the same, this giftedness of created being by no means cancels the integrity and the autonomy proper to existence as such. Rather, the point is that even this is a gift. (To be fair to Smith, this point could have been more stressed in TA.)

But by comparison, Leibniz, to whom Smith appeals, does *not* have as strong a doctrine of created integrity, just *because* he has abandoned analogical participation. Hence, the "preestablished harmony" falls within the onto-theological fallacy of imagining that the higher divine cause "competes" with finite causes at the lower level even though this interruptive case operates only at the finite outset and not continuously, as for occasionalism. It violates created integrity by reducing apparent free interaction between creatures to an epiphenomenon.

This is not to deny though that, as Smith contends, much can be learned from Leibniz's incarnational model for the soul/body relation. And, in general, Smith is right to insist that the Christian doctrines of the incarnation of Christ and the general resurrection do indeed suggest an even higher view of matter than that entertained by theurgic Neoplatonism. Here, indeed, matter and body can more ultimately remain because there is a yet stronger sense that all beneath the first cause is in one sense ontologically equal in its dependency. Even though Proclus could fascinatingly see matter in its simplicity as in one sense "closer to" and more directly informed by the One than are intellect and soul (and this may have influenced later Christian christological reflection), it remains the case that a doctrine of creation *ex nihilo* implies more fully a kind of equality of matter. This, however, should not be taken, as it perhaps is by Smith, to mean a *necessity* of matter within the created order. The doctrine of creation led Aquinas to insist that humans were a soul/body unity, but against the Franciscans (whose view is echoed by Leibniz, as Smith mentions), it also led him to insist that angels lacked even subtle bodies, since the state of intellectual being can still be a state of dependent created being, given that the Creator/created ratio is now for Christianity more fundamental than the spirit/body one. If, nevertheless, for Aquinas the soul/body unity of humans possesses some special significance, then this is because it microcosmically reflects the entire span of reality.

Nevertheless, it must be conceded to Smith that he raises an interesting point about the beatific vision. Its pure intuition need not, as he supposes, be thought of as "unmediated," since here the lack of mediation by *species* or by human *verbum* is supplied by a mediation by the divine *Verbum* itself—since we will then be seeing God and ourselves through God alone. All the same, he is right to ask whether this ultimacy of contemplation passes entirely beyond an active donation of images on our part. Should beatitude not also involve a maximum identification with divine creative providing? Should not our final end be theurgic as well as contemplative? Iamblichus, within paganism, thought just this, and perhaps such an outlook survived in Dionysius, even if it was then lost to later Christian tradition. This may very well be an important and valid modification of the received understanding.

Smith, as we have seen, rightly makes central the overcoming of a nature/grace duality. He also rightly insists on an equal overcoming of a spirit/matter duality, stressing again and again the RO idea of the "suspension" of the material. Here the argument is that all reductive materialism must paradoxically ensure that matter "does not matter" and is ultimately evacuated by the void (Bulgakov already put forward a similar view in his *Philosophy of Economy*). Matter can only "matter" if it expresses that which, unlike matter, has its cause in itself, which must be spiritual or trans-spiritual. Smith also rightly highlights an emergent sense in RO (in the wake of Catholic thinkers such as Jean Trouillard and Stanislas Breton) that such a notion was thoroughly explored by Iamblichus, Proclus, and Damascius and then transmitted to Christian tradition through Dionysius the Areopagite, Maximus the Confessor, Eriugena, and later thinkers. For this theurgic tradition, which later informed the Christian sacramental one, it is logically the case that, if the soul is too preoccupied with matter, then matter—which always effects its own return to God, like the sunflower following the sun—can nonetheless help homeopathically to cure the stricken soul. This is part of the reason why, as Smith stresses, sacramentality must be so central for our religious outlook.

It is also part of the reason why, as Smith also stresses, the work of the imagination is not incidental to the work of reason and is never just left behind. Already, without referring to Iamblichus or Proclus, Catherine Pickstock realized that this insight is consummated in the centrality of liturgy. Here, in order to invoke God and in order for God to be first present to us at all, we must imaginatively shape God at the point that is the very consummation of our participation in God's own shaping work. And it is important to insist that all art is paradigmatically liturgy; otherwise it sinks to mere fiction and spectacle and can become a drug, a distraction, or an incitement to sadistic violence. This, in fact, as Smith fails to grasp, is Plato's and then Augustine's point about art and drama. They worry about *fiction*, not about *poiesis* as such, and part of this worry is that whereas the liturgical image *does* revert to the highest source and so in a sense "remains," the fictional "image of an image" is simply cancelled out in favor of an illusory abstract message or private delusory consolation. Hence, there is a suspicion of the stage here that is not at all a suspicion of the image—indeed, it is perhaps the very opposite. One can confirm this point by noting that Balthasar, who had a strange aversion to Proclus and made "drama" not "liturgy" his central category, tends in the end to instrumentalize the "appearing" and "aesthetic" aspect of drama in favor of pure ethical praxis and imageless interpersonal interaction.

This, of course, is not to denigrate, as much as Plato or Augustine did, either fiction or drama. But does not the best drama "redeem" itself as liturgy? Think of Puccini's *Tosca*, in which opera seems to bend back upon its oratorical, liturgical roots: Set in a church, Floria *Tosca's* erotic and justice-seeking pleas against the "spectacle" of misleading clues, treacherous pictorial images corrupted by sexual infidelity, and sadistic enjoyment of the spectacle of torture in the safety of the "off-stage" on the part of the state is at times blended into an actual liturgical and hymnic mode when the characters directly address both God and the audience.

This is the logic of RO's theurgic liturgical turn: It celebrates images but also retains a sense of how images may corrupt. As with our insistence that God causes even freedom, any true Calvinist should surely understand. Also, I would hope, any true Calvinist would appreciate that we tend to have a far more realistic and robustly ontological doctrine of the fall than any other contemporary theologians apart from the Russians. I have always insisted, after St. Paul, that death (in its current form) as well as sin is an intruder upon the original creation and that, after the fall, sinister cosmic forces became (literally) in charge of the world. But to have a doctrine of the fall does not mean to believe that creation is totally corrupted or that it is corrupted in part. In a kind of negative version of the causality of gift, it rather remains entirely perfect—else it would not exist at all—and yet also entirely corrupted through and through. Existentially, we know this. It is not when we learn that the world contains active paedophiles as well as celebrators of the innocence of childhood that we know that the world is fallen. It is rather when we learn, for example, that the author of one of the most remarkable series of fictional celebrations of childhood of all time, the British author William Mayne, was also for a time a systematic sexual abuser of little girls (as has recently been exposed in the English courts) that we know that the world is indeed abysmally fallen. Because then the terrible truth has to be faced that innocence and corruption may in our world lie so close together that the sources of inspiration and the sources of perversion are hard to disentangle.

But the Calvinist view that the world and human intellect are totally depraved violates the equally Calvinist doctrine of the sovereignty and majesty of God, for without God, things do not exist, and what exists shares at least somewhat in God's goodness. Hence, the traditional Catholic view, at which Smith seems to protest, that God *immediately* gives grace to a fallen world (or simply continues to give grace) is an aspect of the view that he went on sustaining creation in being. (For grace was part of the original creation of Adam and is after the fall now doubly required: as the continuing provision of the ultimate human supernatural end and now also to mend fallen nature.) This is no new insistence in my own thought, as Smith indicates, but is found also in TST. Everywhere on earth Christ is typologically foreshadowed, and all are faced with the choice whether to accept or refuse Jesus—as he himself told us. Also, St. Paul is transparently clear that all men at all times *could* have recognized the Creator and so are "without excuse."

In this regard, it would be true to say that Smith stresses just a little more the centrality of specific doctrine and the institutional church than does RO. Here, incidentally, he fails to point out that the *British* members of RO (including myself) are less hostile to the institution of the state *tout court* than are the American ones, even though this is a matter of degree.

But all within RO distance themselves from the pure postmodern emphasis on particularity, even though we thoroughly agree with Smith's own philosophically astute verdict that Derrida in truth ultimately denigrates the particular. For us, rather, the problem is as Alain Badiou has defined it: how to overcome the emptiness of souls divided between an empty market/state universalism on the one hand and purely private arbitrary allegiances on the other. To do so we need to discover a difference that yet has a universal claim and that harmonizes but does not cancel out all other differences. It would seem that Badiou knows in a secular fashion that the name of this concrete universal (as Hegel saw) is Christ. Affirming this in a fully theological mode, RO claims that in the form of Christ we both see and may (in principle) ourselves ecclesially shape and further provide the gift of peace (this is exactly the central theology of Dionysius the Areopagite as well as of Augustine).

Here the utterly specific and remarkable event yet exceeds the merely general conditions of creation that remain somewhat too abstract to command a universal allegiance. As specific, fully identical with positive life as such, as fully and entirely affirming and expressive without any hidden substantive reserve (the Deleuzian echoes here pay homage to Smith), the Christic form is yet without bounds. Increasingly, as Smith surmises (with some needless worry), RO is stressing the generosity and the universality as well as the specificity and the contingency of the Christic gift. If Christianity refuses the conflict of gods, it does not refuse "other gods" (sometimes spoken of by the church fathers as synonymous with angels) intimated by other traditions, simply because these can in no way impinge upon, but rather confirm, the sovereignty of the One God who is one beyond mere oneness and manyness. In a similar fashion, the Christian enterprise of a "universal gift exchange" focused on the specificity of Christ pays a kind of homage to the universal prevalence of gift-exchange economies in all human societies prior to the onset of capitalism, and the Christian fulfillment of theurgy as the descent of God himself in order to provide the true worship of himself impossible to fallen humanity in order to unleash his power of love in the world is able to appreciate and situate all the other "theurgic" attempts to captivate divine power in order to heal finite reality.

Likewise, following the great Russians, RO increasingly insists that the Triune God is the God who in himself brings about the other to God who must also be "created God" (Eriugena). In this case, as the Wisdom literature of the Bible suggests, the gift of God to creation must first be received "psychically" (by angels and whatever psychic powers sustain the entire cosmos in being) and then to a lesser degree by human beings, for since it is a "giving of gift to gift" that establishes being as originally gift without prior non-given supposition, this gift of God must be first of all received also as a further gift of this gift by creation to itself—thereby (as Proclus suggests) establishing the realm of reflective intelligence. This follows, because the subordinate, received intelligence of humans and angels and other psychic powers (unlike the higher divine purely intuitive intelligence) is clearly characterized in this lower degree of understanding by "return to self" (to think, as Aquinas still insisted, is to receive the reflection of things in our minds, including ourselves and our own thinking) and therefore any perfectly reflexive "giving of creation to itself" that must characterize the initial constitution of the creation, ought, it would seem, to coincide with conscious understanding. (The Catholic philosopher Claude Bruaire, following the Proclean reflections of Cusansus and Berulle later echoed by Laberthonnière and Henri de Lubac, has put forward a contention somewhat upon these lines.)

But since "return to self" is not after all quite perfectly reflexive at that point at which it must also seek to be a return to its own higher origin, which is inseparable from its inner selfhood, one can see that self-reflection (as Plotinus already taught) is equally a "failed" attempt (though this failure has the positive value of *apophasis*) at perfect reflection, which in its "failure" constructs the world beneath the psyche and is thereby the "giving" to be of material reality in its diverse modes—even though, for Proclus already, this is the work of higher not human souls, since the latter are rather "fully descended" into the body (and therefore have *their* realm of donation within the realm of the imagination, culture, and history). Notice here also that since the higher divine intellect as pure intuition is already something that "gives" and that this prior cause remains more fundamentally at work even in lower self-reflective intellect, donation as the outworking of self-reflection is still *more primarily* donation, even for Neoplatonism, never mind Christianity. Equally, one must make the qualification that for a Christianized Procleanism the

divine cause, as alone creative of being as such, remains the cause
that is the most powerfully operative even at the lower levels of reality
that are nevertheless in one sense the outworking of psychic reflection
(the work of angelic and astral "influence" invoked by many medieval
theologians)—and so always point upward in their "return" (even for
Aquinas) to spiritual creatures as well as to God.

As was the case for Dionysius, Maximus, Eriugena, and Aquinas,
while it remains true that there is an absolute chasm between Creator
and created, it is nonetheless the case that, if creation is a gift, the hierarchical primacy of self-giving must be reflected (roughly in the sort
of mode just indicated) within the structures of creation itself, as the
Wisdom books of the Bible explain. Else how should we be able to see
that creation is the work of love? But many Calvinists, like Jonathan
Edwards, have been able to recognize something of this sort.

This stress on "communication" within the created order broadens
to include a strong RO emphasis on the idea of a "double descent" of
the Son with the Spirit as an expression of the divine Sophia as identical with the divine essence. The divine work of the incarnate Son in
perfect worship of the Godhead is completed in an active human social
response under the prompting of the Spirit, which also aims to complete
this worship universally (in a non-identically repeated fashion), even if
this must in reality await the eschaton.

Thus, to its emphasis on the *metaxu* (the "between" of analogy) and
methexis (participation), I suspect that RO in the future will increasingly add one on *Sophia, dosis* (gift), and *theurgia* as complementing
theosis.

John Milbank

Acknowledgments

Books—even books that I write—are, for me, gifts: They are the fruit of relationships and are undergirded by the reflections and support of many. To the following I owe my gratitude.

Thinking and reflection on these themes was supported by the Radical Orthodoxy Faculty Working Group (2002–3) funded by a grant from the Calvin Center for Christian Scholarship. I profited from wonderful lunchtime conversations with an interdisciplinary team of insightful Christian scholars from Calvin College and Seminary: John Bolt, Jim Bratt, Rebecca Konyndyk DeYoung, Ronald Feenstra, Susan Felch, Lee Hardy, David Hoekema, Rick Plantinga, Laura Smit, Jerry Stutzman, and Tom Thompson. Special thanks to Jim Bratt, director of CCCS, and Donna Romanowski for their support of the project.

Writing the book was made possible by release time afforded by a Calvin Research Fellowship in the fall of 2003. My thanks to the college; our provost, Joel Carpenter; and the dean of research and scholarship, Janel Curry, for their continued support of my labors. The Calvin College community as a whole has been a wonderful environment for sustaining confessional scholarship, as well as intentional discipleship, and I count myself blessed to call this my institutional home.

Pieces of the book were read by colleagues and friends who provided helpful advice, even if I did not always heed it. I would like to thank my colleagues in the philosophy department, especially Rebecca Konyndyk DeYoung, John Hare, and Terence Cuneo, for fruitful discussions about Aquinas and Scotus. John Monda read the entire manuscript with care and raised helpful questions. My research assistant, Jerry Stutzman, provided critical feedback that helped me to refine matters (particularly on Edwards) and also labored carefully on editing, footnotes, and the index. An ongoing conversation with Hans Boersma, who I consider one of my most valued theological dialogue partners, pushed me to rethink and reformulate my position on a number of crucial points. His thorough reading of the manuscript was then coupled with the careful attention given to it by D. Stephen Long. Both Hans and Steve offered wonderfully perceptive criticisms and suggestions that much improved the book. The errors that remain are likely due to my stubbornness in failing to listen to them.

I am grateful to John Milbank and Graham Ward for their work, which continues to provoke thought, as well as their support of my own labors. I am happy to be considered something of an adopted son of Radical Orthodoxy, even if a bit of the black sheep (i.e., Protestant evangelical) of the family, and I am especially grateful to John for writing the foreword.

The book would not have been written without the prodding and support of a wonderful acquisitions editor, Robert N. Hosack. I am excited by Bob's vision for theology and the direction of Baker Academic and am happy to collaborate on this project. Above all, I am grateful for his friendship and for his and Lisa's hospitality since we made the move to Grand Rapids.

My greatest debts are to those who are closest: special friends and a wonderful family. Our life in Grand Rapids has been singularly blessed by our friendship with Mark and Dawn Mulder—and now baby Seth!—who are truly kindred spirits in Christ (Phil. 2:20) and who have nourished our hearts and minds. Their friendship has been transformative for us, and some of the themes in this book stem from that. (If this book has a "soundtrack," it is a two-disc set: Coldplay's *Rush of Blood to the Head* and Radiohead's *Hail to the Thief,* both provided courtesy of Mark.) We also have found gifts of God in our neighbors, Sue and Melissa Johnson, who have embraced us and loved us in radical ways.

Above all, and without question, my thought and work is buoyed by the encouragement and support of a family who loves me despite many shortcomings. If I have slowly come to appreciate the role of community and the church for both Christian discipleship and reflection, it is because Deanna has modeled a life of authentic communion: She not only craves friendship but also knows how to *be* a friend. As those closest to her would testify, no one could ask for a better friend than Deanna. Our children, Grayson, Coleson, Madison, and Jackson, continue to be a wonderful sacramental gift to us—a means of grace given for our joy (and sanctification!). I dedicate this book to Grayson, who, as our firstborn, has borne the brunt of too many of my mistakes but who continues to inhabit the world with a forgiving charm that invites me to do the same.

Some of this material appeared previously in different versions. My thanks to Graham Ward, editor of *Literature and Theology,* and Oxford University Press for permission to reprint a piece of my article "Staging the Incarnation: Revisioning Augustine's Critique of Theatre," *Literature and Theology* 15 (2001): 129–33. Thanks also to Brill and editor Frank Macchia for permission to use material from my article "What Hath Cambridge to Do with Azusa Street? Radical Orthodoxy and Pentecostal Theology in Conversation," *PNEUMA: Journal of the Society for Pentecostal Studies* 25 (2003): 97–114.

Abbreviations

AW   Catherine Pickstock, *After Writing: On the Liturgical Consummation of Philosophy* (Oxford: Blackwell, 1998).

BR   John Milbank, *Being Reconciled: Ontology and Pardon*, Radical Orthodoxy Series (London: Routledge, 2003).

CG   Graham Ward, *Cities of God*, Radical Orthodoxy Series (London: Routledge, 2001).

Herman Dooyeweerd, *In the Twilight of Western Thought: Studies in the Pretended Autonomy of Philosophical Thought*, Collected Works, vol. B/4, ed. James K. A. Smith (1960; repr., Lewiston, N.Y.: Mellen, 1999).

NC   Herman Dooyeweerd, *A New Critique of Theoretical Thought*, 4 vols., Collected Works A/1–4 (1953–55; repr., Lewiston, N.Y.: Mellen, 1997).

RO   Radical Orthodoxy as a movement, distinguished from the collection of essays, *Radical Orthodoxy: A New Theology*.

John Milbank, Catherine Pickstock, and Graham Ward, eds., *Radical Orthodoxy: A New Theology* (London: Routledge, 1999).

TA   John Milbank and Catherine Pickstock, *Truth in Aquinas*, Radical Orthodoxy Series (London: Routledge, 2001).

TR   Graham Ward, *True Religion*, Blackwell Manifestos (Oxford: Blackwell, 2003).

TST   John Milbank, *Theology and Social Theory: Beyond Secular Reason* (Oxford: Blackwell, 1990).

WMS   John Milbank, *The Word Made Strange: Theology, Language, Culture* (Oxford: Blackwell, 1997).

Introduction

A Theological Cartography

Between Cambridge and Amsterdam: Outline of a Project

My goal in this book is to play the role of a cartographer—mapping the coordinates of recent developments in contemporary theology and philosophy to navigate a way forward for both practice and theory (which is its own practice). On the one hand, a cartographer is inevitably a surveyor—returning with reports of discovery and dispatches from the front. In that sense, a cartographer is not out to discover and is not governed by a fascination with the new. He or she begins by following trails first blazed by others. (Following Hauerwas, I think there is a certain theological virtue that resists the cult of the new.) So in this way, this work plays the mediating role of introducing a broader audience to Radical Orthodoxy and related currents in contemporary philosophical theology. A surveyor, of course, is faced with certain challenges and must make certain decisions. In its introductory intentions, this book is not intended to be exhaustive, though I do hope it is comprehensive. Writing an exhaustive account of Radical Orthodoxy would be akin to drawing a map that is the same size as the region itself. Moreover, insofar as Radical Orthodoxy is developing and in flux, trying to map its coordinates is a little like trying to draw the boundaries of an island whose coast is given to ebb and flow. On the other hand, a cartographer hopes to be more than merely a surveyor. When a cartographer turns his or her attention to the lay of the land, he or she will discover certain elements. A focus on orientation can be the occasion for a reorientation, providing reasons for renavigation and pursuing previously untraveled paths. In

25

this sense, I hope this book goes beyond a mere report from the front and can contribute to a constructive vision for how the church should orient itself in a postmodern, post-secular world. The book's two parts reflect these goals: Part 1 is intended to provide an orientation to the issues and context that inform Radical Orthodoxy; part 2 is intended to do the work of navigation, charting a constructive path with and through Radical Orthodoxy.

If the publication of this book constitutes a birth, the offspring has come through an extended period of gestation. My first introduction to what would come to be called Radical Orthodoxy was when James H. Olthuis—then my graduate mentor at the Institute for Christian Studies—placed in my hands John Milbank's *Theology and Social Theory*. What intrigued us at the institute was somewhat different from the general splash this book made on the theological scene. For most, Milbank's unapologetic claims regarding the Christian metanarrative sounded a clarion call to stop doing theory according to "the rudiments of this world, rather than according to Christ" (Col. 2:8). For most on the North American (and European) theological scene, Milbank was offering a radically new vision for a Christian account of being-in-the-world (even if there were some similar rumblings from the Yale school of postliberalism). But what intrigued us at the institute was not the newness of Milbank's claims but the way in which they echoed what we had heard for almost a century in the Reformational tradition of Abraham Kuyper, particularly as unfolded in the thought of Herman Dooyeweerd. Thus, one of my goals in this book is to consider parallels between the vision of Radical Orthodoxy and the Reformed tradition, with the correlate goal of signaling the unique contributions to be made by distinctly Reformational thought in our postmodern context.

A Reader's Guide: For the Perplexed

This book is a tad immodest in its intended targets. In particular, I tried to write the book with several—somewhat disparate—audiences in mind. This created some challenges, but I employed some strategies to help these different audiences navigate the text.

The first audience is the community of theologians and philosophers working within the confessional Christian tradition (but also perhaps beyond it). My goal for this audience is both introductory and constructive: On the one hand, I hope to introduce them to the movement known as Radical Orthodoxy; on the other hand, I hope to sketch a constructive vision for Christian thought and cultural engagement in the context of this dialogue with RO. Because of the breadth of this audience,

I tried not to assume too much (e.g., about continental philosophy); thus, the text is generally accessible to a wide variety of theorists but also graduate students and advanced undergraduates. To point them to representative resources, each chapter opens with a few suggested background and primary source readings; a full bibliography is located at the end of this volume. Together, these selections constitute a kind of "Radical Orthodoxy Reader." I hope this facilitates the use of this book in undergraduate and graduate courses. For readers already familiar with RO, these references will indicate the texts under discussion in the chapter. This should provide readers with a horizon of expectation for each chapter. Discussions that are particularly technical and could be passed over by the reader interested—at this stage—in the forest rather than the trees are carried on within footnotes.

A second audience is made up of those particularly concerned with Radical Orthodoxy, perhaps even as adherents of the movement. My goal for this audience is twofold: to provide an account of the state of the question regarding Radical Orthodoxy and to offer insights from the Reformed tradition that can make contributions to the development of Radical Orthodoxy. But the engagement is intended to be reciprocal. Therefore, I point to several places where the Catholic vision of Radical Orthodoxy offers a helpful critique of contemporary instantiations of Reformed theology and worship. As a result, I hope this book will be of interest to those in the Reformed tradition who are interested in what Reformed thought and practice should look like in the contemporary world.[1] In addition, I hope that my identification of some shifts and tensions within Radical Orthodoxy, as well as some of my more programmatic suggestions in chapters 5–7, will constitute an agenda for further research—offering an account not just of where we are but also of where RO might go.

Finally, Christian scholarship—particularly Christian philosophy and theology—should be done in the service of the church. Radical Orthodoxy has important things to say to the worship life of our churches and how we pursue discipleship in a postmodern, post-secular world. In this respect, I follow the lead of Robert Webber in his wonderfully visionary book *The Younger Evangelicals*, in which he points to Radical Orthodoxy as a resource for "the emerging church."[2] I use the term

1. Those interested in this dialogue between Radical Orthodoxy and the Reformed tradition should also consult the collection of essays stemming from the 2003 conference on this theme held at Calvin College in Grand Rapids. See James K. A. Smith and James H. Olthuis, eds., *Creation, Covenant, and Participation: Radical Orthodoxy and the Reformed Tradition* (Grand Rapids: Baker Academic, forthcoming).

2. See Robert Webber, *The Younger Evangelicals* (Grand Rapids: Baker, 2002), 72–73.

"the emerging church" to describe a trajectory of possibilities for the (evangelical) church in postmodernity—sketched by visionaries such as Webber (*Ancient-Future Faith, The Younger Evangelicals*) and Brian McLaren (*A New Kind of Christian, The Church on the Other Side*). Seeing the "pragmatic evangelicalism" of megachurch marketing as the zenith of modernity, I (like Webber and McLaren) am interested in sketching an alternative account of the church that is truly postmodern precisely because it draws on the resources of historic—particularly patristic and medieval—Christianity. Therefore, a third audience for this book is a community of pastors, worship directors, and other church leaders—particularly within the broader evangelical tradition. While I hope these readers will find the book generally accessible (particularly because I believe the leadership of the church must be formed theologically), I have tried in places to conduct a more targeted analysis of the implications of Radical Orthodoxy for worship, spiritual formation, and the life of the church. Given the nature of this project, however, the dialogue between Radical Orthodoxy and the emerging church remains at the nascent level of hints and suggestions here. I explore this next layer of reflection more fully in my forthcoming *Who's Afraid of Postmodernism? A Radical Orthodoxy for the Emerging Church.*[3]

---

3. *Who's Afraid of Postmodernism?* will be the first book in a new series I am editing for Baker Academic called Critical Theory for the Postmodern Church. The series will include works from John D. Caputo, Merold Westphal, and others.

Part 1

Orientation

The task of part 1 is to provide an initial orientation to Radical Orthodoxy and the project of a post-secular faith through a movement from
the general to the particular. Following the cartographer metaphor
suggested in the introduction, part 1 is a kind of reconnaissance mission—a first survey of the territory to get a sense of the lay of the land.
This proceeds by means of a progressive strategy that takes us from a
broader consideration of RO in the context of contemporary theology
to more substantive themes of RO. Chapter 1, therefore, attempts the
large-scale project of mapping RO in the contemporary theological and
cultural terrain of postmodernity. Chapter 2 enumerates core themes
or movements of RO. Chapter 3 provides a substantive analysis of RO's
own history of philosophy and theology, which is important for the
movement's self-understanding. The concluding chapter of part 1 offers
an axiom to guide further exploration: Behind the politics of RO lies an
epistemology that is undergirded by an ontology. This initial orientation makes possible the exploration of specific themes and questions
in part 2.

1

Inhabiting the Post-secular

Why Radical Orthodoxy? Why Now?

Related Reading

Long, D. Stephen. "Radical Ortho-doxy." In *The Cambridge Companion to Postmodern Theology*, edited by Kevin J. Vanhoozer, 65–85. Cambridge: Cambridge University Press, 2003.

Milbank, John. *"Postmodernité."* In *Dictionnare Critique de Théologie*, edited by J. Y. Lacoste, 916–17. Paris: Cerf, 1998.

Pickstock, Catherine. "Reply to David Ford and Guy Collins." *Scottish Journal of Theology* 54 (2001): 405–22.

Ward, Graham. "In the Economy of the Divine: A Response to James K. A. Smith." *PNEUMA: Journal of the Society for Pentecostal Studies* 25 (2003): 115–16.

Mapping the Postmodern Terrain: From Tübingen to Cambridge

The news of modernity's death has been greatly exaggerated. The Enlightenment project is alive and well, dominating Europe and increasingly North America, particularly in the political drive to carve out "the secular"—a zone decontaminated of the prejudices of determinate religious influence.[1] In Europe, this secularizing project has been translated, ironically but not unsurprisingly, into a *religious* project with increasing numbers of devotees of "secular transcendence"[2]—all the while marginalizing forms of determinate religious confession as "dogmatic." In the United States, the march of the secular

---

1. For an insightful and critical account of this project, see Christian Smith, ed., *The Secular Revolution: Power, Interests, and Conflict in the Secularization of American Public Life* (Berkeley: University of California Press, 2003), especially Smith's preface and extensive introduction (1–96).

2. See Gianni Vattimo, *After Christianity*, trans. Luca D'Isanto (New York: Columbia University Press, 2002); and Luc Ferry, *Man Made God*, trans. David Pellauer (Chicago:

finds its expression in the persistent project to neutralize the public sphere, hoping to keep this pristine space unpolluted by the prejudices of concrete religious faith. The religious response to this has been the confused "Constantinian" project of the Religious Right, which has sought to colonize the public and political spheres by Christian morality (or the morality supposedly disclosed by "natural law").[3] As we will see below, this kind of theological response *to* secular modernity actually ends up operating on the basis *of* modernity.

If the core of modernity is the Enlightenment, and the heart of the Enlightenment is a "prejudice against prejudice"[4]—where the most dangerous prejudice is the religious—then political (and academic) rhetoric indicates that modernity is a thriving project. Indeed, the supposed advent of postmodernity is in fact merely an intensification of modernity.[5] But despite this continued public viability of the modern project, for the past several decades, we have been receiving dispatches from the front that indicate problems internal to the Enlightenment endeavor. The challenges to modern orthodoxy have generally trafficked under the banner of postmodernism—though other, hyper-modern agendas have also fallen under this label.[6] The Enlightenment "prejudice against prejudice" has been called into question, and of late, the implications of this for public religious discourse

---

University of Chicago Press, 2002). One could locate the heir of death-of-God theology in the same vein. Here I would include Thomas A. Carlson, *Indiscretion: Finitude and the Naming of God* (Chicago: University of Chicago Press, 1999); and Clayton Crockett, *A Theology of the Sublime* (London: Routledge, 2001). In the end, I would argue that Jacques Derrida's and John D. Caputo's projects cannot really be distinguished from these.

3. On the "Constantinian" (or accommodationist) project, which attempts to accommodate and synthesize the gospel with the interests of the nation-state, see Stanley Hauerwas and William H. Willimon, *Resident Aliens: Life in the Christian Colony* (Nashville: Abingdon, 1989), 17–24. For an example of the way in which the revival of natural law feeds into this Constantinian project, see Jay Budziszewski, *What We Can't Not Know* (Dallas: Spence Publishing, 2003). Hauerwas and Willimon offer an interesting contrast to Budziszewski's claim: "The church, as those called out by God, embodies a social alternative that the world cannot on its own terms know" (17–18). As I will demonstrate in chap. 5, the difference between these two competing theological visions is rooted in a different epistemology.

4. Hans-Georg Gadamer, *Truth and Method*, rev. ed., trans. Joel Weinsheimer and Donald G. Marshall (New York: Continuum, 1989), 276.

5. What is taken to be postmodern relativism is usually allied to a very modern skepticism, coupled with the Enlightenment emphasis on the autonomy of the self, which is intended to secure the right for the individual to do whatever he or she wants. The pervasiveness of rights language and identity politics is a hyper-modern phenomenon, not a mark of postmodernity.

6. See Anthony Giddens, *Modernity and Self-Identity: Self and Society in the Late Modern Age* (Stanford: Stanford University Press, 1991).

have begun to be explored.[7] In fact, the very notion of "the secular" has been called into question. While it may remain a powerful aspect of contemporary political rhetoric, the theoretical foundations for the secular have been systematically dismantled. So if we are witnessing the advent of the *post*modern (and not merely the *hyper*-modern), then we should also be seeing the advent of the *post*-secular.[8] And insofar as twentieth-century Christian theology (sometimes unwittingly) allied itself with the Enlightenment project, resigning itself to an "apologetic" project of correlation with secular thought, the demise of modernity must also spell the demise of such theology. In other words, the critique of the Enlightenment project now calls for a critique[9] of modernist theology that manifests itself across the range of liberal and conservative options. The result is—or should be—a new space for confessional proclamation in the so-called "public"[10] or political sphere, but at the same time a public theology that eschews the Constantinian project. This critical and constructive agenda is precisely that articulated by Radical Orthodoxy—and before it, the Reformational tradition.

While not quite a Barthian bombshell, John Milbank's *Theology and Social Theory* did land with considerable impact on contemporary

7. One could note the critical work of Hans-Georg Gadamer, Alasdair MacIntyre, Richard Rorty, and Charles Taylor (following the lead of earlier dissenters such as Pascal, Kierkegaard, and Hamann). For a helpful survey of this development, see Hendrik Hart, "Conceptual Understanding and Knowing *Other*-wise: Reflections on Rationality and Spirituality in Philosophy," in *Knowing* Other-*wise: Philosophy at the Threshold of Spirituality*, ed. James H. Olthuis, Perspectives in Continental Philosophy Series (New York: Fordham University Press, 1997), 19–53. See also Stephen Louthan, "On Religion: A Discussion with Richard Rorty, Alvin Plantinga, and Nicholas Wolterstorff," *Christian Scholar's Review* 27 (1996): 177–83.

8. What this term signals will be discussed more fully below. Here we should note that it is used to name two different projects: on the one hand, something like the project of Radical Orthodoxy (see Phillip Blond, ed., *Post-secular Philosophy: Between Philosophy and Theology* [London: Routledge, 1998]); on the other hand, John D. Caputo's notion of a "religion without religion" (see, for example, *The Prayers and Tears of Jacques Derrida: Religion without Religion* [Bloomington: Indiana University Press, 1997]).

9. As Herman Dooyeweerd puts it, "Theology itself is in need of a transcendental critique of theoretical thought" (ITWT, 6), which he carries out in part 3 of ITWT. We return to these matters in chapter 5.

10. Christian Smith's Habermasian articulation of "public life" is a helpful shorthand, meaning by it "those fields of social life in which culturally different groups of people must live together with common normative and institutional arrangements that govern or influence important dimensions of their lives. These include the areas of law, education, science, medicine, the mass media, and so on" (Smith, *Secular Revolution*, vii). Smith's articulation of a "structural pluralism" bears deep affinities with the reformational articulation of public life as found in Abraham Kuyper, Herman Dooyeweerd, Nicholas Wolterstorff, James Skillen, and others.

theology. In retrospect, it was this tome that became something of a manifesto for an agenda that would later be described as Radical Orthodoxy.[11] Dubbed a "Cambridge movement,"[12] and proudly British (largely Anglican),[13] RO has turned theological attention back to the UK and has even garnered significant journalistic attention.[14] It has begun to have a significant impact on theological and philosophical discussions in North America and, to some extent, on the Continent.[15]

Before attempting to define RO more fully in chapter 2, here I would like to document its birth by engaging in something of a cartographical project—briefly mapping the terrain of contemporary theology in order to get a sense of the location of RO as a theological agenda. Let's imagine a (very heuristic) map that highlights not state capitals but certain centers of theological intensity and vision: Tübingen, New Haven, Amsterdam, Cambridge, and Durham, N.C. Each of these cities would

---

11. In an earlier response to my claim here, Graham Ward protested that (1) TST did not define the later project of Radical Orthodoxy, and (2) similar themes were already present in the work of Ward and others. See Graham Ward, "In the Economy of the Divine: A Response to James K. A. Smith," *PNEUMA: Journal of the Society for Pentecostal Studies* 25 (2003): 115–16. I am happy to grant that Radical Orthodoxy is not a "Milbank movement," nor is TST any kind of intentional manifesto for the movement. However, it was the reception of TST that put these central questions on the theological table, particularly in North America. Henceforth I will abbreviate Radical Orthodoxy as RO.

12. In the acknowledgments of RONT, RO is described as a Cambridge movement in both a present sense (including authors who are current teachers and students at Cambridge or have past connections) and a heritage (hearkening back to the "Cambridge Platonists").

13. In particular, Anglicans "of a High Church persuasion" (see RONT, xi). We consider matters of ecclesiology in chapter 7. This has already been an issue with Catholic interlocutors: One of Laurence Paul Hemming's consistent questions is whether and how the adherents of RO can lay claim to the vast resources of Catholic thought but arbitrarily, he would suggest, reject a Roman Catholic view of the church and the role of the magisterium. See Hemming, introduction to *Radical Orthodoxy? A Catholic Enquiry*, ed. Laurence Paul Hemming (Burlington, Vt.: Ashgate, 2000), 7–8. Below I argue—as Ward and Pickstock have conceded—that such a High Church ecclesiology is not required by the central movements of RO, though RO does demand reflection on the importance of liturgy and sacramentality.

14. Coverage has included David van Biema, "God as a Postmodern: Radical Orthodoxy," *Time*, December 17, 2001, 34; Jay Tolson, "Academia's Getting Its Religion Back," *U.S. News & World Report*, August 28, 2000, 52; Jeff Sharlet, "Theologians Seek to Reclaim the World with God and Postmodernism," *Chronicle of Higher Education* (June 23, 2000): A20; and David Ford, "British Theology: Movements and Churches," *Christian Century*, April 19, 2000, 467–74 (the concluding installment of a helpful three-part series on British theology).

15. For discussions, see David Burrell, "Radical Orthodoxy in a North American Context," in Hemming, *Radical Orthodoxy?* 20–30; Stephen H. Webb, "Stateside: A North American Perspective on Radical Orthodoxy," *Reviews in Religion and Theology* 8 (2001): 319–25; and Olivier-Thomas Venard, "Radical Orthodoxy: une première impression," *Revue thomiste* 101 (2001): 409–44.

also have sister cities representing allies—perhaps competing allies—of the represented theological vision. For instance, the project associated with Tübingen emigrated to Union Seminary in New York and the University of Chicago (David Tracy's Catholic correlationist project carries on this tradition); the Barthian project in New Haven's "Yale school" is something of an immigrant community from Basel that has a competing but related vision in contemporary Princeton; the Amsterdam vision is now best articulated in Grand Rapids and Toronto; the "Duke school" finds a certain correlate at the University of Virginia; and as RO is wont to claim, Cambridge has a deep affinity with the Paris of the *nouvelle théologie* (Henri de Lubac) and, to a degree, Jean-Luc Marion.[16] Now, let's consider the features of these theological capitals.

We could associate Tübingen with the center of the classic liberal theological project that could be described as "correlationist." Here the agenda is to correlate the claims of Christian revelation with the structures of a given culture or politico-economic system such that both, in some sense, function as a normative source for the theological project.[17] Classic representatives would include Rudolf Bultmann, Paul Tillich, Reinhold Niebuhr,[18] and, more recently, David Tracy.[19] The Tübingen agenda is, in the end, deeply apologetic: The act of correlating and formulating the claims of Christian revelation in terms of given cultural frameworks (sometimes masking as the human condition) aims at ultimately making sense of revelation in terms that are (supposed to be) universally accessible. As Milbank summarizes, "Modern theology on the whole accepts that philosophy has its own legitimacy, its own autonomy apart from faith." Theology, then, merely articulates "the knowledge of God" in terms of the "categories of being in general" disclosed by a supposedly autonomous philosophy. As such, "various

16. However, Milbank ultimately criticizes Marion for adopting a correlationist strategy vis-à-vis phenomenology: "If, therefore, Marion continues to develop the characteristic twentieth-century theology of divine word as gift and event, he also effects the most massive *correlation* of this theology with contemporary philosophy, but in such a fashion that at times it appears that he usurps and radicalizes philosophy's own categories in favour of theological ones" (WMS, 36).

17. For a brief, lucid overview, see David Tracy's foreword to Jean-Luc Marion, *God without Being*, trans. Thomas A. Carlson (Chicago: University of Chicago Press, 1991). Though Tracy distinguishes his own correlational approach from liberalism, in what follows, I argue that it remains a version of liberalism (as do some strains of evangelical, supposedly "conservative," theology).

18. See Stanley Hauerwas, *With the Grain of the Universe: The Church's Witness and Natural Theology* (Grand Rapids: Brazos, 2001), 87–140.

19. One would have suspected that the paradigmatic representative would be Schleiermacher. However, Graham Ward's recent reading of Schleiermacher should cause us to reconsider. See TR, chap. 3.

currents of 'liberal theology' seek to articulate this knowledge in terms of philosophically derived categories of being and knowing, the legitimacy of which liberal theology has forfeited the right to adjudicate" (RONT, 21). Thus, central to the Tübingen liberal project is a confidence in the neutrality of the "secular" sciences such as philosophy, sociology, and economics, which are then synthesized with Christian revelation as part of a mediating project.[20] For instance, for Bultmann, the New Testament discloses the universal existential condition of being-in-the-world that is confirmed by the purportedly "neutral" philosophical investigations of Martin Heidegger.[21] Or for Tillich, the claims of Christian revelation simply confirm the more universal disclosure of our dependence on "the ground of Being." Even what might appear to be radical challenges to this tradition—such as Gustavo Gutiérrez's liberation theology—end up conceding its fundamental tenets insofar as they retain the notion of a neutral sphere of knowledge yielded by secular social sciences (TST, 206–55). The result of the correlationist project tends to be what Graham Ward describes as the "diremption" or "liquidation" of religion such that religion is evacuated of determinate theological content and divorced from concrete practices (TR, 115).[22] This deeply modern correlationist project is replayed in much that goes under the rubric of "postmodern theology," particularly as embodied in the religious work of Jacques Derrida and John D. Caputo.[23] Determinate religious confession becomes, instead, a bland "concern for the ultimate" (Tillich) or a "passion for the impossible" (Caputo)—which one could take to be one more ver-

20. This kind of project trickles down and manifests itself even in popular, conservative Christian rhetoric. For instance, Christian counseling manuals on everything from parenting to marriage simply accept the "findings" of the health sciences and then build a supposedly "Christian" model of the family from this "data." Often, the very secularity of the source is invoked precisely to show why it *must* be true. For just one example, see the persistent best-seller Willard F. Harley Jr., *His Needs, Her Needs* (Grand Rapids: Revell, 1986); or more recently, James Dobson, *Bringing Up Boys* (Wheaton: Tyndale, 2001).

21. For a criticism of Bultmann's project—particularly his blindness to the very *un*neutral origins of Heidegger's analyses in the New Testament itself—see James K. A. Smith, *The Fall of Interpretation: Philosophical Foundations for a Creational Hermeneutic* (Downers Grove, Ill.: InterVarsity, 2000), 104–11.

22. Ward specifically includes Tillich here but then later opposes Tillich and Schleiermacher in this respect: "It *is* quite specifically the Christian God, and the specificity is fundamental. The return to a theological tradition in opposition to the liquidation of religion must be a return to what Schleiermacher understood as the 'positive,' material aspects of faithful practice" (TR, 151).

23. I will return to both Derrida and Caputo when considering initial criticisms of RO. For my critique of their evacuated "religion without religion," see James K. A. Smith, "Determined Violence: Derrida's Structural Religion," *Journal of Religion* 78 (1998): 197–212; and idem, "Re-Kanting Postmodernism: Derrida's Religion within the Limits of Reason Alone," *Faith and Philosophy* 17 (2000): 558–71.

sion of the *theologia gloriae* devoid of the particularity of the *crucis*.[24] In seeking to correlate the religious with the parameters of secular reason, the Tübingen project must remove that which scandalizes the secular: the scandal of the cross.

In some version or another, much of twentieth-century theology was colonized by the Tübingen empire. In fact, one could argue that, ironically, even fundamentalist or early evangelical theologies (such as that of Carl F. H. Henry) paid allegiance to such a project insofar as they presumed upon a neutral, "objective" reason to warrant their theological project.[25] By doing so, such theologies ended up being correlationist and accommodationist,[26] subjecting revelation to an alien criterion of justification—while at the same time allying theology with a Constantinian project that identified the interests of the church with the interests of the state (whether in the name of the culture wars or a war on terror). In other words, evangelical *theology* paved the way for the Religious Right. Further, both liberal and early evangelical projects engender a very thin ecclesiology because the specificity of the church's confession and practice is minimized in Tübingen. In this sense, fundamentalism, even in its critique, is but a mirror of modernism. In this respect, one might wonder whether old Princeton, Philadelphia, and Dallas are not outposts of the Tübingen empire.[27]

24. This despite Caputo's claims that he and Derrida are developing a postmodern *theologia crucis,* in which the cross is diremptively generalized as emblematic of suffering "in general." See John D. Caputo, "Toward a Postmodern Theology of the Cross: Augustine, Heidegger, Derrida," in *Postmodern Philosophy and Christian Thought,* ed. Merold Westphal (Bloomington: Indiana University Press, 1999), 202–25. A cross without the incarnation is just one more execution, not the cross that funds Christian theology.

25. David Burrell suggests the same link, noting the parallels between the modernist, Cartesian desire for certitude and the propensity of fundamentalism. See Burrell, "Radical Orthodoxy in a North American Context," in *Radical Orthodoxy?* 22–23. For a related discussion of fundamentalism's modernity, see James K. A. Smith and Shane R. Cudney, "The Growth of Fundamentalism: Was the Grand Inquisitor Right?" *Studies in Religion/ Sciences Religieuses* 25 (1996): 35–49.

26. Thus, Dooyeweerd sets genuine "inner reformation" in opposition to the "scholastic device of accommodation" (ITWT, 132). What has been described above as correlationist Dooyeweerd would describe as scholastic, by which he means a mode of Christian theorizing that, perhaps unwittingly, adopts presuppositions that are antithetical to Christian revelation (ITWT, 96–116).

27. This would also include what I have described elsewhere as the "Biola school" in Christian philosophy. See James K. A. Smith, "Who's Afraid of Postmodernism? A Response to the Biola School," in *Christianity and the Postmodern Turn,* ed. Myron Penner (Grand Rapids: Brazos, 2004). After noting the extent to which North American Catholic theology is "immersed in a 'correlationist' model of inquiry, [tempted] to adopt thought patterns ready-to-hand," Burrell also criticizes the establishment of (analytic) philosophy of religion in North America, which, he says, "seems more intent on putting the categories of analytic philosophy to a theological use than it is in querying how appropriate such

One of the most significant challenges to the Tübingen empire was voiced from Basel in the work of Karl Barth. If the Tübingen liberal project is correlationist, we might describe the Barthian project as revelationist— eschewing any notion of a neutral or secular "point of contact" between the gospel and public or sociopolitical structures, proclaiming instead a revealed gospel that subverted cultural givens.[28] In his bombshell, which landed on the playground of liberal theology, Barth asserted:

> The Gospel is not a truth among other truths. Rather, it sets a question mark against all truths. . . . So new, so unheard of, so unexpected in this world is the power of God unto salvation, that it can appear among us, be received and understood by us, only as a contradiction. The Gospel does not expound or recommend itself. It does not negotiate or plead, threaten, or make promises.[29]

Directly confronting the dominant Tübingen strategies that dominated both theology and preaching in his day, Barth eschewed such correlational, apologetic projects. "Anxiety concerning the victory of the Gospel," he continued, "—that is, Christian Apologetics—is meaningless, because the Gospel is the victory by which the world is overcome."[30]

This Barthian challenge was taken up in its contemporary form in New Haven with the advent of what came to be known as the Yale school or postliberal theology associated with Hans Frei and George Lindbeck. Following Barth, the Yale school sought to revalue the revelational pole of Scripture in theological formulation, emphasizing not the correla-

---

categories may (or may not) be to the subject at hand" (Burrell, "Radical Orthodoxy in a North American Context," 29). In that respect, one might have to include South Bend as a colony of Tübingen.

28. See Barth's articulation of this in his Gifford Lectures of 1937–38, published as *The Knowledge of God and the Service of God according to the Teaching of the Reformation*, trans. J. L. M. Haire and Ian Henderson (New York: Scribner's, 1979). For a discussion, see Hauerwas, *With the Grain of the Universe*, 141–71.

29. Karl Barth, *The Epistle to the Romans*, trans. Edwyn C. Hoskyns (New York: Oxford University Press, 1968), 35, 38–39. In his preface to the critical second edition, Barth points to Franz Overbeck as a critical influence on his thinking about the antithesis (3). Overbeck also exerted influence on the young Heidegger. Overbeck's challenge to correlationist strategies in theology remains important, particularly his retrieval of early Christianity's polemic against paganism. For access to his work in English, see Franz Overbeck, "How Christian Is Our Present-day Theology?" trans. Martin Henry, *Irish Theological Quarterly* 66 (2001): 51–66. For an introduction, see Martin Henry, "Franz Overbeck: An Introduction," *Irish Theological Quarterly* 65 (2000): 307–18.

30. Barth, *Romans*, 35. Cf. Graham Ward, "Reformed Apologetics: Why Barth Needed Hegel," in *Creation, Covenant, and Participation: Radical Orthodoxy and the Reformed Tradition*, ed. James K. A. Smith and James H. Olthuis (Grand Rapids: Baker Academic, forthcoming).

tion or synthesis of revelation with secular frameworks but rather the *antithesis* between them and the way in which revelation subverts secular frameworks.[31] The difference between Barth and postliberals, we might say, is that the Yale school made the linguistic turn in a way that Barth had not. The Yale school took part in a certain Wittgensteinian direction (resisted by the Princeton Barthians) that would eventually produce a satellite project in Durham, N.C., embodied in the work of Stanley Hauerwas.[32] Here Barth's Reformed thought is melded with the Anabaptist theology of John Howard Yoder (Reformed anathemas of the Anabaptists notwithstanding). But this mixture raises a question: What have Basel and Goshen to do with one another? While it remains a curious amalgam, the possibility of the synthesis is found in Barth and Yoder's shared emphasis on the antithesis of revelation vis-à-vis given cultural forms.[33] Both deeply resist the correlational and Constantinian projects of modern theology, and both emphasize the practices of *being* the church, informed by the narrative of Scripture, constituting an alternative community and a peculiar people. Echoing Barth, Yoder emphasizes that the norm for Christian existence—and hence theology and proclamation—must derive from the gospel as modeled by Jesus, not from the supposedly neutral norms of a public social ethics independent of revelation. Arguing against what he called the "mainstream ethical consensus," rooted in "an epistemology for which the classic label is the *theology of the natural*," Yoder criticizes the attempt to discern the shape of Christian theology under the guidance of public norms; the Tübingen consensus claims that "it is by studying the realities around us, not by hearing a proclamation from God, that we discern the right."[34]

31. For a helpful introductory discussion of Barth and the Yale school, see John R. Franke, "God Hidden and Wholly Revealed: Karl Barth, Postmodernity, and Evangelical Theology," *Books & Culture* 9 (September/October 2003): 16–17, 40–42.

32. The Barth/Wittgenstein amalgam is important for Hauerwas. As he puts it, "I read Barth my way—a way I tried to exhibit in *With the Grain of the Universe*—by suggesting not only that the *Dogmatics* should be read as a training manual for Christian speech but also how that speech shapes the speaker in a manner appropriate to that which the speech speaks" (Stanley Hauerwas, "Hooks: Random Thoughts by Way of a Response to Griffiths and Ochs," *Modern Theology* 19 [2003]: 93). See a related discussion in Stanley Hauerwas, "The Church as God's New Language," in *The Hauerwas Reader*, ed. John Berkman and Michael Cartwright (Durham: Duke University Press, 2001), 142–62; and commentary in Brad J. Kallenberg, *Ethics as Grammar: Changing the Postmodern Subject* (Notre Dame: University of Notre Dame Press, 2001).

33. The emphasis here should be on *given* cultural forms, not culture *as such*. For Hauerwas's narrative of how Barth and Yoder can be correlated under the banner of "witness," see *With the Grain of the Universe*, 205–41.

34. John Howard Yoder, *The Politics of Jesus*, 2nd ed. (Grand Rapids: Eerdmans, 1994), 8–9.

Thus, he sought to make a case against "the modern ethicists who have assumed that the only way to get from the gospel story to ethics, from Bethlehem to Rome or to Washington or Saigon, was to leave the story behind."[35] Therefore Hauerwas's Barth/Yoder synthesis arises from their deep critique of what we would now call modernity (and more specifically, liberalism), sketching a vision for an alternative, postmodern—and hence post-secular—manner of being a living witness. Behind this is a trenchant rejection of the Enlightenment value of autonomy both in epistemology (as in secular foundationalism) and politics (with the idolization of rights).

Quite independent of the Barthian protest against Tübingen, though also rooted in the Reformed tradition, a similar criticism of the liberal project was launched from Amsterdam, first in the work of Abraham Kuyper and later in the thought of Herman Dooyeweerd.[36] As Nicholas Wolterstorff observes, what Basel and Amsterdam (or New Haven and Grand Rapids) share in common is "the call to *reverse the direction of conformation*" such that Christian theologians or scholars need not conform to the secular criteria of knowledge or justice.[37] This critical call rests on an earlier critique of the notion of autonomy or neutrality, whether within the secular halls of politics or the academy. "Common to Yale theology and Neo-Calvinism," Wolterstorff adds, "is their rejection of [the] self-image of acceptable learning as an autonomous, generically human, foundationally structured practice which is grounded and situated within universal structures by philosophers."[38] Thus, it is not surprising that Abraham Kuyper has been described as the first "postmodernist" insofar as his thought called into question these sacred tenets of modernity—particularly notions of secularity or neutrality with a view to the public role of determinate religious

35. Ibid., 13. For further and more recent articulations of this project, see Stanley Hauerwas, "How 'Christian Ethics' Came to Be" and "On Keeping Theological Ethics Theological," in *Hauerwas Reader*, 37–74; and D. Stephen Long, *The Goodness of God* (Grand Rapids: Brazos, 2001).

36. A case of overlap between Basel and Amsterdam might be found in G. C. Berkouwer.

37. Nicholas Wolterstorff, "What New Haven and Grand Rapids Have to Say to Each Other," in *Seeking Understanding: The Stob Lectures, 1986–1998* (Grand Rapids: Eerdmans, 2001), 256. One can hear the same call to nonconformity in Alvin Plantinga, "Advice to Christian Philosophers," *Faith and Philosophy* 1 (1984): 253–71, where he emphasizes the need for boldness to resist the hegemonic research programs of the "secular" academy.

38. Wolterstorff, "New Haven and Grand Rapids," 259. In the Yale school—as in Barth—this tends to issue in a generally antiphilosophical stance, as if philosophy were implacably Greek and thus pagan. In the Reformational tradition, there is a more positive sense that we can also have a philosophy that is rooted in revelation (and without that philosophy *becoming* theology). I discuss this further in chapter 5.

confession.[39] As Wolterstorff notes, the elements of this critique of reason had been articulated by Kuyper in the 1880s:

> I have long thought, and I continue to think, that that was remarkable. It's remarkable that Karl Barth should have arrived in the 1920s at the views which I characterized as those of the Yale theologians, views which we can now recognize to be—I stifle my dislike for modish language—*postmodern* views. But it's even more remarkable that Abraham Kuyper should have arrived at postmodern views of academic learning fifty years before that, more than a hundred years ago.[40]

This seminal critique was further unfolded by Dooyeweerd, who undertook a comprehensive analysis of the committed or religious nature of theoretical thought, predating Gadamer's critique of the Enlightenment "prejudice against prejudice."[41] What Kuyper, Dooyeweerd, and the Reformational tradition were pointing toward was an early understanding of the post-secular.

The RO voice reverberating out of Cambridge bears a deep affinity with these other critical voices, all directed against Tübingen (or Dallas). As Catherine Pickstock surveys the situation, she concludes, "It seems to me that there are no sharp boundaries between radical orthodoxy and other identifiable tendencies within what one might generically call post-secular theology: One can mention, for example, the Yale School, Radical Traditions at Duke University, and Scriptural Reasoning, associated with Peter Ochs at the University of Virginia."[42] As such, before defining RO more substantively in chapter 2, it is most helpful for us to see RO in its relationship with these other critical voices—mapping a certain (sometimes uneasy) alliance between Cambridge, Amsterdam, New Haven, and Durham, N.C. What all these centers share in common is an assertion regarding the *antithesis* between Christian revelation and the direction of given cultural forms—an antithesis between the revealed

---

39. For this provocative description of Kuyper as the first postmodern, see Malcolm Bull, "Who Was the First to Make a Pact with the Devil?" *London Review of Books* (May 14, 1992): 22–24.

40. Wolterstorff, "New Haven and Grand Rapids," 278.

41. Thus, one can discern an affinity between Dooyeweerd's critique of the modern subject and recent feminist criticisms of the Kantian model of the subject. For a discussion, see Janet Catherine Wesselius, "Points of Convergence between Dooyeweerdian and Feminist Views of the Philosophic Self," in *Knowing Other-wise*, 54–68.

42. Catherine Pickstock, "Reply to David Ford and Guy Collins," *Scottish Journal of Theology* 52 (2001): 406. Ward echoes this "big tent" understanding, describing Rowan Williams, Fergus Kerr, Nicholas Lash, Stanley Hauerwas, David Burrell, and Peter Ochs as "theologians engaging in social, political, and critical theory and metaphysics, on the basis of tradition-based reasoning" (Ward, "In the Economy of the Divine," 115).

wisdom of Jerusalem and the pagan logic of Athens—as well as a refusal to concede the criteria for responsible public discourse to the supposed neutrality of the secular. They are all particularly wary of the danger of adopting secular frameworks for Christian theological and theoretical reflection insofar as such secular paradigms are, ultimately, pagan (i.e., religious but misdirected or apostate). In short, *there is no secular,* if by "secular" we mean "neutral" or "uncommitted"; instead, the supposedly neutral public spaces that we inhabit—in the academy or politics—are temples of other gods that cannot be served alongside Christ. Instead of a baptism of (supposedly) secular philosophy or the supplementation of (supposedly) secular social sciences, what is required is an "inner reformation of the sciences" (Dooyeweerd) and the development of a distinctly Christian theoretical framework, informed by revelation and shaped by the practices of the Christian community. Radical Orthodoxy is a recent, particularly intense call for the development of a theoretical framework and sociopolitical involvement that are distinctly Christian at their foundation.

Augustine in Paris: Sources and Influences

In addition to situating RO on the contemporary theological map, a second prelude to a more substantive definition involves tracing something of its intellectual genealogy. We will undertake this genealogy regressively.

Given RO's critique of modernity, the advent of postmodernism in the work of thinkers such as Jacques Derrida, Jean-François Lyotard, and Gilles Deleuze has provided a welcome platform to articulate a distinctly theological postmodernism. Engaging contemporary currents in philosophy and critical theory, particularly new French thought,[43] RO has

43. In this respect, Graham Ward, a key figure in RO, has put the entire theological community (both teachers and students) in his debt by providing two important texts for understanding the relationship between theology and postmodernism. His *Theology and Contemporary Critical Theory: Creating Transcendent Worship,* 2nd ed. (New York: St. Martin's Press, 1999) provides a comprehensive overview of major currents in contemporary thought, particularly French theory, with lucid expositions of figures such as Derrida, Foucault, Irigaray, Ricoeur, and Levinas, as well as less discussed but important thinkers such as Judith Butler, Julia Kristeva, Jean-Luc Nancy, and Michel de Certeau. This text is nicely complemented by Ward's edited volume, *The Postmodern God: A Theological Reader* (Oxford: Blackwell, 1997), which provides selections of primary texts from these figures, introduced by leading scholars in the field. See also Graham Ward, ed., *The Blackwell Companion to Postmodern Theology* (Oxford: Blackwell, 2001). Together, these volumes would provide the perfect foundation for advanced undergraduate or graduate seminars in contemporary theology or theology and postmodernism. His other important book,

taken on postmodernism in a dual sense: On the one hand, it is a theological movement that speaks in the idiom of contemporary continental thought, engaging in theological reflection in the language of French phenomenology and critical theory; on the other hand, it has taken on such thought in a polemical sense, seeking to demonstrate the paucity of postmodern nihilism[44] and then to recover an alternative, Christian vision by returning to decidedly premodern sources (without wanting simply to recover premodernity). So while RO speaks the language of postmodernism—at times to the point of obscurantism, some have charged—it is at root a critique of postmodernism, or at least certain incarnations of such. The conceptual tools of RO, then, owe a great deal to the rubrics of contemporary continental philosophy, largely because of the legacy of Heidegger, Derrida, Foucault, and others who, though subjected to sustained critique by RO, are nevertheless seen to be grappling with the internal breakdown of the Enlightenment project.[45]

But if contemporary continental theory provides something of a launching pad for RO, its substantive claims draw on a much older tradition. Again, this should be seen regressively. The closest influence is the *nouvelle théologie* of Henri de Lubac, Yves Congar, and others.[46]

Barth, Derrida, and the Language of Theology (Cambridge: Cambridge University Press, 1995), is a careful, specialized study of similarities between Barth's account of language and revelation and contemporary theories of language operative in Derrida, Levinas, and other continental thinkers. As he concludes, the book is meant to function as "the basis for a postmodern theology of the Word" (256).

44. This is RO's consistent characterization of postmodernism, including figures such as Nietzsche, Derrida, Foucault, and Lyotard. Some critics such as Caputo, citing the deep ethical concerns in Derrida's thought, have rejected RO's claim concerning Derrida's nihilism as outlandish. But nihilism, for RO, does not signal a mere abandonment of morality for an anything-goes mentality; rather, nihilism has a distinct *metaphysical* meaning: At root, such nihilism rests on an ontological *monism*. For a discussion, see Conor Cunningham, *Genealogy of Nihilism*, Radical Orthodoxy (London: Routledge, 2002), xii–xviii. Nevertheless, nihilism can play a positive, propaedeutic role (akin to the role of boredom in Heidegger or vanity in Marion's *God without Being*). An early document circulated around Cambridge claimed that "nihilism is nearer the truth than humanism, because it recognizes the unknown and indeterminate in every reality and because it is true that without God there is nothing. One can add that humanism is nihilism unable to recognize itself and therefore also naïve or cynical or both" ("Radical Orthodoxy: Twenty-four Theses," thesis 7).

45. Unlike, say, Anglo-American or analytic philosophy, which has generally been happy to leave these more fundamental questions unexamined, operating on the basis of what we could call, following Dooyeweerd, an "absolutization" of the logical aspect. In this respect, Plantinga and Wolterstorff's (postfoundationalist) "Reformed epistemology" would signal a departure within the analytic tradition.

46. Interestingly, Dooyeweerd saw the *nouvelle théologie* as a welcome development in Catholic thought, contrary to what he saw as Barth's antiphilosophical "dualism." In fact, Dooyeweerd suggests a deep agreement: "It is a heartening symptom of a re-awakening of biblical consciousness that, under the influence of Augustinianism, an increasing

While many originally saw an alliance between Barthian neo-orthodoxy and RO, Milbank is critical of Barth and points instead to the *nouvelle théologie* as a crucial resource: "Radical Orthodoxy considers that Henri de Lubac was a greater theological revolutionary than Karl Barth, because in questioning a hierarchical duality of grace and nature as discrete stages, he transcended, unlike Barth, the shared background assumption of all modern theology. In this way one could say, anachronistically, that he inaugurated a postmodern theology."[47] A formative voice surrounding the Second Vatican Council, the *nouvelle théologie* was critical of the received Thomistic tradition—both the manual tradition of Vatican I scholasticism as well as Karl Rahner's "transcendental Thomism"—which tended to rend the cosmos into natural (autonomous) and supernatural elements. In contrast, de Lubac and his confreres emphasized a strategy of *ressourcement,* going back to the sources, particularly the early fathers and patristic theology.[48] In particular, de Lubac sought to undo the dualistic understanding of nature and grace that had emerged from scholastic Thomism—a dualism that suggested the notion of a pure nature or *saeculum* that was autonomous and devoid of grace. Instead, he argued, there is a sense in which nature is always already graced. As a dependent creation, nature is gift and therefore cannot be autonomous; correlatively, reason always participates in grace, so any dualistic opposition of faith and reason is a product of modernity. The natural and the supernatural are not to be understood as two different levels or realities but rather varying intensities of grace (TA, 21).

This revolution of neoscholastic dualism came to be described as the integralist revolution (integrating grace and nature, sacred and secular) and was closely associated with shifts in political theology around

number of Roman Catholic thinkers, belonging to the movement of the so-called *nouvelle théologie,* have begun to oppose this dualistic view. They agree with the Reformed philosophical movement in the Netherlands in advocating the necessity of a Christian philosophy" (ITWT, 97).

47. John Milbank, "The Programme of Radical Orthodoxy," in *Radical Orthodoxy?* 35. His charge is that "Barthianism, as much as Natural Theology, is operating in a specifically modern space" (34). We revisit these questions in chapter 5. The "Twenty-four Theses" referred to above are quite concerned to assert that RO is *not* neo-orthodoxy.

48. In an insightful comment, George Lindbeck notes a common concern at Vatican II between those who advocated *ressourcement* ("back to the sources") and the strategy of *aggiornamento* ("updating"): "The *ressourcement* [*nouvelle théologie*] and *aggiornamento* people at the Council thought of themselves as collaborators. *Ressourcement* and *aggiornamento* were understood to be two dimensions of the same reality. But the dimension labeled '*aggiornamento*' could be used in a program of *accommodation* to the modern world, rather than one of an openness to the modern world; and when that happened, *aggiornamento* fell into opposition to *ressourcement*" ("Re-Viewing Vatican II: An Interview with George A. Lindbeck," *First Things* 48 [1994]: 45). We might suggest that RO is trying to recover the productive tension of both *ressourcement* and *aggiornamento.*

Vatican II (TST, 206). The neoscholastic model, which had consigned nature to the secular and understood it as an autonomous, un-sacred realm, was called into question by two quite different theological movements in the twentieth century. On the one hand, one found resources for integration in the German tradition stemming from Karl Rahner and transcendental Thomism; it was this tradition that spawned the revolutionary work of liberation theologians such as Gustavo Gutiér-rez, Leonardo Boff, and Juan Luis Segundo. On the other hand was a different model of integration articulated by the French tradition of de Lubac and Congar, drawing on Maurice Blondel and eventually finding articulation in the work of Hans Urs von Balthasar. But for Milbank, while both of these traditions subscribe to the "integralist revolution," there is a "drastic difference between the two versions of integralism" (TST, 207). Recalling our mapping above, we could say that the Rah-nerian version of integration (and therefore also liberation theology) is ultimately a Tübingen-inspired project of correlation and accom-modation.[49] As Milbank articulates the difference between the German and the French versions of integralism—admittedly crudely—"whereas the French version 'supernaturalizes the natural,' the German version 'naturalizes the supernatural.' The thrust of the latter version is in the direction of a mediating theology, a universal humanism, a *rapprochement* with the Enlightenment and an autonomous secular order" (TST, 207). Thus, the development of liberation theology is rooted in an uncritical acceptance of the findings of Marxist theory as the neutral data of a secular science. As such, "their theology of the political remains trapped within the terms of 'secular reason,' and its unwarranted foundationalist presuppositions" as if the "basic Marxist conclusions were inviolable" (TST, 207).[50] The consequence of such correlationist strategies in political theology is critical:

> From the Rahnerian version of integralism to an embracing of Bonhoeffer's dialectical paradoxes of secularization is an easy step: the social is an autonomous sphere which does not need to turn to theology for its self-understanding, and yet it is already a grace-imbued sphere, and therefore it is *upon* pre-theological sociology or Marxist social theory that theology must be founded. In consequence, a theological critique of society be-

49. This echoes Lindbeck's observation above that the *aggiornamento* strain of Vatican II tended toward an accommodation to modern culture.

50. It should be immediately noted that Milbank's critique of liberation theology is not in the service of a theology allied with capitalist market economies. (As Milbank puts it, "Not without distress do I realize that some of my conclusions here coincide with those of reactionaries in the Vatican" [TST, 208]). As I discuss in chapter 7, RO sees the only authentic Christian politics to be socialism (TST, 208; BR, 162).

comes impossible. And, therefore what we are offered is *anything but* a true theology of the political. Theological beliefs themselves, however much a formal orthodoxy may still be espoused, tend to become but a faint regulative gloss upon Kantian ethics and a somewhat eclectic, though basically Marxist, social theory. (TST, 208)

In other words, what we get in the name of a theology of liberation is but one more project that has been colonized by the Tübingen empire. In contrast, the French version is more closely allied with the antithetical projects of New Haven and Durham, even if, admittedly, "thinkers like de Lubac and von Balthasar do not fully follow through the implications of their integralism" (TST, 209). It is precisely at this point of *nouvelle théologie*'s failure that RO begins to develop a postmodern social theology.

In addition to constructive and substantive influences of the *nouvelle théologie* on RO, perhaps its most significant influence is discerned in the historical method and strategy of RO. The *nouvelle théologie* of de Lubac and Congar was very much concerned with subverting the hegemony of modernity within the church, and its primary strategy for doing so was the retrieval of ancient and medieval sources, including the Eastern fathers. In de Lubac, this meant primarily a retrieval of a deeply Augustinian vision, and the centrality of Augustine is echoed in RO.[51] The vision and program that concludes Milbank's *Theology and Social Theory* is something of a postmodern translation of Augustine's *City of God* (TST, 380ff.)—a project taken up more concretely in Ward's own *Cities of God*. Before taking on the moniker of "Radical Orthodoxy," Milbank described his project as a "postmodern critical Augustinianism."[52]

What is it about Augustine that makes him such a crucial resource for a post-secular theology? In addition to the sheer genius of Augustine's theological insight, several reasons exist for this retrieval.[53] First, for a movement that wants to subvert theological allegiances to modernity, the (not uncritical) recovery of premodern sources provides a worldview not yet contaminated by the invention of the secular. In a basic sense, therefore, Augustine is important because he is not modern.[54] Second,

---

51. See Henri de Lubac, *Augustinianism and Modern Theology*, trans. Lancelot Sheppard (New York: Herder, 1969). I owe much of my understanding of the relationship between de Lubac and Augustine to Wayne Hankey and appreciate his assistance on these matters.

52. John Milbank, "Postmodern Critical Augustinianism: A Short *Summa* in Forty-two Responses to Unasked Questions," in *The Postmodern God: A Theological Reader*, ed. Graham Ward (Oxford: Blackwell, 1997), 265–78. RO's retrieval of Augustine is also heavily mediated through Vico, Nicholas of Cusa, and the Cambridge Platonists.

53. I grapple with the more substantive aspects of Augustine and RO in chapter 3.

54. However, philosophical reception of Augustine has tended to paint him as a simple precursor to Descartes, one of the founding fathers of modernity. This reading of Augustine

there is a sense in which Augustine's cultural situation mirrors our own postmodern predicament. As Ward observes, "It seems to me we stand, culturally, in a certain relation to Augustine's thinking. Poised as he was on the threshold between radical pluralism (which he called paganism) and the rise of Christendom, we stand on the other side of that history: at the end of Christendom and the reemergence of radical (as distinct from liberal) pluralism."[55] Like Augustine, we are constructing theology and engaging in Christian witness in the shadow of both a dominant empire and a religious pluralism. Third, the substance of Augustine's thought—in particular his epistemology, his cultural analysis, and his theological vision—resonates with the postfoundationalist project that rejects the autonomy of reason and hence also the autonomy of the sociopolitical sphere. In short, for Augustine there is no secular, non-religious sphere as construed by modernity; there is only paganism or true worship.

If contemporary continental theory provides much of the discursive framework for RO, and the *nouvelle théologie* provides it with a central theological impetus, pointing RO back to patristic sources, especially Augustine, we must also note the important role that Aquinas has come to play in the shape of RO.[56] Admittedly, this is an Aquinas mediated through the lens of the *nouvelle théologie* and thus

---

has been comprehensively challenged in Michael Hanby, *Augustine and Modernity*, Radical Orthodoxy (London: Routledge, 2003).

55. Graham Ward, "Questioning God," in *Questioning God*, ed. John D. Caputo, Michael Scanlon, and Mark Dooley (Bloomington: Indiana University Press, 2001), 277. What Ward here calls "radical pluralism" has been described in the Reformational tradition as directional pluralism. For a helpful discussion, see Richard J. Mouw and Sander Griffioen, *Pluralisms and Horizons: An Essay in Christian Public Philosophy* (Grand Rapids: Eerdmans, 1993).

56. I say that Aquinas "has *come* to play" this role in RO because I do not think that Aquinas's thought was central in some of the earlier aspects of Milbank's or Ward's thought (unlike Pickstock), certainly not on a level equivalent to Augustine (no one suggested the agenda could be described as a "postmodern critical Thomism!"). This is an instance in which already, in a young theological movement, we need to discuss questions of development (the other is the account of reason vis-à-vis apologetics, particularly as seen in the changing relationship to Hauerwas [see chap. 5]). It seems that to some degree RO (or at least Milbank) has changed its tune with respect to Aquinas. One wonders how we can reconcile the claims of *Truth in Aquinas* with Milbank's earlier charge that Aquinas (in contrast to Augustine) "moved not very far down the road which allows a sphere of secular autonomy; nevertheless, he has moved a little, and *he has moved too far*. By beginning to see the social, economic, and administrative life as essentially natural, and part of a political sphere separate from the Church, Aquinas opens the way to regarding the Church as an organization specializing in what goes on inside men's souls" (TST, 407, emphasis added). My hunch is that this gradual forestaging of Aquinas is part of a broader increased "Catholicism" in RO but also perhaps a response to criticisms, especially articulated by Hemming and Kerr, in *Radical Orthodoxy?*

a very Augustinian Aquinas who rejects the notion of an autonomous nature and hence rejects a notion of a "universal, natural, unaided human reason."[57] In other words, this is an Aquinas who eschews any rationalist account of the human person as well as an overly confident notion of natural law that would traffic under the banner of a universal human reason.[58] Moreover, because adherents of RO make the Eucharist so central to their ontology—and a distinctively *transubstantiationist* account of the Eucharist—Aquinas must be retrieved within a postmodern context. As with Augustine, Aquinas's very premodernity means that his theological vision is able to outwit the dualisms of modernity.[59]

Finally, our regressive genealogy of sources and influences must bring us back to the Neoplatonism that shaped the thought of the early fathers, Augustine, and Aquinas.[60] From its earliest intimations, RO has been allied with a (certain) retrieval of (a certain) Platonism, such that Milbank could speak of a "Platonism/Christianity" (TST, 290) and the "neo-Platonic/Christian infinitization of the absolute" as crucial for the theological ontology that marks the radical distinction between Christianity and nihilism. As we will discuss further in chapter 3, this retrieval of Neoplatonism is not the retrieval of more Gnostic strains of "henological" Neoplatonism that one would find in Plotinus and the Valentinian tradition.[61] Rather, RO counters the nihilism and flattened materialism of post/modernity with the *theurgical* Neoplatonism in the tradition of Iamblichus (and a certain Socrates/Plato derived from the *Phaedrus* and *Symposium* [AW]). This invocation of the Platonic philosophical and theological tradition is meant to counter the reductionisms of both nihilism and naturalism, pointing instead to a vision of

57. Ward points to an account offered by Joseph DiNoia, who suggests a connection between "a recovery of Aquinas . . . and the refreshing postmodern agenda" insofar as "Aquinas . . . speaks with pristine clarity to a host of postmodern theological questions," including concerns with participation, embodiment, temporal embeddedness, and non-foundationalism. See J. A. DiNoia, "American Catholic Theology at Century's End: Post-conciliar, Post-modern, and Post-Thomistic," *The Thomist* 54 (1990): 500, 511, as cited in Ward, "Radical Orthodoxy and/as Cultural Politics," in *Radical Orthodoxy?* 107–8.

58. As such, the RO retrieval of Aquinas stands in stark contrast to evangelical Protestant retrievals of Thomas in philosophy of mind (Scott Rae, J. P. Moreland, and others) and ethics (J. Budziszewski and others). In both cases, Aquinas is put in the service of a correlationist, Constantinian agenda.

59. See a more extended discussion of Aquinas in chaps. 3 and 5.

60. For those who would doubt Aquinas's profoundly Neoplatonic commitments, see Wayne J. Hankey, *God in Himself: Aquinas' Doctrine of God as Expounded in the Summa Theologiae* (Oxford: Oxford University Press, 1987).

61. For a critique of the Plotinian tradition, see Cunningham, *Genealogy of Nihilism*, 3–9, 157–63.

creation—and the material world—being "suspended" from the Good that transcends it (RONT, 3–4).

Defending the Secular: A Survey of Criticisms

If we can get an initial impression of RO by mapping its relation to other theological agendas as well as by tracing a genealogy of its sources and influences, this initial impression can be further crystallized by considering the criticisms RO has provoked. There is a sense in which knowing who rejects RO tells us a bit more about it. Not surprisingly, RO has no shortage of critics. Some of the criticisms have been friendly calls for refinement and development, as in the engagements by Stanley Hauerwas and Nicholas Lash.[62] Others have been generated along more confessional or denominational lines, as Laurence Paul Hemming's charges from the Catholic tradition, or Colin Gunton's remarks from the perspective of Reformed Christianity, or my earlier engagement from a charismatic/Pentecostal perspective.[63] Another common refrain has concerned the lack of sustained biblical engagement and reflection in RO and questions regarding its potential for the life and worship of the church.[64] To determine further the shape of RO as a program, this sec-

62. See Stanley Hauerwas, "Creation, Contingency, and Truthful Nonviolence: A Milbankian Reflection," in *Wilderness Wanderings: Probing Twentieth-Century Theology and Philosophy* (Boulder: Westview Press, 1997), 188–98; idem, "Explaining Christian Nonviolence: Notes for a Conversation with John Milbank," in *Must Christianity Be Violent? Reflections on History, Practice, and Theology*, ed. Kenneth R. Chase and Alan Jacobs (Grand Rapids: Brazos, 2003), 172–82; and Nicholas Lash, "Where Does Holy Teaching Leave Philosophy? Questions on John Milbank's Aquinas," *Modern Theology* 15 (1999): 433–44.

63. See Laurence Paul Hemming, "Introduction: Radical Orthodoxy's Appeal to Catholic Scholarship" and *"Quod Impossible Est! Aquinas and Radical Orthodoxy,"* in *Radical Orthodoxy?* 3–19, 76–93; Colin Gunton, "Editorial: Orthodoxy," *International Journal of Systematic Theology* 1 (1999): 113–18; and James K. A. Smith, "What Hath Cambridge to Do with Azusa Street? Radical Orthodoxy and Pentecostal Theology in Conversation," *PNEUMA: Journal of the Society for Pentecostal Studies* 25 (2003): 97–114. Recent dialogues at the annual meeting of the American Academy of Religion have also put RO in critical conversation with the Mennonite tradition (2002) and with Judaism (2002). Another set of partisan criticisms would come from those who, more generally committed to the analytic or Anglo-American tradition of philosophy, would be ideologically opposed to RO simply because of its sustained engagement with continental philosophy. See, for instance, Paul O'Grady's review of RONT in *Religious Studies* 36 (2000): 227–31.

64. On the former, see David Ford, "Radical Orthodoxy and the Future of British Theology," *Scottish Journal of Theology* 54 (2001): 397–99; on the latter, see R. R. Reno, "The Radical Orthodoxy Project," *First Things* (February 2000): 37–44. I find Reno's critique to be tinged with a hint of anti-intellectualism. For a "churchman" who sees much potential in RO, see Robert Webber, *The Younger Evangelicals* (Grand Rapids: Baker, 2002), 72–75.

tion considers three particular camps of criticism: first, the historical or apologetic critique of Wayne Hankey and Douglas Hedley; second, the deconstructive critique of John D. Caputo; and third, the atheological or secular critique of Clayton Crockett and Gavin Hyman. For all three schools of criticism, there is a sense in which RO is either too Christian, too confessional, or too dogmatic. Thus, all three of these critiques remain committed to defending some version of the secular. (While it may not be immediately self-evident, what is at stake in most criticisms of RO is ultimately a matter of politics. By that I mean that our epistemologies and attendant theologies spawn political agendas, even where such political implications are neither suggested nor glimpsed.[65] Conversely, the theological critiques of RO are also funded by an allegiance to classical [political] liberalism. The secular will almost always be in allegiance with classical liberal polity.[66] Wayne Hankey's critique of RO, for instance, deals with a somewhat Tory defense of the status quo through a defense of an autonomous nature. Caputo's Derridean critique of RO is a critique funded by a fairly uncritical allegiance to the kind of American left that allows one to care passionately about mutual funds and at the same time celebrate a simply more radical individualism.)

One strain of critique is historical or apologetic, as evidenced in the responses by Wayne Hankey, Robert Dodaro, James Hanvey, and Douglas Hedley. Central to their critique of RO is a critique of its unique history of philosophy and their narrative regarding philosophical development and decline from Plato through Augustine and Aquinas, with a downward turn in Scotus toward Descartes. While chapter 3 deals more specifically with their challenge to RO's history, here we are interested in their broader historical interest in positing a deep continuity between ancient, medieval, and modern philosophical formulations—contrary to RO's articulation of a discontinuity between, say, the fathers and the moderns, between Augustine and Descartes. Central to RO's critique of (post-Scotus) modernity is its claim that the secular—as neutral, objective, and universally rational—is a modern invention intended to secure a universal reason that could ground a public politics. This same neutral reason shared in

65. One of Milbank's claims in "A Critique of the Theology of Right" is that "theology proceeding in the wake of [Kantian] transcendentalism is partially reducible to a liberal rights ideology. This verdict will be applied both to theologies seeking for themselves epistemological foundations, and to theologies which assume that ethics has some extra-theological and well-grounded autonomy" (WMS, 7). Ward makes the point even more concrete in his analysis of the natural theology at work behind the "cities of eternal aspiration" in Frank Lloyd Wright and Le Corbusier (CG, 39–41).

66. The most curious historical piece of this reality is the strange allegiances between Aquinas and Kant, or at least between contemporary retrievals of each.

common by all could also underwrite an apologetics or natural theology that would secure foundational truths of theism by appeal to natural, unaided reason. In many cases, these political and apologetic interests merge to underwrite a Constantinian religious political project. In other words, the epistemological confidence of a natural theology often translates into a notion of natural law that, more often than not, feeds into the colonizing of the political by the religious that also tends to cut the other way—namely, the church becomes allied with the interest of the state.[67] RO, on the other hand, seeks to articulate a fundamental incommensurability between the Christian and the pagan that entails both an epistemological and a political consequence: On the one hand, the project of a natural theology is undercut because the very notion of a neutral, secular reason is a myth; therefore, on the other hand, there can be no Constantinian natural law project that could appeal to self-evident moral norms as criteria for shaping the state. Rather, such criteria must depend on the narratives that shape a particular community or *polis*, in particular, the *ecclesia* (TST). The *ecclesia*, as the community that by faith receives the revelation of the Word, sees the world in a way that is radically different from that of the pagan. As Milbank puts it, "Either the *entire* Christian narrative tells us how things truly are, or it does not. If it does, we have no other access to how things truly are, nor any additional means of determining the question" (WMS, 250). Thus, distinctly Christian thought is "a thinking out of the resources of revelation alone" (WMS, 36).[68]

It is precisely RO's rejection of a natural or neutral secular reason that Hankey and Hedley seek to contest. Each of them steps up as an advocate of natural reason and therefore natural theology. As a consequence, each is also an ardent defender of the continuity between the ancient and the modern (especially between Augustine and Descartes).[69] While chapter 3 deals with these historical claims and chapter 5 grapples with the question of natural theology and apologetics, here it is important to see that Hankey and others are most critical of RO because it rejects the notion of an autonomous reason or philosophy. Central to Hankey's concern

---

67. Christian Smith describes this as the "accommodationist" project advocated by "those who want the state to advantage one or all religions in public life" (*Secular Revolution*, ix).

68. Cf. Ward: "From the specific standpoint of Christian theology, orderings and accounts of the world proceed from that which has been revealed" (CG, 83).

69. The Augustine/Descartes relation is particularly helpful in seeing the difference here. On the one hand, RO commentators are wont to distinguish the Augustinian self from the Cartesian ego (see esp. Hanby); on the other hand, Hankey, Dodaro, and Hedley all want to paint a picture of the Augustinian self as characterized by "self-reflexive self certainty" to show the continuities with Descartes's later account. For an overview of these matters, see Hanby, *Augustine and Modernity*, 6–26.

is what he describes as RO's dissolution of philosophy into theology or *sacra doctrina*.[70] By suggesting a metaphysics that would be "properly Christian"—a theontology (TA, 35, 44, 47, 51)—RO ends up collapsing metaphysics into theology proper.[71] For Hankey, this mitigates precisely the universality and autonomy of the philosophical project that underwrites the project's apologetic possibilities. Philosophy "must retain an autonomy," Hankey argues, because philosophy "belongs to nature, which grace and *sacra doctrina* presuppose and do not destroy but perfect."[72] For Hankey, RO's project of developing a distinctively Christian metaphysics, or social theory, or psychology, is a confusion of nature and grace that pollutes the purity and autonomy of a secular nature. Philosophy as a distinct, natural—and therefore secular—discourse must abide. Thus, Hankey, perhaps unwittingly, ends up an advocate of the secular under the rubric of an autonomous philosophy.[73]

Like Hankey, Hedley is critical of RO insofar as it claims that there is a distinctly Christian philosophy, thought, or worldview. As Hedley puts it (though he disagrees), "Milbank posits a distinctively 'Christian thought' that is clearly opposed to pagan models and yet gravely obscured and perverted by modernity."[74] In contrast, Hankey and Hedley are eager to defend secular reason as the common ground between believer and unbeliever, Christian and pagan.[75] For Hedley, at least, the interest is unabashedly apologetic: "Might not the pursuit of natural theology," he asks, "notwithstanding the inflammatory rhetoric of Kierkegaard, Barth, and Milbank, still constitute much the best way of defending the faith today?"[76] Too quickly painting Milbank's project

---

70. Wayne J. Hankey, "Why Philosophy Abides for Aquinas," *Heythrop Journal* 42 (2001): 329–48, especially 335, 336, 343, where he uses the metaphor of "dissolving."

71. Wayne J. Hankey, "'Poets Tell Many a Lie': Radical Orthodoxy's Poetic Histories," *Canadian Evangelical Review* (forthcoming): 10, 12 (ms. pp.).

72. Hankey, "Why Philosophy Abides," 336. In chapter 3, I return to this question of nature and grace as a matter of Aquinas interpretation.

73. Hankey sides with Jean-Luc Marion precisely because of what I have criticized as Marion's "scholasticism." See James K. A. Smith, "Liberating Religion from Theology: Marion and Heidegger on the Possibility of a Phenomenology of Religion," *International Journal for Philosophy of Religion* 46 (1999): 17–33.

74. Douglas Hedley, "Should Divinity Overcome Metaphysics? Reflections on John Milbank's Theology beyond Secular Reason and Confessions of a Cambridge Platonist," *Journal of Religion* 80 (2000): 275.

75. Ibid., 275–76. Those in the Reformed tradition will hear echoes of the Barth/Brunner debate concerning the possibility of a "point of contact" with culture. Those in the evangelical tradition will hear echoes of a similar debate between "classical" and "presuppositional" apologetics, which revolves around the same question regarding the possibilities for a "point of contact" (Schaeffer). I return to this in further detail in chapter 5.

76. Ibid., 297–98. The rhetorical question assumes, of course, that the church has some interest in "defending" its faith. To whom? For what? I will resist drawing too much of a

as Barthian and fideist, Hedley argues that "attacking rationality may fend off the cultured despisers of religion, but it also removes one of the important sources of religious belief, reason as the 'candle of the Lord.'"[77] But what is meant by "rationality" here, and what is being attacked? One could hardly describe the lineaments of RO as antirational (TA, 22–23). The RO critique of reason is not a critique of rationality as such, as if RO sought to reject theoretical or scientific investigation.[78] Nor does it entail, as Hedley seems to think, a rejection of pagan learning, let alone some kind of de-Hellenizing attempt to "rescue the Christian theological tradition from any contagion of 'Greek' metaphysics"[79]—a strange charge to lay at the feet of a movement deeply interested in recovering Platonic metaphysics! What has drawn Hedley's ire is the rejection of a neutral, natural, and secular reason that is universal to all. In other words, for Hedley, rationality simply means a reason that is autonomous and universal. In the RO critique of rationality, therefore, he hears what to him is an oxymoronic concept: a "reason within the bounds of religion."[80] What Hedley protests is the loss of a reason uncontaminated by religion—a secular, neutral reason common to both believer and nonbeliever. For him, the RO position can only amount to the simple thesis that "everything is theology,"[81] but such a claim must be rejected, he concludes, because it mitigates the apologetic project—which, in the end, is allied with the project of liberal polity.[82] But rather than actually demonstrating that RO's critique of secular reason fails, Hedley merely invokes the supposedly negative ramifications of such a critique—namely, the loss of both the apologetic and the Constantinian project—as reasons to

---

conclusion from Hedley's nostalgic observation regarding "the Church of Rome's" loss of "secular power" (297), though it is my suspicion that such apologetic projects are almost always interested in reinstituting some version of the Holy Roman Empire, even if it is the Protestant version of the American Religious Right.

77. Ibid., 272. On Milbank's supposed "Barthianism" and "fideism," see 272–75.

78. Hedley simply mistakenly over-reads Milbank on this score: "My contention," he says, "is that Milbank's presentation of the strict alternative of *either* the Christian *or* the secular story is quite misleading. The modern Christian cannot simply dismiss, say, evolutionary theory because it is part of a counternarrative" (ibid., 276–77). Of course not, and Milbank would be the first to agree. Hedley sounds remarkably like Bultmann here, who also claimed that "modern" Christians could not just believe certain things in an era of the wireless and electric lights!

79. Ibid., 274.

80. Ibid. He does not cite the (reformational) book of which this is the title: Nicholas Wolterstorff, *Reason within the Bounds of Religion* (Grand Rapids: Eerdmans, 1984).

81. Hedley, "Should Divinity Overcome Metaphysics?" 272. Interestingly, similar charges were leveled against Dooyeweerd.

82. Ibid., 291–93.

think Milbank is wrong. But what if both apologetics and the politics that attend it are well lost?

It would be somewhat disconcerting to both Hankey and Hedley to point out a basic affinity between their thought and the critique of RO articulated by John Caputo. Nevertheless, Caputo's deconstructive critique remains, in the end, deeply committed to the secular project of the Enlightenment. What Caputo finds most disconcerting about RO, beyond its critique of Derrida,[83] is its dogmatism. For him, the very idea of a radical orthodoxy is "in the strictest and most rigorous terms incoherent, for the 'radical' strains against and bursts the seams of the 'orthodox.'"[84] Caputo shares RO's critique of a neutral, autonomous, secular rationality—"the central point on which both Derrida and radical orthodoxy agree"[85]—and is right to discern that postmodern ought to mean post-secular, echoing a critique of reason first articulated by Augustine and reformulated in Kierkegaard's counter-modernity.[86] Nevertheless, Caputo is reticent to describe his deconstructive "religion without religion" as post-secular because the term has already been taken up in a reactionary way by others who oppose the Enlightenment.

> The "post-" in "post-secular" should not be understood to mean "over and done with" but rather *after having passed through* modernity, so that there is no danger of the emergence of an irrational relativistic left, on the one hand, or of a lapsing back into a conservative pre-modernism masquerading under the guise of the post-modern, on the other, which is the sort of thing that is going on right now in a "post-secular" movement that describes itself with the unnerving, angry, and resentful title "Radical Orthodoxy." Radical Orthodoxy is a good deal more orthodox than radical, has managed to convince itself that God came into the world in order to side with Christian Neoplatonism against poststructuralism, and appears utterly dumbfounded by the fact that medieval metaphysics has lost its grip on contemporary thinkers.[87]

83. Caputo's central concern is RO's consistent claim that Derrida is a nihilist. He protests this reading in "What Do I Love When I Love My God? Deconstruction and Radical Orthodoxy," in *Questioning God*, 291–317. Dooley, as usual, simply repeats Caputo's criticism in "The Catastrophe of Memory: Derrida, Milbank, and the (Im)possibility of Forgiveness," in *Questioning God*, 129–49. I have more systematically engaged Caputo's model in my "On (True) Religion: Contesting Postmodern Augustines," in *Encounters with Augustine*, ed. Elizabeth Hoppe and Mark Zlomsic (Albany: SUNY Press, forthcoming).

84. Caputo, "What Do I Love," 306.

85. Ibid., 296.

86. See Caputo's account of "How the Secular World Became Post-secular," in *On Religion* (New York: Routledge, 2001), 37–66.

87. Caputo, *On Religion*, 60–61. Caputo seems to (mistakenly) think that RO is "taken in by the dream of Pure Objectivity" (61), and he charges Ward with denying the reality

What bothers Caputo, then, is the assertion of an orthodoxy, the proclamation of a particular, confessional account of the world as true. But could anything be more modern than the systematic preclusion of determinate, confessional accounts of the world? In the name of the "post-secular," does not Caputo offer a critique that repeats the Enlightenment prejudice against prejudice? In fact, he is happy to own up to the fact: "I insist," he says, "that the 'post-secular' style should raise by way of a certain *iteration* of the Enlightenment, a continuation of the Enlightenment by another means, the production of a New Enlightenment."[88] What aspects of the Enlightenment are reiterated in Caputo's version of the post-secular? The modern allergy to particularity and the liberal construction of individual rights. "Far be it from me," Caputo exclaims, "to say that modernity and secularization were a bad idea." On the contrary, Caputo is happy to hitch his post-secular wagon to Descartes:

> I am not prepared to dismiss Descartes, who started something that led to the most modern idea of all, the idea that in a way defines modernity: that we have the right to say what we think, to think what we want, to publish what we think, to think or publish or doubt or believe *anything*, without fear of censorship, excommunication, exile, or execution. The only limits on such rights are the rights of others to do the same and to enjoy the same freedoms.[89]

Thus, Caputo's version of the post-secular remains deeply liberal and modern in its individualist politics, which is precisely why it is interested ultimately in protecting the secular, for the secular, he thinks, protects us from the dangers of people who actually believe something determinate. That is why under the rubric of a supposedly postmodern "religion without religion" we hear the (intensified) repetition of the most classical Enlightenment views concerning religious particularity. For Caputo, the very specificity of religious belief can mean only danger for his still-hoped-for (American) dream of a neutral public square. "I do not see," he concludes, "how any religious tradition or theological language can take shape *without* violence (particularly one, God save us, bearing the

---

of mediation ("What Do I Love," 312–13). Neither charge holds however: RO's project is predicated upon denying the very idea of pure objectivity, and while they claim to think on the basis of revelation, this does not require thinking that revelation is unmediated. To claim that something *gets through* does not deny mediation per se. For a discussion of revelation in these terms, see James K. A. Smith, *Speech and Theology: Language and the Logic of Incarnation*, Radical Orthodoxy (London: Routledge, 2002).

88. Caputo, *On Religion*, 60.

89. Ibid., 62.

name 'radical orthodoxy'), whether institutionally or in the readings it
makes of texts which differ from its point of view."[90] Particularity and
tradition are linked, in good Prussian fashion, to corruption and violence.
The antidote to this supposed danger of concrete religious confession,
therefore, is the evacuation of a secularized sphere where, admittedly,
it is not reason that bars access to determinate religious discourse but
rather freedom. But what if the freedom of the individual is a creedal
commitment we are not willing to confess? What if we value community
over individual rights? What if being post-secular entails the rejection
of this quasi-American dream? What if we reject the logic that equates
particularity with violence?

The deconstructive critique of RO—and the general Derridean notion
of a "religion without religion"—is ultimately a Kantian (and therefore
Enlightenment) project.[91] Clayton Crockett's "atheological" critique takes
up this Kantian strain in an unapologetic fashion (whereas Caputo
and Derrida are still a bit reticent to describe their project in Kantian
terms). In particular, Crockett follows Kant in the direction of Paul
Tillich, Thomas Altizer, and Gordon Kaufmann, defining theology as a
perpetual questioning that defers answers.[92] Thus, he shares Caputo's
allergy to dogmatism, assuming that "representatives of dogmatic institutions promote confessional theologies which serve the interests
of already-established interpretations, and such theologies comfort
lay members of such institutions who would sooner allay doubts and
discrepancies than open them up." For this reason, "theology is inherently conservative."[93] In contrast, Crockett proposes a radical Kantian
theology that embraces Kant as the culmination of the Enlightenment
and takes seriously Kant's "transcendental critique of theology."[94] But
such a Kantian theology seems plagued by a distinctly Cartesian anxiety: Unable to know with certainty the Thing-in-Itself, such a theology
makes the merely skeptical move of perpetual deferment and lack of
finality. Such a theology does not make a confession and has no determinate credo. But the only reason a specified confession is precluded

90. Caputo, "What Do I Love," 307.

91. I have articulated this in more detail in my "Re-Kanting Postmodernism" and
"Determined Violence." This critique is expanded in James K. A. Smith, *Holy Wars and
Democratic Crusades: Deconstructing Myths of Religious Violence and Secular Peace* (forth-
coming). Ward and Milbank both point out Derrida's Kantianism in their roundtable
discussion with him, in Richard Kearney, "On Forgiveness: A Roundtable Discussion with
Jacques Derrida," in *Questioning God*, 61–62, 64.

92. Crockett, *Theology of the Sublime*, 1.

93. Ibid. One can hear more of a Freudian suspicion in Crockett's assumption than
in Caputo's.

94. Ibid., 2, 35.

is because of the supposed criterion of mathematical certainty that is required for knowledge. But why should we accept that as the criterion for knowledge? What if we reject the flattened epistemologies of post-Cartesian modern philosophy—which reduce knowledge to cognitive certainty—and unpack an epistemology that recognizes other modes of knowing? Then the supposed dangers of determinate confession are erased and the supposed failure of a credo to meet the standards of certainty is, in fact, no failure at all. As Milbank observes, "Radical Orthodoxy does not situate itself in a post-Kantian intellectual space that tends to identify a correct insistence on the *finitude* of our knowledge with the false idea that we can once and for all specify the bounds of possible knowledge for finite minds."[95]

But because Crockett clings to this modern, Kantian project—fostered later by Tillich—his critique of RO echoes the deeply modern critique of Caputo. Aside from criticisms that are simply mistaken,[96] Crockett is an advocate of an autonomous reason and sees secularization as the completion of Christianity.[97] As such, he rejects RO's fundamental critique of secular, autonomous reason and sees RO, in fact, as simply a new version of totalization: "Milbank works against a certain totalizing viewpoint, that of autonomous modern reason, and yet his opposition forces him to articulate a totalizing view of his own, that of a Radical Orthodoxy that ends up looking much more orthodox than radical."[98] Insofar as RO boldly articulates a distinctive, Christian, theological vision, Crockett sees in this a desire to transcend the conditions of human knowing marked out by the Kantian critique—a critique whose goal is to mark the boundaries and trace the limits of knowledge. "Theological claims are in some ways the most grandiose," he remarks, "because they are statements concerning (and constitutive of) the divine. Finite humans,

---

95. Milbank, "Programme of Radical Orthodoxy," 38. For further critique of Kant, see 38–40.

96. For instance, Crockett claims that, for RO, "secular modernity is bad because it divorces reason from its ground in traditional faith and communal practice" (*Theology of the Sublime*, 23). The RO critique of secular modernity is not that it lacks "traditional faith" but rather that it does not own up to its own particular faith commitments. Further, he says that "Milbank indicts modern secular reason, condemning all of modern thought as autonomous and therefore necessarily implicated in violence" (24). This is mistaken on two fronts: First, Milbank indicts modern secular reason for *thinking* it is autonomous and neutral when such neutrality is impossible. Second, it is not autonomy that entails implication in violence (since autonomy is a myth). Rather, it is the specifically *pagan* and *heretical* religious commitments of secular reason that lead it to begin from presuppositions regarding original violence. In general, the question of violence comes up very little in Milbank's discussion of Kant.

97. Ibid., 25–26. On the latter point, cf. Vattimo, *After Christianity*.

98. Crockett, *Theology of the Sublime*, 33.

however, cannot simply, immediately, or adequately speak or write about the divine, which is why Milbank and others want to overcome human finitude as a limit."[99] Given the Cartesian/Kantian criteria of knowledge as an impossible ideal, any particular finite formulation cannot count as knowledge. The result is a kind of radical, negative theology for which to say anything specific is to act from a deep hubris that, in the very act of confession, corrupts the divine. But this is to operate on the basis of a "logic of determination," which posits an impossible, pure ideal and therefore sees finitude itself as a corruption. In opposition to this logic of determination we must adopt a logic of *incarnation* that rejects such binary oppositions.[100] The logic of determination that engenders Crockett's Kantian negative theology also stands behind his assumption that the neutrality of secularity can keep us from the dangers of particularity.

As such, Crockett's critique is reiterated by Gavin Hyman, who also plays the role of a cartographer, mapping the terrain of contemporary theological options and then charting a course that offers, he would suggest, not a way out of the predicament but a way to get lost in and through the predicament in "a movement of perpetual departure" toward the Other.[101] Hyman's privileged (non)guide for this nomadic wandering is Michel de Certeau, who, according to Hyman (and in contrast to the readings offered by his *Doktorvater*, Graham Ward),[102] offers something of a third way in postmodern theology, in contrast to both RO (Hyman selects Milbank as its representative) and the "textualist nihilism" of Don Cupitt and Mark C. Taylor. Hyman's critique of both Radical Orthodoxy and textualist nihilism can, following de Certeau's topics, be articulated in terms of place: In this respect, for Hyman, RO is a little too settled, a little too tied to the particularities of a place and a tradition; on the other hand, Cupitt's and Taylor's a/theologies are a little too disconnected, attempting even to escape place by passing over it rather than moving through it.[103] In contrast to both, de Certeau advocates a nomadic wandering that "moves through embodied particularities, *through* traditions and *through* locations" to other locations and traditions.[104] Thus, de Certeau's Labadie presents a paradigm that neither settles down in one place (in contrast to RO) nor escapes place-ment as such.[105]

99. Ibid., 35.

100. Smith, *Speech and Theology*, 127–33.

101. Gavin Hyman, *The Predicament of Postmodern Theology: Radical Orthodoxy or Nihilist Textualism?* (Louisville: Westminster John Knox, 2001), 130.

102. Graham Ward, introduction to *The Certeau Reader*, ed. Graham Ward (Oxford: Blackwell, 2000), 1–14; and idem, *Theology and Contemporary Critical Theory*, 146–56.

103. Hyman, *Predicament of Postmodern Theology*, 139.

104. Ibid., 134.

105. Ibid., 129–40.

Hyman's rejection of Ward's reading of de Certeau is instructive for discerning the commitments that undergird his project: "To 'name' de Certeau's 'other' theologically compromises its essential otherness and therefore necessarily entails a certain betrayal."[106] Note the logic at work here: To name something—to determine it—is to compromise its alterity and, ultimately, to violate this other. Here Hyman repeats the logic of determination, which assumes that the determination of an other is a violation of the other. One would operate with that logic only if one held out a regulative ideal of purity that colluded with pretensions to infinity. Thus, not surprisingly, Hyman is sympathetic to Derrida's American ambassador, John Caputo, who, like Hyman, operates with such a logic of determination and thus advocates a religion evacuated of content—a religion without determination whose Other is subject to slippage due to anonymity and indetermination—which is at the same time a very Kantian and modern reduction of religion to ethics.[107] Therefore, it is not clear just how postmodern this option really is.

Further, Hyman's argument, particularly his critique of Milbank, raises reservations. While the opening chapters (1–3) of Hyman's *Predicament of Postmodern Theology* do a nice job of mapping the terrain of contemporary theology in the context of postmodernity, the discussion of Milbank is maddeningly slippery. In particular, in chapter 3, Hyman provides a helpful Wittgensteinian account of theological debates that take place *between* frameworks rather than *within* frameworks. Such debates are made difficult by a certain incommensurability between languages that is mitigated when the disputants recognize that the dispute is between different frameworks.[108] But Hyman forgets this advice in his critique of Milbank, consigning him to a place within Hyman's framework and thus shutting down the "otherness" of Milbank's position (see esp. 92–93).[109]

Second, echoing Crockett's claim above, Hyman's entire critique of Milbank rests on the premise that Milbank is advocating "a totalizing, absolute metanarrative" that "must necessarily entail a certain violence and exclusion of difference in spite of his claims to the contrary."[110] This is problematic on two fronts: (1) In contemporary theology, the language of metanarrative is batted about (and not just by Hyman) with an initial tip of the hat to Lyotard, but then turns into a notion of metanarrative that has nothing to do with Lyotard's analysis. For Lyotard, metanar-

106. Ibid., 135.
107. Ibid., 147–48, 144.
108. Ibid., 59.
109. Ibid., 92–93.
110. Ibid., 66.

ratives are distinctively modern systems of legitimation that appeal to
(illusory) universal human reason as the ground of their legitimation
(because, for Lyotard, the postmodern condition is a legitimation crisis).[111] Milbank, therefore, is obviously not offering a metanarrative since
his work sets out to critique the very idea of a universal secular reason.
Further, it is not at all a question of their *scope* (tribal narratives tell all-
encompassing stories, but these are not metanarratives). For Lyotard,
therefore, the problem with metanarratives has nothing to do with their
being totalizing or exclusionary. As a result, if Hyman wants to charge
that the problem with Milbank's metanarrative is that it is totalizing
and violent because it is exclusionary, he must first concede that he is
no longer working within the Lyotardian universe of discourse. Instead,
Hyman criticizes Milbank for offering a metadiscourse that positions
other discourses, making theology a "master discourse" that thereby
masters other discourses.[112] But this critique holds only if one adopts
the logic of determination noted above. Further, Hyman's view seems
to commit him to a notion that any principle of organization is unjust
and violent. (2) Part of the problem stems from Milbank's own lack of
precision regarding what he means when he (sometimes) asserts that
theology is a metanarrative or a metadiscourse. Here again, it cannot
mean what Lyotard means since Milbank's project is a confessional one:
The story is told not by reason but by and from faith (a term conspicu-
ously absent from Hyman's analysis).

What is common to all of these criticisms—the apologetic critique
of Hankey and Hedley, the deconstructive critique of Caputo, and the
(a)theological critique of Crockett and Hyman—is that they reject RO
insofar as they are interested in defending the secular. Their defense of
the secular is rooted in a deeply liberal suspicion regarding the purported
dangers of determinate religious confession, to which their response is
the advocacy of an autonomous reason and an autonomous individual
subject, endued with certain inalienable rights.[113]

111. See James K. A. Smith, "A Little Story about Metanarratives: Lyotard, Religion,
and Postmodernism Revisited," *Faith and Philosophy* 18 (2001): 261–76.

112. Hyman, *Predicament of Postmodern Theology*, 4, 79. This sounds to me like the
liberal notion that we are not allowed to say anyone is wrong.

113. Throughout this analysis, by "liberalism" I mean a worldview that prioritizes individual freedom and thus values autonomy as a fundamental value. Beginning with this
creedal commitment to individual freedom as "the Good," liberalism entails both political
autonomy (rights and freedoms constrained only by the rights and freedoms of others)
and epistemological autonomy (neutral, secular reason unconstrained by nonrational
commitments). All of this can be legitimately called into question, particularly within
the thick theological framework of Christian theology, which suggests that redemption is
found in *submission* to a Lord (contra political autonomy) and that wisdom is found only
on the basis of receiving revelation (contra epistemological autonomy).

Inhabiting the Post-secular

But what if our postmodernism were more persistent? If we are going to take seriously the postmodern critique of reason, then it must entail calling into question the very project of the secular, such that the post-modern should entail the post-secular. And if that is the case, then we cannot retain those vestiges of Enlightenment modernity that coddle our continued liberal interests in individual rights. Nor can we accept the logic of determination that characterizes such modern and hyper-modern thought. What we need is a more consistent postmodernism, one that follows through on the internal deconstruction of the Enlight-enment project rather than halting it at the point of liberal politics and the classical critique of religion. The church, authentically conceived, should be the quintessential site of such a post-secular engagement.

Radical Orthodoxy represents just such a consistent postmodern-ism. Thus, while the occasion for this book is an introduction to RO, its primary goal is constructive, not merely expository. The goal is to sketch the elements of a post-secular worldview that should shape the understanding and practices of the church—and Christian thought and practice more generally—in our engagement with the contemporary world. This requires both a critique of the persistent modernity and secularity of our culture as well as a formulation of how to navigate an alternative being-in-the-world that refuses modern idolatries. Radical Orthodoxy, intensifying earlier insights in the Reformational tradition, provides critical resources at a crucial juncture of opportunity. The investigations in part 2 explore the substantive shape of such a vision.

2

Elements of a Manifesto

The Movements of Radical Orthodoxy

Related Reading

Milbank, John. "Postmodern Critical Augustinianism: A Short *Summa* in Forty-two Responses to Unasked Questions." In *The Postmodern God: A Theological Reader*, edited by Graham Ward, 265–78. Oxford: Blackwell, 1997.

———. "The Programme of Radical Orthodoxy." In *Radical Orthodoxy? A Catholic Enquiry*, edited by Laurence Paul Hemming, 33–45. Burlington, Vt.: Ashgate, 2000.

———, Graham Ward, and Catherine Pickstock. "Suspending the Material: The Turn of Radical Orthodoxy." In *Radical Orthodoxy: A New Theology*, edited by John Milbank, Graham Ward, and Catherine Pickstock, 1–20. London: Routledge, 1999.

Ward, Graham. "Radical Orthodoxy and/as Cultural Politics." In *Radical Orthodoxy? A Catholic Enquiry*, edited by Laurence Paul Hemming, 97–111. Burlington, Vt.: Ashgate, 2000.

Defining Radical Orthodoxy: School, Movement, or Sensibility?

The goal of the opening chapter was to situate Radical Orthodoxy first by mapping its relation to other theological projects, second by considering its sources and influences, and third by outlining common criticisms. This project of situating RO helped locate it at the intersection of certain historical trajectories in response to the contemporary situation, which now brings us to the point where we can take up a more substantive definition of RO as a project. As the proponents themselves have discovered, the claim of Radical Orthodoxy can be quickly misunderstood. Before proceeding, therefore, we should consider what RO is *not:* It is not, for instance, a new *Fundamentals* or a list of infallible doctrines erected to determine what (or who) is orthodox. A new missive from another magisterium this is not. RO would be a fan of neither Cardinal Ratzinger nor Carl F. H. Henry; the movement is consistently critical of such "positivism" in theology as seen in both "Protestant biblicism [or fundamentalism] and post-tridentine Catholic positivist authoritarian-ism" (RONT, 2). RO argues that both are theological aberrations that are ultimately modern in origin.[1]

Rather, RO is a deeply ecumenical program: "The designation 'ortho-dox' here transcends confessional boundaries" (RONT, 2). Therefore, contrary to those, such as John D. Caputo, who think that RO wants to revisit us with postmodern crusades commissioned by a Cambridge curia, Graham Ward seems to argue for only a minimal core orthodoxy in this regard:

> There is not *one* Christian tradition and yes we can speak to a certain extent about orthodoxies. For orthodoxy is broader than might at first be believed. . . . *Filioque* may divide, views on the Eucharist or even the sacraments more generally, may differ, but these are not grounds for het-erodoxy. But if I claim that Jesus was a man adopted by God; if I claim that God is three people; if I claim the resurrection did not occur but that the disciples staged it—then I am no longer speaking the language of the Christian church.[2]

It is a movement unafraid to speak of boundaries but not at all in a manner that seeks to establish a narrow orthodoxy.[3] Thus, Catherine Pickstock, commenting on the contradictory charges leveled against RO (that it is at once "ecclesiastically rootless and yet at the same time, biased against several parts of Christendom"), suggests that an

> alternative reading of the radically orthodox position might point out that it is an explicitly ecumenical theology. How is this envisaged? It is quite

---

1. I have elsewhere argued for a similar account of the modernity of fundamentalism and hence the necessity for Pentecostal theology to excise such elements from its world-view, which is fundamentally *un*modern. See James K. A. Smith and Shane R. Cudney, "Postmodern Freedom and the Growth of Fundamentalism: Was the Grand Inquisitor Right?" *Studies in Religion/Sciences Religieuses* 25 (1996): 35–49; and James K. A. Smith, "The Closing of the Book? Pentecostals, Evangelicals, and the Sacred Writings," *Journal of Pentecostal Theology* 11 (1997): 49–71.

2. See Graham Ward, "Radical Orthodoxy and/as Cultural Politics," in *Radical Orthodoxy? A Catholic Enquiry*, ed. Laurence Paul Hemming (Burlington, Vt.: Ashgate, 2000), 106.

3. Of course, the very articulation of boundaries and even a generous orthodoxy run counter to liberal sensibilities that want everybody to be "in." If, like John D. Caputo or Clayton Crockett, one accepts the logic of determination, then *any* specification of bound-aries or orthodoxy is suspect. Their liberal individualism is allergic to any communal or hierarchical specification of what is to be believed. But RO rejects this fallacious logic of determination. However, chapter 7 notes that Ward, and to some extent Milbank, remains somewhat reticent to demarcate such boundaries.

common for ecumenical conversations to arise between representatives rooted in particular church traditions. In the case of radical orthodoxy, however, ecumenism was envisaged from the outset of its formation; for a radically orthodox position can be—and already has been—espoused by people from widely differing ecclesial backgrounds, from Roman Catholic and Orthodox, to the independent evangelical churches.[4]

For Pickstock, therefore, RO translates into a "concrete ecumenical proposal" regarding both the history of philosophy and theology as well as more constructive theological questions, including ecclesiology. RO's vision for a "reformed catholicism" has found "many surprising sympathizers amongst Baptists, Methodists, Mennonites, Nazarenes, and others."[5] As John Milbank articulates it, "Radical Orthodoxy, if catholic, is not a specifically Roman Catholic theology; although it can be espoused by Roman Catholics, it can equally be espoused by those who are formally 'protestant,' yet whose theory and practice essentially accords with the catholic vision of the Patristic period through to the high middle ages."[6]

Second, though seeking to retrieve premodern resources for theological reflection, RO is not simply a nostalgic preoccupation or a simplistic return to old paths. Rather, it seeks to rethink tradition as the very condition for theological reflection—something that evangelicals would do well to consider.[7] Even its critique of modernity should not be construed as a simple antimodernity; rather, "Radical Orthodoxy, although it opposes the modern, also seeks to save it. It espouses, not the pre-modern, but an alternative version of modernity."[8]

4. Catherine Pickstock, "Reply to David Ford and Guy Collins," *Scottish Journal of Theology* 54 (2001): 407.

5. Ibid., 407–8.

6. John Milbank, "The Programme of Radical Orthodoxy," in *Radical Orthodoxy?* 36. My burden below is to demonstrate the ways in which Reformed theology stemming from Calvin resonates with this "catholic" theology, while also offering a critical voice to it.

7. Catherine Pickstock responds to this criticism with careful reflections on the nature of time and the very meaning of the "past" in her "Radical Orthodoxy and the Meditations of Time," in *Radical Orthodoxy?* 63–75. There she argues that "a radically orthodox perspective sees time not as something to be lamented or circumvented by means of the instruments of nostalgia, but rather as our very condition of possibility *per se*" (64). I argued a similar point in "The Time of Language: The Fall to Interpretation in Augustine," *American Catholic Philosophical Quarterly,* Supplement: Annual ACPA Proceedings 72 (1998): 185–99. Protestants, especially evangelical Protestants, have traditionally had an ambivalent attitude to tradition that demands to be rethought. I made a first attempt to rethink both the necessity and the possibilities of "traditionality" as constitutive of finitude in *The Fall of Interpretation: Philosophical Foundations for a Creational Hermeneutic* (Downers Grove, Ill.: InterVarsity, 2000), 149–59.

8. Milbank, "Programme of Radical Orthodoxy," 45.

Third, while sympathetic to the insights of the Eastern fathers, especially Gregory of Nyssa (WMS, 194–216; CG, 87–91), the "O" of RO is not to be confused with Eastern Orthodoxy, which lacks the ecumenicity that RO seeks to embody.

Finally, while RO might have a program, we should not therefore conclude that it has a singular agenda built "on a discrete edifice that purports to be a stronghold."[9] Rather, RO describes a certain spirit that is "a call to look again at things one has too often assumed." As such, it is not a system, method, or formula but "a hermeneutic disposition and a style of metaphysical vision."[10] It is orthodox insofar as it seeks to be unapologetically confessional and Christian; it is radical insofar as it seeks to critically retrieve premodern roots (*radix*).[11]

If RO is not a rigid set of doctrines, nor a merely nostalgic return to premodern ways of being and knowing, nor a monolithic ideology, then what is it? Can we speak of it as a school? Or a theological movement? What are the boundaries of RO? Is it fair to ask who is in and who is outside the pale of RO? What tenets must a radically orthodox theologian affirm? And if we cannot mark the boundaries of RO, can we at least locate a center?

Graham Ward, John Milbank, and Catherine Pickstock are all wary of designating RO as a school or a movement in any kind of institutional sense.[12] Pickstock emphasizes that "radical orthodoxy has never seen itself as an exclusive movement, but rather as a loose tendency."[13] Ward echoes this qualification by noting that "RO has no program, it has no headquarters, it has none of the definitiveness of, say, the Yale School (a 'School' both Frei and Lindbeck wished to downplay)."[14] Instead of a movement with a defined agenda or a school with established doctrines,

---

9. Pickstock, "Radical Orthodoxy and the Meditations of Time," 63.

10. Ibid.

11. RONT, 2. Cf. Herman Dooyeweerd, *Roots of Western Culture: Pagan, Secular, and Christian Options* (Toronto: Wedge, 1979).

12. While the introduction to RONT describes it as a "Cambridge movement," its ties there are thin and in some ways tendentious. Only Pickstock remains at Cambridge (Ward is at Manchester, Milbank at Nottingham, formerly at Virginia, and the graduate students have scattered), and it is hardly the case that Cambridge is under the "sway" of RO.

13. Pickstock, "Reply to David Ford and Guy Collins," 405.

14. Graham Ward, "In the Economy of the Divine: A Response to James K. A. Smith," *PNEUMA: Journal of the Society for Pentecostal Studies* 25 (2003): 117. In general, I find Milbank more comfortable with thinking of RO as a fairly unified "movement" and more likely to use "we" to describe those who are "with the program," so to speak. But Milbank, too, is quick to emphasize the plurivocity of this "we." See John Milbank, "Alternative Protestantisms," in *Creation, Covenant, and Participation: Radical Orthodoxy and the Reformed Tradition*, ed. James K. A. Smith and James H. Olthuis (Grand Rapids: Baker Academic, forthcoming).

Ward describes RO as a certain "theological sensibility, a sensibility shared to a greater or lesser degree with several other contemporary theologians."[15] Pickstock speaks of "the 'spirit' of Radical Orthodoxy." More specifically, RO should be understood as a "hermeneutic disposition and a style of metaphysical vision; and it is not so much a 'thing' or 'place' as a 'task.'"[16] RO, therefore, does not have a postmodern creed or statement of faith to which one must subscribe, nor is it a movement to which one either belongs or does not belong, nor is it a school with respect to which one is either in or out. As a theological sensibility and spirit, RO is more of a substantive set of alliances and agreements to which many might subscribe. Indeed, as Pickstock notes, "Radical orthodoxy can be taken as potentially embracing all those who espouse a basically orthodox theology, but do not regard themselves as simply ecclesiastical or political traditionalists. The point, however, is to work out just what this position involves in the face of modern and postmodern thought."[17]

Nevertheless, it is clear that this is not orthodoxy as usual; in other words, the remarkable reception of the work of Milbank, Ward, and Pickstock demonstrates that RO is touching a certain nerve in the contemporary church and theology. As a result, while RO is not a movement in a heavy-handed institutional sense, it is a movement in the sense of a network of common allegiances and concerns with which a number of confessional scholars resonate—including those working within the Reformational tradition.[18] The sensibility that is RO has something unique to say and to contribute not only to the contemporary theological scene but also to the shape of Christian practice in a post-secular world. Despite the fuzziness of boundaries, the label Radical Orthodoxy is effective in naming a certain spirit of theologically driven cultural engagement.

What is the shape of this theological sensibility? What is the essence of this spirit? If we cannot define RO's boundaries, can we at least locate its core or center? Ward helpfully proposes a basic, unifying principle: "Employing the tools of critical reflexivity honed by continental thinking, taking on board the full implications of what has been termed the linguistic turn, Radical Orthodoxy reads the contemporary world through the Christian tradition, weaving it into the narrative of that

---

15. Ward, "In the Economy of the Divine," 117. The theologians Ward names include Rowan Williams, Fergus Kerr, Nicholas Lash, Stanley Hauerwas, David Burrell, and Peter Ochs (115).

16. Catherine Pickstock, "Radical Orthodoxy and the Meditations of Time," 63.

17. Pickstock, "Reply to David Ford and Guy Collins," 405.

18. RO is an academic and theological "movement" that finds a strongly ecclesial correlate and ally in the Ekklesia Project (www.ekklesiaproject.org).

tradition."[19] This take on the sensibility of RO highlights both a methodological approach as well as a constructive task. On the one hand, methodologically, RO finds its voice in the discourses of contemporary continental thought, which it takes to have opened up a space for cultural analysis that Anglo-American or analytic philosophy has not.[20] Its adoption of continental discourse, therefore, is not accidental. Whether Ward's appropriation of Michel de Certeau, Daniel Bell's engagement with Foucault,[21] or Milbank's more recent engagements with Gilles Deleuze, Alain Badiou, and Slavoj Žižek, RO's theological vision is articulated in the language of—and in response to—the critical insights of contemporary critical theory haling from the Continent.[22] On the other hand, constructively, RO's project is not one of correlation, trying to demonstrate the affinity between the insights of Foucault and the apostle Paul. Rather, RO seeks to retrieve the deep theological resources of the Christian tradition—particularly premodern resources in the fathers and medievals—to let them speak *to* postmodernism. It eschews both the modern hubris that characterizes liberal theology (which, in its ahistorical pride, imagines only a narrative of progress whereby we overcome our infantile and immature commitments to myths) and the postmodern hubris that characterizes contemporary theology (which, in its reactionary philosophical naïveté, imagines that we can give up the project of metaphysics). This is why a movement that is so contemporary is nevertheless deeply committed to tradition, convinced that the insights of the Spirit given to the early church have much to say to the contemporary church—and to the world.

This world-oriented proclamation is essential to RO, for RO is not intended to be just an interior—albeit prophetic—monologue within the church. Rather, it is intended to motivate a *kerygmatic* engagement with contemporary culture. Ward is careful to emphasize this when addressing questions about the tone of the initial RO collection:

> One source of the misconception of RO among fellow Christian theologians has been that the "Introduction" was setting up a new and better Christian theology than anything else on offer. This misconception arises because it is assumed that the volume is addressed to other Christian theologians

19. Ward, "Radical Orthodoxy and/as Cultural Politics," 106.
20. On the poverty of analytic philosophy in this respect, see David Burrell, "Radical Orthodoxy in a North American Context," in *Radical Orthodoxy?* 29–30.
21. Daniel M. Bell Jr., *Liberation Theology after the End of History: The Refusal to Cease Suffering*, Radical Orthodoxy (London: Routledge, 2001).
22. For an overview of this kind of project, see Graham Ward, *Theology and Contemporary Critical Theory: Creating Transcendent Worship Today*, 2nd ed. (New York: St. Martin's Press, 2001).

in order to point up their deficiencies. But that assumption is wrong. That first volume is not primarily addressed to Christian theologians but to the imploding world of secular reasoning with which it opens. Hence the titles of the essays act as interdisciplinary bridges for opening wider cultural conversations: aesthetics, music, sex, nihilism, the city, the body, and so forth. The essays explore areas in which contemporary society has invested much of its thinking, money, manipulations, and values.[23]

Thus, RO is advocating a distinctly theological engagement with the world—and the academy that investigates this world—undergirded by the belief that the way to engage the contemporary world is not by trying to demonstrate a correlation between the gospel and cultural values but rather by letting the gospel confront these (apostate) values. If, for instance, we want to think about the nature of society, "only (Christian) theology"—for example, only accounts that are funded by revelation and recognize the world as God's creation—can provide a proper account of the nature of social relationship. Thus, the regnant sociologies currently on offer (Weberian, Geertzian, etc.)—which deny creation and reject revelation—must be confronted on their own turf. This is why the true *telos* of the RO project is not simply a theology but a comprehensive Christian account of every aspect of the world—a properly and radically Christian account of social relationships, economic organization, political formation, aesthetic expression, and so on, engendering a radically Christian sociology, a radically Christian economics, and so forth.[24] In other words, while it articulates a theologically funded reflection on the world, RO is not only (or even properly) a *theology*.[25] Because of this conviction, RO has (in)famously eschewed "dialogue" with secular disciplines.[26] Unlike correlationist strategies that defer the "truth" of the natural sphere to secular sciences (as in liberation theology's deferral to Marxism as the

23. Ward, "In the Economy of the Divine," 116–17.

24. In this respect, RO is closer to Amsterdam than to New Haven. As Nicholas Wolterstorff notes, the Yale school articulated the project of "reversing the direction of conformation" largely only for *theology*, whereas neo-Calvinism thinks of this more broadly (Nicholas Wolterstorff, "What New Haven and Grand Rapids Have to Say to Each Other," in *Seeking Understanding: The Stob Lectures, 1986–1998* [Grand Rapids: Eerdmans, 2001], 259). Cf. Stanley Hauerwas's concluding reflections on "The Church and the University," in *With the Grain of the Universe: The Church's Witness and Natural Theology* (Grand Rapids: Brazos, 2001), 231–40.

25. We return to these questions in detail in chapter 5.

26. Obviously, this does not entail, as Douglas Hedley seems to suggest, that RO is cutting off any engagement with "secular" theory or "pagan" learning (Douglas Hedley, "Should Divinity Overcome Metaphysics? Reflections on John Milbank's Theology beyond Secular Reason and Confessions of a Cambridge Platonist," *Journal of Religion* 80 [2000]: 275–76). Even a cursory survey of their work would show that this is a mistaken conclusion. Nor does their (qualified) rejection of dialogue entail the "suicidal sectarianism" Hedley suggests (276).

"expert" on the social sphere), RO claims that there is not a single aspect of human existence or creation that can be properly understood or described apart from the insights of revelation. "It regards no element in secular discourse as sacrosanct and sees no limit as to how a theological discourse may change our perspective on anything. Therefore, Radical Orthodoxy defers to no experts and engages in no dialogues because it does not recognize other valid points of view outside the theological."[27] Instead, RO thinks about these aspects of being-in-the-world through theoretical lenses informed by the resources of revelation.

A Symphony in Five Movements

Since RO is not a clearly delineated "school" or "movement" whose doctrines can be neatly listed but rather a "sensibility" or a "spirit" energized by common practices and commitments, the strategy employed here for defining RO is heuristic. In particular, we will use the metaphor of a symphony made up of different movements—though we could also consider it a chorus of voices producing a harmonious new song that, while sung by a plurality of tongues, is characterized by enough similarity and consensus that we can speak of a "program" of Radical Orthodoxy. Based on the unifying principle articulated by Ward above, I want to suggest five key movements or themes that characterize the "sensibility" of RO. The descriptions of themes here will be brief since they are intended to provide just an initial sketch of the core of RO and to point us to the more systematic engagements of each of these themes in the following chapters. At the end of this chapter, after this initial sketch, I will introduce one of the central projects of this book: the attempt at a Reformed "rendition" of RO. In the chapters that follow, each of these movements is further unpacked in detail, all in the service of this Reformed rendition.

1. *A critique of modernity and liberalism.* If Milbank's *Theology and Social Theory* expressed the spirit of what would come to be known as RO, then at its roots, RO is a trenchant critique of modernity as a flawed, imploding project. The key figures in RO see in modernity the institution of dualisms that are grounds for excluding the divine and the transcendent, hence modernity's implosion or what others have called the "end" of metaphysics. "The end of modernity," Milbank argues, "which is not accomplished, yet continues to arrive, means the end of a single system of truth based on universal reason, which tells us what

reality is like."[28] Modern dualisms, such as the opposition between faith and reason, became the rules of the game in which modern theology had to play. RO, instead of operating within those confines, questions the very rules of the game by calling into question the assumptions of modernity itself. Thus:

> with this ending [of modernity], there ends also the modern predicament of theology. It no longer has to measure up to accepted secular standards of scientific truth or normative rationality. Nor, concomitantly, to a fixed notion of the knowing subject, which was usually the modern, as opposed to the premodern, way of securing universal reason. This caused problems for theology, because an approach grounded in subjective aspiration can only precariously affirm objective values and divine transcendence.[29]

While RO criticizes theological liberalism, which it views as accommodating theology to modernity rather than grounding itself in revelation, RO is also a strident critic of classical political liberalism because of its assumptions regarding human nature (as in Thomas Hobbes, for instance) and its atomistic account of the social sphere.

However, though RO is grounded in a critique of modernity, it is not antimodern. To be antimodern in the sense of Protestant fundamentalism is to be the simple negation of modernity and hence still within a modern paradigm. RO is critical of modernity in a way that seeks to circumvent its assumptions; thus, as some proponents of RO suggest, only RO is truly postmodern because it is precisely *other than* modern. "Hence Radical Orthodoxy, although it opposes the modern, also seeks to save it. It espouses, not the pre-modern, but an alternative version of modernity."[30]

What this means is that Christian theologians and theoreticians are, in a sense, empowered to call into question the foundational metaphysical, epistemological, and anthropological assumptions—or faith commitments—that undergird modernity. We can briefly discern the shape of this critique in practice by considering three examples (each considered in more detail in part 2). In Milbank, for instance, this means calling into question the "ontology of violence," which construes human intersubjective relationships as governed by power and war. But he does more than just call this into question. He seeks to show the internal inconsistencies of such a construal.[31] Further, he

---

28. John Milbank, "Postmodern Critical Augustinianism: A Short *Summa* in Forty-two Responses to Unasked Questions," in *The Postmodern God: A Theological Reader,* ed. Graham Ward (Oxford: Blackwell, 1997), 265.

29. Ibid., 265.

30. Milbank, "Programme of Radical Orthodoxy," 45.

31. This is the burden of the later sections of TST, esp. 278–325.

then offers an "ontology of peace," which considers human intersubjective relationships as grounded in a fundamental harmony.[32] This is confessedly and unapologetically grounded in a Christian, particularly Augustinian, metaphysics—which, of course, the modern academy claims must be excluded because it operates from a particular faith perspective. But Milbank's analysis has demonstrated that even these modern, supposedly secular, accounts of intersubjectivity are founded on particular faith perspectives. The "fundamental shifts" that characterize modern, secular social theory—which Milbank argues are in fact simply modifications or rejections of Christian orthodoxy—are "no more rationally 'justifiable' than the Christian positions themselves" (TST, 1).[33] In another instance, Catherine Pickstock criticizes the "immanentism" of modernity in its accounts of language, which shuts down any reference to transcendence and thus undoes the liturgical or doxological foundation of language (AW, 47–100).[34] The result of significant shifts in Ramus, Scotus, and Descartes, modernity eternalizes the present and sacralizes the immanent, such that "space becomes a pseudo-eternity which, unlike genuine eternity, is fully comprehensive to the human gaze, and yet supposedly secure from the ravages of time" (AW, 48). But again, the burden of Pickstock's argument is to demonstrate that we need not play the game by these modern rules, that we are not constrained to accept these assumptions, and that we can, in fact, consider space, time, and language differently—as the

32. Ibid., 380–438.

33. In "Postmodern Critical Augustinianism," he goes on to argue not just for the right of Christian accounts to "compete" as just another perspective but that in fact Christian accounts are better or more viable than these others: "Christianity, therefore, is not just in the same position as all other discourses *vis-à-vis* postmodernity; it can, I want to claim, think difference, yet it perhaps uniquely tries to deny that this necessarily (rather than contingently, in a fallen world) entails conflict" (268; see also 267–69). Milbank wants not only to clear the space for radically Christian accounts to be admitted into the marketplace of ideas as yet another option for consumers of ideas but also to show that such Christian accounts have an internal consistency and ability to account for reality that non-Christian perspectives do not have. In this way, there is a deep continuity with the project of Reformed philosophy as developed by Kuyper and Dooyeweerd, who also argue for the primacy of faith commitments and then seek to demonstrate the inconsistency of other worldviews. For a helpful introduction to this theory and strategy, see ITWT, 1–42. (Again, on this point, Amsterdam and Durham are allies, for as Hauerwas emphasizes, "Christians owe it to themselves and their neighbors to put descriptions of the world that presume that God does not exist into what MacIntyre calls 'epistemological crisis'" [*With the Grain of the Universe*, 208n4]).

34. Cf. Phillip Blond, "Introduction: Theology before Philosophy," in *Post-secular Philosophy: Between Philosophy and Theology*, ed. Phillip Blond (New York: Routledge, 1998), 1–66; and James K. A. Smith, *Speech and Theology: Language and the Logic of Incarnation*, Radical Orthodoxy (London: Routledge, 2002).

space of creation that liturgically and sacramentally points us to the transcendent.

In a third instance, Graham Ward's analysis of secular utopias in the work and thought of Frank Lloyd Wright and Le Corbusier unveils the way in which their "cities of eternal aspiration"—whether Wright's ideal community of Broadacres or Le Corbusier's "Radiant City"—are in fact parodies of the eschatological city (CG, 38–43). As such, urban planners and architects become priests of this immanentized New Jerusalem, and city planning is, in fact, a covert natural theology (CG, 40–41). The proper response to this unveiling of the theologies at work in the secular city is a more radical and integral theological account of urban reality, particularly the nature of relationships within this city.[35] As a final instance of this project, one can see similar movements in Phillip Blond's critique of modern assumptions regarding art and his proposal for a radically incarnational account of aesthetics.[36]

2. *Post-secularity.* By calling into question the dualisms of modernity, RO eliminates a significant distinction between the secular and the sacred, thus undoing the very notion of secular reason. As a result, the modern distinction—or better, opposition—between faith and reason is also called into question. Thus, RO

> protests equally against assertions of pure reason and of pure faith; equally against denominational claims for a monopoly of salvation and against indifference to church order; equally against theology as an internal autistic idiolect, and against theology as an adaptation to unquestioned secular assumptions. . . . However, it further asserts that the apparently opposite poles refused are in secret collusion: more specifically it contends that the pursuit of pure faith is as much a *modern* quest as the pursuit of pure reason; that the investing of salvific security entirely in institutions and formulae is as modern as the individualistic neglect of such matters, while the eschewing of all apologetics is likewise as modern as regarding apologetics as the essential foundation for a truthful theology.[37]

In this way, RO attempts to be a kind of *via media,* without being middle-of-the-road. It seeks to articulate not only a confessional theology but

35. We discuss this in more detail in chapter 7.

36. See Phillip Blond, "Perception: From Modern Painting to the Vision in Christ," in RONT, 220–42; and idem, "The Primacy of Theology and the Question of Perception," in *Religion, Modernity, and Postmodernity,* ed. Paul Heelas (Oxford: Blackwell, 1998), 285–313.

37. Milbank, "Programme of Radical Orthodoxy," 33. In regard to Milbank's list of pairings, evangelicals should consider whether they find themselves on the side of "pure faith," the individualistic neglect of institutional ecclesiology, and a historical eschewing of rational reflection.

also a confessional account of human experience in all of its elements: a Christian social theory, a Christian aesthetics, a Christian account of sexuality, and so on. It sounds a call for radically Christian reflection across the disciplines.

RO, therefore, challenges *the* orthodoxy of the academy: secularity, or the belief in purportedly objective accounts of human life untainted by faith perspectives. As already suggested, RO sees the very notion of "the secular" as a myth, and a late one at that.[38] ("Once, there was no 'secular'" [TST, 9].) Thus, Phillip Blond's manifesto-like claim: "To say we should now bring an end to the secular is to say that we should reverse the dreadful consequences of the liberal erasure of God and take myth back from out of the hands of the fascists where it has all too often fallen."[39] Rejecting modern dualisms and the myth of secularity allows theology in mainstream discourse to be unapologetically confessional and Christian research across the disciplines to be unapologetically theological. The hope is that, once the theoretical foundations of secularity are dismantled—and demonstrated as such—the spaces for public discourse (in both politics and the academy) will provide new opportunities for the expression of a properly theological or Christian account of reality. RO, therefore, seeks to foster the kind of confessional pluralism sketched in George Marsden's vision of the academy in which, ultimately, *everyone* is a confessional theorist.[40]

3. *Participation and materiality.* The first two, more epistemological themes of RO are grounded in and grow out of an ontological commitment to participation as the only proper metaphysical model for understanding creation, the Creator/creation relation in particular.[41] This movement is the crescendo of the RO symphony. The emphasis on participation (*methexis*) again emphasizes that the target of RO is not primarily Christian theology per se but rather the contemporary theoretical currents of our day that traffic under the banner of postmodernism. What characterizes postmodern ontology, according to RO, are a flatness and materialism that ultimately lead to nihilism—a loss of the

38. I considered the same themes in "Re-Kanting Postmodernism? Derrida's Religion within the Limits of Reason Alone," *Faith and Philosophy* 18 (2000): 261–76.

39. Blond, "Introduction," 54.

40. See George Marsden, *The Outrageous Idea of Christian Scholarship* (Oxford: Oxford University Press, 1998). Cf. also Christian Smith, "Secularizing American Higher Education," and Kraig Beyerlein, "Educational Elites and the Movement to Secularize Public Education," in *The Secular Revolution: Power, Interests, and Conflict in the Secularization of American Public Life,* ed. Christian Smith (Berkeley: University of California Press, 2003), 97–195.

41. Ward describes participation as a "fundamental theme" of RO ("In the Economy of the Divine," 118).

real squandered into nothing. When the world is so flattened that all we have is the immanent, the immanent implodes upon itself. In contrast to such nihilism and materialism, only a participatory ontology—in which the immanent and material is suspended from the transcendent and immaterial—can grant the world *meaning*.[42] "The theological point here," Pickstock remarks, "is that Christianity is as equally removed from nihilism as it is from finite positivism, because, following Augustine, every created reality is absolutely nothing in itself. . . . This point is fundamental to radical orthodoxy's pitting of participation against postmodern tendencies to nihilism."[43] If nothing *is* autonomously or in itself but *is* only insofar as it participates in the gift of existence granted by God (a clearly Augustinian model), then we can see how the first two themes are in fact grounded in this central movement: As articulated in the introduction to RONT, participation is central

> because any alternative configuration perforce reserves a territory indepen-
> dent of God. The latter can lead only to nihilism (though in different guises).
> Participation, however, refuses any reserve of created territory, while al-
> lowing finite things their own integrity. Underpinning the present essays
> [in RONT], therefore, is the idea that every discipline must be framed by
> a theological[44] perspective; otherwise these disciplines will define a zone
> apart from God, grounded literally in nothing. (RONT, 3)

Thus, while the call for Christian reflection across the disciplines is grounded epistemologically in terms of insight and revelation, here it is grounded ontologically in terms of participation: Every sphere of creation, and our inhabitance of it (including the labors of human *poiesis* and culture making), participates in the primal gift of the Creator.[45] Simply because the world is creation demands that every aspect of that world

---

42. In chapter 6, I compare this with Dooyeweerd's claim that "*meaning* is the *being* of all that has been *created*" (NC, I.4).

43. Pickstock, "Reply to David Ford and Guy Collins," 416. David Ford welcomes this discussion of participation insofar as it is "vital for the Church" to reflect on "how God comes together with the world" ("Response to Catherine Pickstock," *Scottish Journal of Theology* 54 [2001]: 424).

44. One of the most vexing aspects of RO, especially from a Reformed perspective, is the somewhat equivocal use of the terms *theology* and *theological* to indicate phenomena that range from revelation and confession to creeds and scientific theology. This is the focus of chapter 5.

45. This is central to Milbank's work. As he has most recently put it, "I have always tried to suggest that participation can be extended also to language, history and culture: the whole realm of human *making*. Not only do being and knowledge participate in a God who is and who comprehends; also human making participates in a God who is infinite poetic utterance: the second person of the Trinity" (BR, ix).

be investigated *as created*—which must also mean *in light of the cross* (so that this perspective cannot become another "natural theology").

This is why the nihilistic postmodern valorization of appearances (Jean Baudrillard following Nietzsche) or the body (Judith Butler and others) ends up dissipating the reality of the immanent, material world. "In contrast, the theological perspective of participation actually saves the appearances by exceeding them. It recognizes that materialism and spiritualism are false alternatives, since if there is only finite matter there is not even that, and that for phenomena really to *be* there they must be more than there" (RONT, 4, emphasis added). RO, therefore, is characterized by a genuine theological materialism because it affirms what is beyond the material; its affirmation of transcendence funds a proper valuation of immanence—a valuation that is not really legitimate for nihilism, despite all the postmodern theorizing about the body and so on. "One of the most central aims of a radically orthodox perspective," Pickstock informs us, "is to restore time and embodiment to our understanding of reality."[46] This is indicative of an even broader goal of revaluing materiality and embodiment as part of what we might describe as an incarnational ontology.[47] Undoing one more dualism of modernity—namely, body and soul, where the body is relegated to non-necessity[48]—RO emphasizes the material and bodily as a site of both revelation and redemption: God both appears in the flesh and seeks to redeem it. Indeed, only such a "suspension of the material" in relation to a transcendence that exceeds it can do justice to the material as such without lapsing into a simple materialism.[49] Historically:

> the great Christian critics of the Enlightenment—Christopher Smart, Hamann, Jacobi,[50] Kierkegaard, Péguy, Chesterton and others—in different ways saw that what secularity had most ruined and actually denied were

46. Pickstock, "Radical Orthodoxy and the Meditations of Time," 64.

47. I have tried to sketch the outlines of such an incarnational or creational ontology (in contrast to both a Platonic ontology and a nihilistic ontology) in James K. A. Smith, "Staging the Incarnation: Revisioning Augustine's Critique of Theater," *Literature and Theology* 15 (2001): 123–39; and in more detail in chapter 6.

48. The paradigmatic case would be Descartes's account of the human person as essentially a "thinking thing" that only accidentally "occupies" a body. Thus, Descartes's project is to demonstrate the "immortality of the soul" without any reference to resurrection (a marked departure from Aquinas, for instance). Christian theology, particularly fundamentalism, has unwittingly adopted such a dualistic ontology, which places complete emphasis on the soul and denigrates embodiment with all of its characteristics (art, sexuality, language, political relationships, etc.).

49. See Blond, "Perception," 221.

50. Milbank closely considers Hamann and Jacobi's critique in "Knowledge: The Theological Critique of Philosophy in Hamann and Jacobi," in RONT, 21–37.

the very things it apparently celebrated: embodied life, self-expression, sexuality, aesthetic experience, human political community. Their contention, taken up in this volume [RONT], was that only transcendence, which "suspends" these things in the sense of interrupting them, "suspends" them also in the other sense of upholding their relative worth over-against the void. (RONT, 3)[51]

The connection is simple: Because we are embodied, we are gendered, sexual beings; we speak and express ourselves; we can view a painting and listen to a symphony; we can relate to others in a community. Downplaying embodiment (emphasizing the soul over the body, the spiritual over the sensible) is to devalue these modes of being-in-the-world. Conversely, revaluing the body is to see the way in which these aspects of human be-ing are integral aspects of being embodied creatures. This is why Ward argues that contemporary critical theory can offer important resources for Christians to rethink the material in terms of incarnation. In Luce Irigaray, for instance, "a new age of spiritual incarnation is suggested, of a transcendent that is material (what Irigaray has termed a 'sensible transcendental')."[52] It is just such a transcendence revealed in the material that constitutes the truth of the incarnation. Because God has become flesh and dwelt among us, we have beheld his glory (John 1:14); thus is established the general principle that God reveals himself in the sensible or material. "Theology, then, re-describes the created world, not as nothing, nor indeed as any self-sufficient something, but as the real testimony and loving expression of God who donates the ideal to the real that we might make it so."[53]

   4. *Sacramentality, liturgy, and aesthetics.* A consequence of this incarnational account of the revelation of transcendence, coupled with a participatory ontology, is a renewed appreciation for the liturgical or doxological character of creation and the role that liturgy plays in leading us to the divine.[54] Material or sensible modes of revelation—such as dance, the visual arts, gesture, scent, etc.—are important "iconic" indicators. These embodied modes of worship are valued as important means of reflecting (in a dual sense) the divine. "Since God is not an item in the world to which we might turn," Milbank concludes, "he is only first there for us in our turning to him. And yet we only turn to him when he reaches us; herein lies the mystery of liturgy—liturgy that for theology is more fundamental than *either* language *or* experience,

   51. RO roots this revaluing of the material in both the incarnation and a Platonic ontology of "participation." I address the Platonic moorings of this ontology in chapter 3.
   52. Ward, *Theology and Contemporary Critical Theory*, 25.
   53. Blond, "Perception," 221.
   54. This is most fully developed in AW.

and yet is both linguistic and experiential."[55] A particular consequence of revaluing embodiment is an emphasis on aesthetics and the arts as a medium of revelation and worship. As Ward observes, new models of personhood in postmodernity give "renewed dignity to the affective side of human nature."[56] This points to the centrality of an experiential aspect in postmodernity—but such a role for "the experiential aspect has been fundamental in Christianity as one element in the mechanism of repentance and conversion."[57] Such affectivity, recovered in post-modernity, points to a knowledge that is "more profound and prior to rationality."[58] Thus, Ward, drawing on Jean-François Lyotard and Hélène Cixous and repeating key moves in the history of mysticism, explores the parallels and relationships between aesthetic and religious experience, both deeply affective experiences of the sublime. More sustained analyses of the aesthetic are found in the work of Phillip Blond, which we will engage in chapter 6. The core of RO's emphasis on liturgy and the aesthetic is captured in a recent claim by Jean-Luc Marion:

> Where, then, is the paradigmatic kenosis of the image for the benefit of the holiness of God accomplished? In the liturgy. The liturgy proposes to demonstrate a visible spectacle, which summons and possibly fills vision, but also the senses of hearing, smell, touch, and even taste. It accomplishes an entire possible aesthetic and perhaps thus appears to be a complete spectacle, more than opera, which moreover is its mimic and, by the *oratio*, results from it. . . . The attitude of my gaze before the liturgy determines my general attitude before the crossing of the visible by invisible.[59]

If Pickstock claims that outside the liturgy there is no meaning (AW), such that only a liturgical account could underwrite the operation of language in general, then RO's aesthetic correlate might be that outside the liturgy there is no visible, such that only a doxological account can underwrite the arts.

5. *Cultural critique and transformation.* Grounded in a participatory ontology that revalues time and embodiment, RO articulates a distinctive Christian approach to being-in-the-world, or what in evangelical circles is referred to as "this world"—which, too often, we write off as a world "under the sway of the wicked one" (1 John 5:19). One of the important

55. Milbank, "Programme of Radical Orthodoxy," 43.

56. Ward, *Theology and Contemporary Critical Theory,* 121. He examines these theories of personhood in chapter 3.

57. Ibid., 121.

58. Ibid., 123.

59. Jean-Luc Marion, *The Crossing of the Visible,* trans. James K. A. Smith (Stanford: Stanford University Press, 2004), 64–65.

contributions of RO, in ways similar to certain strains of Reformational thought, is to call into question the ubiquity or extent of this sway. Given its incarnational account of God's revelation in the world, building on the participatory account of the relationship between creation and Creator, RO emphasizes both God's revelation of himself in the material world (in art, for instance) and God's concern for the redemption and transformation of this world (socially, politically, and economically). One sees the first theme in the latter essays of RONT, such as Frederick Christian Bauerschmidt's sociopolitical reflections on aesthetics; Blond's essay on incarnation, painting, and art; and Pickstock's concluding consideration of music.[60] RO emphasizes the fact that participation spills over into the sphere of human culture and making—the sphere of *poiesis*. As Milbank puts it, "I have always tried to suggest that participation can be extended also to language, history and culture: the whole realm of human making. Not only do being and knowledge participate in a God who is and who comprehends; also human making participates in a God who is infinite poetic utterance: the second person of the Trinity" (BR, ix). Thus, the project of cultural unfolding (cultivation of the creation [Gen. 1:27]) participates in the redemptive process.

We see the second theme of transformation in Graham Ward's description of RO as "cultural politics" or "constructive cultural criticism."[61] In a lucid essay, Ward argues that one of the aspects of the church's mission is to "read the signs of the times" (Matt. 16:3; 24; cf. 1 Chron. 12:32).[62] This demands both discernment and transformation. Thus, Ward suggests that

> Radical Orthodoxy is involved in reading the signs of the times in such a way. It looks at "sites" that we have invested much cultural capital in—the body, sexuality, relationships, desire, painting, music, the city, the natural, the political—and it reads them in terms of the grammar of the Christian faith; a grammar that might be summed up in the various creeds. In this way Radical Orthodoxy must view its own task as not only doing theology but being itself theological—participating in the redemption of Creation.[63]

60. Frederick Christian Bauerschmidt, "Aesthetics: The Theological Sublime," 201–19; Blond, "Perception," 220–42; and Catherine Pickstock, "Music: Soul, City, and Cosmos after Augustine," 243–77.

61. Ward, "Radical Orthodoxy and/as Cultural Politics," 97–111. See, more recently, CG.

62. Ward, "Radical Orthodoxy and/as Cultural Politics," 103. While Ward grounds this "cultural imperative" in the gospel and the church's mission, one could also root such a program in a creational imperative, as in the Reformed tradition of Abraham Kuyper. The two are complementary, not mutually exclusive.

63. Ibid.

RO's project, therefore, is de(con)structive, "unmasking the cultural idols, providing genealogical accounts of the assumptions, politics, and hidden metaphysics of specific varieties of knowledge—with respect to the constructive, therapeutic project of disseminating the Gospel."[64] Thus, for Ward, the "radical" of RO carries left-wing political connotations: "In the collapse of socialism as a secular political force I see Radical Orthodoxy as offering one means whereby socialism can be returned to its Christian roots."[65] RO thus has a very practical consequence for the church, understanding part of its mission to be Christian *Kulturkritik* in the vein of Walter Benjamin, Herbert Marcuse, and Jürgen Habermas—a kind of Christian baptism of social theory or, more properly, a rededication, since Ward and Milbank would both argue that, at root, such social critique relies on a Christian foundation.[66] But the church does not *have* a cultural critique; it *is* a cultural critique. Its politics is an ecclesiology. Central to the project of RO, then, is a radical consideration of politics—and the political nature of the church and gospel—in a way that does not simply concede political expertise to the secular but rather attempts to unfold a distinctively Christian politics, such that even this "socialism by grace" is not confused with its secular parodies.

A Reformed Rendition

While many other themes characterize RO, these five summarize the major movements of this symphonic chorus. But the task of this book is not simply a repetition or reproduction of this symphony of RO themes but rather a specifically *Reformed* rendition of these movements. One task of the book, then, is the "reforming" of RO. To understand such a project, we must understand what is meant by Reformed, the multilayered sense of reforming RO, and why such a project is warranted.

First, in seeking to bring RO into an engagement with the Reformed tradition, we must understand this Reformed tradition as generously as possible. More specifically, I will draw on two strains within the Reformed tradition: the "Reformational" or "Neo-Calvinist" strain of Dutch Calvinism associated with Abraham Kuyper, Herman Dooyeweerd, and others, as well as the Scottish-American and more Pres-

---

64. Ibid., 104.
65. Ibid., 103.
66. This is the burden of Milbank's TST. Ward suggests the same, arguing that such theories of social critique can be "redeemed" by being returned to their Christian roots. "The ethics and politics many of these thinkers are attempting to construct, the new incarnationalism many of them insist upon, is given a new, non-nihilistic coherence within a theological framework" (ibid., 105).

byterian strain of Calvinism. The Reformational sub-tradition, with its distinct emphasis on the goodness of creation, revalues all spheres of culture as sites for both revelation and redemption. At the same time, because of its emphasis on the radical and structural nature of religious commitment, the Reformational tradition offers a strident critique of claims to secular or neutral accounts of the world. The Scottish Calvinist tradition, while able to give an account of the prior Reformational themes, is characterized by a distinct emphasis on sin and its effects.[67] While my point of entry into the Reformed tradition is its Dutch strain as articulated by Kuyper and Dooyeweerd, I have no interest in being parochial about this. In fact, unlike others operating from within this tradition, I am interested in situating this specifically Dutch strain of Reformed theology within the broader currents of continental Reformed Christianity, particularly Karl Barth (and G. C. Berkouwer), as well as the more Scottish Reformed tradition that has tended to influence the American Reformed and Presbyterian traditions of theological reflection.[68]

Moreover, I hope to undo a certain long-term memory loss that often accompanies the Dutch Reformational tradition insofar as it tends to have difficulty remembering back beyond Kuyper. I am interested in rehabilitating Calvin as a resource for postmodern theological reflection, particularly his account of a sacramental theology and Eucharistic "real presence."[69] With Michael Horton and Richard Muller, I am also convinced that in the (so-called) post-Reformation "scholastics" we find, in fact, theological insights that speak to our postfoundational context.[70] Indeed, Horton's most recent work in a sense already stages the kind of dialogue I want to pursue here.

67. Both traditions find their confessional sources in the Heidelberg Catechism, the Belgic Confession, and the Canons of Dort. For the Scottish tradition, the Westminster Confession and Catechisms take center stage. The Dutch Reformational tradition in its current manifestation tends to downplay Dort.

68. One finds the confluence of all of these strains in the recent work of Michael Horton, *Covenant and Eschatology: The Divine Drama* (Louisville: Westminster John Knox, 2002).

69. For a recent, relevant articulation, see Keith A. Mathison, *Given for You: Reclaiming Calvin's Doctrine of the Lord's Supper* (Phillipsburg, N.J.: Presbyterian & Reformed, 2002).

70. See Michael Horton and Richard Muller's essays in *A Confessing Theology for Postmodern Times*, ed. Michael Horton (Wheaton: Crossway, 2000). Of course, if we want to undertake this retrieval of post-Reformation thinkers in connection with RO, we will bear the burden of demonstrating that they were not captivated by Scotist thought, as is generally assumed. For helpful research to this end, see Paul Helm, "Synchronic Contingency in Reformed Scholasticism: A Note of Caution," *Nederlands Theologisch Tijdschrift* 57 (2003): 207–22.

There is a certain analogy between Michael Horton's *Covenant and Eschatology* and Michael Graves's famous *Portland Building*. Graves's work, like those of other "postmodern classicists,"[71] arose out of the ruins—soon to be rubble—of Le Corbusier's architectural modernism. "Modernism," Charles Jencks observed, "has left us."[72] Of course, modernist structures, such as modernist buildings, continue to surround us, but they exist only as monuments because of cultural and intellectual upheavals since the 1960s.[73] "Modernism cut architectural expression off from the past," Jencks claimed. Thus, "paradoxically, the only way forward was a return to a richer language . . . since innovation, as is now well advertised, depends on convention."[74] In his design for the Portland Public Service Building, Graves mined the resources of the classical architectural tradition as the only site for meaning in a postmodern world. After Le Corbusier, the best we can do is go back—not as a matter of simple repetition, mimicking ancient forms, but in a more Kierkegaardian repetition that "recollects forward."[75] Michael Horton is a kind of theological Michael Graves, and as such, his project of a postmodern theological classicism finds deep affinity with the project of RO. His project in *Covenant and Eschatology* effects the same kind of forward recollection in the wake of modernity. Perhaps only now, he suggests, are we in a place to mine unlikely resources for a postmodern classicist theology in the work of the Reformers and post-Reformation theology.[76]

Indeed, one of the most striking claims of Horton's work is his oblique suggestion that Francis Turretin and Geerhardus Vos are the first postmodern theologians—because for Turretin and other post-Reformation scholastics (the term hardly fits now), Christian theology is a decidedly postfoundationalist enterprise that does not try to "justify" its claims

71. This is the term coined by architectural analyst and commentator Charles Jencks in his *Post-modern Classicism: The New Synthesis*, *Architectural Design Profile* (London: Architectural Design and Academy Editions, 1980).

72. Ibid., 5.

73. In Grand Rapids, there has been debate as to just why we would want to retain the hideous modernist glass box that is our city hall. In the end, the only justification was a kind of antiquarian value: We don't *believe* in Le Corbusier anymore, but we want to keep it around to remind ourselves of the epoch in which we believed in it—kind of like high school yearbooks or prom tuxedos.

74. Jencks, *Post-modern Classicism*, 5.

75. See Kierkegaard, *Repetition*, alluded to in Alain Robbe-Grillet's new novel, *Repetition*, trans. Richard Howard (New York: Grove Press, 2003).

76. As such, Horton's project is distinguished from Thomas C. Oden's "paleo-orthodoxy," which is a little suspicious of anything after the fifth century. Horton thinks the sixteenth- and seventeenth-century Reformed theologians picked up what the fourth century started.

by appeal to neutral reason. Their method, then, is not bringing a prior philosophical construction to the Scriptures; rather, their method—centered around covenant—grows out of the narrative and canon of Scripture itself. In other words, Reformed theology does not apologize for beginning with the presupposition that God speaks to his covenant people in the Scriptures. For the Reformers, Horton observes, "having to justify that God has spoken here and now [in the canon of Scripture] is equivalent to having to justify that one has heard one's spouse this morning at breakfast."[77] Appealing to "Calvin the nonfoundationalist," Horton argues that when we properly retrieve the theological project of post-Reformation systematics, as well as the biblical theology of Vos and Herman Ridderbos, "a real conversation could begin between erstwhile unlikely partners, namely, post-Reformation scholasticism and contemporary philosophy, hermeneutics, and science."[78]

Horton's point echoes the claims of RO, but with a Reformed twist: In a postfoundationalist context, confessional theology need no longer play handmaiden to naturalistic science or philosophy as neutral arbiters of what gets to count as true. As he rightly discerns, the crumbling of the modern metanarrative and Enlightenment construals of science opens the possibility for "a fresh account of traditional Christian claims concerning divine action."[79] By freeing theology to be *un*apologetic, Horton's postmodern classicism—like the Radical Orthodoxy of Ward and Milbank or the postliberalism[80] of Hans Frei and Stanley Hauerwas—begins from a determinate, robust Christian confession, not just

---

77. Horton, *Covenant and Eschatology,* 201.

78. Ibid., 199, 183.

79. Ibid., 51.

80. The most perplexing aspect of *Covenant and Eschatology*—which I cannot fully articulate here—is Horton's persistent criticism of postliberals such as Frei, Lindbeck, and Hauerwas. Methinks he doth protest too much because, on the one hand, he senses how close his proposal is to their project but, on the other hand, feels some need to say that he is *not* one of them. His criticisms of postliberalism are reactionary and miss their target due to significant misunderstandings regarding the question of reference. For instance, on the testimony of the Spirit and the self-authentication of Scripture, Horton suggests that "when one reads this text, one encounters God speaking so clearly by the Spirit's work. . . . Having to justify that God has spoken here and now is the equivalent to having to justify that one has heard one's spouse this morning at breakfast" (200–201). But who is this *one*? Do the Scriptures speak "so clearly" to Northrop Frye? Or Robert Funk? Is not this *one* only the one who has been regenerated by the Holy Spirit so as to hear? And isn't this the heart of Reformed theology? "Our full persuasion and assurance of the infallible truth, and divine authority thereof, is from the inward work of the Holy Spirit, bearing witness by and with the word in our hearts" (Westminster Confession I.v; cf. Belgic Confession, art. 5). And isn't this closer to what Hauerwas is saying—that only the *one* who is a member of the community of the Spirit—the *ecclesia*—will be able to hear this "so clearly"? "The meaning of the text," Horton goes on to say, "does not depend on

a thin Christian consensus or tip of the hat to some big notion such as incarnation or Trinity, but a highly specified account of the story of God in Christ as informed by the Reformed confessions. Horton's rigorous opening salvo, therefore, is a significant challenge to a growing Arminian consensus in evangelical thought (contrary to Roger Olson on the one hand and open theism on the other) while at the same time being engaged with some of the most significant movements in contemporary theology and theory.[81] Horton's rigor and erudition in *Covenant and Eschatology*—unlike in some of his more popular and polemical works—issues a twofold challenge to contemporary Reformed theologians. On the one hand, Horton's postfoundationalist model offers a critique of those branches of Reformed theology that have bought into the modernist project by adopting a rationalist construal of doctrine as merely a body of "propositions," a univocal understanding of theological language, and an Enlightenment notion of a universal reason undergirding a classical apologetics. On the other hand, Horton sketches the possibility for a postfoundationalist Reformed theology that unapologetically speaks to contemporary culture. After all, why should the Anglicans and Anabaptists have all the fun? The kind of project sketched by Horton should embolden Calvinists to enter the contemporary conversation *as Calvinists*, with a renewed sense that the deep wells of Calvin, Edwards, and Kuyper have something important to say in a culture engaged with Derrida, Foucault, and Lyotard.

If we want to join Horton in this project, it is along the lines of this counter-cultural track that the most work remains to be done—even if this might not be a desideratum of Horton himself. Too often, calls for the renewal of Reformed theology are wedded to the most static of status quos that—allied to Reformed understandings of law—feed into a Constantinian project for a repristination of American civil religion. What is unique about Horton's project is the way in which it subverts

---

human receptivity or resistance, conversation or contempt, sympathy or suspicion. But its perlocutionary force does. One can resist the general summons of scripture, both law and gospel. But one's resistance cannot make an utterance untrue any more than one's acceptance can render it true" (201). But isn't Horton's primary interest in the *perlocutionary force* of the text—as commanding and promising? Granted, the fact that the Scriptures are the commands and promises of God in an "objective" sense does not depend on their reception. But that they are received *as* promises and commands—"so clear" for one to see—depends on *recognition* of their provenance and authorship (cf. 100, 102). And this recognition requires regeneration. Horton sometimes wants a kind of "public" theology in which the Scriptures' perlocutionary force is "clear" to just *any* "one." This can feed into a Constantinian agenda.

81. This is also why the "Reformed tradition" I have in mind must include the voice of Jonathan Edwards. See George Marsden, *Jonathan Edwards: A Life* (New Haven: Yale University Press, 2003); and forthcoming research of Jerry Stutzman.

such Constantinian strategies, even if the anti-Constantinian elements of his project are underdeveloped. As he hints in the opening of *Covenant and Eschatology*, "The believing community today in the United States has more in common with the believing community in first-century Asia Minor than it has with the late capitalist culture of Los Angeles and New York."[82] Descriptively, without question, the American evangelical church mirrors late-capitalist culture, but *Covenant and Eschatology* demonstrates why it should not: "Our identity [should be] preeminently shaped by the role that we play in the drama of redemption."[83] We, as a believing community, need to be more discerning about the roles we play. Too often we end up like Nicholas Cage—an Oscar-caliber actor who seems to appear in far too many B-grade movies. But the Reformed tradition does have the resources for just this kind of counter-cultural *Kulturkritik*—particularly when we draw on the unique confluence of Basel and Amsterdam, New Haven and Princeton.

Therefore, by the Reformed tradition I mean a catholic Reformed tradition that has a broad geographical identity (Basel *and* Amsterdam, New Haven *and* Princeton) but also a deep history (beyond Kuyper and Barth to Edwards, Turretin, and Calvin). But *why* this project of reforming RO? What motivates and warrants such an engagement? What is to be gained from such a dialogue? Several reasons come to mind.

First, this project demonstrates the deep allegiances between the program of Radical Orthodoxy and a long tradition of reflection within the Reformed tradition. There are several ways in which core movements of RO were anticipated in the work of Kuyper and Barth, and pointing out such affinities helps us to see reasons for increased consensus and collaboration. Reforming RO, therefore, means first of all the task of lining up the concerns of RO with those of the Reformed tradition in order that both might see themselves in a new light. Second, I want to reform RO in terms of a mutual critique: on the one hand subjecting RO to critique from the perspective of the Reformed tradition, while on the other also giving critical voice to the insights of RO with respect to the Reformed tradition. It is in this sense that RO can profit from an engagement with the Reformed. The Reformed tradition has a long history of reflection on a number of themes on which RO has only begun to reflect. Third, and ultimately, the constructive task of sketching the shape of Christian cultural and academic engagement in a postmodern world demonstrates the relevance of the Reformed theological tradition for the task of inhabiting the post-secular.

---

82. Horton, *Covenant and Eschatology*, 14.
83. Ibid.

3

Radical Orthodoxy's "Story" of Philosophy

From Plato to Scotus and Back

Related Reading

Milbank, John. "Only Theology Overcomes Metaphysics." Chap. 2 in *The Word Made Strange: Theology, Language, Culture.* Oxford: Blackwell, 1997.

Pickstock, Catherine. "Socrates Goes Outside the City." Chap. 1 in *After Writing: On the Liturgical Consummation of Philosophy.* Oxford: Blackwell, 1998.

———. "Modernity and Scholasticism: A Critique of Recent Invocations of Univocity." *Antonianum* 78 (2003): 3–47.

Radical Orthodoxy's History of Philosophy: Of Narratives, Tall Tales, and Meta-history

The incarnational emphasis of RO, briefly outlined in chapter 2, entails an affirmation of time and therefore history as essential aspects of creation. History is the site for the unfolding of revelation, which requires that we take the history of thought seriously.[1] Radical Orthodoxy has a story to tell. It constitutes something of an oral rather than official history and goes roughly as follows.[2]

Once upon a time, there was no secular (TST, 9). All things were understood as participating in the divine, and thus

---

1. On these matters, see Catherine Pickstock, "Radical Orthodoxy and the Meditations of Time," in *Radical Orthodoxy? A Catholic Enquiry,* ed. Laurence Paul Hemming (Burlington, Vt.: Ashgate, 2000), 64–65.

2. In what follows, I attempt to pull together a coherent narrative from the pieces of historical claims made across the RO corpus. I intentionally employ the language used by RO (already encountered in chaps. 1 and 2) and unpack the more technical terms below.

every sphere of reality and human life was understood as being suspended, as it were, from the transcendent. For Christian confession, this translated into the more specific understanding that creation participated in and was suspended from the Creator. As a result, no sphere of creation or creaturely *poiesis* was thought to reside outside the religious or theological—there was no reserve of created territory that was unhooked from this relationship to the transcendent (RONT, 3–4). The entire created and social order, civic life, and reason itself were understood to be undertaken within religious or mythic horizons oriented beyond the material. Indeed, the material world of nature itself was not simply "nature" but creation—a materiality or "charged immanence" curved toward the transcendent and thus saved from the flatness of mere nature. Insofar as there was no secular, there was no objective, autonomous, or neutral reason (RONT, 21–39), no state (RONT, 182–200), no public or private sphere, and no space that was not always already understood to be liturgical and doxological—oriented toward praise of the divine (AW, 37–46).[3] Beginning from a sense of creation and the belief that humankind was created for communion (RONT, 182)—both with the Creator and with creation—this participatory worldview generated an ontology of peace that saw differences as harmoniously rather than oppositionally related (TST, 279, 289), which in turn generated an account of social life that, at the very least, posited peace as a real possibility. This vision of social harmony directed toward the *telos* of divine friendship was undergirded by an ontology that refused both Gnostic dualisms, which opposed the transcendent to the immanent, and atomistic materialisms, which flattened the world to sheer immanence.

This is the story based on a long tradition: from Plato (AW; TST) and the theurgical Neoplatonism of Proclus and Iamblichus, recounted with slightly different intonations in the East by Gregory of Nyssa, passed on to Augustine and picked up by Aquinas, reiterated from the margins of modernity by radical pietists such as Kierkegaard, Hamann, and Jacobi (RONT, 22), recaptured by the *nouvelle théologie*, and most recently narrated from Cambridge by Radical Orthodoxy.

But then came the secular—which is to say, modernity. Ushered in as a process, modernity generated the invention of the secular by rejecting the participatory ontology that had preceded it. In place of a participatory framework that understood the immanent as suspended from the transcendent, modernity assumed an ontology based on the univocity of being, which denied the "depth" of being (Scotus)—an ontology that both flattened the world and unhooked it from the transcendent, thus creating a new space untouched by the divine and an autonomous reserve of reality outside the religious. In short, the secular emerged and along with it the notion of an autonomous reason that was supposedly neutral and

---

3. This does not entail the benighted notion that there was only *one* liturgy or *one* theology. Unlike as some have suggested (Robert Dodaro), RO is able to take into account the reality of competing theologies. What it rejects is the notion of a "neutral" or "rational" discourse about these matters that is not already religious.

objective, offering an account of the world uncontaminated by the theological. Thus, a univocal ontology that flattened the world engendered a
neutral rationality that was supposedly universal. These ontological and
epistemological inventions contributed to anthropological and political
developments—in particular, the construction of a decidedly unliturgical
social world (AW, 48–60). Unfettered from dependence on the transcendent and no longer understood within an ontology of peace and original
harmony, the human self was reduced to an isolated "subject"—a thinking thing (Descartes) later endued with autonomy and inalienable rights
(Locke, Kant). The result was a picture of the social order as an aggregate
of competing atomistic, self-interested subjects (Hobbes, Adam Smith)
quasi-united in a supposedly neutral space called the "public," where relationships were no longer governed by charity but by contract. The *polis*
was no longer a space for liturgical relationships—with both the Creator
and other creatures—but rather a non-teleological, agonistic space where
only the invisible hand of self-interest procedurally governed the subjects
of this order. The modern subject became a parody of God, the modern
state became a parody of the church (RONT, 182–88), the modern city
became a parody of the New Jerusalem (CG, 27–51), modern social theory
became a parody of theology (TST), and so on.

The advent of modernity took place earlier than most people think—the
late Middle Ages—and, despite postmodern pronouncements to the contrary, has yet to come to an end. We find the culmination of the secular in
the nihilism of a postmodernity that is the culmination of the modern. The
logic of nihilism is directly linked to the univocity of being, and insofar
as the supposedly postmodern assumes this modern ontological confession, it can only be hyper-modern. In contrast, a genuinely postmodern
ontology and praxis must subvert the ontology, anthropology, and politics
of modernity. As such, we will find resources in the pre- and otherwise-
than-modern participatory framework of Christian theology.

To say that RO has a story to tell is, on the one hand, a methodological
point: The nature of the theoretical task is necessarily narrative.[4] On
the other hand, this is also a historical point: Central to RO's articulation of a post-secular faith is an account of the history of philosophy
and theology.[5] This is a rich epic narrative, full of heroes and villains,
that recounts the story of theology's fate, particularly in the chapters
of modernity. The last stage of part 1's preliminary project of sketching
the horizons of RO involves getting a sense of this sweeping historical
narrative, since it informs the backdrop of particular criticisms and
more constructive proposals. In fact, there is a sense in which RO's

4. In TST, Milbank argues that narrative is "a more basic category than either explanation or understanding" (267). We return to this aspect of narrativity in chapter 5.

5. My thanks to Jim Bratt for helping me appreciate how central this history is to the
constructive project of RO.

own identity is narratival and thus must be articulated within and by this story. Lucy Gardner is right to suggest that "fundamental to the Radical Orthodoxy programme, and to its own sense of identity, is a story of opposition." Thus, "the history which Radical Orthodoxy must narrate in order to articulate its own identity involves a genealogy of error, an archaeology of sorts—an answer to the question: what went wrong, where?"[6] Gardner seems to think this somehow illegitimate, but given RO's very project as outlined by Ward—"reading the signs of the times"[7]—there is a deep sense in which it must be historically situated. Indeed, RO calls into question the ahistorical project of a "systematic theology" and articulates instead a theology *of* and *for* culture in response to the times without sacrificing proclamation on the altar of relevance. As such, RO's polemical histories are an effort to read the signs of the times genealogically—asking with a critical edge how we got here. The history itself resonates with the antithetical aspect of RO that we already heard from Basel and Amsterdam—taking seriously the claim that God's having spoken "in Son" (Heb. 1:2) constitutes a genuine *apokalypsis,* an unveiling and opening up of reality in a way different from any other account. It finds precedent in Augustine's own project of reading the contemporary world theologically[8] in his *City of God,* in which he takes pains to articulate the difference between pagan and Christian readings of the world, including the culturally dominating project of empire at the time. And there is a sense in which RO's polemical history echoes the Pauline polemics regarding the "foolishness of the Greeks" in contrast to the message of the cross (1 Cor. 1:18–31).

From a meta-historical perspective, the historical account offered by RO exhibits two notable aspects. First, RO's histories tend to be narratives of (qualified) *rupture* and *discontinuity* rather than tales of continuity and progress.[9] In particular, RO provides a historical narrative in the

6. Lucy Gardner, "Listening at the Threshold: Christology and the 'Suspension of the Material,'" in *Radical Orthodoxy?* 135–36.

7. Graham Ward, "Radical Orthodoxy and/as Cultural Politics," in *Radical Orthodoxy?* 103.

8. In chapter 5, I qualify this use of the term *theology* or *theologically.* There I suggest that we make a distinction that RO does not—between theology as ecclesial confession and theology as second-order, theoretical science (or theology[1] and theology[2]).

9. Pickstock and Milbank are both drawn to Alain Badiou's articulation of the "event" as a "break" or "rupture." See Alain Badiou, *L'Être et l'événement* (Paris: Seuil, 1998); and idem, *Saint Paul: The Foundation of Universalism,* trans. Ray Brassier (Stanford: Stanford University Press, 2003). For a discussion, see Catherine Pickstock, "Modernity and Scholasticism: A Critique of Recent Invocations of Univocity," *Antonianum* 78 (2003): 40–46. Daniel Bell also describes Scotus's ontology as "a rupture with the Thomistic *analogia entis*" (Daniel M. Bell Jr., *Liberation Theology after the End of History: The Refusal to Cease Suffering,* Radical Orthodoxy [London: Routledge, 2001], 33).

wake of modernity and situates itself—not naively—in relation to modernity as one of the formative currents of the signs of the times. This, of course, requires all kinds of definitions and demarcations—of the origin of modernity, its boundaries and demise, the nature of *post*modernity, and so forth. To engage in such a project is risky business, open to the criticism of a thousand qualifications at the hands of specialist scholars. But RO discerns something of a paradigm shift in Western culture that gave birth to remarkably new, quite unparalleled accounts of the world and social relationships. These philosophical and theological shifts gave birth to new social arrangements, new political ideals, new economic models, and new accounts of human nature, all of which were slowly globalized through the exportation of liberal democracy and capitalist economics. In other words, if RO's history tells a certain story about the West—especially European Christendom and the birth of modernity—this story constitutes the genealogy of now global phenomena.

Of course, many current accounts of where we are operate on the assumption of a break with the past, generally taking our *post*modern situation to be a rupture with modernity such that we find ourselves in a radically new cultural configuration. But this is precisely where RO's history departs from the now standard postmodern account that posits a supposed superiority of the current age, which has risen above the modern, issuing in a kind of ahistorical hubris that denies tradition.[10] Such postmodern histories assume a discontinuity with the modern and posit a fundamental continuity of all that has gone before: the "history of metaphysics from Plato to Husserl," as it is often suggested.[11] This is why the question of Augustine is so contested: Many philosophical accounts of Augustine—particularly his notion of selfhood—construe Augustine as simply the precursor to Descartes.[12] On this score, the Augustinian self is taken to be a proto-Cartesian subject, indicating a fundamental continuity between ancient (or medieval) and modern. Wayne Hankey, for instance, is wont to establish this continuity, speak-

10. "Radical Orthodoxy utterly rejects the cynicism and pseudo-adulthood of the present age which scorns (or fetishizes) childhood, nature, romance, and hope" ("Radical Orthodoxy: Twenty-four Theses," thesis 11).

11. It would be hard not to lay some blame for such a history at the feet of Martin Heidegger's "destruction of metaphysics" in both his early and later work—a tendency picked up in Derrida's early work as well. While qualified elsewhere, Derrida's *Of Grammatology* is riddled with such claims regarding the story of metaphysics from Plato to Hegel (or Plato to Husserl). See Jacques Derrida, *Of Grammatology*, trans. Gayatri Chakrovorty Spivak (Baltimore: John Hopkins University Press, 1976), e.g., 3, 33, 301.

12. See the works of Stephen Menn, Charles Matthews, and Wayne Hankey. For a fuller account, see Michael Hanby, *Augustine and Modernity*, Radical Orthodoxy (London: Routledge, 2003), 6–26, 134–45.

ing of "the self-reflexive and self-certain Augustinian *cogito*" in terms
that obviously invoke the Cartesian model.[13] The story is then taken a
step farther by tracing the lineage of this modern subject back through
Augustine ultimately to Plato: "On the way from Plato to Descartes
stands Augustine," Charles Taylor recounts.[14] Thus, the filiation of the
modern self is narrated by positing a continuity between the Platonic,
Augustinian, and Cartesian accounts of the subject, ultimately "locating in Plato an anticipation of the modern self."[15] As Michael Hanby
suggests, there is a reason supposed postmoderns want to tell such a
story: Having linked Christianity to modernity, in rejecting modernity,
they are also able to reject Christianity.

> Charles Taylor has provided the architecture for a grand story of modern
> origins now taken as axiomatic by thinkers who otherwise have little in
> common. Augustine's place in this narrative is crucial as one of the great
> pillars of the "Western metaphysical tradition" that concludes in the birth
> of Cartesian subjectivity, a tradition which has fallen into disrepute in the
> wake of Nietzsche, Heidegger, and their disciples. Since Augustine is the
> father of the Western church par excellence, the discrediting of this tradi-
> tion as intrinsically nihilistic is thought, by those inclined toward such
> unmaskings, to expose the intrinsic nihilism of Christianity.[16]

So at stake in the postmodern account of the basic continuity of the
Western tradition is a decidedly theological thesis.

In contrast to this grand story of Western continuity and a recent postmodern rupture with this tradition, RO observes a deep continuity between
the modern and (supposedly) postmodern such that what goes under the
banner of postmodernism is really just hyper-modernism. Milbank, Pickstock, Hanby, and Conor Cunningham all emphasize the degree to which
supposedly postmodern thinkers such as Derrida, Deleuze, and Foucault
replay and play out the ontology of modernity.[17] Moreover, RO contests

13. Wayne Hankey, "'Poets Tell Many a Lie': Radical Othodoxy's Poetic Histories,"
Canadian Evangelical Review (forthcoming), 14 (ms p.). Cf. similar accounts in Menn
and Eric Alliez.

14. Charles Taylor, *Sources of the Self* (Cambridge: Harvard University Press, 1989), 127.

15. Catherine Pickstock, "The Soul in Plato," in *Explorations in Contemporary Con-
tinental Philosophy of Religion*, ed. Deane-Peter Baker and Patrick Maxwell (New York:
Rodopi, 2003), 115. One must concede that Kierkegaard undertakes a similar strategy in
Philosophical Fragments. Pickstock counters this in the conclusion to AW.

16. Hanby, *Augustine and Modernity*, 135.

17. See AW, chaps. 1–3; TST, chap. 10; Hanby, *Augustine and Modernity*, chap. 5; and
Conor Cunningham, *Genealogy of Nihilism*, Radical Orthodoxy (London: Routledge, 2002).
There is an interesting layer of complication and tension here regarding the degree of
continuity between the ancient and the medieval. While RO routinely posits a line of continuity from Plato to Christianity, Milbank's earlier work seemed much more interested

the supposed continuity between the medieval and the modern, locating a decisive rupture in the late Middle Ages. While postmoderns tend to posit a line of simple progress from Augustine to Aquinas to Scotus to Descartes, RO contests this account, arguing that Scotus signals a paradigm shift in ontology that eventually issues in both what we call modernity as well as (ultimately) nihilism—an ontological framework that denies the transcendent and thus leaves the realm of immanence to its own resources (entailing, RO concludes, the dissipation of immanence itself).[18] Scotus's shift away from a metaphysics of participation to an ontology predicated on the univocity of being rent the cords of suspension that hooked the immanent to the transcendent, the material to the more than material. The result—the following section explores this in more detail—was modernity's "flattened" ontology, which eventually issued in nihilism.[19] This account points us to a second meta-historical aspect of RO's history.

In addition to being a narrative of (late medieval) rupture, RO's history of philosophy is a *genealogical* or *archaeological* account of knowledge that reflects a mode of inquiry not unlike that articulated by Nietzsche and later Foucault (TST, 281).[20] Thus, Milbank's project in *Theology and*

---

in asserting an *antithesis* between the Greek and the Christian in important respects. For instance, in *Theology and Social Theory*, he argued, against Alasdair MacIntyre, that "from the perspective of Christian virtue, there emerges to view a hidden thread of continuity between antique reason and modern, secular reason. This thread of continuity is the theme of 'original violence'" (TST, 5; further unpacked in TST, chap. 11; and "Can Morality Be Christian?" in WMS). But lately, Milbank seems to retract such accounts of antithesis. He suggests, for instance, that "for Aristotle as well as Plato, dialectics is finally subordinated to the enticement of the Good, rendering them both more the anticipators of Augustine than I allowed in *Theology and Social Theory* . . . chapters 11 and 12" (Milbank, "Beauty and the Soul," in John Milbank, Graham Ward, and Edith Wyschogrod, *Theological Perspectives on God and Beauty* (Harrisburg, Pa.: Trinity Press International, 2003), 25n55. This seems a point of development, even change, in Milbank's version of the narrative.

18. We consider nihilism in more detail below. There are a couple of interesting twists on this narrative. First, Conor Cunningham suggests a certain Western legacy that gave us Scotus, tracing a "genealogy of nihilism" that begins with Plotinus, whose henological Neoplatonism must be distinguished from the theurgical Neoplatonism of Iamblichus and Proclus (see Conor Cunningham, *Genealogy of Nihilism* [London: Routledge, 2002]). Second, Michael Hanby argues that in Descartes (or what he calls "the nihilism occasioned by the advent of the *res cogitans*") nihilism results from the triumph of a Stoic conception of the will that Augustine had refused (*Augustine and Modernity*, 135–36).

19. Modernity's univocal ontology gives us a "flattened" world insofar as the created, immanent order no longer participates in the divine and thus is no longer characterized by the depth of that which is stretched toward the transcendent. The metaphor suggests a picture in which the created order is "suspended" from the Creator, stretching and "thickening" it; once that connection is "unhooked," the created order is no longer stretched or elongated but rather snaps back into a thin, flattened zone of immanence.

20. There is also a sense in which RO's history is methodologically akin to Heidegger's destruction of metaphysics or critique of "onto-theo-logy," even though it would dispute

Social Theory, aimed at "demonstrating the questionability of the assumptions upon which secular social theory rests" operates on the basis of "an
'archaeological' approach" that traces "the genesis of the main forms of
secular reason, in such a fashion as to unearth the arbitrary moments
in the construction of their logic" (TST, 3). The particular shape of the
genealogy is quite different, but the methodological sense of suspicion
is similar: Our contemporary ontologies commonly described as postmodern are not what they claim to be. While claiming to be remarkable
inventions—virgin births, as it were—their paternity can be discerned;
their filiation traces to the father they have attempted to depose: modernity itself. And even modernity, characterized by either proclamations
of a similar miracle of invention or alternative pedigrees, has an unrec-
ognized father: the late Middle Ages. In other words, genealogies always
contest the official story or public pedigree of structures and ideas to
discern a different line of descent. Both modernity and postmodernity
have fathers whom they refuse to recognize, either because they do not
know their own history or because they have a stake in denying such
a legacy (and claiming a different one). For instance, while Descartes
may attempt to portray himself as the son of an Augustinian heritage,
Hanby points to the way in which Descartes's father is Stoicism and late
medieval scholasticism.[21] While Kant, in some ways, claims to arrive
almost without filiation (offering a Copernican revolution), in fact he
remains a scholastic.[22] And while Derrida or Deleuze may want to suggest
a rejection of ancient and modern fathers, a little time in the archives
suggests that their fathers are located in modernity, with grandfathers
in the late Middle Ages. Postmodernism was not created *ex nihilo;* it
was born and thus has a specific family history.

Central to RO's genealogy, characterized by a certain hermeneutics
of suspicion, is the contention that "aspects of late medieval theological
thought underpin later characteristically 'modern' ideas."[23] Further,
modern thought underpins characteristically postmodern ideas. Hence,
Scotus is, we might say, the grandfather of what is commonly called postmodernism: "Scotus' proto-modernity involves also the 'post-modern.'"[24]

the conclusions of Heidegger's histories. Both would agree, however, that Duns Scotus
undoubtedly qualifies as an "onto-theo-logian." See Catherine Pickstock, "Reply to David
Ford and Guy Collins," *Scottish Journal of Theology* 54 (2001): 412.

21. Hanby's complex account is important here, for he argues that the "dueling cosmolo-
gies" of Scotus and Aquinas replay Augustine's critique of Stoic materialism. Stoicism,
then, is a kind of proto-modernism (Hanby, *Augustine and Modernity*, 72–90, 106–16).

22. Catherine Pickstock, "Modernity and Scholasticism," in WMS, 5; and John Milbank,
"Critique of the Theology of Right," in WMS, 8–16.

23. Pickstock, "Modernity and Scholasticism," 4.

24. Ibid., 10.

What we have in postmodernity is a persistent Middle Ages: "The issue," Pickstock summarizes, "does not involve a contrast between the modern and the postmodern. It is rather that both represent a certain middle ages (with roots that reach back before Duns Scotus in his Franciscan forebears and in Avicenna), within which our culture still mostly lies, and whose assumptions we might at least want to examine."[25] RO's project is to call into question the structure of post/modernity by first unveiling this filiation and then subjecting the Scotist ontology to critique. It is to this critique of Scotus that we now turn.[26]

Beginning from the Middle: The Modern Turn (to Nihilism)

Given RO's project, there is a strange sense in which we begin the story in the middle by documenting the fall.[27] If modernity is the heuristic label used to name what's wrong, this does not make matters simple, for we need to discern the shape and scope of modernity and then undertake a genealogy that might give us a glimpse of where and when this began to take shape (as well as its persistence, despite many claims to its demise). One of the unique contributions of RO's history is the claim that the supposed origins of modernity are not where many go looking. In standard (supposedly) postmodern accounts, the matrix of modernity is identified with the eighteenth-century Enlightenment, particularly the figure of Kant, or early modern revolutions in science and philosophy, particularly Descartes. RO does not deny the deep modernity of Kant or Descartes, but its genealogy asks just what made a Kant and a Descartes possible. For RO, the root and condition of the possibility of modernity are found in a late medieval paradigm shift in ontology—away from a metaphysics of

25. Ibid., 30 (cf. 32, 36). For an account of Avicenna's role in this narrative, see Cunningham, *Genealogy of Nihilism*, 9–13.

26. A question that must be raised but cannot be adequately addressed here is, If Calvin is a nominalist, does not the RO critique of Scotus also apply *mutatis mutandis* to Calvin as well? Here I reject the premise: Calvin's ontological framework is not nominalist. This, however, is an agenda for future research. (One aspect of such a claim would have to demonstrate that a commitment to *voluntarism* does not necessarily require a commitment to nominalism.) For a survey of the issues, see Richard Muller, "Scholasticism in Calvin: A Question of Relation and Disjunction," in *The Unaccommodated Calvin: Studies in the Foundation of a Theological Tradition* (Oxford: Oxford University Press, 2000), 39–61. My thanks to Jerry Stutzman for pointing me to Muller.

27. Or what Hanby describes as a "fall from grace"—the "collapse of the Augustinian theological vision" in early modernity (*Augustine and Modernity*, 1).

participation and toward the univocity of being—crystallized most comprehensively in the work of John Duns Scotus. While RO's critique of Scotus—bordering on a fixation—has been subject to wide criticism,[28] it is not without precedent; indeed, it picks up the interpretation of Etienne Gilson and more contemporary readings offered by Jean-Luc Marion, J.-F. Courtine, and Olivier Boulnois.[29] Further, RO concedes that Scotus is indicative of broader currents: "He is one figure among many—although a crucial one—in a general shift away from a focus upon the metaphysics of participation . . . , and he is noteworthy in particular because he gave attention to these matters in a comprehensive fashion."[30] Scotus, then, is privileged as a kind of case study in univocal ontology.[31]

The Scotus Case

But just what problem does Scotus bequeath to us? What is so wrong with an ontology predicated on the univocity of being? This must be understood in contrast to Aquinas's participatory metaphysics, which affirms the *analogy* of being. For Aquinas, to say that God "is" can be understood only by analogy with the sense in which a creature "is": The mode of being of the Creator is different, in an important sense, from the mode of being of creatures. God's very essence *is* existence, whereas the creature "is" only to the extent that it receives the gift of being from the Creator or, in other words, to the extent that the creature

28. The criticisms here come in two forms: First, some argue that Scotus simply does not think or believe what RO attributes to him; second, some agree with the reading of Scotus but disagree regarding the *evaluation* of this shift. See, for example, Richard Cross, "Where Angels Fear to Tread: Duns Scotus and Radical Orthodoxy," *Antonianum* 76 (2001): 1–36; idem, *Duns Scotus* (Oxford: Oxford University Press, 1999); Orlando Todisco, "L'univocità scotista dell'ente e la svolta moderna," *Antonianum* 76 (2001): 79–110; and Isidoro Manzano, "Individuo y sociedad en Duns Escoto," *Antonianum* 76 (2001): 43–78. The latter is particularly interested to appropriate Scotus as a proto-liberal. This explains why these critiques tend to view positively what RO seeks to reject.

29. See Pickstock's almost comprehensive review of the literature in "Modernity and Scholasticism," 5n2. Of particular importance is Olivier Boulnois, "Quand Commence L'Ontothéologie? Aristote, Thomas d'Aquin et Duns Scot," *Revue Thomiste* 95 (1995): 84–108.

30. Pickstock, "Modernity and Scholasticism," 5n2.

31. Scotus's role as villain in this account is sometimes rivaled by Suárez. See John Montag, "Revelation: The False Legacy of Suárez," in RONT, 38–63. This echoes a similar line of critique in Jean-Luc Marion, *Sur la théologie blanche de Descartes: Analogie, creation des verites eternelles, fondement* (1981; repr., Paris: Presses universitaires de France, 1991), §§6–7; and J.-F. Courtine, *Suárez et le système de la métaphysique* (Paris: Presses universitaires de France, 1990).

participates in the being of the Creator.[32] Creation "is" only insofar as it participates in—or is suspended from (RONT, 3–4)—the Creator.[33] In contrast, Scotus asserts that "to be" is predicated univocally; that is, both the Creator and the creature exist in the same way or in the same sense. Being, now, becomes a category that is unhooked from participation in God and is a more neutral or abstract qualifier that is applied *to* God and creatures in the same way.[34] As Phillip Blond puts it, "Duns Scotus, when considering the universal science of metaphysics, elevated being (*ens*) to a higher station over God, so that being could be distributed to both God and His creatures."[35] The result is that the vertical suspension of creation from the Creator is unhooked, and because being is "flattened," the world is freed to be an autonomous realm.

Thus, in "Only Theology Overcomes Metaphysics," Milbank contrasts Aquinas's theological metaphysics[36] with Scotus's autonomous metaphysics. The point seems to be this: For Aquinas, metaphysics—as an account of being—cannot be divorced from theological considerations. "For Aquinas," Milbank suggests,

> the difference of *esse* from essence in the *ens commune* of creatures . . . is "read" in *entirely* theological terms as the site of the internal fracture of creatures between their own nothingness and their alien actuality which is received from God. This means that the domain of metaphysics is not simply subordinate to, but completely *evacuated* by theology, for metaphysics refers its subject matter—"Being"—wholesale to a first principle, God, which is the subject of another, higher science, namely God's own, only accessible to us via revelation (Aquinas, *In metaphysica*, prologue). (WMS, 44)

---

32. See Aquinas, *De ente et essentia*. I am following here the broad lines of Etienne Gilson's canonical reading in *Being and Some Philosophers* (Toronto: Pontifical Institute of Mediaeval Studies, 1949).

33. RO employs the metaphor of "suspension" in a dual sense: On the one hand, it indicates the way in which the created, immanent order is *linked* to the transcendent divine. In this respect, the metaphor of suspension does not really do justice to the richer theme of participation. On the other hand, the created order is "suspended by" the transcendent in the sense that it is always interrupted by the transcendent, the site for the in-breaking of the transcendent.

34. For a discussion, see James F. Ross and Todd Bates, "Duns Scotus on Natural Theology," in *The Cambridge Companion to Duns Scotus*, ed. Thomas Williams (Cambridge: Cambridge University Press, 2002), 196–97.

35. Phillip Blond, "Introduction: Theology before Philosophy," in *Post-secular Philosophy: Between Philosophy and Theology*, ed. Phillip Blond (London: Routledge, 1998), 6. This echoes Jean-Luc Marion, *God without Being*, trans. Thomas A. Carlson (Chicago: University of Chicago Press, 1991), 80–82.

36. In TA, he refers to this as Aquinas's "theontology."

For Milbank, following Aquinas, there is no metaphysics apart from rev-elation. This contrasts with the autonomous, non-revelational metaphysics of Scotus—who resolved an "ambiguity" in Aquinas "in an untraditional direction" by affirming that we speak of God by first speaking of finite beings "because one can first understand Being in an unambiguous, sheerly 'existential' sense, as the object of a proposition, without refer-ence to God, who is later claimed 'to be' in the same univocal manner" (WMS, 44). Milbank takes this to be the advent of "ontotheological idolatry" insofar as Scotus subjects God to a conception of being that is anterior to God's self-revelation.

However, for Milbank, the problem with Scotus's account is its implica-tions not just for the Creator but also for creatures. According to Milbank, Jean-Luc Marion sees Scotus's idolatry with respect to God but fails to acknowledge "Scotus' *idolatry toward creatures.*" Scotus's autonomous (and secular) metaphysics treats finite creatures as wholly available for comprehension. This stems from a consequence of Scotist univocity: By asserting "that finite things univocally 'are' as much as the infinite," Scotus grants to finite being its own subsistence and autonomy (TA, 33–34). "By contrast, the Christian thought which flowed from Gregory of Nyssa and Augustine was able fully to concede the utter unknowability of creatures which continually alter and have no ground within them-selves" (WMS, 44).[37] This is why there is such a marked rupture between the ontology of Aquinas and that of Scotus. For Aquinas, "finite being is not on its own account subsistently anything, but is only *granted to be* in various ways" (TA, 34, emphasis added). Scotus's univocal ontology, then, reduces God while at the same time exalting creatures; the result is a double idolatry that stands in contrast to Aquinas's metaphysics of participation (WMS, 47).[38] In a way, RO is more concerned about the idolatrous autonomy ascribed to creation than the idolatrous reduction of God (though they are opposed to that too).

The way in which Scotus's univocal ontology opens the space for modernity is traced most carefully by Pickstock. She sees Scotus launching a project of "immanentization" that, in some sense, flat-tens the world—in contrast to the Platonic account of participation

37. This "pliability" of creatures who participate in God is further developed in Gra-ham Ward's account of materiality as a kind of "transcorporeality" in CG. I consider this more fully in chapter 6.

38. Milbank goes on to see Meister Eckhardt as the anti-Scotus in this respect, insofar as Eckhardt "closed the window of ambiguity left slightly ajar by Aquinas and insisted that analogical attribution means that no transcendental predication—of Being, Intellect, Unity and Goodness—belongs positively to any creature, but that all in them that 'is,' or is united, or 'thinks,' or wills the good, reverts ecstatically back to its uncreated source" (WMS, 45).

(*methexis*), which suspends the immanent order from a transcendent source. According to Pickstock, the implication of the univocity of being is a radical separation of Creator from creature, entailing a discrete, secular order.[39] "Scotist univocity," she suggests, "unmediably separates the creation from God, precisely because the infinity of that distance can be the object of no concept other than Being. . . . One cannot peer through such an interminable *quantity* of sameness, for God's infinite intensity of Being exceeds every measure" (AW, 122–23). Starting from the univocity of being paradoxically produces "a kind of equivocity, for the difference of degree or amount of Being disallows any specific resemblance between them, and excludes the possibility of figural or analogical determinations of God that give us any degree of substantive knowledge of His character. . . . Thus, the 'same' becomes the radically disparate and unknowable" (AW, 123).[40] The result, again, is the unhooking of creation from the Creator and reason from revelation, carving out an autonomous or secular realm of both being and thought. In this sense, the production of "the secular" finds its impetus in late medieval ontology. "Duns Scotus and his successors . . . opened a space for univocal treatment of finite being without regard to any theology, rational or revealed. Although this space was not immediately exploited in a secularizing fashion, in the long run this came to be the case."[41]

This is why the critique of Scotus is the historical side of RO's systematic critique of modernity and modernity's development of the secular. Behind the *politics* of modernity (liberal, secular) is an *epistemology* (autonomous reason), which is in turn undergirded by an

---

39. It is interesting that the charges leveled against Scotus by RO mirror the charges leveled against Aquinas by Francis Schaeffer. See Francis Schaeffer, *The God Who Is There* and *Escape from Reason* in *Trilogy* (Minneapolis: Crossway, 1988).

40. Pickstock also finds in Scotus "a new leaning towards voluntarism" in the emphasis on "the sovereignty of God's will, which, because the universe had now been desymbolized, becomes the only explanation for the way things are" (AW, 122–23).

41. Pickstock, "Reply to David Ford and Guy Collins," 415. RO is not alone in this reading of Scotus and his legacy. In his Gifford Lectures, Alasdair MacIntyre makes a similar claim: "Paradoxically Scotus, whose philosophical enquiries were at every point controlled by his theological conclusions and whose primary interest was in protecting the autonomy of Augustinian theology from the inroads of either Averroist or Thomistic Aristotelianism, set the scene instead for the emergence of philosophy as an autonomous discipline or set of disciplines. . . . Viewed from a Thomistic perspective, it is at this point that philosophy is redefined as an autonomous academic discipline" (Alasdair MacIntyre, *Three Rival Versions of Moral Enquiry* [Notre Dame: University of Notre Dame Press, 1990], 155–56). Stanley Hauerwas notes a tension, then, in MacIntyre's own claim for the independence of philosophy from theology (*With the Grain of the Universe: The Church's Witness and Natural Theology* [Grand Rapids: Brazos, 2001], 23n18).

ontology (univocity and the denial of participation).[42] The modern turn to epistemology—and specifically, representational epistemologies—is predicated upon the shift to a univocal ontology.[43] So also, Scotus's marking out of an autonomous creation opens up the space for a new emphasis on human autonomy in the political sphere. As critics of RO, such as Isidoro Manzano, concede—and want to celebrate—Scotus's "proto-liberalism" meshes with his "proto-empiricism and modest rationalism." This takes modernity back to its Scotist roots, recognizing that "for Scotus, human beings are not political or else social animals, as they are for Aristotle and Aquinas respectively. Instead, they are able to negotiate culture as a work of freedom, and the only 'common good' one should recognize is a contractually produced state of empirical peace."[44]

RO's Scotus interpretation continues to be the most contested aspect of its historical narrative. Much work on this remains to be done, but as a way forward, it is important to try to distinguish the systematic/conceptual question from the contingent/historical issue. In other words, RO tends to pack two claims into its account: (1) the historical claim that Scotus's development of a univocal ontology generated what would become the secular philosophies of immanence that dominate modernity; (2) the systematic or conceptual claim that adherence to the univocity of being engenders a secular, nontheistic metaphysics that makes no reference to the transcendent. One could perhaps grant (1) without holding (2). That is, one could perhaps contend that adhering to a univocal ontology does not entail the denial of transcendence that RO suggests.[45] However, the complexities of the issue require further reflection and should be an agenda for research, particularly if RO hopes to engage (and convince) those working within the analytic tradition.

From Univocity to Nihilism

RO's genealogy of modernity does not end with discerning its late medieval filiation. Central to the project is also tracing its heritage in the development of nihilism. But how do we get from univocity to nihilism? What is meant by nihilism in this context? Contrary to many reaction-

---

42. The same is true of the alternative that RO envisions: Behind the *politics* (socialism) lies an *epistemology* (illumination), which is in turn undergirded by an *ontology* (participation).

43. Pickstock, "Modernity and Scholasticism," 6.

44. Ibid., 14.

45. My thanks to Terence Cuneo for helping me see these matters a little more clearly.

ary responses,[46] for RO, nihilism is not a shorthand for a dangerous amorality. In fact, Pickstock remarks, "It is not even taken for granted that nihilism is amoral and dangerous, but rather, it is presented as a matter which has to be argued."[47] Gavin Hyman correctly observes that "for Milbank, the nihilist narrative is the only serious rival to the Christian narrative because all other ideologies, whether of secular reason, scientific truth, or Enlightenment humanism, are 'masked' or 'disguised' versions of nihilism, for any ideology that attempts to exclude God must ultimately be nihilistic."[48] This issue is not primarily ethics but ontology. Therefore, if RO charges that Derrida's philosophy is ultimately nihilistic, it is not thereby claiming that it lacks an ethics or a politics but rather that the ethics or the politics of deconstruction is generated by an ontology plagued by internal contradictions.[49] Nihilism does not lack an ethics but rather provides an inadequate (and at the same time utopian) ethic grounded in a problematic ontology. Thus can Pickstock charge even Emmanuel Levinas with nihilism, for "the ethical impulse is for Levinas born with our 'persecution' by the sufferings of others. That is to say, his ethic assumes death and violence as the fundamental facts of ethical relevance; such a perspective is perfectly compatible with nihilism and in some ways Levinas appears to offer an ethic for nihilists."[50]

46. For instance, John D. Caputo, "What Do I Love When I Love My God? Deconstruction and Radical Orthodoxy," in *Questioning God*, ed. John D. Caputo, Michael Scanlon, and Mark Dooley (Bloomington: Indiana University Press, 2001), 292; Mark Dooley, "The Catastrophe of Memory: Derrida, Milbank, and the (Im)possibility of Forgiveness," in *Questioning God*, 130, 135–36; and Guy Collins, "Defending Derrida: A Response to Milbank and Pickstock," *Scottish Journal of Theology* 54 (2001): 344–65. Confusion about the charge of nihilism explains why Caputo could not quite understand Pickstock's charges in her review of his *Prayers and Tears of Jacques Derrida: Religion without Religion* (Bloomington: Indiana University Press, 1997). See Pickstock, "Postmodern Theology?" *Telos* 110 (1998): 167–70.

47. Pickstock, "Reply to David Ford and Guy Collins," 416. In the "Twenty-four Theses," RO is more affirmative of nihilism than either humanism or evangelicalism (theses 7, 14), and Cunningham's project is, in some sense, to use the accomplishment of nihilism as the springboard for articulating a theology of creation *ex nihilo* (*Genealogy of Nihilism*, 235–38).

48. Gavin Hyman, *The Predicament of Postmodern Theology: Radical Orthodoxy or Nihilist Textualism?* (Louisville: Westminster John Knox, 2001), 29.

49. As Pickstock so clearly states, "I do not doubt that Derrida is a just and democratically-minded man; but this is not enough to prove that his philosophy fulfills the criteria for justice and democracy" ("Reply to David Ford and Guy Collins," 417).

50. Pickstock, "Modernity and Scholasticism," 37. Insofar as Derrida's ethics is basically Levinasian, the critique applies *mutatis mutandis* to Derrida. I articulate a similar critique of Derrida in James K. A. Smith, "Determined Violence: Derrida's Structural Religion," *Journal of Religion* 78 (1998): 197–212; and idem, "Determined Hope: A Phenomenology

If nihilism is not primarily identified with amorality, or even Nietzsche, how are we to understand the charge? And how is it the product of the Scotist shift and its modern development? Nihilism is a consequence of the ontological flattening of the cosmos by univocity; in other words, once immanence was unhooked from its suspension from transcendence and granted an autonomous self-sufficiency, it also enclosed itself within a closed system. We can think of it this way: Nihilism is obviously linked to the *nihil*, to nothingness. According to a Christian theological understanding, creation in itself is nothing; that is, created things depend so radically on God for their existence that "without God, created things can only be perceived as *nothing* since they are, indeed, in themselves nothing."[51] With the advent of a Scotist ontology, created things were unhooked from their participation in God, such that they are now taken to be independent realities. But these "nothings-in-themselves" were also unhooked from the something (or Someone) that granted them being. Thus, the "logic of nihilism," as Cunningham defines it, is "a sundering of the something, rendering it nothing, and then having the nothing be after all *as* something."[52] The "sundering" was accomplished by a univocal ontology. The investment of this unhooked nothing-in-itself *as* something has been the task of modernity and postmodernity. Nihilism, unlike humanism (which operates, in a sense, on borrowed capital), recognizes this ontological nothingness of the immanent order—which is precisely why nihilism can operate as a kind of "pre-evangelistic" *preambula fidei* (preambles to faith) for a participatory, creational ontology.[53]

Up to this point, the critique of nihilism is a transcendent one. In other words, it simply locates the original faith of nihilism's ontological commitments and points out the antithesis with the Christian confession of creation. But RO also offers a transcendental or internal critique of nihilism. For Cunningham, and Milbank following him, nihilism implodes upon itself precisely because it cuts itself off from what it wants and needs. It inevitably falls into antinomies because it is forced to oscillate between two internal poles—what Milbank, echoing

---

of Christian Expectation," in *The Future of Hope: Essays on Christian Tradition amid Modernity and Postmodernity*, ed. Miroslav Volf and William Katerberg (Grand Rapids: Eerdmans, 2004), 200–227.

51. John Milbank, "Knowledge: The Theological Critique of Philosophy in Hamann and Jacobi," in RONT, 26.

52. Cunningham, *Genealogy of Nihilism*, xiii.

53. This is precisely Cunningham's project. I am reminded here of Jean-Luc Marion's account of the way in which vanity—in which the image becomes nothing, is emptied of any meaning—can be the precondition for recovering the image as icon (*God without Being*, chap. 4).

Cunningham, describes as "the logic of a 'double shuttle' between two nullities."[54] As Cunningham puts it, such nihilisms are plagued by "a dualism within a monism."[55] Thus, one can show how they tend toward a certain implosion. Nihilism is simply the consequence of a univocal ontology that denies the depth of things, shutting us up in a suffocating immanence (RONT, 3–4).

Once upon a Time There Was Plato

If modernity gave birth to nihilism by adopting an ontology predicated on the univocity of being, the antidote, according to RO, must be a metaphysics of *participation*—an account of the being of creation that recognizes its "suspension." In other words, if we are to find an alternative to nihilism (and its correlate market economy and liberal polity), we need to find an ontology that recharges immanence with transcendence. Thus, more recently, Pickstock has linked the ontological and the political in this respect: "Given that attempts to improve society in a secular way via the state and market have so visibly failed, then perhaps this revised genealogy that stresses the legacy of a distorted religious theory and practice could also point us indirectly towards a more serious alternative future polity than the liberal and postmodern critiques."[56] Crucial to RO's constructive project, then, is a retrieval of a participatory ontology that counters modernity's univocal, flattened ontologies—and central to such an ontological project is a retrieval of Plato.

Platonism/Christianity

This central link between Platonism and Christianity has been articulated since the earliest rumblings of RO. In *Theology and Social Theory*, Milbank already evoked both participation and Platonism as allies of the project, offering an ontology nourished by "Platonism/Christianity" (TST, 290). One of the core claims of Pickstock's *After Writing* is the no-

54. John Milbank, "Materialism and Transcendence," in Theology and the Political, ed. Creston Davis, John Milbank, and Slavoj Žižek (Durham, N.C.: Duke University Press, forthcoming), 12 (ms. p.). Cf. TST, 302–28.

55. Cunningham, *Genealogy of Nihilism*, xiv. This echoes what D.Th. Vollenhoven, working in the Reformational tradition, describes as a "contradictory monism" (D.Th. Vollenhoven, *Schematische kaarten: Filosofische concepties in probleem historische verband* [Amstelveen: De Zaak Haes, 2000]).

56. Pickstock, "Modernity and Scholasticism," 4.

tion that, contra Nietzsche and Derrida, Plato is a theurgical philosopher of sacramental materiality. As she summarizes, "The strongly positive view of *methexis* (participation) in the *Phaedrus* frees [Plato] from the charge of otherworldliness and total withdrawal from physicality, for the philosophic ascent does not result in a 'loss' of love for particular beautiful things, since the particular participates in beauty itself" (AW, 14). Thus, in the introduction to RONT, the editors could call for a Christianity that is at once "more incarnate" and "more Platonic," rooted in a "participatory philosophy and incarnational theology" (RO, 3–4). If the Reformed tradition sees it as necessary to *overcome* Platonism, there is a sense in which RO sees it as necessary to *recover* Platonism.[57]

The recovery of Platonism is, one might assert, really just a recovery of Neoplatonism, and what is being recovered is not the dualistic Neoplatonism of Plotinus but rather the *theurgical* Neoplatonism of Iamblichus (ca. A.D. 250–325) as well as that of Augustine.[58] In this theurgical Neoplatonism, one finds a much more robust valuation of the body, materiality, and sacramental practice, such as that sketched in AW. While this is a possible account, it is not one open to Pickstock, for her central claims concern not just the Platonic tradition but the Platonic corpus. In other words, RO does not attach itself simply to Neoplatonism but directly to Plato.

Suggesting that the immanentism of (nihilistic) modernity generates a dualism-within-a-monism, RO consistently contends that nihilism is unable to value the material *as* material; rather, its flattening of materiality's depth ends up evacuating materiality. In this respect, modern rationalism is but the inversion of Nietzschean nihilism—and both have much in common with more traditional dualisms and their account, for instance, of the body. Contemporary scholarship in a plurality of fields has demonstrated that how we think about the body has a direct impact on our politics and our construction of social reality. In other words, dualistic understandings that devalue embodiment often give rise to totalitarian organizations of social arrangements. Further, such dualistic devaluations of the body are reductionistic, producing notions of being human that are driven by factors that consider many aspects of embodiment unnecessary or at least merely supplemental. The body—the

57. In this chapter, focused on RO's history of philosophy, I largely bracket my critique of their account of participation retrieved from Plato. I return to a more critical analysis of this in chapter 6.

58. Iamblichus, a student of Porphyry, is best known for his work *Theurgia*, or *On the Mysteries of Egypt* (a digital edition is available online at www.esotericarchives.com/oracle/iambl_th.htm). For a discussion of Iamblichus, see Gregory Shaw, *Theurgy and the Soul: The Neoplatonism of Iamblichus* (University Park, Pa.: Penn State Press, 1995).

site of immanence—is rejected in the pursuit of transcendence. Or if immanence is all we have, the body is, in a sense, nothing. The result, then, is the same: a denigration of the body and the material. Thus, Pickstock argues that Scotus's ontology, insofar as it rejects sensible mediation as essential to human knowing, devalues mediation as such: "Everything that depends upon this mediation—science, the arts, philosophy, even the sacramental practice of religion—must partake of this re-evaluation. The entire sphere of culture, like politics, for Scotus can only figure as a kind of semi-sinful emergency measure."[59]

One of the ironies of this critique of univocity is that its ontological consequences mirror those of what we would traditionally understand as Platonism—the Platonism Nietszche loved to hate. In Plato's *Phaedo*, for instance, the body is understood as an "evil" and "contamination" from which the soul seeks purification (*Phaed.* 66a–67b). Thus, the body is described as a prison for the soul from which we (ought to) seek escape by death (79a–81d). The connection between this conception of the body and totalitarian politics is evident in Plato's account of social organization in the *Republic:* The philosopher-kings, detached from their bodies as a practice for death, rule over those lower classes who are too attached to their bodies, consumed by worldly desire (*Resp.* 414b–415c). While this politics grows out of a philosophical anthropology that devalues embodiment, this anthropology is rooted in a deeper ontology that devalues materiality per se.

This is the account of Plato yielded by the traditional reading. This reading is also represented in continental philosophy by those who most disagree with Plato: Jacques Derrida and Gilles Deleuze, who follow a tradition spawned by Nietzsche.[60] Both Derrida and Deleuze see in Plato a devaluing of the temporal and the material in favor of the eternal and the intelligible. For Derrida, this is most acutely seen in Plato's denigration of writing in the *Phaedrus:* There Plato devalues writing because of its exteriority to the soul (275a–e). Writing is a mode of material mediation and embodiment. Insofar as writing is linked to embodiment, it is subject to the same evaluation as the body (*Phaed.* 81d).[61]

---

59. Pickstock, "Modernity and Scholasticism," 18.

60. See Alain Badiou, *Deleuze: The Clamor of Being* (Minneapolis: University of Minnesota Press, 2000), 97–101.

61. Jacques Derrida, "Plato's Pharmacy," in *Dissemination*, trans. Barbara Johnson (Chicago: University of Chicago Press, 1981), 61–171. For Deleuze, the devaluing of the material or "immanent" is located in Plato's ontological distinction between "appearance" and "reality" as found in the *Republic:* "The whole of Platonism . . . is dominated by the idea of drawing a distinction between 'the thing itself' and the simulacra. . . . Overturning Platonism, then, means denying the primacy of original over copy, of model over image; glorifying the reign of simulacra and reflections" (*Difference and Repetition*, trans. Paul

The New Plato

Recent scholarship, however, has challenged this reading of Plato as a dualist who devalues embodiment and immanence.[62] The RO interest in Platonic ontology seems to stem from its central attempt to contest the nihilist ontologies of immanentism or reductionistic materialism (cf. AW, 48). This has been described as the necessary "suspension of the material," which alone can avoid materiality being reduced to inert substance—in which case it would not be properly material. Only the suspension of the material from the ideal or transcendent is able to guard the material from nothingness, from dissolving into the *nihil*. This interest in a participatory ontology contra reductionistic materialism forms the horizon for Pickstock's reading of Plato.[63] It is in a move different from—though related to—Badiou's that Pickstock, explicitly criticizing Derrida's reading, suggests that the Platonic notion of participation (*methexis*), particularly as unpacked in the *Phaedrus*, offers a better paradigm for understanding Plato's fundamental affirmation of embodiment. Drawing on an interpretation of Plato in the Iamblichian tradition of Neoplatonism, Pickstock argues that Plato's account of embodiment is sacramental or liturgical, generating an account of sociopolitical life that revalues embodied existence rooted in an ontology that espouses, we might now say, a nonreductive materialism. Contrary to Derrida's reading, she locates a theurgical aspect of Plato's thought in a concept of liturgy that "forms the soul through an experience of transcendence" (AW, 19, 39). As a result, "the Socratic subject finds itself in and through its liturgical role in the *polis*" (AW, 45). Thus, we have a fundamental affirmation of materiality and embodiment (in language and the liturgy of the *polis*) as integral to Platonic knowledge and care of the soul. This is what Pickstock describes as Plato's positive view of physicality (AW, 14).

Patton [New York: Columbia University Press, 1994], 66). According to Deleuze, the "plane of immanence" for Plato can at best "only *lay claim* to quality in a secondary way, and only to the degree that they *participate* in the Idea" (Gilles Deleuze and Felix Guattari, *What Is Philosophy?* trans. Hugh Tomlinson and Graham Burchell [New York: Columbia University Press, 1994], 30). Thus, Deleuze thinks that the Platonic account of *methexis* is precisely what devalues immanence.

62. See especially Badiou, *Deleuze*. RO would argue that what is described as Platonism in the "traditional" account is, in fact, a version of Neoplatonism, in particular the henological, non-theurgical Neoplatonism of Plotinus. Thus, Cunningham would propose drawing a line of continuity from Plotinus, through Avicenna, to Scotus (*Genealogy of Nihilism*, chap. 1).

63. Again, our interest here is *historical;* in chapter 6, I return to a more *systematic* or *constructive* consideration of participation.

The case study for this positive account of physicality is the *Phaedrus*, where, Pickstock claims, "Plato portrays the transcendence of the good, its beyond presence-and-absence, as a kind of *contagion*, for its plenitude spills over into immanence, in such a way that the good is revealed in the beauty of the physical particulars" (AW, 12). The philosopher who seeks to "glimpse" the transcendence of the good in the mundane order is thus "given to revere all physicality according to its participation in this spiritual sun" (AW, 12). The physical, on this reading, is not a fallen distraction but rather an incarnational index of the transcendent. In sum, the physical bears a positive relation to the transcendent. Therefore, both the physical and the temporal are revalued as sites for the "arrival of transcendence within immanence" (AW, 12). For instance, "temporality does not compromise . . . knowledge, but rather constitutes its condition of possibility for us: the good arrives through time, and therefore time is not merely a ladder of access which can be kicked away, its job performed" (AW, 13). Or, to take another example, "in the *Phaedrus*, the encounter with an actual lover in time plays a positive role, stimulating the memory of the Forms" (AW, 14). Socrates describes an encounter with such a "beautiful boy" (*Phaed.* 244a):

> A recent initiate, however, one who has seen much in heaven—when he sees a godlike face or bodily form that has captured Beauty well, first he shudders and a fear comes over him like those he felt at the earlier time; then he gazes at him with the reverence due a god, and if he weren't afraid people would think him completely mad, he'd even sacrifice to his boy as if he were the image of a god. (251a–b)

This physical embodiment of Beauty excites the soul's desire such that its wings sprout and are nourished, and it both desires and is capable of flying to new heights (251c).[64] The important insight in this context is the way in which the physical visage of the young Phaedrus has a positive role to play in knowledge and philosophical ascent. But Pickstock further intensifies the claim in two ways: First, she argues that temporality and materiality constitute necessary conditions of possibility for knowledge (AW, 13, 19). Second, she seems to suggest that this condition of temporal and material mediation is perpetual: The "philosophical life," she claims, is "*hermeneutical* because it involves the perpetual discernment of divine mediation through physicality" (AW

---

64. This comes after Socrates has recounted something of a "history of the soul," in which he recounts an earlier time when the soul enjoyed "the ultimate vision, and we saw it in pure light because we were pure ourselves, not buried in this we are carrying around now, which we call a body, locked in it like an oyster in its shell" (*Phaed.* 250c). It seems to me that the soul sprouts wings to fly *from* embodiment.

20, emphasis added). More recently, Pickstock has tried to generate this reading of Plato from a more surprising dialogue, the *Phaedo*. Trying to demonstrate the deep discontinuity between the Platonic soul and the modern self, she argues that this dialogue contains the antecedents of a certain nonreductive materialism—even resurrection.[65]

The Platonic legacy is crucial for developing a participatory ontology that resists the flattened ontologies of Scotus and his modern heirs. But RO is not *simply* a Platonism; it is, as Milbank suggests, "Platonism/ Christianity." Thus, its complement is found in RO's recovery of key late ancient and medieval sources: Augustine and Aquinas.

Back to Augustine

What RO is after is an alternative ontology. While this is traced to Plato, such a retrieval is possible only through an Augustinian filter. Thus, Milbank could describe the project as a "postmodern critical Augustinianism." This is an important point of contact between RO and the Reformed tradition, which quite explicitly understands itself to be situated within the legacy of Augustinian Christianity.[66] (In Jonathan Edwards, this is also quite explicitly linked to a certain Platonism.)[67]

Postmodern Augustines: Caputo and Derrida

There has been no shortage of postmodern retrievals of St. Augustine,[68] but RO's retrieval must be marked off from these other "postmodern Augustines." Seeing the contrast between them is instructive for under-

65. Pickstock, "Soul in Plato," 115–26. Again, I reserve criticism of this interpretation until a more thematic discussion of participation and materiality in chapter 6.

66. The role of Augustine is central in my own contribution to the RO project. See James K. A. Smith, *Speech and Theology: Language and the Logic of Incarnation*, Radical Orthodoxy (New York: Routledge, 2002), chap. 4.

67. See, for example, Michael J. McClymond, "Salvation as Divinization: Jonathan Edwards, Gregory Palamas, and the Theological Uses of Neoplatonism," in *Jonathan Edwards: Philosophical Theologian*, ed. Paul Helm and Oliver Crisp (Burlington, Vt.: Ashgate, 2003), 142–44. My thanks to Jerry Stutzman for conversations along this line. Edward's "Platonism" demands further exploration as a possible point of rapprochement between RO and the Reformed tradition (Stutzman's own work takes up this project). For a positive evaluation of Calvin's "Platonism," see John Milbank, "Alternative Protestantism," in *Creation, Covenant, and Participation: Radical Orthodoxy and the Reformed Tradition*, ed. James K. A. Smith and James H. Olthuis (Grand Rapids: Baker Academic, forthcoming).

68. Jacques Derrida, "Circumfession," in Geoffrey Bennington and Jacques Derrida, *Jacques Derrida* (Chicago: University of Chicago Press, 1991); Jean-François Lyotard, *The Confession of Augustine*, trans. Richard Beardsworth (Stanford: Stanford University Press,

standing why and how Augustine is such an important figure for RO.
Therefore, here we consider two quite different postmodern Augustines:
the Derridean Augustine suggested by Derrida and developed by John D.
Caputo, and the radically orthodox Augustine unpacked by Ward and
Milbank.[69] The contrast between these two Augustines is expressed rather
succinctly in the titles of two recent books, both of which we might
describe as manifestos: In 2001, Caputo published his provocative *On
Religion*—a little tract *de religione*. The next year, Ward offered his own
account in a work titled *True Religion*. Not just the titles but also the
projects themselves intentionally echo a little book by St. Augustine, *De
vera religione: On True Religion*. Are these projects faithful[70] to Augustine's
project? If Augustine has something to say to a postmodern context,
is it in a discourse on religion (or a "religion without religion"), or is it
an account of "true religion"? Could it be that a discourse simply "on
religion" is not only not Augustinian but not really postmodern either?
In other words, could it be that this Derridean Augustine is, in fact, quite
modern?[71] Would a truly postmodern Augustine be radically orthodox?
Or does Ward's Augustine also have only tendentious ties to the Bishop
of Hippo? Is the radically orthodox Augustine the one we have been
awaiting, or should we look for still another—a third Augustine? This
section stages an encounter between Caputo and Ward, replaying their
encounter in *Questioning God*, and then considers Caputo's *On Religion*
and Ward's *True Religion* in light of Augustine's own *De vera religione*.[72] I
will argue that Augustine's unique contribution in a postmodern context
stems not simply from his question[73] but from his determinate answer:

2000); and Foucault, *The Politics of Truth*, ed. Sylvère Lotringer (New York: Semiotext,
1997), 171–235.

69. Milbank's appropriation of Augustine is considered in more detail in chapter 7.

70. I am trying to choose my words carefully here. It is not quite a question of who gets
Augustine "right." As Ward notes, in the context of describing the "holographic" Augustine
hovering behind his work, "I wish to emphasize that the Augustine I am conjuring, and
whose thinking has shaped my own, bears some relation to the late-fourth- and early-fifth-
century Bishop of Hippo. But that relation, while historically true, is tenuous. I have learnt
too much from Gadamer to pretend that my Augustine or interpretation of Augustine is
Augustine or the true interpretation of Augustine" (CG, 262n18).

71. This would correlate with my criticism of Derrida's account of "religion" as deeply
modern. See James K. A. Smith, "Re-Kanting Postmodernism: Derrida's Religion within
the Limits of Reason Alone," *Faith and Philosophy* 17 (2000): 558–71.

72. Augustine, "Of True Religion," in *Augustine: Earlier Writings*, ed. J. H. S. Burleigh
(Philadelphia: Westminster, 1953), henceforth abbreviated in the text as DVR.

73. Both Caputo and Ward find the virtue of Augustine to be in his *questioning* (e.g.,
"What do I love when I love my God?"), and both seem to celebrate the notion that Augustine's questions remain unanswered (QG, 275). I think the questions do get answered,
and I think the *answers* make Augustine "Augustine."

that the incarnation of God in Christ is the condition of possibility for meaning in creation.

Caputo was an Augustinian before being an Augustinian was cool.[74] *Quaestio mihi factus sum* (I have become a question to myself)[75] was the *cri de coeur* of his radical hermeneutics long before it was sanctioned by Derrida's deconstruction. However, Augustinian themes animated Derrida's later *Circumfession* and *Memoirs of the Blind* and thus reanimated Caputo's commitment to an Augustinian vision (which resonated with the Augustinian heritage of his own Villanova University). The result is a confession that identifies itself as Augustinian but disavows any particular, determinate Christian confession and instead professes a "religion without religion." Let's consider two questions: First, what are the contours of this Augustinian religion without religion? In other words, what about it warrants the descriptor "Augustinian"? Second, how would this square with Augustine's account of religion in *De vera religione*?

Caputo's *On Religion* opens with an axiomatics that he describes as Augustinian or at least a "post-modern or post-secular repetition of St. Augustine."[76] Beginning with the admittedly Augustinian assumption that religion is at root a question of love and, more specifically, love of God, Caputo moves on to the Augustinian question that motivates his project: "What do I love when I love my God?" echoing *Confessions* X. Caputo finds ambiguity in the question:

> Is it the case, as Augustine the bishop thought, that whenever we are carried away by the love of something, anything at all, it is really God whom we are seeking, but we simply have not come to realize that it is God whom we love, rather the way I might see Peter coming even if I do not know it is Peter? Or might it be the other way around, that the name of God is a name we confer on things we love very dearly, like peace or justice or the messianic age? (OR, 25)

We will return to these questions below when we tackle Augustine himself, since Augustine really offers a third way of thinking through this ambiguity.[77] For the moment, let's return to Caputo's Augustinian

---

74. See John D. Caputo, *Radical Hermeneutics* (Bloomington: Indiana University Press, 1987). (I am thinking here, I must confess, of an old country song by Barbara Mandrell: "I was country, when country wasn't cool.")

75. Augustine, *Conf.* 4.4.9; 10.33.50.

76. John D. Caputo, *On Religion*, Thinking in Action (London: Routledge, 2001), 132, henceforth abbreviated in the text as OR.

77. It is not a matter of everyone anonymously loving God or baptizing their desires *as* God but rather recognizing a structure of human identity that *should* desire God the

axiomatics, by which he offers the following string: "God is love. God is the name of love.[78] God is the name of what we love" (OR, 134).[79] The ambiguity of the opening question is now inscribed in this chain, such that "what is loved" and "God" have a certain interchangeability, and we know not which is which. Therefore, *quaestio mihi factus sum* (I have become a question to myself) (OR, 18). For Caputo, religion is found in the deferral of an answer: "I would keep Augustine's question open," he offers, "give it a full throttle *as a question*, and treat it as a crucial and permanent part of the passion of our lives, of the *quaestio mihi factus sum* of which he spoke. When we put our head down and love God with all our strength, we do not know[80] whether love is an exemplification of God or God is an exemplification of love. Or whether justice is one of the names we use to speak about God or whether the name of God is a way we have of speaking about justice" (OR, 26).

Now, admittedly, a certain Augustinian structure is at work here.[81] While doing a masterful job of replaying the rich poetics of Augustine (in contrast to the laborious medieval Latin of Aquinas), Caputo, following Derrida, offers a rendition of two deeply Augustinian themes: (1) the structural primacy of faith before knowledge, and (2) the centrality of love in the understanding of religion. The two of these go together be-

---

Creator but which can take an idolatrous direction, in which case it is not God who is loved but idols. We return to these matters in chapter 7.

78. The former statement is from the New Testament (1 John 4:8); the latter statement is not, and is, I would argue, a transposition that is not consistent with the New Testament. In other words, the New Testament does not offer the reversible equation of God and love that Caputo needs to make his argument work.

79. In addition to the transposition noted above, it seems that Caputo also plays a little too fast and loose with the ontology of these matters, suggesting that God is a "how," not a "what" (*On Religion*, 134–35). Quite apart from philosophical interests, my experience in ministry—even in inner-city churches—has taught me that the faithful take questions of ontology very seriously, even if they do not name them as such. No "how" ever answered a prayer.

80. Significant epistemological questions are behind this concern (my discussions with James Olthuis have helped me to see this, even if we might still disagree). Just what is meant by knowledge here? Are we still expecting something like "Cartesian certainty," and if we cannot have that, must we say that we don't "know"? Can we not imagine—in postmodernity—a very different account of knowledge, a more Augustinian account of noncognitive knowing such that I can say that I do know what I love when I love my God? A *faith*-ful mode of knowing? (Cf. 2 Tim. 1:12: "I know whom I have believed.") In fact, in *Soliloquies*, Augustine's most fundamental desire—repeated in Calvin's *Institutes*—is to "know God and the soul . . . nothing else" (2.7). He then goes on to investigate the *how* of this knowing, which is by a *committed reason*.

81. I have earlier considered such a "formal" or "structural" Augustinianism in Derrida and Caputo in James K. A. Smith, "Is Deconstruction an Augustinian Science?" in *Religion without Religion: The Prayers and Tears of John D. Caputo*, ed. James H. Olthuis (New York: Routledge, 2002), 50–61.

cause, for Augustine, religious faith is not a matter of logical assent to propositions but rather a commitment of the heart. But the question is, Is such a formalized Augustine really Augustinian? Having elsewhere articulated the structural overlap, here I would like to take the opposite tack. More specifically, I would argue that this Derridean Augustine, offering a religion without religion, is an Augustine with too many "withouts," a little too much *sans*. In particular, despite its emphasis on faith, this Derridean religion without religion—offered in the name of Augustine—is an Augustinianism without revelation. Despite all its talk about love, it is an Augustinianism without the *ordo amoris*, and despite its attentiveness to injustice, it is an Augustinianism without sin.

To put this another way, Caputo ontologizes the *inquietude* of the Augustinian heart (OR, 36), inscribing this restlessness of the Augustinian self into the very structure of creation. But this is to read the first half of *Confessions* X without reference to the narrative of books I–IX.[82] Certainly, Augustine articulates the angst of a restless, questioning self throughout the *Confessions* (1.1.1; 1.18.28; 2.10.18; 4.4.9; 10.33.50), but this anxiety and restlessness, for Augustine, (1) are the result of fallenness, not finitude or creaturehood per se, and (2) are countered by the rest and peace that are found in Christ (8.12.29; 9.4.11).[83] One sometimes gets the impression, reading Derrida or Caputo, that they are working with an anthology that lifts out book I and the first half of book X, without reference to the conversion narrative of II–IX.[84] The Augustinian self, once it discovers (or better, recollects) that it is created in the image of God, finds its identity and meaning (*only*) in that relationship. Thus, book X concludes with an answer to the questions "Who am I?" and "What do I love when I love my God?" The answer is found in the reconciliation accomplished by the passion of a "true Mediator" (10.42.67–10.43.68).[85] The answer, for Augustine, is christological.

82. Which, of course, one is free to do; I just don't think we should then describe our account as "Augustinian" except in a weak sense.

83. I have discussed this in more detail in James K. A. Smith, "Confessions of an Existentialist: Reading Augustine after Heidegger," *New Blackfriars* 82 (2001): 273–82 (part 1) and 335–47 (part 2).

84. Book X steps out of the historical, narrative structure of the *Confessions*, which culminates in book IX. Books X–XIII are more systematic treatises written "in the present." On the structure of the *Confessions* and relation of I–IX to X–XIII (a hotly contested issue in Augustinian scholarship), see the work of Ferrari and Brian Stock, *Augustine the Reader* (Cambridge: Harvard University Press, 1996), 126–27.

85. Contrary to the baptisms of theurgy by Milbank and Pickstock, it is precisely in this context that Augustine condemns the strategies of Neoplatonic theurgy: "They sought a mediator to purify them, and it was not the true one. For it was 'the devil transforming himself into an angel of light' (2 Cor. 11:14)" (*Conf.* 10.42.67).

But from whence does the answer spring? This is crucial and constitutes the heart of anything that would claim to be Augustinian: the *interruption* of Augustine's musing by the infusion or surprise of revelation (DVR, 3.4, 6.12).[86] We see this first and most importantly in book VII of the *Confessions,* where what disturbs Augustine's reading of those Platonic books is the very un-Platonic idea of incarnation found in John's Gospel.[87] Indeed, the narrative in books VII and VIII, particularly at the culmination of Augustine's conversion, is persistently interrupted by the insertion of the Word of God. And the concluding sections of book X are riddled with the constant interruptions of revelation (10.43.70). Caputo's Derridean Augustine seems to disqualify such revelation a priori.[88] But is an Augustine without revelation really Augustine?

It is precisely revelation that functions as the criterion that establishes not just the centrality of love but also a right order of such love—the *ordo amoris.* Interestingly, even Caputo's religion without religion contains a certain latent orthodoxy or "Right Teaching" (25–26), since evidently, people who are passionate about their mutual funds and the Dow Jones are *not* religious (OR, 2, 3). In fact, Augustine himself grants that they are religious; it is just that they are idolaters. So despite Caputo's protests to the contrary (OR, 3), at root this is a question of theology—of "true" religion—not just religion, and for Augustine, theology is a question of Christology.

Unlike for Caputo, for Augustine there is no virtue in being religious. This is because, for Augustine (and earlier St. Paul and later John Calvin), being religious is constitutive of being human (cf. TR, 38). Human beings—as created in the image of God—cannot help but be religious. Hence, being religious is not a notable achievement. We might describe this as Augustine's account of formal or structural religion, but his account does not end there. Augustine is the author of a treatise titled not simply *De religione* (*On Religion*) but *De vera religione—On True Religion.* It is here that we locate the most fundamental sense in which

---

86. Unfortunately, I cannot deal with all the implications (and problems) of this here (I made a start in "Nietzsche's Faith: Why We Need an Even More Radical Hermeneutics"). Here I point out that by revelation I do not mean some kind of modernist dream that pulls us out of the flux history but a speaking of God *into* history, paradigmatically in the incarnation. If I were to suggest a paradigm, Barth might be the best place to start.

87. I have analyzed this in more detail in my *Speech and Theology,* chap. 4. A striking parallel can be found in Kierkegaard's account of the "mad" idea of the incarnation in *Philosophical Fragments* III.

88. Caputo seems to think that to accept a particular, determinate revelation is to claim to have a "God's-eye-view" ("What Do I Love When I Love My God?" in *Questioning God,* 312; and idem, *More Radical Hermeneutics* [Bloomington: Indiana University Press, 2000]). But the faithful accept the gift of revelation *as* mediated, and the acceptance is one of faith.

the Derridean Augustine is not really very Augustinian—an Augustine whose project never gets beyond structural religion.

Let's unpack Augustine's account by considering an example from Caputo's *On Religion:* By emphasizing the general structure of love for God as religious (coupled with the slipperiness of reference in the name of God), Caputo can suggest that both those who attend Mass on Sunday mornings in rural areas of Mexico and those who stay home on Sunday mornings to read the *Sunday Times* are religious, insofar as both are passionate about something—the impossible, justice, God. Thus, Caputo concludes that "it seems to go without saying, for Derrida as for Augustine, that we love God."[89] In fact, Caputo articulates this in terms that deeply resonate with Augustine's *De vera religione:* "I would rather speak of the religious *in* people, in all of us. I take 'religion' to mean the being-religious of human beings, which I put on par with being political or being artistic. By 'the religious,' I mean a basic structure of human experience. . . . I do not confine religion to something confessional or sectarian" (OR, 9). This is why both those who participate in the liturgical formation of the sacraments and those who stay home to read the *Sunday Times* are religious for Caputo (OR, 9). The problem is that Caputo is not consistent on this score, because we must admit that most of those people who stay home to read the *Sunday Times* are pretty passionately concerned about their mutual funds (as are a few of those at Mass, admittedly). But earlier, Caputo indicated that those who are so passionate about tax breaks don't love God and thus aren't religious (OR, 2).

What this demonstrates is that Caputo's account lacks the criteria for naming false religion, or what Augustine would simply describe as idolatry.[90] It is not that there aren't idolatries for Caputo (ardent capitalism seems to be one); it is just that he does not offer criteria to distinguish true religion from false religion because he has baptized the structurally religious as authentic.[91] Augustine, however, offers a framework that permits a more nuanced account of this situation. For Augustine, the communicant, the *Sunday Times* reader, and the lover of mutual funds are *all* religious; however, only the worshiper is truly religious—that is, for Augustine, Christian. How is true religion determined? For Augus-

89. Caputo, "What Do I Love When I Love My God?" 291 (henceforth abbreviated in the text as DRO). Below I argue that this misreads Augustine in a very important way.

90. For Augustine, there is false religion precisely because there is idolatry, and there is idolatry only because there is a right order of love: "Let it be clearly understood that there could have been no error in religion had not the soul worshipped *in place of its God* either a soul or a body or some phantasm of its own" (DVR, 10.18).

91. Or perhaps I should say that for Caputo, idolatry has less to do with the *what* of religious confession and more to do with the *how*.

tine, following Paul (Rom. 1:18–31),[92] all of humanity is constituted by a religious structure. However, this structure is misdirected by sin such that we become religiously committed to aspects of creation instead of the Creator (DVR, 10.18–11.21).[93] In other words, the ineradicable religious structure of human selfhood, when marred by sin, does not lead to irreligion or to no religion but to a distorted religion—in short, idolatry. The human self, created in the image of God, is to find its true meaning and identity in a religious commitment to the Creator as Triune God ("You have made us for yourself . . ."). Thus, the religious structure of human existence finds its proper direction only when related to the Creator revealed to humanity in Christ. And so the right order of love, revealed in the Word, is what prescribes the criteria for what constitutes true religion (DVR, 12.23, 15.29).[94]

How does this change our analysis of the example above? For Augustine, not only the avaricious individual worshiping the God of Mammon is an idolater. Even the democratic *Sunday Times* reader—committed to justice as some kind of end in itself—is committed to false gods. Only the one who recognizes her identity in the Creator through the revelation of God in Christ can be *truly* religious. Therefore, not everyone loves God. Every human being is created and structured in such a way that he or she desires transcendence, but when this desire is directed to anything other than the Triune God, the desire is not *caritas* but a *cupiditas* that has erected false gods.

Therefore, beginning from the revelation[95] of God in Christ (DVR, 16.30) attested to in the Scriptures (7.12), Augustine outlines the criteria for the right order of love that defines true religion and thus authentic

92. This structure is unpacked most carefully by a later Augustinian: John Calvin, *Institutes* I.iii.

93. Here William Cavanaugh's discussion of religion as a distinctly *modern* invention is mistaken. He suggests that Marsilio Ficino's "1474 work entitled *De Christiana Religione* is the first to present *religio* as a universal human impulse common to all" (William T. Cavanaugh, "'A Fire Strong Enough to Consume the State': The Wars of Religion and the Rise of the State," *Modern Theology* 11 [1995]: 404). In fact, we already see such a claim in Augustine.

94. In *Speech and Theology*, chap. 4, I unpack in more detail Augustine's phenomenology of sin and idolatry. For a related account, see Dooyeweerd, ITWT, chap. 2.

95. It seems to me that we cannot underestimate the difference that this beginning makes. In fact, *De vera religione* itself was penned in response to "those who refuse to own the light of the Holy Scripture and the grace of the spiritual people of God" (DVR, 7.12). But it seems that the Derridean Augustine stems from just such a refusal. However, I would suggest that to refuse, or to choose *not* to accept the revelation of God in Christ, is not to refuse revelation per se but only to commit oneself to the revelations of reason, or liberal tolerance, or whatever. It is no different from choosing the Qur'an. To not choose is to choose, to invoke a Pascalian dictum.

humanity. But after this brief tour through Augustine, doesn't it seem that we are a long way from Paris? If this is Augustine, is not the Derridean Augustine much more Parisian than North African?

A Radically Orthodox Augustine: Ward and Milbank

The difference between the Derridean Augustine and St. Augustine is *religious*. They begin from very different fundamental commitments. In particular, the Bishop of Hippo does not share the Derridean Augustine's commitment to what was described elsewhere as the logic of determination.[96] Simply stated, Derrida—and Derrida's Augustine, as sketched by Caputo—believes and confesses that any determinate, particular structure is always violent and unjust. As Caputo confesses, "I do not see how any religious tradition or theological language can take shape *without* violence."[97] Why is that? Because as soon as a confession or institution takes on a particular, determinate shape, it is necessarily exclusionary and therefore violent.[98] But it is important to recognize that this is an assumption—and it seems to be a (democratic, American) "liberal" one at that, with all of its allergy to the scandal of particularity.

And it is certainly an assumption that is completely foreign to St. Augustine. It is significant to note that Augustine emphasizes this particularity (as exclusivity): "From one particular region of the earth in which alone the one God was worshipped and where alone such a man could be born, chosen men were sent throughout the entire world, and by their virtues and words have kindled the fires of the divine love. Their sound teaching has been confirmed and they have left to posterity a world illumined" (DVR, 3.4). Caputo seems to see this difference[99] but

---

96. I cannot do justice to this complex problem here, but I have unpacked this logic and subjected it to critique in "Determined Violence" and "Re-Kanting Postmodernism." The argument is further developed in James K. A. Smith, *Violence of Finitude: Derrida and the Logic of Determination* (forthcoming). Here I set Derrida's logic of determination in opposition to what I have described elsewhere as a logic of incarnation (*Speech and Theology*).

97. Caputo, "Deconstruction and Radical Orthodoxy," 307.

98. I am simply not convinced that "exclusion" is a bad thing or inherently violent. One reaches this conclusion only if one accepts the logic of determination and the faith of liberal toleration. My hunch is that anyone who wants to take the notion of sin seriously cannot accept these assumptions.

99. "The difference [between Derrida and Augustine] is that Augustine has seized and settled upon a determinate historical name for the object of his faith and hope and love, that he has 'entrusted' or 'delivered' himself over to the proper names that have been transmitted to him by his tradition, while for Derrida faith and hope and love make their way in the night as best they can" (DRO, 311). Aside from the fact that this seems to construe Augustinian faith as some kind of Cartesian knowledge (faith is *undecidable* for Augustine),

then goes on to reject Augustine precisely because of the particularity of his confession: "The *difference* between Augustine and Derrida should be seen to lie in the *relative*[100] *determinacy* of the figures in which their faith, hope, and love are lodged. *Unless*, of course, one has dogmatically decided that Augustine's determinately *Christian* faith, hope, and love is the one definitive way of having faith, hope, and love and those who disagree with Augustinian Christianity are wrong" (DRO, 313). First of all, at least we are clear at this point that Derrida—even Derrida's Augustine—is not really Augustinian. Second, it seems that behind this rejection of dogmatism lies simply a different dogmatism: a dogma of something like American liberal toleration. But is there any good reason to believe this other gospel? If it is simply a question of degrees of determinacy (it is not clear that this is the case for Derrida), then why is one determinate confession dogmatic but the other is not? The charge of dogmatism cannot really stick in a postfoundationalist context.

In this respect (though I launch a critique below), Ward's Augustine—or Augustinianism—is in one sense closer to the spirit of St. Augustine. In particular, Ward emphasizes the way in which even Augustine's questioning arises out of a covenantal relationship, and "for this relationship to be a relationship, a history of practiced believing is required, the memory (one's own and one's communities') of past engagement, past epiphany, past revelations" (QG, 276). There is no Augustine apart from the practices of Christian liturgy. Thus, Augustine's questioning—highlighted in the Derridean Augustine as an end in itself—is a questioning-within-relationship, within covenant, rather than a musing about the *tout autre* (wholly other) as such (QG, 276–77). It is this particularity of tradition and, more importantly, revelation[101] that animates Ward's Augustine, for it is precisely revelation that reveals that the world as

---

does Caputo really mean to suggest that Derrida's faith is *not* determinate or historical or "delivered over" to a tradition? Below (DRO, 312) Caputo seems to conclude (à la John Hick?) that historical *contingency* is equivalent to some kind of *translatability*—that God in Christ and Allah are just two different determinations of the same faith. I simply do not see any good reason to think that, and certainly Augustine would not think so.

100. This is a crucial concession, where Caputo is trying to save Derrida, since Derrida himself does not speak of a "relative" determinacy but indeterminacy as such. The problem with then admitting a *relative* determinacy is that now the question concerns who gets to decide how much determination is too much. How could that not be a simply dogmatic determination?

101. Ward emphasizes that revelation, for Augustine, is first inscribed in creation itself, rather than a later "addendum" to the world in the incarnation (TR, 282). While this is certainly true, the very Pauline Augustine would also emphasize the obfuscation of this creational revelation (Rom. 1:18–31) and hence the almost "medicinal" necessity of the incarnation's revelation to heal our perception of this creational revelation (DVR, 16.30). In other words, the affirmation of revelation in creation does not entail a natural theology.

"given" is, in fact, not a simple "given" at all but a gift that is to be understood and constituted as creation (QG, 281).

This revelational particularity, in the vein of Augustine's *De vera religione*, marks the contrast between Ward's *True Religion* and Caputo's *On Religion*. Within the narrative of *True Religion*, we find the precursors to Derrida and Caputo in Ward's analysis of Novalis's "diremptive" religion, which empties religion of the contingent and the concrete (TR, 76).[102] In contrast, Augustinian true religion is articulated by Schleiermacher (who is something of the hero of *True Religion*).[103] Schleiermacher is a critic of Romantic abstraction and instead "defines his experiences within the context of a specific religious revelation, practice, and tradition. That is, for Schleiermacher, we can only name this original moment as religious from within an understanding and knowledge of a particular tradition" (TR, 91). Thus, what funds Schleiermacher's project is not some kind of Kantian "religion within the limits of reason alone" but rather a specifically Christian and theological starting point (TR, 93)—specifically echoing Augustine by beginning with the Christian notions of incarnation and the *imago Dei* (TR, 92–93).

We can understand Ward's sketch of post-secular religion only if we see him operating in the same stream that runs from Augustine through Schleiermacher—which is precisely what distinguishes his proposal in *True Religion* from Caputo's Derridean vision in *On Religion*. According to Ward, authentic religion in a post-secular climate is not a liquidated religion of diremption, denuded of any particularity; rather, there is the growth of confessional religion, of public theology (TR, 133), suggesting something like a new Reformation (TR, 134). In a postmodern context still dominated by liberalism (TR, 139), theological and confessional communities constitute "resistance identities" (TR, 134), which is not without danger of war (TR, 153). But Ward suggests that

> in a neo-tribal culture, only theological communities have the resources—in terms of history, tradition, transcendent truth-claims, and pedagogical

---

102. Ward elucidates Schleiermacher's analysis that "natural religion is the Spinozist, monist religion of Schlegel and Novalis that 'consists wholly in the negation of everything positive and characteristic in religion,' that is everything that gives religion form. The refusal to engage with specific form of religion combined with the exultation of a general religious spirituality, Schleiermacher suggests, fails to understand true religion" (QG, 92).

103. I found the role of Schleiermacher the most fascinating and surprising aspect of Ward's manifesto. While the extended and insightful analysis of Schleiermacher's project (which should send Schleiermacher scholars working in the wake of Barth back to the texts) in chapter 3 is simply presented as part of the narrative, it seems that at the end of the book (151) he reappears precisely as an example of the "theological" response to postmodernity, embodying what I am trying to describe here as an Augustinian religion of revelational particularity.

practices for the formation of moral subjects—to resist the collapse into pragmatic and transitory values associated with media-driven "lifestyles." Only theological communities have the resources to cultivate forms of relationality that can resist the dissolving of the social into the cultural (TR 152).[104]

In sum, while Derrida's Augustine could write *Circumfession*, only Ward's Augustine could write *The City of God*.

In a certain sense, then, Ward's Augustine takes seriously the particularity of determinate, theological confession in a way that the Derridean Augustine does not. If the Derridean Augustine is religious, the radically orthodox Augustine is theological; that is, the latter Augustine is formed and shaped by determinate liturgical practices and a contentful theological confession. By retrieving such an Augustine in the contemporary context, Ward is suggesting that the only viable, authentic religions in postmodernity are theological, confessing communities. However, in the vein of *De vera religione,* this would seem to require another Augustinian chapter conveying the way in which Christianity alone is the true theology. Is this a chapter Ward would write? In other words, it seems that Ward's account in *True Religion* simply valorizes particularity per se—the theological as such (in contrast to the ambiguously religious)—without specifying the criteria of what would constitute authentic particularity or true theology.[105] "True religion," according to Ward, is theology. But what is "true theology"? Given that Ward does not articulate an answer to this question, it is here that we need to stage a further retrieval of a robustly christological Augustine, for Augustine would agree that true

---

104. In some ways, Ward here echoes the proposal of Daniel M. Bell Jr., *Liberation Theology after the End of History: The Refusal to Cease Suffering,* Radical Orthodoxy (New York: Routledge, 2001). I return to Bell in detail in chapter 7.

105. Ward's account is also characterized by a disturbing "blurring" of the Augustinian vision. In developing a "theology of commingling" (CG, 229) or *permixtum* (227–28), Ward makes Augustine seem quite a bit more agnostic than the Bishop of Hippo. Unable to draw the borders of the church, Ward's Augustine is left with a blurred distinction between the *civitas Dei* and the *civitas terrena.* The result seems to be the dissolution of the church by means of diffusion; thus, Ward concludes that the "displacement" of Christ's body entails that "all human bodies participate in this one body and this participation and belonging constitutes the ecclesial body, the Church" (CG, 225; cf. BR, 121–22). It is hard to see how this does not feed into the worst sorts of "Protestant" notions of the church invisible. Furthermore, Ward's Augustine seems beset by a Cartesian anxiety that leaves him a skeptic. Indeed, at the conclusion of CG, Ward sounds remarkably like Caputo: "From Augustine I take the insight that we need to suspend judgment. I take it in a way that differs from him. As Christians we have to suspend judgment concerning other faiths. . . . We must suspend our judgment about those who pursue love, mercy, justice, and righteousness in other practices. . . . We do not know what we say when we say 'Abba,' 'Lord,' 'Christ,' 'salvation,' 'God'" (CG, 257–59).

religion is confessional and theological, but he would also claim that "Jesus is Lord" is the true confession and that only an account of the Triune God rooted in revelation constitutes authentic theology. Here the Augustinian retrievals of Milbank and Hanby seem more substantive and christologically robust.

A New Aquinas: Graced Nature

The earliest emphases of RO focused on a retrieval of Augustine (echoing the project of the *nouvelle théologie*). But given its catholicity and increasing emphases on the doctrine of transubstantiation (Ward, Pickstock), Aquinas has come to play an increasingly important role in the story that RO wants to tell. However, the Aquinas that takes the stage in RO's narrative is, like its Plato, a "new" creation.

Historically, many of the charges that RO levels against Scotus have been laid at the feet of Aquinas, particularly by those within the Reformed camp.[106] In particular, the nature/grace schematic has drawn the charge that it is Aquinas, not Scotus, who first unhooked creation from Creator, granting autonomy to nature, which could be properly (though partially) understood apart from revelation.[107] In fact, earlier, Milbank himself makes just this point, suggesting that Aquinas "has moved too far" down the road that allows a sphere of secular autonomy (TST, 407). "By beginning to see social, economic, and administrative life as essentially *natural*," he continues, "Aquinas opens the way to regarding the Church as an organization specializing in what goes on inside men's souls" (TST, 407).[108] So also, Daniel Bell's critique of Jacques Maritain's account of the relation between an autonomous, secular nature and a sphere of supernatural grace is, at root, a critique of a deeply Thomistic paradigm.[109]

Such notions of an autonomous nature, of course, run counter to the core thesis of RO, namely, that a participatory ontology "refuses any reserve of created territory" (RONT, 3).[110] Thus, if Aquinas is to be

---

106. E.g., Francis Schaeffer, Herman Dooyeweerd, Cornelius Van Til.

107. I address the specifically *epistemological* implications of this in more detail in chapter 5.

108. Later, Milbank lumps Aquinas with Scotus insofar as both "denied participation in creation by creatures"—in contrast to Eriugena. Therefore, "Eriugena's ontology, based on God as internally 'maker' and then on different degrees of participation in creation, is . . . more profoundly Christian than that of Aquinas" (TST, 425).

109. Bell, *Liberation Theology after the End of History*, 45–48.

110. Cf. Kuyper's oft-quoted claim, "There is not a single square inch of creation concerning which Christ does not say, 'Mine!'"

enlisted as a resource for the RO project, a new reading is required.[111] What worries Milbank and Pickstock is a notion of nature as autonomous, which can then become secular. But on this score, they argue two key theses: First, for Aquinas, it is not possible to have any kind of secular or neutral metaphysics because the world can be properly understood only in its dependence on and relation to God. Therefore, second, there can be no neutral epistemic access to the structures of the world—and thus no notion of an autonomous reason. Since this second claim is considered in chapter 5, here we will expound just the first claim.

According to their reading, nature, for Aquinas, is not a neutral realm of autonomy that can be considered in abstraction (as for Scotus); in other words, to speak of nature is not to speak of a world devoid of grace. Rather, insofar as all of creation—all that exists—exists by virtue of gift (the gift of being), there is a sense in which we must speak of creation as originally graced—grace as a "proper accident" (TA, 12) or original supplement.[112] For (RO's) Aquinas, then, there can be no such thing as a secular metaphysics that operates irrespective of the created nature of being. Rather, in the place of (Scotist) ontology (or ontotheology), Aquinas offers a theo-ontology, because "it did not need first to be situated in a 'general discourse' about being, essence and substance, indifferent to finite and infinite, as later articulated by Scotus" (TA, 35).[113] Thus, "it is surely clear that this new theological ontology of constitutive supernatural supplementation and ecstatic relationality reveals a cosmos already in a sense graced, and in such a fashion that the supplement of grace will not seem in discontinuity with existing principles of ontological constitution" (TA, 44). When Milbank and Pickstock describe nature as essentially graced, they do not mean to say that nature/creation is inherently deficient and always already in need of redemption. Rather, they want to emphasize its dependence—its creaturehood. Creation cannot be understood as autonomous in any way, and thus "grace goes all the way down." The "leading characteristic" of Aquinas's theological ontology, therefore, "is a grasp of creation in the light of grace, as itself graced or supplemented" (TA, 51). Insofar as nature is always already graced, there can be no dualistic demarcation of an autonomous nature to which a relationship to the divine is appended. Nature—which "is" only insofar as it participates in God—is suffused with the divine and

111. My thanks to Rebecca Konyndyk DeYoung for several helpful conversations on the matters that follow.

112. "It has been seen how not only Creation as a whole is a gift for Aquinas, but each creature is ceaselessly re-constituted through supplementation, in such a way that the 'more' and 'later' is taken paradoxically to define it" (TA, 43).

113. "Metaphysics is already, in some weak sense, *sacra doctrina*" (TA, 35).

hence with grace. Thus, Milbank later claims that "everything is therefore 'engraced'" (BR, 115).

It is certainly true that, for Aquinas, nature does not have a *sui generis*
autonomy. Rather, as created it is structured by a "natural orientation
to the supernatural" (BR, 115). However, Aquinas does not describe
this gifted nature as grace. Milbank and Pickstock's argument for an
"engraced nature" seems to collapse the orders of creation and redemption such that the fall is either ignored or immediately undone in such a
way that it has no enduring impact on the present postlapsarian world.
Milbank, therefore, refers to "the lost and renewed gift of grace" (BR,
27) and later, more specifically, speaks of "the aporetic loss of divine
glory in the world through the Fall, *which God immediately corrects*,
although our own realization of this correcting must be gradual" (BR,
42, emphasis added).[114] As a result, Nicholas Lash legitimately remarks
that "Milbank is so (admirably) concerned to keep the 'graciousness'
of creation centre stage that he risks effacing those further distinctions
between creation and election, for example, and between creation and
Incarnation, without which Christian narratives crumble into incoher-
ence."[115] But this criticism of RO's history does not mitigate its more
constructive account; that is, while the notion of a graced nature may
not be found in Aquinas, the constructive theological vision is an important account. However, in the constructive aspect, this tendency to
elide creation and redemption—and thus downplay the fall—is a theme
to which we must return. It is to the more constructive aspects of RO
that we now turn in part 2.

114. In chapter 7, I discuss the way in which RO's broadening of grace blurs distinctions
not only between creation and redemption but also between church and world.

115. Nicholas Lash, "Not Exactly Politics or Power?" *Modern Theology* 8 (1992): 353.

Part 2

Navigation

The task of part 1 was to provide an initial orientation to Radical Orthodoxy and the project of a post-secular faith through a spiraling movement that proceeded from the general to the more particular. This task moved from a large-scale project of mapping RO on the contemporary theological and cultural terrain of postmodernity (chap. 1), to an enumeration of core themes or movements of RO (chap. 2), and finally to a more substantive analysis of RO's own history of philosophy and theology, which is important for the movement's self-understanding (chap. 3).

Part 2 continues this spiral movement into the core thematic and constructive issues of RO by expanding themes first sketched in chapter 2. The spiral now operates on the basis of an axiom suggested in chapter 3: Behind a *politics* lies an *epistemology*, which is in turn undergirded by an *ontology*. Chapter 4, therefore, begins by considering the politics of secularity and RO's critique of such a project. Chapter 5 moves on to consider modernity's attendant epistemological claim regarding autonomous reason and RO's constructive alternative. Chapter 6 arrives at the center of the spiral by examining the ontology of participation (vs. univocity). The final chapter then explores the consequences of this politics/epistemology/ontology nexus by taking us back to the outside of the spiral through a consideration of ethics, politics, and community (ecclesiology).

4

Postmodern Parodies

The Critique of Modernity
and the Myth of the Secular

If the goal of RO is ultimately to foster post-secular confession and practice, then it needs to grapple with the nature of secularity, which, in turn, requires a sustained engagement with modernity and its heir, postmodernity. As shown in chapter 3, RO is a confessional strategy that situates itself in critical relation to both modernity and postmodernity. However, it neither celebrates postmodernity (as do more Derridean strains of contemporary philosophical theology) nor simply demonizes modernity.[1] It is important to highlight the latter, since it has so often been ignored: RO is not antimodern. Rather, it takes seriously the

1. Nor is it a simplistic call for a restored premodernity, as some seem to think (John D. Caputo). As John Milbank stated from the beginning, RO "offers no proposed restoration of a pre-modern Christian position" (TST, 2). The point is the articulation of a historic Christian orthodoxy *in* postmodernity, having come *through* modernity.

125

accomplishments of modernity and subjects them to critical scrutiny. As Graham Ward carefully notes, "These observations, let me quickly add, are not to be taken as outright condemnations of secularism or modernity or liberalism. . . . Even today it might be remarked that in certain countries in the world a good dose of secularism would break the repressive holds certain state-ratified religions have over people's lives. Nor can we say that nothing good came from modernity, or that nothing good still comes from its traditions" (TR, 1–2). RO's radical critique of modernity, therefore, does not commit adherents to being intellectual Luddites, nor does it require a rejection of the "fruits of modernity," such as advances in science and medicine or the undoing of forms of institutionalized repression (TR, 2). As such, "Radical Orthodoxy, although it opposes the modern, also seeks to save it. It espouses, not the pre-modern, but an alternative vision of modernity."[2] RO's attitude toward modernity (and postmodernity) is complex: neither "outright refusal, nor outright acceptance. More like an attempt at radical redirection of what we find" (BR, 196).

The goal of this chapter is to unpack RO's critique of modernity, first more formally (in John Milbank), and then more substantively (in Ward's analysis of modern cities and William Cavanaugh's and Daniel Bell's accounts of the modern state). All seek to foster a critical stance toward modernity and its fruits (epistemological and political autonomy, secularization, democratic liberalism, and capitalism). In particular, RO's project is aimed at unveiling the ultimately religious status of this modern vision, thus alerting us to the ways in which these core values or doctrines of modern life are, in the end, competitors of the gospel of Christ. As a result, the stance of the church and disciples of Christ in regard to these values should be one of critical distance rather than easy appropriation. Rather than being merely neutral political phenomena or the supposed political outworking of Christianity, the institutions of modernity are covert idols—rivals of a more radical understanding of the gospel. Without being alarmist, RO seeks to point out the fundamental antithesis[3] between modernity and the Christian faith.

2. John Milbank, "The Programme of Radical Orthodoxy," in *Radical Orthodoxy? A Catholic Enquiry*, ed. Laurence Paul Hemming (Burlington, Vt.: Ashgate, 2000), 45.

3. This is why the "redirection" suggested by Milbank must be "radical": Even some of the achievements of modernity stem from "roots" that are problematic. Milbank seems to suggest that even if we affirm some of the fruits of modernity, they could (should?) be produced by different roots. For instance, ending the oppression of women is a good to be affirmed but not the particularities of liberal discourse that, in this historical case, brought about this modern achievement. The achievement could have been accomplished otherwise.

Modernity as Heresy

Secular modernity, despite all its protests and pretensions to the contrary, is deeply religious and fundamentally theological. This is the core thesis of Milbank's *Theology and Social Theory,* which was a precursor of what would become Radical Orthodoxy. Focusing on modern social theory, Milbank argues that "the most important governing assumptions of such theory are bound up with the modification or the rejection of orthodox Christian positions" (TST, 1). Two important claims about secular modernity are encapsulated here: (1) Modernity, while claiming to be secular and therefore religiously neutral, is in fact governed by (ultimately religious) assumptions that are "no more rationally 'justifiable' than the Christian positions themselves" (TST, 1); and (2) the shape of these assumptions indicates a certain perverse debt to Christianity, such that secular modernity—and secular social theory in particular—is undergirded by a heterodox theology. According to Milbank's reading, "Secular discourse does not just 'borrow' inherently inappropriate modes of expression as the only discourse to hand (this is Hans Blumenberg's interpretation) but is actually *constituted* in its secularity by 'heresy' in relation to orthodox Christianity, or else a rejection of Christianity that is more 'neo-pagan' than simply anti-religious" (TST, 3). Secular theory, then, is supported not by a neutral, universal rationality (as it claims) but by "simply another *mythos,*" an alternative confession.[4] Hence, "'scientific' social theories are themselves theologies or anti-theologies in disguise" (TST, 3). In this way, Milbank's claim echoes Lyotard's critique of metanarratives: Though they claim to rise above the realm of myth, narrative, and *doxa,* in fact they are predicated upon just such mythical narratives (cf. TST, 263–67).[5] In fact, there is a sense in which modern secular theories are predicated upon the advent of the Christian narrative in an almost parasitic fashion. Here Herman Dooyeweerd, working from within the Reformational tradition, anticipates Milbank's critique. Describing the emergence of the (apostate) "humanistic ground-motive" or worldview (the equivalent of what Milbank describes as a "quasi-theology"),[6] Dooyeweerd claims that

> the freedom-motive originated in a religion of humanity, into which the biblical basic-motive had been completely transformed. . . . This meant

4. The focus of chapter 5 is to spell out the consequences of this *status* of modern, secular discourse as "theological" or "confessional."

5. I discussed Lyotard's account in much more detail in James K. A. Smith, "Little Story about Metanarratives: Lyotard, Religion, and Postmodernism Revisited," *Faith and Philosophy* 18 (2001): 261–76.

6. Dooyeweerd's account of ground-motives is considered in more detail in chapter 5.

a Copernican revolution with respect to the biblical basic-motive of the Christian religion. The biblical revelation of the creation of man in the image of God was implicitly subverted into the idea of a creation of God in the idealized image of man. The biblical conception of the rebirth of man and his radical freedom in Jesus Christ was replaced by the idea of a regeneration of man by his own autonomous will. (ITWT, 33)

This new, secular religious orientation was foreign to Greek thought precisely because "it presupposed the Christian motive of creation, fall into sin, and redemption," but this biblical theme is immanentized in modernity: "After having emancipated himself from all belief in a supernatural sphere in its scholastic-ecclesiastical sense, and having made himself into the only master of his destiny, modern man seeks in nature infinite possibilities to satisfy his own creative impulse" (ITWT, 34). The result is an autonomous nature and a liberated humanity. But this stems from distinctly religious commitments of modernity—commitments that are parasitic on orthodox Christian faith.

Marxism, in this case, is paradigmatic. Rooted in the Enlightenment claim of having a scientific basis—thereby eschewing any taint of prejudice—Marxism offers a comprehensive account of sociality with eschatological pretensions. Even the *telos* of the Marxist vision resonates with the Christian vision of shalom, but both the mechanism and the site of its arrival is immanentized, such that what we get in Marxism—in the name of a scientific economics—is an eschaton without kingdom or grace.[7] Thus, "the utopian phase, which Marx envisages as inevitably supervening upon the collapse of capitalism, is conceived primarily in terms of the unleashing of human freedom and the unlimited possibility of human transformation of nature. This essentially liberal and secular goal is no longer secured through market competition or state policing, but instead through the mysterious return of a lost harmony with nature" (TST, 177–78). While Milbank recognizes Marx's penetrating critique (which unveiled that "capitalism is somewhat like a religion" and that "the 'religiosity' of capitalism is also, and preeminently, the paradoxical religiosity of the secular itself" [TST, 196]), he faults Marx's modernism, which blinded him to the contingent, confessional status of his science and in fact appropriated an ultimately liberal, voluntarist priority on freedom (TST, 178).[8]

7. I unpacked this critique further in James K. A. Smith, "Determined Hope: A Phenomenology of Christian Expectation," in *The Future of Hope: Essays on Christian Tradition amid Modernity and Postmodernity*, ed. Miroslav Volf and William Katerberg (Grand Rapids: Eerdmans, 2004), 200–227.

8. For further discussion of Marx, see D. Stephen Long, *Divine Economy: Theology and the Market* (London: Routledge, 2000), 97–102.

The parasitic (and heterodox) nature of secular modernity is sketched most substantively in Milbank's account of early modern shifts to a secular political economy. The emergence of the secular, for Milbank, stems from distinctly religious or theological decisions that informed a new ontology and account of human nature. This new theological framework was characterized by a heretical appropriation of orthodox Christian themes melded with decidedly neo-pagan elements, all under the banner of a new scientific neutrality. But the received wisdom of modern social theory sees this transformation not as a heterodox deformation but rather as the culmination of a certain Christian logic. As Milbank describes it, modern social theory

> interprets the theological transformation at the inception of modernity as a genuine "reformation" which fulfills the destiny of Christianity to let the spiritual be spiritual, without public interference, and the public be secular, without private prejudice. Yet this interpretation preposterously supposes that the new theology simply brought Christianity to its true essence by lifting some irksome and misplaced sacred ecclesial restrictions on the free market of the secular, whereas, *in fact*, it instituted an *entirely different* economy of power and knowledge. (TST, 10, emphasis added)[9]

The political—like nature—is carved out as an autonomous realm and is "defined as a field of pure power" (TST, 10). Beginning with the affirmation of an autonomous nature—and hence autonomous humanity—the new theology places central emphasis on human "making" (*poiesis*) as a mode of power. Within this new paradigm, classic Christian themes are reconfigured such that, while their semantic filiation is orthodox, they are put to work in a way that departs from authentic Christian teaching. For instance, Adam's dominion over creation is now defined in terms of power, and more specifically, a power *over* things in terms of property (TST, 12–13). "One can conclude that 'unrestricted' private property, 'absolute sovereignty' and 'active rights,' which compose the 'pure-power' object of the new politics, are all the emanations of a new anthropology which begins with human persons as individuals and yet defines their individuality essentialistically, as 'will' or 'capacity' or 'impulse to self-preservation' [*conatus essendi*]" (TST, 14). The new politics (of autonomous sovereign power) is undergirded by a new anthropology (of individual self-determination), and both are "theologically promoted"

9. Milbank contends that, to a significant degree, this was the product of "the self-understanding of Christianity arrived at in late-medieval nominalism, the protestant reformation and seventeenth-century Augustinianism, which completely privatized, spiritualized and transcendentalized the sacred, and concurrently reimagined nature, human action and society as a sphere of autonomous, sheerly formal power" (TST, 9).

(TST, 14) through the appropriation of a Christian semantics of *dominium*, equating the *imago Dei* with a conception of radically autonomous will and translating covenantal relationships into contractual ones (TST, 15). In this respect, what may appear to be different accounts of the secular political sphere—Thomas Hobbes's and Machiavelli's—end up with a deep similarity: Both construe the space of the secular fundamentally in terms of autonomous power.[10] "If the Hobbesian field of power seems to be constructed by a perverse theology, then the Machiavellian field of power is constructed by a partial rejection of Christianity and appeal to an alternative *mythos*" (TST, 21). In both cases, however, we have a politics and an anthropology rooted in a *mythos* antithetical to orthodox Christian faith. At stake here is the fact of "the 'neo-pagan' character of this clear-sighted vision of political economy and its outright celebration of what Christian theology rejected, namely the *libido dominandi*. Here again, the 'autonomy' of secular reason involves as a condition of its very independence, the endorsement of a viewpoint which Christianity earlier presumed to call into question" (TST, 37).

Milbank goes on to consider the shift from this "new science of politics" (Hobbes, Machiavelli, Benedict Spinoza) to "political economy" (Adam Smith, Thomas Malthus). If the new science of politics was concerned with freedom and autonomy (articulated with the Christian lexicon of *imago Dei* and *dominium*), political economy was interested in the regulation of power by the operations of the market and articulated this with the Christian lexicon of providence. "Political economy *turns away* from the seemingly ultra-modern themes of anarchy and autonomy mooted in the seventeenth century by Hobbes and others, and seeks to supplement science as making with a science of providence, or a social theodicy. There is a concern to display history as the natural process of the self-emergence of an immanent reason, *within which* 'man' or 'humanity' arises" (TST, 29). The result is the same: a perversion of Christian orthodoxy and the development of a new theology founding the new science of economics. "Here again, the institution of the 'secular' is paradoxically related to a shift *within* theology and not an emancipation *from* theology" (TST, 29). Milbank's analysis of these two strands of modernity (the new science on the one hand and political economy on the other) and the dialectical tension between them interestingly parallels Dooyeweerd's account of the dialectical tensions within the

10. Milbank takes these to be foundational to later social science: "Both the natural rights [Hobbes] and the Machiavellian traditions in 'scientific politics' are heavily presupposed by all later social science. Yet from both a Christian *and* a metacritical perspective . . . it might seem that we have here only to do with heresy on the one hand and the half-return of paganism on the other" (TST, 23).

modern "humanistic" ground-motive, oscillating between the poles of nature and freedom (ITWT, 33–36). In other words, modern secular accounts are characterized by an internal tension because they tend to "absolutize" a particular pole or sphere of experience, which calls forth its opposite in ways that cannot be reconciled.

So "in effect," Milbank surmises, "theology encounters in sociology only a theology, and indeed a church in disguise, but a theology and a church dedicated to promoting a certain secular consensus" (TST, 4). Thus, modernity and its institutions offer what RO describes as a "parody" of Christian faith and the church.

Modernity as Parody

The relation of modernity to Christianity is one of both debt and distance, but for RO, the relationship can generally be described in terms of parody—a kind of skewed *mimesis* or perverse imitation by which modern secular institutions attempt both to replace and to subvert the church and its gospel.[11] This modern, secular "logic of parody" involves a movement of displacement and replacement. For instance, in the line of Milbank's analysis discussed above, Ward assays an important shift in the sixteenth century whereby the theme of sovereignty led to a blurring by which God and the monarch were confused. The blurring entailed a shift in the vocation of the state: "If, in the old world order, it was the sacrament of the Eucharist administered and interpreted by the church that was the focus for the material presence of God on earth, then, in the new world order, the monarch was the new focus for God's sacramental presence. The monarch replaced the mass, the body of Christ becoming the body of the king, and in this transposition was forged a new understanding of communion in terms of commonwealth" (TR, 43). Therefore, the logic of parody on the one hand capitalizes on the religious capital of the Christian legacy but on the other hand seeks to set up secular institutions founded on quite different theological paradigms to subvert Christianity. The public is not so much desacralized as it is de-Christianized to bathe the new secular public in a kind of sacral secularity. New rituals of formation take the place of Christian liturgy and serve quite different ends. The secular is not areligious, just differently religious—a religion of immanence and autonomy.

---

11. One could question whether *parody* is the right term to describe this phenomenon of skewed mimesis. Perhaps *travesty* better conveys the sense. However, in this discussion, I follow the RO practice of employing the term *parody*. My thanks to Matt Halteman for raising this issue.

RO's analysis of this logic of parody is found in two crucial sites: Cavanaugh's and Bell's accounts of the state's soteriological pretensions, and Ward's careful analysis of urban planning as a new soteriology.[12]

Statecraft: A Secular Ecclesia

Daniel Bell suggests that RO's account of the modern logic of parody is in fact a restatement of Augustine's project in *City of God*, in which he criticized the empire's pretensions to being a commonwealth in decidedly liturgical terms; that is, what was at stake was worship, and only the city of God could be the site of authentic human community because only there could one find true worship.[13] So also, Bell argues, the articulation of a radically orthodox account of sociality "begins with the recovery of the Augustinian insight that politics as statecraft is but a secular parody of the true politics that is the fellowship of the saints."[14] This notion of the state as a parody of the *ecclesia* is picked up in further detail in Cavanaugh's contribution to the Radical Orthodoxy collection.[15]

Both the church and the modern state have a story to tell: The modern state is "founded on certain stories of nature and human nature, the origins of human conflict, and the remedies for such conflict in the enactment of the state itself"; the Christian story is a narrative of creation, fall, and redemption. But, Cavanaugh argues, "*both* ultimately have the same goal: salvation of humankind from the modern divisions which plague us" (RONT, 182). Thus, "the modern state is best understood . . . as a source of an alternative soteriology to that of the Church" (RONT, 182). The advent of modernity and the birth of the secular, therefore, do not entail the creation of a secular public space where the state merely manages temporal goods, distinguished from a private sacred space where individuals and communities are free to pursue a supra-temporal *telos*. The state does not take a merely temporal regulatory role and leave

12. Cavanaugh, Bell, and Ward all posit an alternative vision to that of the secular state and secular city. However, here I am interested in only their critique or "read" of the state/city. I return to a discussion of their constructive visions in chapter 7.

13. Augustine, *City of God*, book XIX. Peter Leithart advocates a revival of this Augustinian critique: "What the Church needs is a renewal of the Augustinian project. We need to disentangle the American story from the Christian story" (*Against Christianity* [Moscow, Idaho: Canon Press, 2003], 64).

14. Daniel M. Bell Jr., *Liberation Theology after the End of History: The Refusal to Cease Suffering*, Radical Orthodoxy (London: Routledge, 2001), 72.

15. William T. Cavanaugh, "The City: Beyond Secular Parodies," in RONT, 182–200. This argument is unpacked and extended in William T. Cavanaugh, *Theopolitical Imagination* (Edinburgh: T & T Clark, 2002).

salvation in the hands of the church; rather, the modern state seeks to replace the church by itself becoming a soteriological institution.[16] It is in this sense, then, that the modern state is a parody of the church: "The body of the state is a simulacrum, a false copy, of the Body of Christ" (RONT, 182). As a result, while political rhetoric may suggest that the state is confined to a "public" sphere or that the reign of the secular is circumscribed, in fact the modern state demands complete allegiance, and the reign of the secular does not tolerate territories of resistance.[17] The state is happy to absorb all kinds of private pursuits under the umbrella of civil society, but it cannot tolerate a religious community that claims to be the only authentic *polis* and proclaims a king who is a rival to both Caesar and Leviathan. In such a case, this community's allegiance to its king ultimately trumps its allegiance to the state or empire, and its understanding of the nature of human persons does not fit the normative picture of liberalism. This the state cannot tolerate. It is in this sense that "every worship service is a challenge to Caesar."[18] Thus, Cavanaugh defines the state as "that peculiar institution which has arisen in the last four centuries in which a centralized and abstract power holds a monopoly over physical coercion within a geographically defined territory" (RONT, 182–83).[19]

The story that orients the modern state echoes that expounded by Milbank above: Beginning from an ontological and anthropological assumption of an original "war of all with all" in a state of nature (hence, this opposition is taken to be "natural"), the state's mission is to "make peace" between competing individuals (RONT, 186–87). "As in Christian soteriology, salvation from the violence of conflicting individuals comes through the enacting of a social body" (RONT, 188). But there is an immanentization of this social organism such that the resources for salvation are thought to reside within the power of autonomous human

---

16. Of course, insofar as the modern state operates on the basis of an ontology of immanence, its conception of salvation is *immanentized* to this plane.

17. Elsewhere Cavanaugh considers the way in which "revulsion to killing in the name of religion is used to legitimize the transfer of ultimate loyalty to the modern State" (William T. Cavanaugh, "'A Fire Strong Enough to Consume the House': The Wars of Religion and the Rise of the State," *Modern Theology* 11 [1995]: 397). In *Torture and Eucharist*, Cavanaugh expands his analysis of "the state's claim to omnipotence over its citizens" and the way in which torture functions as a liturgy to produce docile subjects (William T. Cavanaugh, *Torture and Eucharist: Theology, Politics, and the Body of Christ* [Oxford: Blackwell, 1998], 22–34). His constructive argument claims that "the Eucharist is the church's 'counter-politics' to the politics of torture" (205).

18. Leithart, *Against Christianity*, 67.

19. In chapter 7, I argue that Cavanaugh confuses a particular *direction* the modern state has taken with the *structure* of the state as such. My thanks to Hans Boersma for helpful conversations on this point.

beings, even if they need to choose to give up some of their autonomy for this peace. "Leviathan, then, is the new Adam, now of human creation, which saves us from each other" (RONT, 188). The consequence is the civil religion of state-induced peace.[20] (In a post-9/11 America, the state's penchant for a monopoly on allegiance is coupled with its soteriological mission of peace in what is described as a war on terror, which is a war against those who would refuse unity. The state's war *for* unity and *against* terror demands an uncompromised allegiance to the new Leviathan.)[21]

However, in seeking to achieve peace without grace (a correlate of an original war without sin), the state not only pretends to *be* a church or soteriological institution but must also save us *from* the church. If the *telos* of the state's mission is a unity without difference, a peace without faction, then "the Church is perhaps the primary thing from which the modern state is meant to save us" (RONT, 188), for the church, as a transnational body,[22] must necessarily both transcend the boundaries of the state and also be a fractive force *within* the state precisely because it asserts difference—an antithesis. This is why "Leviathan must swallow the Church whole; a commonwealth is a church is a state," such that there are "as many Churches as there are states" (RONT, 188–89). Hence, religion—the civic religion of the state—"becomes a means of binding the individual to the sovereign" (RONT, 189).[23] Thus, the narrative of the modern state—its *euangelion*—ends with a Glorious Revolution: "We are saved bloodlessly from the most serious cause of division among people, and all religion is tolerated. All religion, that is, except those forms which continue to consider the Church a transnational body" (RONT, 190).

What most concerns Cavanaugh (here he echoes Stanley Hauerwas) is the degree to which "Christians have tended to succumb to the power of the state soteriology" and "have done so often on Christian grounds" (RONT, 190). Cavanaugh and Bell would suggest several reasons for this. First, Christians have failed to recognize the status of this state soteriol-

---

20. An oblique critique of contemporary civil religion can be found in Harry S. Stout, "'Baptism in Blood': The Civil War and the Creation of an American Civil Religion," *Books & Culture* 9 (2003): 16–17, 33–35, which is something of a précis of his *Upon the Altar of the Nation: A Moral History of the Civil War* (London: Viking/Penguin, forthcoming).

21. For additional suggestions along this line, see John Milbank, "Sovereignty, Empire, Capital, and Terror," in *Dissent from the Homeland: Essays after September 11*, ed. Stanley Hauerwas and Frank Lentricchia (Durham, N.C.: Duke University Press, 2003), 63–82.

22. In chapter 7, I engage Bell's important analysis of the transnational character of capitalism, which supercedes the functional power of the state.

23. While Hobbes is the focus of Cavanaugh's analysis, he notes similar themes in Rousseau (RONT, 189).

ogy as a *mythos;* in other words, the church bought modernity's story that this account of the political is a neutral and scientific account of social realities. From an epistemological perspective, the church conceded analysis of the social sphere to rationality. This was linked to a second concession: Ecclesiologies conceded the temporal plane to the secular. Here Bell and Cavanaugh are deeply critical of the "New Christendom" ecclesiology offered by Jacques Maritain. This model posits the church as a "social rather than political witness" whereby the church is "an apolitical custodian of moral values . . . [that] conceded politics to the state."[24] Granted, on the one hand, this model tried to mitigate stark oppositions between the secular and the sacred (the temporal realm is valued as a site for a certain grace), contributed to "the formation of voluntary associations that would contribute to re-Catholicizing society by creating a critical mass of Catholic laity active in society," "created space for reformist and progressive voices in the Church," and ultimately valued cultural engagement by the laity "as a sort of 'leaven' of the temporal realm."[25] On the other hand, this model resulted in a certain evacuation of the church from the political as such, engendering "the creation of the temporal as an autonomous space from which the church was removed."[26] New Christendom ecclesiology did nothing to subvert the state's soteriological pretensions. In Bell's terms, modern ecclesiologies "embraced a conception of politics as statecraft" such that "the state was left as the uncontested overseer of the political realm."[27] Finally, because the church failed to recognize the mythical status of this secular story and conceded the temporal to the state, it also failed to discern the antithesis between this story and the Christian story. But for Cavanaugh (and Bell), this "state soteriology offers a false unity and a false peace which are fundamentally at odds with the Christian story" (RONT, 190). This is because, following Augustine, "there can be

24. Bell, *Liberation Theology after the End of History,* 45.
25. Ibid., 45–48. One must be struck by how much this "New Christendom" model parallels Abraham Kuyper's notion of the "Church as organism" (as distinguished from the "Church as institution"). Indeed, Kuyper valorizes the "mystical body of Christ" as a kind of Kantian "noumenon" (and for Kuyper, the model of this is the supposed "dichotomous" nature of the human person, with invisible soul and physical body), echoing the very language of Maritain and New Christendom ecclesiology (see Cavanaugh, *Torture and Eucharist,* 207–21). But because of this overlap, Kuyper's ecclesiology is subject to the same critique as that of Maritain. We return to these matters in chapter 7.
26. Cavanaugh, *Torture and Eucharist,* 206.
27. Bell, *Liberation Theology after the End of History,* 48, 51. Bell and Cavanaugh both go on to note the way in which Jacques Maritain embraces liberal democracy as the "truth" about the political. For an analysis that confirms this but is sympathetic to Maritain, see Eduardo J. Echeverria, "Nature and Grace: The Theological Foundations of Jacques Maritain's Public Philosophy," *Journal of Markets and Morality* 4 (2001): 240–68.

no justice and no common weal where God is not truly worshipped"
(RONT, 185). As a result, Christians need to reconsider their capitulation to the state soteriology and the liberal project it has spawned. This
will require revisiting the church's capitulation to key themes of secular
modernity that grew out of a *mythos* that was deeply antithetical to the
Christian narrative.

Divine Cities: A Secular Kingdom

Cavanaugh's account of the state as a parody of the church is complemented by Ward's rich analysis of another social unit: the city.[28] In
particular, Ward observes a bivalent parody at work in the secular city:
on the one hand, modern "cities of eternal aspiration" that are parodies
of the eschaton's city, New Jerusalem; on the other hand, postmodern
"cities of endless desire" whose libidinal dynamics make a travesty of
the desiring nature of creatures.[29] In both cases, a secular institution or
sphere, supposedly evacuated of the religious, assumes a quasi-ecclesial
function and, in fact, operates on the basis of a particular theological
ontology (of social atomism rooted in the univocity of being).[30] Far from
being religiously neutral regimes of social organization, "the communities of desire, dreamt and engineered by modernity, are parodies of
the Christian *ecclesia*" (CG, 125). But because the parody is based on
a univocal ontology of social atomism, the modern city is not able to
secure authentic, genuine community. This is why "only a theological
or analogical account of bodies safeguards the concreteness of community" (CG, 117).

As with Cavanaugh, Ward's first burden is to get the ecclesial community to appreciate the *mythos*-grounded character of the modern
urban project, contrary to the pretensions of scientific neutrality under
which it traffics. Only after the religious nature of the modern urban
project is appreciated can we appreciate the antithesis between the anthropology and ontology of secular modernity and that of the church.
In the wake of secular modernity's advent, by which social life was

28. Though there is also a significant sense in which the city Ward considers is a
metaphor for the state, the nature of the *polis*. In this sense, Cavanaugh's and Ward's
analyses overlap.

29. There is a sense, then, in which the logic of parody represents what we could describe as a misdirection of creational structures. However, in Kuyperian or Dooyeweerdian
terms, the logic of parody also involves a confusion of spheres insofar as the state or city
attempts to assume the role meant for the church. (In general, RO does not recognize such
a notion of sphere sovereignty.) We return to these matters in chapter 7.

30. For Ward's analysis of modernity's anthropology of social atomism, stemming from
its nominalism, rooted in the univocity of being, see CG, 126–37.

unhooked from transcendence and secured as an autonomous realm (CG, 37), urban planning became religious in its grammar and goals of constructing "secular Edens" (CG, 39). Urban planners became the new Johns of Patmos, recording visions of a coming city—a utopian "heteropolis" (CG, 33; cf. Heb. 11:16). Therefore, despite the alleged secularity of the project, cities became sites of eternal aspiration. Frank Lloyd Wright's "Broadacres" was envisioned as the ideal community in which he saw "a social harmony allied to a natural harmony, fostered by a political egalitarianism" (CG, 40). Thus, there is a sense in which Wright's project was informed by a kind of "natural theology." And as Cavanaugh pointed out with regard to the modern state, the modern city is here given a salvific mission. Where social disharmony is linked to the war of all with all, Broadacres is prophesied to be the site where such sin is eradicated: "To build Broadacres as conceived," Wright proclaimed, "would automatically end unemployment and all the evils forever" (cited in CG, 40).

The vision of the city as parody of the New Jerusalem is intensified in another paragon of modern architecture and urban planning: Le Corbusier. At the same time Wright was sketching his vision of Broadacres, Le Corbusier was planning his "Radiant City" (CG, 40). The Radiant City "is informed by, and parodies, the Christian heteropolis itself—the city made and built by God Himself towards which we, like Abraham, move" (CG, 40–41). But Le Corbusier's ideal differs in its realized eschatology and its immanentization of the conditions for this city's advent. His work "announces that perfection is possible in this world through human efforts alone. Buildings and cities can be designed and built which will satisfy our deepest religious desires" (CG, 41). This will be a city without a church, not because the Lamb is there (Rev. 21:22–23) but because humanity has been enthroned and has replaced God (CG, 41, 43). There is no temple or church because there is no transcendence to worship. The realized eschatology, coupled with a univocal ontology, shuts down any reference to transcendence and leaves the city to its own devices—and Le Corbusier is characteristically confident in these devices, for the powers of human design and planning are able to occasion the advent of this parodied eschaton. "Resurrection life is to be lived now. Again the end times, the total presence of the eschaton, is realized or realizable now. Today is salvation—through the city; a city which has no need of a Temple because it is the Temple" (CG, 42).

Central to the project of secular modernity, then, is this movement of immanentization whereby the *telos* of transcendent desire is flattened to be encased by an autonomous nature.[31] "The Christian heteropolis,

---

31. This theme of immanentization is carefully analyzed by Pickstock in AW, chap. 2.

its cosmology and metaxis, becomes, with Le Corbusier, the kingdom of this world. The city comes of age—men and women have resurrection life and have it now in 'the radiant city,' the metropolis. . . . This city has no need of God (or religion), for its values (aesthetic, moral, and spiritual) all lie at hand. The cities of aspiration can embody transcendence in the sublime heights of their towers" (CG, 42)—though these heights remain within the plane of immanence. This is why, while the secular city may be organized around modes of ritual, it is not and cannot be properly liturgical or doxological insofar as these require transcendence—precisely what is excluded by secular modernity's univocity or naturalism (AW, 48–49). Therefore, the rituals of Le Corbusier's Radiant City can give us only the nihilistic lineaments of a virtual community: "Cities like Le Corbusier's radiant city are transcendent, sublime and atheistic cities—cities where light, space, freedom and harmony can penetrate into the very heart of buildings and bodies. They are virtual cities, cities of the imagination, cities of light. They express a secular dream that will reach its apotheosis in cyberspace and its electronic communities" (CG, 42).

But Wright's and Le Corbusier's modern cities of eternal aspiration are no longer the primary mode of parody—though their effects (and structures) continue to surround us. Indeed, the 1972 dynamiting of the Pruitt-Igoe Housing Development in St. Louis—which exemplified Le Corbusier's "dream for social engineering by architectural design" (CG, 55)—signaled a crisis for these utopian visions. But the vacuum created by their demise was not filled with a robustly Christian vision of the city. Rather, the forces of secularity in postmodernity instead constructed "cities of endless desire" in which we see "the libidinal dynamics of contemporary urban life, primed with fantasy, hyped with ecstasy, dazzling in the allure of promised, sybaritic pleasures" (CG, 53). Here the vision is less hopeful and aspiring and the *telos* markedly different: "The market turns us all into consumers who produce only to afford to be more powerful consumers. Cities become variants on the theme-park, reorganized as sites for consumption, sites for the satisfaction of endless desire. The *libido dominandi* is implicitly both economic and sexual" (CG, 56). But even here the postmodern secular city remains a parody of the ecclesial community, for it draws on the capital of the fact that creatures are created as desiring animals who crave the Creator (cf. Augustine, *Conf.* 1.1.1: "You have made us for yourself, and our hearts are restless until they rest in you"). Therefore, the ecstatic orientation of desire, or *eros*, is subverted and perverted, reduced and redirected to merely immanent and largely sexual (or econo-sexual) ends.[32] As a

---

32. One of the core pieces of Ward's constructive argument is to recover the centrality of *desire* and *eros* for Christian theological reflection by first unhooking it from its reduc-

result, the logic of parody in postmodern cities of endless desire is again manifested in a dis/replacement strategy whereby immanent sites are invested with the task of fulfilling transcendent desires. The city is not just about buses or rent control but the configuration of a secular space that is invested with salvific significance or, better, the endless deferral of salvation in favor of immanence.

The burden of this analysis of modernity's penchant for parody is to indicate the complex relationship between Christianity and secular modernity. If secular modernity and its institutions are ultimately religious or theological visions—but heretical parodies of orthodox Christian faith—then the stance of the church must be one of critical distance. Rather than being apologists for the liberal, secular state, Christians should be naming its idolatry *as* idolatry. Rather than celebrating the "end of history" with the globalization of democratic capitalism, the church should be lamenting the globalization of false theology imbedded in the free market.

More Modernity: On the So-Called Postmodern Turn

There is a common tendency in contemporary Christian reflection to ask what must change for Christian theorizing and witness given the advent of postmodernity. How has postmodernity changed our cultural landscape? How are we to grapple with the epistemological shifts of the past several decades? What does the demise of modernity mean for Christian theological reflection and proclamation?

For RO, this is a somewhat misleading way to formulate the contemporary task of confessional scholars. As already noted in chapter 3, RO sees continuities where others see ruptures. This is particularly true in its account of postmodernity as the completion of modernity and hence a kind of hyper-modernity.[33] As Ward's account of modern and postmodern cities suggests, despite their difference, there is a deep continuity between the ontology and the anthropology that they assume, all within the broader framework of an autonomous secularity. While it may be that the foundationalist paradigms of modernity have largely collapsed (except in La Mirada), the dogma concerning the autonomy

---

tion to *sexual* desire and then reconceiving the ecclesial community as a community of desire (CG, 121–81). This anthropology of desire is also central to Bell and Hanby and is unpacked in more detail in chapter 7.

33. In this respect, RO's evaluation of postmodernity has some intriguing parallels to Jürgen Habermas's critique of Derrida and Foucault in *The Philosophical Discourse of Modernity* (Cambridge, Mass.: MIT, 1987).

of theoretical thought has not really been dislodged in postmodernity. In other words, the issue is not modernity or postmodernity per se but rather the politics of secularity rooted in an ontology of immanence, which is common to both. If, as Ward does, we begin with a consideration of "the brokenness of bodies in postmodernity," we will see that their brokenness "is a continuity of the logic (and, ironically, humanism) of modernity. Postmodernity does not transcend but deepens, and brings to a certain terminus, the hidden agendas of modernity" (CG, 81). In particular, though postmodernity has called into question the modern ideal of epistemological autonomy (though even here it is not persistent), it has done little to dislodge the idol of freedom generated by the modern ideal of political autonomy. In other words, even more leftist postmodern accounts that critique capitalism still retain the ontology and the anthropology of modernity and therefore cannot offer a genuinely radical alternative. Instead, under the banner of radicalism and postmodernism (and even communitarianism), they offer simply more radical affirmations of autonomy. If, as Peter Leithart suggests, "all moderns are liberals,"[34] I would also suggest that all postmoderns are liberals.

Because of this discernment of a deep continuity between modernity and postmodernity, RO is more ambivalent about contemporary theory. On the one hand, RO does not find in postmodernism anything drastically new or particularly disconcerting that supposedly changes everything or poses a new threat to confessional practice.[35] On the other hand, it also does not find anything particularly new in supposedly postmodern theology or postmodern philosophy of religion (Derrida, Caputo) that is not already found in modernity and thus plagued by the same problems. As Milbank frames it, "It will be contended that the perspective of 'malign' postmodernism is the final, most perfect form of secular reason, in some ways reverting to and developing the neo-paganism of Machiavelli. Christianity reveals that nihilism sustains its ontology as

---

34. Leithart, *Against Christianity*, 35.

35. In an analogous way, RO would not conclude that "everything changed" on September 11, 2001. As Stanley Hauerwas remarks, "The world was not changed on September 11, 2001. The world was changed during the celebration of Passover in A.D. 33" (Stanley Hauerwas, "September 11, 2001: A Pacifist Response," in *Dissent from the Homeland*, 188). Milbank also notes the certain banality (Arendt) of September 11 in this respect: "Concerning the immediate aftermath of the events of September 11, the initial question one should ask is exactly why there was outrage on such a gigantic scale? After all, however unusual and shocking this event may have been, people are killed in large numbers all the time, by terror, politics, and economic oppression. Within a matter of days after the attack on the World Trade Center, the United States already may have killed more people in response to the attacks than died in them" (Milbank, "Sovereignty, Empire, Capital, and Terror," 63).

another *mythos*. The only possible social critique 'beyond' nihilism will therefore have to be theological" (TST, 262–63).

Nevertheless, RO does see the contemporary, postfoundationalist context as a catalyst for the recovery of an unapologetically confessional theory and practice. Thus, Milbank suggests that there is an "inevitable, if wary, affinity, which must exist between Christianity and postmodernism" (BR, 196). This affinity is neither an identification of the two nor an accommodation of one to the other but rather the discernment of an opportunity afforded by the contemporary situation. Postmodernity's critique of modern epistemologies may represent a chink in modernity's armor that provides both an opportunity to launch an internal critique of modernity and an occasion for the church to be alerted to its complicity with modernity.

As Milbank argues, RO is after "an alternative version of modernity."[36] Thus, its genealogical critique of modernity has as its *telos* an alternative model for social life. "Given that attempts to improve society in a secular way via the state and market have so visibly failed," Catherine Pickstock suggests, "then perhaps this revised genealogy which stresses the legacy of a distorted religious theory and practice could also point us indirectly towards a more serious alternative future polity than the liberal and postmodern critiques."[37] RO's strategy is regressive. If we accept the axiom suggested in chapter 3—that the politics of secular modernity rests on an epistemology, which in turn presupposes a distinct ontology—then RO's critique of the parodic politics of secular modernity takes us to its critique of modernity's epistemology. It is to this layer of the project that we turn in chapter 5.

36. Milbank, "Programme of Radical Orthodoxy," 45.

37. Catherine Pickstock, "Modernity and Scholasticism: A Critique of Recent Invocations of Univocity," *Antonianum* 78 (2003): 4.

5

Possibilities for the Post-secular

Faith, Reason, and Public Engagement

Related Reading

Milbank, John. "Knowledge: The Theological Critique of Philosophy in Hamann and Jacobi." In *Radical Orthodoxy: A New Theology,* edited by John Milbank, Catherine Pickstock, and Graham Ward, 21–37. London: Routledge, 1999.

———. "Only Theology Overcomes Metaphysics." Chap. 2 in *The Word Made Strange: Theology, Language, Culture.* Oxford: Blackwell, 1997.

———. "The Other City: Theology as a Social Science." Chap. 12 in *Theology and Social Theory: Beyond Secular Reason.* Oxford: Blackwell, 1990.

Ward, Graham. "The Step Back: The Politics of Believing." A section of chap. 2 in *Cities of God.* London: Routledge, 2000.

Central to RO's project of cultural critique is the axiom laid down in chapter 3: Behind the politics of modernity (liberal, secular) is an epistemology (autonomous reason), which is in turn undergirded by an ontology (univocity and the denial of participation). The same is true of the alternative that RO envisions: Behind the politics (socialism) lies an epistemology (illumination), which is in turn undergirded by an ontology (participation). The invention of the secular and its political project of liberal autonomy, as shown in chapter 4, was attended by the invention of an autonomous reason. Thus, this chapter examines these competing epistemologies. Chapter 6 explores the competing ontologies.

In this opening section, the goal is to demonstrate the parallels between RO's critique of secular reason and the critique of autonomy in the Reformed tradition. Both are crucial for nourishing a genuinely post-secular Christian practice.

The Pretended Autonomy of Secular Thought

Secular Theologies

In a series of lectures in 1959, Herman Dooyeweerd reiterated what he described as a critique of "the pretended autonomy of philosophical thought."[1] As Dooyeweerd observed, one of the last remaining certitudes in philosophy is "the traditional dogma concerning the autonomy of philosophical thought" as the only possible basis for a "truly critical attitude" (ITWT, 3). This dogma entails the notion that philosophical (or, more broadly, theoretical) thought operates on the basis of a "neutral" system of rationality—one that is autonomous with respect to controlling factors such as tradition, religious belief, or other "prejudices."[2] The problem, however, is that what constitutes the autonomy of thought is determined by extra-theoretical commitments or presuppositions—as evidenced by the different notions found in ancient, medieval, and modern versions of the dogma (ITWT, 4). Thus, there are some interior cracks in the edifice of philosophical autonomy. The edifice might be a façade, a pretended autonomy. While drawing on the capital of those who began to call this dogma into question (Pascal, Dilthey, Heidegger, and others), Dooyeweerd offered a critique that he described as transcendental.[3] Instead of piling up de facto evidence of persistent bias, he analyzed the inner structure and necessary conditions of the theoretical attitude. In this way, Dooyeweerd saw his critique of (secular) reason

1. Herman Dooyeweerd, *In the Twilight of Western Thought: Studies in the Pretended Autonomy of Philosophical Thought*, Collected Works B/4, ed. James K. A. Smith (Lewiston, N.Y.: Mellen, 1999). For background on the context of these lectures, see editor's introduction, "Dooyeweerd's Critique of 'Pure' Reason," v–xiii.

2. See Roy Clouser, *The Myth of Religious Neutrality* (Notre Dame: University of Notre Dame Press, 1991). For a suggestion of a certain (qualified) Pascalian link, see Roy Clouser, *Knowing with the Heart* (Downers Grove, Ill.: InterVarsity, 1999). I discuss the Pascalian precedent in James K. A. Smith, *Speech and Theology: The Language and Logic of Incarnation* (London: Routledge, 2002), 80.

3. A "transcendental" critique stands opposed to a merely "transcendent" critique: "A transcendent critique," Dooyeweerd remarks, "has nothing to do with the inner structure of the theoretical attitude of philosophical thinking and its necessary conditions. Much rather, it criticizes the results of a philosophical reflection from a viewpoint which lies beyond the philosophical point of view" (ITWT, 6). Thus, a transcendent critique is merely "dogmatic." On that score, it may seem that RO tends to engage in *transcendent* critique; however, Dooyeweerd's account does not rule out the kind of opposition mentioned here. But such "dogmatic" critiques are effective only *after* the transcendental critique, which undermines the autonomy of philosophical thought. Once it is clear that every theoretical account begins from fundamental presuppositions, then we—as Milbank does, for instance—can point out the fundamental difference between the Greek and the Christian conceptions of virtue. I return to these matters below.

as more radical than the earlier projects of Immanuel Kant or Husserl, both of whom "started from the autonomy of theoretical thinking as an axiom which needs no further justification" (ITWT, 6).

A generation after Dooyeweerd's critique of the "pretended autonomy of philosophical thought," Radical Orthodoxy has generated a similar, though independent,[4] critique of this modern dogma. If we take John Milbank's *Theology and Social Theory* as an index, RO's critique of reason stems directly from its critique of the secular. This is because the very notion of a secular public sphere is predicated upon the notion of a universal, autonomous reason—even if only construed as a thin rationality. Thus, what Milbank seeks to unveil vis-à-vis modern social theory (to choose just one example) is that supposedly neutral, rational conclusions in fact stem from prerational commitments (as shown in chapter 4, those commitments are either classically pagan or heretical modifications of orthodox Christian accounts).[5] Supposedly "'scientific' social theories are themselves theologies or anti-theologies in disguise" (TST, 3).[6] Therefore, Milbank's archaeology of secular reason calls into question "the questionable idea of an autonomous secular realm, completely transparent to secular understanding" (TST, 1); it does so by tracing "the genesis of the main forms of secular reason, in such a fashion as to unearth the arbitrary moments in the construction of their logic" (TST, 3).[7] For example, what Thomas Hobbes concluded is disclosed by mere reason—a fundamental war of all with all—is unveiled as a particular interpretive decision or commitment, not the self-evident truth of a universal logic.[8] And as such, this logic can be contested; indeed, such contestation is the core of TST's project, with the goal of opening the space for a distinctly Christian (or "theological") sociology—"theology as itself a social science" (TST, 380).

4. Even this independence is qualified insofar as both Dooyeweerd and RO are drawing on Augustinian wells.

5. There is an important sense in which Christian Smith's *Moral, Believing Animals* (Oxford: Oxford University Press, 2003) undertakes a similar project. Smith is concerned to demonstrate that the empiricism of contemporary social science—which is supposed to generate a "neutral" account of being-in-the-world—is always already *theory-laden*, such that any description of "human animals" is already working from nonempirical presuppositions. See also Bruce C. Wearne, "Deism and the Absence of Christian Sociology," *Philosophia Reformata* 68 (2003): 14–35.

6. Dooyeweerd makes basically the same point in *A Christian Theory of Social Institutions*, trans. Magnus Verbrugge, ed. John Witte Jr. (La Jolla, Calif.: Herman Dooyeweerd Foundation, 1986), 45–58. My thanks to Elaine Botha for pointing me to this text.

7. Milbank's archaeology, then, tends toward a de facto analysis of the commitments of secular reason (to use Dooyeweerd's language above, ITWT, 4–6).

8. As such, Milbank's critique of secular reason mirrors Lyotard's critique of metanarratives. For a discussion, see James K. A. Smith, "Little Story about Metanarratives: Lyotard, Religion, and Postmodernism Revisited," *Faith and Philosophy* 18 (2001): 261–76.

Milbank is happy to describe this as a theological realism but goes on to say that "it does not seem to me that it at all supports or requires philosophical realism" (TST, 426). What is the difference between these two realisms? For Milbank, theological realism is a kind of confessional realism. Philosophical realism is problematic in terms of both epistemology and ontology. Epistemologically, it tends to assume a sort of neutral access to the way things are, which is then capable of universal rational demonstration. Ontologically, it assumes that there *are* things, substances to be known. But here RO's ontology is most radical. As Milbank puts it, "There are no substances in creation, no underlying matter, and no discrete and inviolable 'things'" (TST, 424).[9] Because everything "participates" in God's being—and therefore does not have an autonomous existence but *is* only by gift—all can be properly known only "in God" (TA, 23).[10]

The critique, then, has a dual aim: On the one hand, Milbank seeks to unveil the deeply religious or even theological commitments that undergird supposedly secular social science (and other modes of knowledge); on the other hand, having unveiled that and thus leveled the playing field (showing that all claims to knowledge are, at root, confessional), Milbank seeks to reinvigorate distinctly Christian accounts of sociality (and other spheres of being-in-the-world).[11] Since "no . . . fundamental account, in the sense of something neutral, rational and universal, is really available," Christian theology[12] itself "will have to provide its own account of the final causes at work in human history, on the basis of its own particular, and historically specific faith" (TST, 380). As a result, RO's project echoes earlier Reformed critiques of autonomous reason—in the continental tradition of Dooyeweerd and in the Anglo-American tradition of Alvin Plantinga and Nicholas Wolterstorff[13]—which funded similar

9. We return to this theme in more detail in chapter 6; the logic of this claim is unpacked most forcefully by Ward's notion of "transcorporeality" in CG.

10. Again, the ontology of participation informs the epistemology here.

11. Cf. RONT, 1. This is why Ward emphasizes that the audience of RONT is not other theologians but rather the broader marketplace of ideas (Graham Ward, "In the Economy of the Divine: A Response to James K. A. Smith," *PNEUMA: Journal of the Society for Pentecostal Studies* 25 [2003]: 116–17). RO has a distinctly world-oriented, almost "missional" sense in which it envisions the academic enterprise.

12. In a section below, we consider in more detail just what Milbank means by "theology" in this context.

13. See Alvin Plantinga, "Advice to Christian Philosophers," *Faith and Philosophy* 1 (1984): 253–71; idem, "The Reformed Objection to Natural Theology," *Proceedings of the American Catholic Philosophical Association* (1980): 49–62; idem, *Warranted Christian Belief* (Oxford: Oxford University Press, 2000); Nicholas Wolterstorff, "Can Belief in God Be Rational If It Has No Foundations?" in Alvin Plantinga and Nicholas Wolterstorff, *Faith and Rationality* (Notre Dame: University of Notre Dame Press, 1983); idem, *Reason*

calls for distinctly Christian accounts of being-in-the-world, entailing a distinctly Christian sociology, psychology, political theory, philosophy, and so on. Therefore, if in chapter 1 we emphasized that RO and the Reformed tradition share a sense of antithesis,[14] here we can note another significant consensus: Both RO and the Reformed tradition are suspicious of epistemologies that assume neutral or objective criteria for determining what counts as rational or true. All pretended autonomous accounts of human nature or social life are funded not only by biases or prejudices but also by religious, even quasi-theological, commitments.[15] What parades itself as a scientific or objective (i.e., neutral) account of economic realities, for instance, is in fact undergirded by a theology—a set of ultimate presuppositions about the shape of the world.[16] Therefore, if every economics, for instance, is always already theological—and if postmodernity means, to some degree, the recognition of this fact[17]—then there should be no disqualification of a distinctly Christian economic theory from the arena of public discourse (in both the academy and the political square).[18] This is precisely why an authentic or persistent postmodernity would also be post-secular (and pluralist). The persistence of secularity's hegemony indicates that, notwithstanding reports to the contrary, modernity is still with us.

---

within the Bounds of Religion (Grand Rapids: Eerdmans, 1976); and idem, *John Locke and the Ethics of Belief* (Cambridge: Cambridge University Press, 1998). For an introduction to Reformed epistemology, see Kelly James Clark, *Return to Reason* (Grand Rapids: Eerdmans, 1990).

14. There I drew on Wolterstorff's analyses in "What New Haven and Grand Rapids Have to Say to Each Other," in *Seeking Understanding: The Stob Lectures, 1986–1998* (Grand Rapids: Eerdmans, 2001).

15. What I am pointing to here has been variously described as "ground-motives" (Dooyeweerd), "worldviews" (Abraham Kuyper, Albert Wolters), and "control beliefs" (Wolterstorff). What qualifies these beliefs as religious is their ultimacy. One could find parallel accounts of such ultimate beliefs in Thomas Kuhn's analysis of the role of "paradigms," which govern both observation and theory formation, as well as Wittgenstein's account. For a discussion, see James K. A. Smith and Shane R. Cudney, "The Growth of Fundamentalism: Was the Grand Inquisitor Right?" *Studies in Religion/Sciences Religieuses* 25 (1996): 35–49.

16. Milbank seems to suggest that these fundamental issues come to the fore when we get to matters of ontology: "Christianity starts to appear—even 'objectively'—as not just different, but as *the* difference from all other cultural systems, which it exposes as threatened by incipient nihilism. However, it is only at the ontological level, where theology articulates (always provisionally) the framework of reference implicit in Christian story and action, that this 'total' difference is fully clarified, along with its ineradicable ties to non-provable belief" (TST, 381).

17. The point of Lyotard's critique is to demonstrate the way in which (modern) science is always informed by myth.

18. For a suggestion along these lines, see D. Stephen Long, *Divine Economy: Theology and the Market*, Radical Orthodoxy (New York: Routledge, 2000).

Scholasticism in Theology

RO's critique of the notion of a secular or neutral science or rational-ity is a two-edged sword: Not only does it undercut the pretensions of secular theory, but it also undercuts much of the project of twentieth-century theology and Christian cultural engagement—particularly in its correlationist modes emerging from Tübingen. This is because theology and the church have been insufficiently radical in these engagements—they have not penetrated to the roots on matters of either theoretical frameworks or perspectival commitments. According to Milbank, this is because Christian theology and practice have accepted the dogma of the autonomy of theoretical thought—and the autonomy of philosophy in particular. "Modern theology on the whole," Milbank observes, "accepts that philosophy has its own legitimacy, its own autonomy apart from faith" (RONT, 21). Thus, the majority of modern Christian theological and ecclesial projects operate as colonies of the Tübingen empire (chap. 1): They assume the neutrality of other sciences (whether philosophy, sociology, economics, or, increasingly, the natural sciences),[19] receive the objective findings of such neutral sciences, and then seek to correlate the claims of Christian confession with these facts—thus furnishing, indi-rectly, an apologetic demonstration of the truth of Christian revelation. In particular, the broad shape of what it means to know, or questions of being, are determined by the neutral discourse of philosophy and metaphysics; Christian theology then builds on these neutral or natural axioms and offers a theological supplement of what it means to know Christ, or what it means to say that God "is." Milbank points to several diverse examples of such a correlationist strategy:

1. Liberation theology (and political theology in general)[20] is char-acterized by an uncritical appropriation of Marxist social science

19. While to date RO has tended to focus its critique on the theological appropriations of social science, one could see the need for a radically orthodox critique of much that currently goes on under the banner of the "science and theology" dialogue, in which it is generally assumed that the findings of the "hard" sciences are neutral dispensations of "the way things are" (John Polkinghorne, Nancey Murphy). In all these cases—across the sciences—much that is offered by supposedly "descriptive" sciences involves a great deal of *evaluation* in the very description, and such evaluation always already operates on the basis of worldview-relative criteria. (A conference on Radical Orthodoxy and science was staged in 2001; the proceedings remain forthcoming.)

20. Moltmann, Metz, Peukert, or, conversely, Novak and his ilk. Whether accepting the findings of Marxism or capitalist economics, both of these projects concede that secular social science is the "authority" on these "secular" matters. For extended analysis of the deep continuities between the "dominant" and the "liberation" models—both anchored by an *analogia liberates*—see Long, *Divine Economy*.

as the "expert" on the natural sphere of politics, as if "basic Marxist conclusions are inviolable, simply in terms of a proper respect
for the autonomy of secular social science" (TST, 207).[21]

2. Jean-Luc Marion, despite what sounds like a *nouvelle théologie*-
   like project that privileges revelation, "effects the most massive
   correlation of this theology with contemporary philosophy" (WMS,
   36). Though he rejects any correlation of philosophy and theology
   in terms of "being," he simply substitutes a different mode of
   phenomenological correlation in terms of donation or gift (WMS,
   37). This is because Marion continues to maintain the notion of
   an "independent phenomenology" (WMS, 49).[22]

3. Neo-orthodoxy, and Karl Barth in particular, confirms the autonomy of philosophy by (supposedly) rejecting it.[23] In protesting
   the correlational strategies of liberal theology, neo-orthodoxy attempts to "articulate this knowledge in terms of categories that are
   proper to theology itself" (RONT, 21). While this entails privileging
   the revelation of God in Christ "over the seemingly more general
   and abstract acknowledgement of God as creator," what remains
   unclear "is the degree to which these theological categories are
   permitted to disturb a philosophical account of what it is to be, to
   know and to act, without reference to God" (RONT, 21). Milbank
   discerns here a liberal residue: "For if philosophy determines what
   it is to be and to know, then will it not pre-determine how we know
   even Christ to be, unless we allow that the structure of this event

21. A similar critique is unfolded in Daniel M. Bell Jr., *Liberation Theology after the End
of History: The Refusal to Cease Suffering,* Radical Orthodoxy (London: Routledge, 2001).
We return to these matters in chapter 7.

22. One can see this project most clearly in Jean-Luc Marion, *Reduction and Givenness,*
trans. Thomas A. Carlson (Evanston: Northwestern University Press, 1999); and most succinctly in idem, "Metaphysics and Phenomenology: A Relief for Theology," *Critical Inquiry*
20 (1994): 572–92. I have elsewhere argued that Marion does retain the notion—inherited
from natural theology—that phenomenology is an autonomous philosophy. See James
K. A. Smith, "Liberating Religion from Theology: Marion and Heidegger on the Possibility
of a Phenomenology of Religion," *International Journal for Philosophy of Religion* 46 (1999):
17–33. Milbank, however, goes on to suggest that "the enterprise of phenomenology itself
is hitherto 'Scotist' in that, independently of any spiritual discipline, it aspires to 'see' the
essences of things" (WMS, 47–48). I contest this claim by offering an Augustinian or *Christian* phenomenology in *Speech and Theology.* Ward is also comfortable articulating what
he describes as a "theological phenomenology" (Graham Ward, "The Beauty of God," in
Theological Perspectives on God and Beauty, ed. John Milbank, Graham Ward, and Edith
Wyschogrod [Harrisburg, Pa.: Trinity Press International, 2003], 47–48).

23. I think one could suggest a parallel in Open theism, which is wont to describe itself
as inherently biblical and rejecting the (Greek) categories of metaphysics (Open theism
sees classical theism as a kind of correlationist theology)—as if one could ever be without
a metaphysics, and as if one could not formulate a *biblical* metaphysics.

re-organizes also our ordinary sense of what is and what we can know, in such a way that the autonomy of philosophy is violated" (RONT, 21–22).

What all of these forms of correlationist theology retain is a dualism between reason and revelation: Reason, the domain of the sciences, is conceded as an autonomous sphere that revelation either supplements (liberation theology) or overwhelms (Marion, Barth). In either case, the autonomy of theoretical thought goes unchallenged. Milbank's concluding critique of Barth is sharp: "While the Barthian claim is that post-Kantian philosophy liberates theology to be theological, the inner truth of his theology is that by allowing the legitimacy to a methodologically atheist philosophy, he finishes by construing God on the model, ironically, of a man without God" (RONT, 22).[24] In this respect, Dooyeweerd had already anticipated Milbank's critique: "The Barthian view of theology as the exclusive Christian science with its negative relation to philosophy, is still entirely penetrated by this dualism. . . . The reason is that Barth, though sharply opposed to the synthetical Thomistic view of nature and grace, did not abandon this dualistic theme itself; a scheme which in the Augustinian [tradition] was unknown" (ITWT, 98). By retaining the wall of dualism between reason and revelation, theology in its Barthian mode cannot call into question the assumptions of the "secular" sciences, and theology itself remains demarcated by the shape of secular science (RONT, 33).

One of the resounding aspects of Milbank's critique, then, is that Christian theological discourse (and ecclesial practice) has uncritically appropriated theoretical frameworks and philosophical categories that, in fact, are funded by commitments that are deeply antithetical to Christian confession and revelation. In other words, twentieth-century theology—even in its neo-orthodox form—was colonized by the "liberal" correlationist paradigm. This brings Milbank to a provocative question: "Has there really been in this century, at least within Protestantism, *any* post-liberal theology?" (RONT, 22). To appreciate the sting of this question, we must recall that the so-called postliberal Yale school is pre-

---

24. Milbank includes a long footnote (RONT, 32–34) concerning whether Barth is radically orthodox. We should trace this concern to one of the most influential teachers of Barth in the UK, Donald McKinnon. In the end, Milbank thinks that Barth offers us a "secular" theology (33). Theology never calls into question the other disciplines. However, this note still indicates the ambiguity of just what Milbank means by "theology." It seems that he needs some distinction between (pre-theoretical) confession and (theoretical) theology—or what I describe below as theology[1] and theology[2]. For critical discussion of Milbank's critique of Barth, see Joseph L. Mangina, "Mediating Theologies: Karl Barth between Radical and Neo-orthodoxy," *Scottish Journal of Theology* 56 (2003): 427–43.

dominantly Barthian.[25] He goes on to ask, "Would not such a theology have to challenge, at least in some sense, the autonomy of philosophy, and articulate a *theological* account of what it is to be and to know in general?" (RONT, 22). Milbank finds just such an undertaking in "radical pietists" such as Hamann, Jacobi, Wizenmann, and Herder (and later, a reassertion of radical pietism in Kierkegaard).[26] They are more radical Lutherans than Luther himself, for they propose a theory of knowledge by faith alone that Luther never entertained, insofar as "he broadly accepted the framework of late medieval nominalist philosophy" (RONT, 23).[27] Scotus and Co. launched modernity by creating the space for an autonomous ontology—"and the Reformation did nothing to disturb this situation" (RONT, 24).[28] Jacobi and Hamann, however, did disturb this "post-Scotist legacy" in two ways: First, "they insisted that no finite thing can be known, *not even to any degree*, outside of its ratio to the infinite"; and second, they asserted that "if the truth of nature lies in its suprarational ordination, then reason is true only to the degree that it seeks or prophesies the theoretical *and* practical acknowledgement of this ordination which, thanks to the fall, is made possible again only through divine incarnation" (RONT, 24).

Milbank emphasizes that Jacobi and Hamann do not struggle with a reason/revelation duality: "True reason anticipates revelation" (RONT, 24). But at this point, a couple of questions arise (assuming that this is not just a restatement of manual Thomism): (1) While there may not be a dualism, there is a duality—and it seems fair to ask which of these (reason or revelation) is accorded primacy? In other words, just how do Jacobi and Hamann know these things about the knowledge of

25. At this juncture, Nicholas Wolterstorff's Stob Lectures are a crucial document both for assessing points of convergence between Radical Orthodoxy and the Kuyperian tradition and for—if we were to find Cambridge and Grand Rapids/Amsterdam agreed on this point—questions regarding Wolterstorff's allegiances to Amsterdam/Grand Rapids.

26. The fact that Milbank finds resources in the Pietist tradition is itself an indicator of contemporary dialogues that should be staged (e.g., with the Pentecostal tradition).

27. Again, Dooyeweerd already anticipates this critique: "This dualistic view betrays the after-effects of the Occamistic [*sic*] Nominalism which has especially influenced the Lutheran view concerning the impossibility of a Christian philosophy" (ITWT, 98).

28. This common RO evaluation of the Reformation (cf. CG, 160–67; TR) seems to have undergone some revision. Milbank, for instance, later remarks that "this stance toward Barth leaves open the question of our attitude toward the first reformers, especially Luther, since sometimes they can be read as at least half-recuperating forgotten aspects of Patristic and high Mediaeval thought" (John Milbank, "The Programme of Radical Orthodoxy," in *Radical Orthodoxy? A Catholic Enquiry*, ed. Laurence Paul Hemming [Burlington, Vt.: Ashgate, 2000], 35). More recently, Milbank has offered an affirmative account of Calvin and his French heirs. See John Milbank, "Alternative Protestantisms," in *Creation, Covenant, and Participation: Radical Orthodoxy and the Reformed Tradition*, ed. James K. A. Smith and James H. Olthuis (Grand Rapids: Baker Academic, forthcoming).

the created order? Is it not on the basis of revelation? In other words, is not this very understanding of reason rooted in the acceptance of a revelation, and does not that acceptance happen by means of faith? (2) What are we to make of this qualifier—true reason? Does it mean that reason can take a false, perhaps apostate, direction (I am alluding to Dooyeweerd here)?[29] We return to such questions below.

In any event, Milbank sees these pietists as more radical than Barth or Luther: "Their apparent merging of reason and faith, and apparent fusion of nature and grace, are not suspicious traces of enlightenment, but rather signs that they were the real conservative revolutionaries" (RONT, 24). But theirs is not a mere recovery: "Their very Lutheran insistence on the priority of faith and language points to a position that allows even less autonomy to universal reason than that permitted by the Church Fathers" (25).[30] And here we discern the link between epistemology and ontology: One of the cores of this radical pietism might also be described as a Christian materialism—the assertion that Enlightenment rationalism (whose founding principle is that "pure reason can accept as real only the identically repeated according to logically necessitated laws") is ultimately a nihilism that cannot account for the reality of the world (RONT, 26–27). Thus, "the central Hamannian insight" is that "worship of God and celebration of corporeality and sensual beauty absolutely require each other" (26). Corporeal things have depth only if they are read as "signs disclosing or promising such a depth"; "if we take things as *only* finite, their solidity paradoxically vanishes" (RONT, 27). So only an affirmation of transcendence can really value the immanent or the finite (cf. RONT, 3–4 on suspending the material).[31]

29. However, even if we were to activate a certain Dooyeweerdian corrective here, the dialogue goes the other way also. Phillip Blond's assertion regarding Christ, the incarnation (and cross) (cited in RONT, 24) are important correctives to the overwhelming emphasis on creation in the Kuyperian tradition. Indeed, I have sometimes heard the doctrine of creation invoked as a kind of natural theology, as though the crucifixion never happened.

30. Milbank goes on to note the overlap (and indebtedness) of the radical pietists with Thomas Reid (RONT, 26–27). Insofar as Reid is an important influence on Reformed epistemology, we should not be surprised to discern overlap between RO and the Reformed tradition. See Nicholas Wolterstorff, *Thomas Reid and the Story of Epistemology* (Cambridge: Cambridge University Press, 2001); and Kelly James Clark, "Reid and Rationality," in *Return to Reason* (Grand Rapids: Eerdmans, 1990), 143–50.

31. In Frederick Christian Bauerschmidt's essay, this theme is considered in terms of "sacrament" as both the reality and the sign (RONT, 214). Along these lines one could discern a deep similarity between RO and Jonathan Edwards. See Jerry Stutzman's paper "Jonathan Edwards' Theological Materialism" (unpublished). For Edwards, the material world is valued for the ways in which it "shadows" or refers to God and the spiritual world. Creation was intended to be a divine communication to intelligent beings, and so it is valued in fulfilling its end, in pointing beyond itself to its Creator. "We see that even

Milbank contrasts the strategy of Jacobi and Hamann with that of Barth and Marion insofar as the former reject the dogma concerning the autonomy of theoretical thought and offer a "theological critique of philosophy." Rather than allowing supposedly secular sciences to establish the methodological rules for confessional reflection, and rather than allowing a secular, autonomous philosophy to determine what it means to know or to be, RO seeks to theorize the nature of knowledge and being "out of the resources of revelation *alone*" (WMS, 36)—allowing the Christ event to restructure just what it means to know or to be.[32] Correlationist theologies are not sufficiently radical in this respect insofar as they accept the results of secular science as the foundation to a supplemental theological reflection. Here, the Reformational tradition offers a simple shorthand to name the problem with this approach: scholasticism.

For Dooyeweerd, theology (in the sense of "a science of the dogmata of the Christian faith") presupposes an account of philosophical questions such as the nature of being (ontology) and knowledge (epistemology). The question, therefore, is not *whether* theology presupposes a philosophy but rather *what* philosophy it will work from: Will Christian theology "seek its philosophical foundations in a Christian philosophy, ruled and reformed by the central biblical basic-motive," or will it "take them from the traditional scholastic or modern humanist philosophy?" (ITWT, 107). Scholasticism, for Dooyeweerd, signals a mode of theological reflection that, accepting the myth of philosophical autonomy, appropriates a philosophical framework that is, in fact, antithetical to authentic Christian confession. Assuming that philosophy was part of an autonomous nature, according to Dooyeweerd, medieval thought, for example, uncritically appropriated the supposedly neutral framework of Aristotelian thought. But at the root of Aristotelian philosophy, he would contend, is a "ground-motive" or a "basic motive"—a constellation of religious commitments (ITWT, 110–15)—which is at odds with Christian revelation (ITWT, 115).[33] The same would be true of contemporary theologies that uncritically appropriate the framework of Kant, Heidegger, or Derrida—as if it were a matter of finding a philosophy

---

in the material world God makes one part of it strangely to agree with another; and why is it not reasonable to suppose he makes the whole as a shadow of the spiritual world?" (Jonathan Edwards, "Shadows of Divine Things," in *Typological Writings*, vol. 11, *The Works of Jonathan Edwards*, ed. Wallace E. Anderson and Mason I. Lowance Jr. [New Haven: Yale University Press, 1993], §8).

32. The latter is most radically developed in Ward's analysis of materiality in light of Christ's resurrection and ascension (CG, 81–116).

33. Dooyeweerd's assertion of the antithesis between the Greek and the Christian is echoed in TST, chaps. 10–11.

and then building a theology on it.[34] In general, if theology accepts the dogma concerning the (pretended) autonomy of theoretical thought, it will inevitably end up bringing on board a philosophical framework with alien freight. "It is a vain illusion," Dooyeweerd remarks, "to imagine that the notions borrowed from such a [so-called autonomous] philosophy could be utilized by the theologian in a purely formal sense. They involve a material content which is indissolubly bound to the total theoretical view of experience and of reality" (ITWT, 105–6).[35] Contemporary theologies are scholastic insofar as they fail to recognize this; in this respect, RO's critique of Barth and Marion could be reformulated in terms of a critique of their scholasticism.

But perhaps there is a lingering scholasticism in RO. Granted, Milbank's agenda is more radical than that of neo-orthodoxy: Rather than conceding the autonomy of philosophy and permitting it to determine the shape of what it means to be and to know, he calls for a foundational disruption of philosophy's autonomy. Our very accounts of being and knowing should be reorganized by the Christ event (RONT, 21–22). If "once, there was no secular" (TST, 9), this is because once there was no philosophy (RONT, 21).[36] This is how Milbank intensifies his earlier critique first formulated in TST; he articulates it in this way because he equates the very idea of philosophy or metaphysics with autonomous reason. Then he is constrained to set this against "a *theological* account of what it is to be and to know in general" (RONT, 22). This will not be philosophy but rather theology (WMS, 50).

34. Dooyeweerd singles out "Protestant scholasticism" as another example of Christian theology that uncritically adopted a philosophical framework that was grounded in "an unbiblical starting point" (ITWT, 108). While this may be true of Philipp Melanchthon and Theodore Beza, Michael Horton has recently argued that later Protestant (so-called) scholastics such as Francis Turretin were decidedly postfoundationalist in their theological methodology—developing their ontology and epistemology on the basis of Christian revelation (Michael Horton, *Covenant and Eschatology: The Divine Drama* [Louisville: Westminster John Knox, 2002]).

35. Admittedly, Dooyeweerd sometimes seems to think there is a "biblical-founded philosophy" that even employs a unique language, untainted by apostate ground-motives. Thus, he sometimes levels the charge of "scholasticism" or "synthesis" simply on the basis of language and categories employed. But as I have demonstrated elsewhere, Dooyeweerd's own language is heavily indebted to Neo-Kantianism and Heidegger's phenomenology, but its fundamental religious orientation is different. Obviously, then, one can—must—adopt an operative framework of philosophical categories and language that, at the same time, subverts the religious ground-motive that spawned them. Indeed, the New Testament notion of *Logos* may do just that.

36. This resonates with antique notions of philosophy as basically *religious* orders (see Milbank's remarks concerning philosophy as a spiritual discipline, WMS, 47, 49). Cf. also Pierre Hadot, *Philosophy as a Way of Life,* trans. Michael Chase (Oxford: Blackwell, 1995).

But he seems to concede, ironically, the autonomy of philosophy by rejecting it, thus establishing a (false) dichotomy: philosophy *or* theology. Indeed, Milbank formulates it in just this way: "It is indeed for radical orthodoxy an either/or: *philosophy* (Western or Eastern) as a purely autonomous discipline, or *theology*: Herod or the magi, Pilate or the God-man" (RONT, 32, emphasis added). Philosophy, then, is first equated with autonomy and then rejected on that basis in favor of theology. But this would seem to confuse the formal structure of philosophical theorizing (regarding, say, foundational questions of being and knowing) with a particular direction the philosophical enterprise has taken (under the aegis of the dogma of theoretical autonomy). In this sense, Milbank's account of philosophy is reductionistic: "Philosophy as autonomous," he concludes, "as 'about' anything independently of its creaturely status *is* metaphysics or ontology in the most precisely technical sense. Philosophy in fact *began* as a secularizing immanentism" (WMS, 50). Theology, then, "if it wishes to think again God's love, and think creation as the manifestation of that love, . . . must entirely evacuate philosophy, which is metaphysics" (WMS, 50).

But does not such a conclusion and program confuse a contingent mode of philosophical orientation with the possibilities of an alternative mode of philosophical research? In other words, isn't Milbank confusing the particular direction (Western) philosophy has taken with the structure of philosophical investigation as such? Could we not entertain the possibility of "a *Christian* philosophy, ruled and reformed by the central biblical basic-motive" (ITWT, 107)—and as "ruled" obviously not autonomous?

Investigating these questions provides an occasion to revisit three key (interrelated) questions: the relationship between faith and reason (particularly in the case of Aquinas and natural theology), the relationship between philosophy and theology, and the consequent question of apologetics in postmodernity. In revisiting these questions, we amplify the project of reforming RO, bringing its claims into critical dialogue with the work of Herman Dooyeweerd.

Faith and Reason Revisited: The Aquinas Case

Questions about the relationship between faith and reason, or revelation and reason, are formulated quite intensely in the work of Thomas Aquinas—and especially RO's unique engagement with his thought. As already suggested in chapter 3, RO offers a new Aquinas—an Augustinian Aquinas distilled through the filter of the *nouvelle théologie*. Here we return to the specifically epistemological issues surrounding this appropriation of the Angelic Doctor. A brief sketch of a more standard or canonical picture of Aquinas's understanding of the faith/reason nexus provides a context for RO's new Aquinas.[37]

The Traditional Thomas

The *locus classicus* for these questions is the opening question of the *Summa Theologiae*. Reflecting on the nature and task of *sacra doctrina*, Aquinas argues that there are, in a sense, two theologies: first, a "theology which is part of philosophy" and is investigated by human reason, and second, "theology included in sacred doctrine" that operates "by way of revelation" (*Summa* Ia.I.1). In other words, there is a mode of knowledge about God that is accessible by human reason, but there is another mode of knowledge about God, inaccessible to human reason and "beyond man's knowledge," that is accessible only by revelation (i.e., Scripture). These two theologies—often referred to as natural theology and revealed theology respectively—differ in both their mode and their content, in both their how and their what: With respect to mode, natural theology knows by means of "the natural light of human reason," whereas revealed theology knows by means of divine revelation; with respect to content, revealed theology is given knowledge of God that exceeds what can be known of God by natural reason. For instance, elsewhere Aquinas argues that whereas human reason on its own can arrive at the knowledge that God exists, or God is simple, "it is an article of faith that God is three and one. Therefore reason is not adequate to perceive this."[38] The preambles of faith are accessible to natural human reason and function as a propaedeutic to the articles of faith, which human reason cannot discern.[39] Aquinas formulates this relationship between natural and revealed theology in terms of the relationship between nature and grace, particularly in terms of the Thomistic axiom that "grace does not destroy nature, but perfects it" (*Summa* Ia.I.8ad2). Philosophical

37. Milbank and Pickstock concede that theirs is not like "most usual interpretations" of Aquinas in which he is seen to be "espousing a sharp [albeit non-oppositional] distinction between reason and faith" (TA, 19). In this "dualistic reading of Aquinas," "this distinction is viewed as both benign and beneficial: on the one hand, it safeguards the mystery and integrity of faith; on the other hand, it allows a space for modern secular autonomy" (TA, 19).

38. Aquinas, *In Boeth. De Trinitate* q. 1, art. 4, translated by Armand Maurer as *Faith, Reason, and Theology* (Toronto: Pontifical Institute for Medieval Studies, 1987), 31.

39. Ibid., 3.1 (67). Cf. *Summa* Ia.2.2.ad1: "The existence of God and other like truths about God, which can be known by natural reason, are not articles of faith, but are preambles to the articles; for faith presupposes natural knowledge, even as grace presupposes nature."

knowledge by means of human reason operates on the basis of a nature that is common to all humanity;[40] thus, the truths about God that are accessible by human reason are universally accessible (Aquinas grants that such knowledge cannot be salvific). This underwrites the project of a natural theology or fundamental theology that purports to lay the groundwork for revealed theology by establishing those matters that can be known by natural, unaided human reason.[41] Moreover, it also supports a notion that metaphysics—a philosophical inquiry into the nature of being—is accessible by natural human reason and therefore does not require reference to theology or revelation. Neutral epistemic access to an autonomous metaphysics spawns a secular politics and natural morality that are both accessible and applicable to all. Thus, it was precisely this Thomistic paradigm that generated Jacques Maritain's vision of a New Christendom in which the temporal realm is granted an autonomy such that (only) nontheological discourse and analysis are proper to this domain and "the [liberal] state [is] left as the uncontested overseer of the political realm."[42]

This Thomistic model of the relationship between revelation and reason (and hence grace and nature) informs a diversity of other models, directly or indirectly, ranging from Rudolf Bultmann's and Paul Tillich's correlationist theologies to what is often described as classical apologetics in the evangelical tradition. All of these models remain colonies of Tübingen insofar as they concede that there is an objective or neutral reason that determines the shape of truth concerning finite existence

40. There is an account of sin at stake here. It does seem that, for Aquinas, the effect of sin is the loss of an original supplement, not the corruption of nature itself. As he states, "The good of human nature is threefold. First, there are the principles of which nature is constituted, and the properties that flow from them, such as the powers of the soul, and so forth. Secondly, since man has from nature an inclination to virtue, as stated above (60, 1; 63, 1), this inclination to virtue is a good of nature. Thirdly, the gift of original justice, conferred on the whole of human nature in the person of the first man, may be called a good of nature. Accordingly, the first-mentioned good of nature is neither destroyed nor diminished by sin. The third good of nature was entirely destroyed through the sin of our first parent. But the second good of nature, viz. the natural inclination to virtue, is diminished by sin" (*Summa* IaIIae.85.1). Included in the "powers of the soul" is the intellect and faculty of knowledge (*Summa* Ia.75–79). Therefore, if there is any "noetic" effect of sin for Aquinas, it is not the corruption of natural human reason but rather the loss of an *addendum* to such. Thus, there would be no distinction between the purely rational capacities or insights of the regenerate versus the unregenerate.

41. In light of RO's project, Aquinas's discussion of *sacra doctrina*'s relation to other sciences is of interest. For Aquinas, "Sacred doctrine is *one* science" that "does not treat of God and creatures equally, but of God primarily, and of creatures only so far as they are referable to God as their beginning or end" (*Summa* Ia.1.4.ad1). RO's sense that an ontology, a sociology, an economics, etc., are all theology may be understood in this sense.

42. For a discussion, see Bell, *Liberation Theology after the End of History*, 46–51.

and then attempt either to demonstrate Christianity's consistency with this rational account (as in Bultmann and Tillich) or to demonstrate the truth of Christianity's account by appealing to neutral principles of truth that are common to all humanity (as in classical apologetics).[43] In almost every case, such a strategy is undertaken with Constantinian goals in mind, namely, establishing principles of natural (though also biblical) morality by appealing to their universal rational basis in secular reason. Having demonstrated the merely "rational" basis of these principles without appealing to (supernatural) revelation, these theologians believe the coercive imposition of these principles on a pluralist culture has also been justified.[44]

However, this Thomistic notion of "natural knowledge" (and a correlative "rational politics") seems to be an analogue to secular reason—a proto-modern notion of autonomous reason.[45] If Scotus's delineation of an autonomous sphere spawned the secular, and in fact such an unhooking of nature was already effected by Aquinas, how can Aquinas be radically orthodox? How can RO, in seeking to move beyond secular reason, appropriate Aquinas for such a project?[46] RO's response is at once pointed and confusing: According to John Milbank and Catherine Pickstock, Aquinas neither offers an autonomous metaphysics (as discussed in chap. 3) nor affirms a notion of autonomous reason. But how can we make sense of the latter given the outline of Aquinas above?

The New, RO Aquinas

The canonical version of Thomism presented above suggests that one can know the world without any dependence on revelation and without commitment to any particular faith. One does not need to receive the Scriptures as the Word of God nor place faith in Christ to understand, for example, what a tree is or even the nature of social and economic structures, insofar as these are both aspects of the autonomous, temporal sphere. The truth of such matters is thought to reside in the proper

---

43. For a critique of the latter, see Timothy R. Phillips and Dennis Okholm, eds., *Christian Apologetics in the Postmodern World* (Downers Grove, Ill.: InterVarsity, 1995); and Kelly James Clark, "An Introduction to Reformed Epistemology," in *Five Views on Apologetics*, ed. Steven B. Cowan (Grand Rapids: Zondervan, 2000), 265–85.

44. This is true of both the revival of natural law theory (Jay Budziszewski et al.) and what I have elsewhere described as the "Biola school."

45. So Schaeffer claims.

46. This move itself has not gone without protest. Most pointedly, Laurence Paul Hemming argues that "Aquinas is simply being co-opted as an authority for this view" (Laurence Paul Hemming, "*Quod Impossible Est!* Aquinas and Radical Orthodoxy," in *Radical Orthodoxy?* 82).

representation or mirroring of these things as they are. Truth is located in this correspondence. Insofar as these things simply "are" in the world, and thus accessible and ready to hand for any finite perceiver, it is possible for anyone to apprehend properly the truth of the world.

But according to Milbank and Pickstock, this is to read later (post-Scotus) correspondence theories of truth back into Aquinas.[47] The difference between Aquinas's theory of truth and more modern theories is ontological rather than epistemological: "Correspondence or adequation for Aquinas is not a matter of mirroring things in the world or passively registering them on an epistemological level, in a way that leaves the things untouched. Rather, adequating is an event which realizes or fulfills the being of things known, just as much as it fulfills truth in the knower's mind" (TA, 5). In other words, the site where truth is located, as it were, is quite different for Aquinas, and this is because at stake is not just an epistemology but an ontology. According to Milbank and Pickstock, Aquinas rejects the key premise of the account above (namely, that the world is an autonomous reality). Rather, "for Aquinas, the place of truth is manifold and hierarchical, and one finds it gradually by means of an ascending scale" (TA, 9). For Aquinas, there is a sense in which truth resides *in* things: "Truth is a property of things" such that "a thing is true if it fulfills itself and holds itself together according to its character and goal" (TA, 9). Here the truth of things is deeply teleological, and the *telos* of things is established by the Creator. "A thing is fulfilling its telos when it is *copying God in its own manner*, and tending to existence as knowledge in the divine Mind" (TA, 9). A tree, for instance, copies God or fulfills its *telos* by being true to its treeness. An important conclusion follows:

> If a thing is truest when it is teleologically directed, and that means when a thing is copying God, this would suggest, as Aquinas indeed affirms, that truth is primarily in the Mind of God and only secondarily in things as copying the Mind of God. Any suggestion, therefore, that Aquinas' realist theory of truth is a simple correspondence of mind to thing is here qualified by this subordination of all things to the divine intellect. (TA, 10)

Truth, therefore, resides in things insofar as things participate in God. "In knowing a tree," then, "we are catching it on its way back to God" (TA, 12). One more radical conclusion follows from this: One can properly *know* the tree only if one discerns this reference, sees it in terms

---

47. They suggest that this is the core of Bruce Marshall's misreading of Aquinas in Bruce D. Marshall, *Trinity and Truth* (Cambridge: Cambridge University Press, 2000), 108–41, 242–75.

of its created *telos*. Truth, then, "is inherently theological" (TA, 19). This is why, for Aquinas, one cannot recognize the truth of things merely by observing features of the natural (albeit created) order "without necessarily recognizing it *as* created" (TA, 23, emphasis added). "Were one to attempt to comprehend a finite reality not as created, that is to say, not in relation to God, then no truth for Aquinas could ensue, since finite realities are of themselves nothing and only what is can be true" (TA, 23; cf. 33–34). So once again the ontology of participation undergirds this account: Things are not anything "in themselves"; therefore, they cannot be understood "in themselves" but only by reference to that from which they are suspended—their Creator (TA, 22). As a result, no secular account of things could possibly be true.[48]

If on the object side of the question of knowledge RO emphasizes the nothing-in-themselves-ness of things, which means that they can be properly understood only by reference to their Creator, on the subject side of the question, it also problematizes the traditional Thomistic distinction between faith and reason. As suggested above (in chap. 3), for Milbank and Pickstock, the distinction between nature and grace is not one of kind but of degree, in particular, the degree of intensity of participation in the divine. Therefore, it is not the case that nature is an autonomous in-itself to which a relationship to the divine is super-added; rather, nature is always already graced in the sense that it participates in the Creator (BR, 115). It *is* only insofar as it *depends;* its being is essentially a gift. Correlatively, insofar as reason is to faith as nature is to grace, the relation (and distinction) must be understood in the same sense: Reason is not an autonomous operation of a pure nature that supernatural faith supplements. Rather, reason is a reception of light, an operation of divine illumination (TA, 11). While one could find passages in Aquinas that suggest a purely autonomous philosophy (TA, 20), to interpret him as advocating such "cannot be rendered consistent with certain other crucial passages in his writings and therefore must be reinterpreted" (TA, 21). More specifically, the distinction between faith and reason (or theology and philosophy) "can at the very most be thought of only as distinct phases within a single gnoseological extension exhibiting the same qualities throughout" (TA, 21). In other words, faith and reason are but two varying intensities along a continuum of

---

48. Elsewhere they formulate this in terms of a phenomenology of discernment (contra Milbank's earlier dismissal of phenomenology [WMS, 47–49]): "The metaphysics of participation in Aquinas is immediately and implicitly a phenomenology of seeing more than one sees, of recognizing the invisible in the visible" (TA, 47). This is because "the invisible really does shine through the visible, and yet this is only apparent for a subtle power of discernment; it is obviously not present in the manner of a 'fact'" (TA, 11). I tried to unpack just such a phenomenology in *Speech and Theology*.

divine illumination. To know (anything), then, is to participate in divine knowledge (TA, 14, 16). As such, "the 'light of faith' is for Aquinas simply a strengthening of the *intellectus* by a further degree of participation in the divine light" (TA, 23).[49] Revelation, then, is not so much the deposit of a *positum* as an "augmentation of human intellect" (TA, 25; cf. BR, 122). Not even reason is autonomous. Rather, as Augustine earlier asserted, it operates only on the basis of an "inner [divine] *illuminatio*" (TA, 23). Thus, in this new Aquinas, there is no neutral space for secular knowledge or an autonomous philosophy.

Doubting (RO's) Thomas: Criticisms

RO's reading of Aquinas has come under heavy fire from several quarters. The critique can be organized along two fronts: First, there are simply "Thomist" critiques articulated by those who seek to orient their thought along the lines of the traditional Thomas; second, a Reformed critique agrees and disagrees with both RO and its Thomist despisers.

Thomist critiques of RO's Aquinas contest RO's reading of Aquinas's faith/reason distinction.[50] In particular, they call into question the suggestion that there is no autonomous philosophy in Aquinas and RO's tendency to dissolve philosophy and metaphysics *into* sacred doctrine. Wayne Hankey is particularly concerned to guard the autonomy of philosophy: "It must retain an autonomy" because "philosophy belongs to the nature which grace and *sacra doctrina* presuppose and do not destroy but perfect."[51] If we follow Milbank, Hankey suggests, we will end up with "the kind of identity of nature and grace against which Aquinas resolutely set himself despite Augustinian persecution."[52] This is because, for Aquinas, the difference between nature and grace, or

49. For Milbank and Pickstock, this increase of "light" means "an increase in the relative *immediacy* of understanding" or intuition (TA, 23; cf. 42). It seems that reason for them is a mode of discursive participation in the divine, whereas faith is a mode of intuitive participation in the divine (TA, 48). This is why the relationship is reciprocal: Faith informs our knowledge of creation, and reason informs our theology of the Trinity (TA, 52). I address these claims in chapter 6, particularly in relation to the necessary role of bodily, material mediation in human knowing.

50. In their defense, Milbank and Pickstock grant that there *is* a distinction between faith and reason, theology and philosophy (contrary to Wayne Hankey, "Why Philosophy Abides for Aquinas," *Heythorp Journal* 42 [2001]: 329). The issue is not *whether* there is a distinction but what *kind* of distinction it is: one of kind or one of degree (TA, 21).

51. Hankey, "Why Philosophy Abides for Aquinas," 336; cf. Hemming, *"Quod Impossible Est!"* 89. As I suggested in chapter 1, those critics of RO who want to guard the autonomy and neutrality of philosophical thought (perhaps unwittingly) end up offering an *apologia* for secularity.

52. Hankey, "Why Philosophy Abides for Aquinas," 344.

natural and revealed theology, is a difference of kind. As Nicholas Lash
carefully points out, when Aquinas discusses the distinction between
these "two theologies," he concludes that "the theology which pertains to
holy teaching differs *in kind* [*differt secundum genus*] from that theology,
that naming of God, which occurs in philosophy."[53] Thus, like Lash,
Hankey "cannot concur with the denial determined by the fundamentals
of Radical Orthodoxy that there is in Aquinas 'a philosophical approach
to God independent of theology.'"[54]

More specifically, Hankey calls into question the alleged Augustinianism of Aquinas's epistemology, in particular the suggestion that, for
Aquinas, all knowledge is illumination. "The neo-Gilsonian Christianiza-
tion of philosophy for which [Milbank] aspires may be Augustinian,"
but it is not Thomist.[55] This is because "Aquinas' treatment of human
knowing cannot be assimilated to a Platonic or Augustinian illumina-
tionism"; in fact, Aquinas explicitly opposes such an illuminationist
account.[56] According to Aquinas, the (natural) light is the operation of
the agent intellect and "has become an internal power to make something in our own minds."[57] Here, Aquinas is more Aristotelian than
the Platonic Augustine, granting a great degree of integrity to nature
and creatures. Aquinas's (albeit oblique) critique of Augustine on this
score is concerned with guarding the integrity of creation as created.
While Aquinas agrees that "the human mind is illumined by a natural
light," he goes on to note that "if this light, because it is created,[58] is not
adequate to know the truth, but needs a new illumination, the added
light with equal reason will not suffice, but will require another light,
and so on to infinity—a process that can never be completed. And so
it will be impossible to know any truth. Therefore, we must depend on
the first light, so that the human mind can see the truth by its natural
light without anything being added."[59] This original intellectual light is
"connatural" to the mind as created. But while Aquinas is criticizing

53. Nicholas Lash, "Where Does Holy Teaching Leave Philosophy? Questions on
Milbank's Aquinas," *Modern Theology* 15 (1999): 439–40.

54. Hankey, "Why Philosophy Abides for Aquinas," 340, citing TA, xiii.

55. Ibid., 336.

56. Ibid., 337, pointing to *De Spiritualibus Creaturis* as the site for this rejection.

57. Ibid., 337.

58. This, of course, is not Augustine's position, at least not in *De vera religione* (we
might find something akin to it, however, in *De magistro* or *Contra academicos*). Augustine
does not say that divine illumination is required because of some inherent deficiency of
human intellect—as if there were a kind of "natural deficiency" that characterized human
knowledge. Rather, for Augustine, such illumination is required by virtue of the intellect's
corruption, its fallenness. I return to this below.

59. Aquinas, *In Boeth.* qu. 1, art. 1 (Maurer, 15–16). Here Aquinas's concern is with the
"occasionalism" that illumination theory seems to entail. In this sense, his critique mir-

a certain kind of (occasionalist) illumination theory, this text could also be cited in support of RO's reading, for here Aquinas emphasizes that this "original light" is a gift, owing to creation, and thus can say that "the human mind is *divinely* illumined by a *natural* light."[60] Within Aquinas's creational framework, what is natural is created and therefore in some sense divine and fundamentally a gift. Thus, he can conclude that "though an additional new light is unnecessary for a knowledge of whatever comes within the reach of natural reason, the divine activity is nevertheless required"—and this in a dual sense: on the one hand, "the act by which God establishes the natures of things" and thus grants the condition of possibility for their operation; on the other hand, by acts of providence, "directing and moving the powers of all of them to their specific acts."[61] In this sense, then, "all created active powers function under the movement and direction of their creator"—even in those operations and powers that are "natural."[62] We might say, then, that Aquinas advocates the integrity of creation versus brute autonomy, or a graced autonomy versus a seized autonomy. For Aquinas, nature is always and only creation. It is not granted any kind of brute autonomy vis-à-vis the Creator.[63]

However, this does not mean that there isn't a problem with Aquinas's account of knowledge. But what is at stake is not creation (or nature) but the fall (and sin). Here is where the Reformed critique is both more complex and more acute than the Thomist critiques. Almost unanimously, RO's Thomist critics seek to guard the autonomy of natural reason and hence the universality of philosophical discourse. But more specifically, they seek to guarantee such even in the current postlapsarian situation. With Aquinas (as described above), we should be willing to grant a certain structural integrity or graced autonomy to human knowing in creation, but after the fall, the proper direction of this structure was corrupted such that confessional pluralism plagues reason in the postlapsarian situation. Reason is not an innately neutral faculty; rather, it is a capac-

rors Leibniz's critique of occasionalism, which was also aimed at guarding the integrity of a good creation (see chap. 6).

60. Ibid., emphasis added (Maurer, 15).

61. Ibid. (Maurer, 17).

62. Ibid. (Maurer, 18).

63. The problem is that Aquinas seems to think it is possible, apart from Christian faith and regeneration, for any human being to recognize nature as creation. This seems to be because he assumes that this original gift of the natural light remains *common* and *commonly available* to all of humanity. Hence, Aquinas's version of a creational illumination concludes to an affirmation of the neutrality of reason. Hence, there can still be a natural theology, and this is certainly true for RO as well (more lately than earlier). This is where I disagree, precisely because I think that sin has distorted this natural light.

ity for grasping the creation, but as with every creational structure, it is corrupted by the fall such that the structure is misdirected.

The test case for appreciating the difference here is the *locus classicus* of Romans 1:20, to which Hankey appeals in his critique of RO's Aquinas. Here Paul asserts that "since the creation of the world [God's] invisible attributes, his eternal power and divine nature, have been clearly seen, being understood through what has been made" (NASB). Aquinas explicitly appeals to this verse as the authority for asserting that God's existence can be demonstrated by natural reason (*Summa* Ia.2.2), underwriting a project of natural theology. As Hankey suggests, "For Aquinas the foundational work of philosophy is an absolutely necessary labor" because natural reason—understood on an Aristotelian register—proceeds from sensible to intelligible. "Without this," Hankey notes, "Romans 1:20, which holds that the invisible things of God are understood from creation, would be false, because we cannot understand God unless we can demonstrate that he is."[64] The apostle's claim regarding the clear visibility of aspects of God through creation is taken as confirmation that such knowledge is universally available on the basis of a common, natural, unaided human reason.

But here the Reformed tradition demurs by continuing to engage the Pauline witness, for as Paul goes on to note in verses 21–31, while there is a sense in which God's nature and attributes are available to be perceived in the structure of creation, sin has marred the perceptive capacities of humanity such that these aspects of creation are not and cannot be recognized. The truth is "suppressed" (v. 18), and foolish minds are darkened (v. 21). What would seem to be neutrally available to the rational perceiver is unable to be perceived because the noetic effects of sin have darkened and distorted rationality.[65] As a result, only the regenerate mind can recognize this almost semiotic reference structure of creation.[66] Again, Aquinas's account of sin is not radical enough insofar as it seems to retain a site within nature—namely, reason—that is not

64. Hankey, "Why Philosophy Abides for Aquinas," 339.

65. On noetic effects of sin, see Alvin Plantinga, *Warranted Christian Belief* (Oxford: Oxford University Press, 2000), 199–240.

66. For Jonathan Edwards, the Holy Spirit dwells in the regenerate as a "vital principle, or as a new supernatural principle of life and action." Through this new "vital principle" (and through Scripture) the regenerate begin to learn the language of God, which is God's typological communication to intelligent beings through all of creation (natural and historical) (Jonathan Edwards, "Misc. 471," *The Miscellanies*, vol. 13, *The Works of Jonathan Edwards*, ed. Thomas A. Schafer [New Haven: Yale University Press, 1994], 512–14; *Typological Writings*, vol. 11, *The Works of Jonathan Edwards*, ed. Wallace E. Anderson and Mason I. Lowance Jr. [New Haven: Yale University Press, 1993], 151). My thanks to Jerry Stutzman for conversations on this point.

(significantly) marred by the fall (cf. TA, 23–24). But the recognition of the radical noetic effects of sin is the basis for what has been the long-standing (and Augustinian) "Reformed critique of natural theology" (see ITWT, 95–96).[67]

The Reformed critique is complicated at this point: The Reformational tradition, in rejecting the notion of a neutral, secular reason, subscribes to the epistemological account offered by RO. But precisely for this reason, the Reformed tradition has been consistently critical of Aquinas's model and has opted for the Augustinian paradigm. As Hankey and Hemming suggest, RO's reading of Aquinas tends to be a re-creation of Aquinas in Augustine's image. But Hankey and Hemming are wrong in thinking that Aquinas's assertion of an autonomous philosophy is a virtue of his thought. This ambiguity in RO might be an indication that what is lacking is a radical understanding of the fall. I have some suspicions that of late, Milbank—under the rubric of universalism—is rehabilitating a quasi-natural theology. This would stem from the fact that, even if he recognizes the noetic effects of sin (it is not clear that he does), for him, grace seems to be universally shed abroad in such a way that these effects are undone for all humanity (BR, 106).[68] The result is a renewed confidence in a general illumination or universal reason—assertions that would seem to contradict the critique of the secular that stands at the heart of RO. (This would also explain his recent critiques of Hauerwas.)[69]

On this score, the Reformational tradition seems more radical in its critique of autonomous rationality. The Reformed tradition asserts the noetic effects of sin in a way that seems to honor the Pauline distinction between the carnal or natural (*psychikos*) person and the spiritual (*pneumatikos*) person (1 Cor. 2:6–16).[70] Because the difference between

---

67. Plantinga, "Reformed Objection to Natural Theology."

68. In TA, this is particularly confusing. To substantiate their claim that "all creatures subsist by grace" (TA, 37), Milbank and Pickstock cite Aquinas, *Summa* Ia.8.3: "And because the rational creature possesses this prerogative by grace, as will be shown later (Q. 12), he is thus said to be in the saints by grace." They then go on to remark that "as to humanity 'the saint' is normative" (TA, 123n73). While that might be the case, it does not follow that this norm is *realized* for all humanity. Who is this "we" for whom this seeing and discernment is possible? Not all humans are saints (in the Pauline sense).

69. In, e.g., John Milbank, "Materialism and Transcendence," in *Theology and the Political*, ed. Creston Davis, John Milbank, and Slavoj Žižek (Durham, N.C.: Duke University Press, forthcoming). In chapter 7, I return to RO's blurring of this matter as it unfolds in its dissolution of the church.

70. See the classic seventeenth-century work of John Owen, *The Holy Spirit* (Grand Rapids: Kregel, 1954). I could recommend no better statement on the noetic effects of sin than his account of "corruption of the depravity of the mind by sin" (144–69). One finds basically the same point articulated in Kierkegaard's *Philosophical Fragments:* To come

the *psychikos* and the *pneumatikos* is the *pneuma,* and it seems clear that the Holy Spirit indwells only believers (1 Cor. 2:14; cf. Rom. 5:5)—not all of humanity—the Reformed tradition (echoing Augustine) emphasizes regeneration as the condition for insight (cf. 1 Cor. 2:10). As John Owen puts it:

> That Jesus Christ was crucified, is a proposition that any natural [i.e., unregenerate] man may understand and assent to, and be said to receive: and all the doctrines of the gospel may be taught in propositions and discourses, the sense and meaning of which a natural man may understand; but it is denied that he can receive the things themselves. For there is a wide difference between the mind's receiving doctrines notionally, and receiving the things taught in them really.[71]

Regeneration[72] is the condition for proper perception, coupled with the lens of scriptural revelation, which is the condition for proper understanding. In other words, the special revelation of Scripture—which can be discerned only by the regenerate (1 Cor. 2:12)—is that alone that makes something like natural revelation intelligible.[73] Or as Jonathan Edwards might put it, only the Bible enables us to read the world well. As a result, the Reformational tradition would be suspicious of what appears to be RO's attempt to rehabilitate a kind of general illumination.

Philosophy and Theology: Anatomy of a Relation

One of the most perplexing aspects of RO is its use and (non)definition of the term *theology* and the qualifier *theological.* The most persistent mantra of RO is that only theology can undo the host of metaphysical, epistemological, and social consequences of the Scotist-nihilist complex: "Only theology overcomes metaphysics" (WMS, 36–52); "only Christian theology now offers a discourse able to position and overcome nihilism itself" (TST, 6) because "the absolute Christian vision of ontological peace now provides the only alternative to a nihilistic outlook" (TST, 434); "in

---

to know the truth, the learner (disciple) must receive from the Teacher (God) not only the *content* of the truth but also the very *condition* for receiving it. The dispensation of the condition is an act of grace by the work of the Holy Spirit.

71. Owen, *Holy Spirit,* 155.

72. This should not be understood as a positivistic guarantee. In other words, we should not divorce regeneration from sanctification. One could also say—with Augustine—that sanctification is a condition for wisdom. At this juncture, the life of worship becomes central to the task of Christian scholarship.

73. This is true for both Calvin and Kuyper. See Abraham Kuyper, *Calvinism: Six Stone Foundation Lectures* (Grand Rapids: Eerdmans, 1943), 120–21. Cf. ITWT, 130.

a neo-tribal culture, only theological communities have the resources
. . . to resist the collapse into pragmatic and transitory values associated
with media-driven 'lifestyles'" (TR, 152); "only theological communities
have the resources to cultivate forms of relationality that can resist the
dissolving of the social into the cultural" (TR, 152); "theology alone"
can grant the nonreductive materialist ontology necessary to undergird
socialism because "the theological appeal to transcendence alone sustains a non-reductive materiality and is the very reverse of any notion
of idealism."[74] The claims are sometimes more specified, as in Catherine Pickstock's assertion that "the event of transubstantiation in the
Eucharist is the condition of possibility for *all* human meaning" (AW,
xv); Phillip Blond's claim that "only a theological realism can properly
acknowledge and affirm what is presented [in perception]";[75] Daniel
Bell's claim that "only a more substantive ecclesiology . . . stands a
chance of resisting capitalist discipline";[76] or Milbank's suggestion that
"it is only the monotheistic doctrine of creation which allows a nonreductive materialism in theory and in practice."[77] Overall, the core of
the RO project is the confident claim that only theology can properly
understand the world and orient just, charitable practice. The essays
in the original collection, then, "seek to re-envisage particular cultural
spheres from a theological perspective which they all regard as the only
non-nihilistic perspective, and the only perspective able to uphold even
finite reality" (RONT, 4). This is why RO "attempts to reclaim the world
by situating its concerns and activities within a theological framework"
and "from a Christian standpoint," contending that "every discipline
must be framed by a theological perspective" (RONT, 1, 3).

In addition to these persistent claims to theology's unique ability to
understand the world, RO is quite explicit that its goal is to once again
establish theology as the queen of the sciences. As stridently formulated
in the "Twenty-four Theses," "Radical Orthodoxy defers to no experts and
engages in no 'dialogues,' because it does not recognize other valid points
of view outside the theological."[78] Secular sciences, which by definition

---

74. Milbank, "Materialism and Transcendence," 4.

75. Phillip Blond, "Introduction: Theology before Philosophy," in *Post-secular Philosophy:
Between Philosophy and Theology*, ed. Phillip Blond (London: Routledge, 1998), 58.

76. Bell, *Liberation Theology after the End of History*, 72. Along these lines, one could also
note Ward's development of a distinctive ontology that flows from the sense of materiality
engendered by Eucharist, resurrection, and ascension (CG); or Phillip Blond's account
of art that could only be spawned by the Christian doctrines of creation and incarnation
(RONT, 220–42); or my own claim that only the incarnation can provide a framework for
a nonreductive understanding of language (*Speech and Theology*).

77. Bell, *Liberation Theology after the End of History*, 5.

78. "Radical Orthodoxy: Twenty-four Theses," thesis 5.

refuse the theological, are not to be accepted on their own terms or as the experts on the natural sphere (as they were by liberation theology, for instance). Thus, secular, autonomous disciplines such as metaphysics or philosophy must be evacuated (WMS, 50). This is formulated most forcefully by Milbank, who decries the "false humility" of theology that has allowed it to be positioned by secular sciences (TST, 1). Once this happens, "theology surrenders its claim to be a metadiscourse" and "it cannot any longer articulate the word of the creator God, but is bound to turn into the oracular voice of some finite idol" (TST, 1). What is required, then, is a reassertion of theology's claim to give an account of every sphere of creation so that theology is not positioned by other disciplines but rather positions them with respect to itself as "the queen of the sciences for the inhabitants of the *altera civitas*" (TST, 380).

Here we hit upon a fundamental ambiguity in RO's project, one that raises distinct concern from the perspective of a Reformed engagement.[79] Just what does theology mean in this context? What does it mean, according to RO, for a discourse or a framework to be theological? How are we to understand the claim that theology alone is able to out-narrate nihilism when theology is left undefined? Theology and the theological seem to indicate several quite different things: First, theology is identified with both Christianity and Christian faith;[80] second, theology is clearly equated with a science, a mode of theoretical discourse, analysis, and reflection; in a third sense, theology is linked to confession and even practice;[81] and still further, theology is linked to revelation and Scripture. But such ambiguity points us to a number of long-standing questions in the Reformational tradition: Is Christian faith to be equated with Christian theology? Is Christian revelation to be equated with theology? Is Christian confession theological in a scientific sense? How are we to do justice to the "sense of the faithful" if Christian faith is collapsed with Christian theology? Must every Christian be a scientist in this respect? At this juncture, Dooyeweerd expresses a deep concern about the place of theology in the life of discipleship:

> Dogmatic theology is a very dangerous science. Its elevation to a necessary mediator between God's Word and the believer amounts to idolatry and

79. Dooyeweerd was frustrated by a similar ambiguity in Augustine's use of the term *theology* (ITWT, 80).

80. That said, this is not always the case, especially in Ward's discussion in TR, where "theology" seems to be used more formally to describe simply "a distinctive mode of discourse and tradition-based knowledge" (TR, 96). In this sense, one would have to specify *which* theology is at stake: Jewish? Muslim? Christian? Ward tends to balk at this point.

81. This is especially true of those in the more Hauerwasian line of RO authors, such as Stephen Long, Daniel Bell, and Michael Hanby.

testifies to a fundamental misconception concerning its real character and position. If our salvation be dependent on theological dogmatics and exegesis, we are lost. (ITWT, 93)

In addition to these concerns, we must add those articulated by Christians working in other disciplines such as sociology, psychology, or economics: Even if we agree that Christian revelation speaks to the whole of creation precisely because creation is subject to the lordship of the Creator, and even if we recognize creational norms for the disciplines and different spheres of life—in short, even if we want to articulate a radically Christian account of social or economic relationships—does this require that the Christian sociologist or economist also be a theologian? Or more ominously, does it suggest that only theologians can properly be economists or sociologists? If we followed RO's model in developing a Christian university, would the theology department direct all others? Or would there even *be* other departments? Would the theology department be "all in all"?[82]

It is in its account of the relationship between theology and philosophy—or theology and the disciplines more generally—that RO's project stands in need of reforming. In particular, Dooyeweerd's framework for articulating the relationship between faith, theology, and the disciplines is more radical than RO's and offers a corrective. However, the corrective is reciprocal insofar as RO pushes the Reformational tradition to consider the substance of its confessional commitments.

Before unpacking Dooyeweerd's framework, it should be noted that the Reformed vision articulated by Kuyper, Dooyeweerd, and others is sympathetic to the claims regarding the utterly unique conclusions yielded by Christian theorizing alone. This is simply to reassert the fundamental point regarding antithesis. The most radical elements of the Reformational tradition would readily concur with RO's (Thomistic) conclusion that "were one to attempt to comprehend a finite reality not as created, that is to say, not in relation to God, then no truth for Aquinas could ensue" (TA, 23). As Dooyeweerd puts it, the "structural data" of our shared world "may be interpreted in different philosophical ways; but this does not mean that the philosophical interpretations are withdrawn from a general standard of truth. These philosophical interpretations turn out to be misinterpretations insofar as they amount

---

82. Not all in the Reformed tradition would be as suspicious of RO's project. Hans Boersma, in fact, has recently called for a certain reinstatement of theology as (qualified) queen of the sciences. See Hans Boersma, "The Relevance of Theology and Worldview in a Postmodern Context," in *Living in the Lamblight: Christianity and Contemporary Challenges to the Gospel*, ed. Hans Boersma (Vancouver: Regent College Publishing, 2001), 1–13. He offers helpful criticism of the Neo-Calvinist "worldview" paradigm (6–8).

to a reasoning away of structural data of our experience" (ITWT, 41).[83]
While all philosophical or theoretical accounts of the world are rooted
in a religious starting point, the "truly absolute standard of truth is not
to be found in man, but only in the Word of God, in its central sense,
which uncovers the source of all absolutizations and which *alone* can
lead man to true knowledge of himself and of his absolute Origin"
(ITWT, 42). Hence, any secular account of our being-in-the-world is
fundamentally false insofar as it refuses to recognize nature as creation
and refuses to understand all creatures and creaturely relationships with
reference to the Creator.[84] Therefore, just as RO points out the inner
paucity of nihilism to account for our experience, Dooyeweerd analyzes
the way in which historicism fails to make this transcendent reference,
which is necessary for properly grasping the world of experience.[85] The
Reformational tradition, then, resonates with RO's claims regarding the
unique disclosures of distinctively Christian accounts of every facet of
being-in-the-world.

However, Dooyeweerd, and the Reformational tradition in general,
is wary of describing such Christian accounts as *theological* accounts,
as it is offered in RONT. This stems from the Reformed tradition's concern—antedating a theme in RO—to emphasize that every aspect of
creation is created and therefore is in some sense religious and can be
properly understood only in relation to the Creator. Against the dualism of fundamentalism, which RO also seeks to subvert, the Reformed
tradition has always emphasized that "life is religion"[86]—that worship
or doxology is not confined to a religious compartment of human existence but rather spills over into every sphere of human activity, from
agriculture to commerce, from recreation to parenting. Insofar as a life
of discipleship must be predicated upon God's revelation of himself, all
of life is to be guided and shaped by this self-revelation of the Creator.
This is especially true of the theorizing that corresponds to these multiple
spheres of existence: A distinctly Christian account of the environment
or economic structures must be fundamentally shaped by God's revelation concerning the norms for these spheres, the impact of the fall on
their current direction, and the shape of redemption in those spheres.
But for all its resonance with RO on this score, the Reformed tradition

---

83. For Dooyeweerd's more detailed account of truth, see NC, 2:571–82.

84. This does not, however, shut down all dialogue with non-Christian discourses.

85. Both, Dooyeweerd would say, are rooted in apostate ground-motives or basic religious
commitments that distort perception of creation by absolutizing one aspect of it.

86. "Life is religion" was a common formulation spawning from H. Evan Runner, *The
Relation of the Bible to Learning* (St. Catherines, Ont.: Paideia Press, 1974). See also Henry
Vander Goot, ed., *Life Is Religion: Essays in Honor of H. Evan Runner* (St. Catherines,
Ont.: Paideia Press, 1981).

has been reticent about describing such shaping and guidance as theological.[87] Why is this? While not representative of the Reformed tradition as a whole, Dooyeweerd's account can shed light on this concern about the "theologization" of both theorizing and human experience. First, however, we must have a broader picture of how he understands the relationship between the disciplines and the role of faith and revelation in relation to them.

In Dooyeweerd's unique ontology, creation itself is structured by multiple aspects or modes that inhere in every created thing.[88] These aspects include, for instance (in an ascending order), the numerical, the biotic, the psychic, the logical, the social, the economic, the jural, the moral, and the faith or "pistic" aspect.[89] These aspects "inhere" in every creature—including products of human *poiesis*—but they are disclosed only by theoretical abstraction or through the lens of the theoretical attitude, to be distinguished from the nontheoretical or natural attitude. In the nontheoretical attitude, for instance, a person experiences a chair as a concrete whole intended for a particular use. But if one "steps back," as it were, from one's immersion and involvement with the world to analyze and reflect on the chair in the theoretical attitude, that person can consider it from a number of different aspects: Its color and design indicate an aesthetic aspect; its place within the classroom denotes a particular social aspect; its material composition indicates a physical or chemical aspect, and so forth. These aspects of the concrete whole, then, are disclosed and opened up when a person's everyday experience of things is refracted through the prism of theoretical analysis. The theoretical attitude refracts the unified whole of everyday experience into the spectrum of creational aspects of things. Each of these aspects, then, corresponds to a special science or discipline that investigates the corresponding aspect of creation: Physics investigates the physical aspect, biology the biotic aspect, law the jural aspect, ethics the moral aspect, and so forth. But insofar as these are aspects of creatures, each of the disciplines must ultimately be grounded in "the radical and central biblical theme [or ground-motive] of creation, fall into sin and redemp-

87. The Reformed tradition has generally been nonplussed by evangelical attempts to think critically about different aspects of being-in-the-world under the rubric of "a theology of *x*" (a theology of the arts, a theology of business, a theology of science, etc.).

88. This ontology is most fully unpacked in his consideration of "thinghood" (NC, 2: 1–413). For a helpful discussion, see Calvin Seerveld, "Dooyeweerd's Legacy for Aesthetics: Modal Law Theory," in *The Legacy of Herman Dooyeweerd*, ed. C. T. McIntire (Lanham, Md.: University Press of America, 1985), esp. 44–62. See also John Witte Jr., ed., *A Christian Theory of Social Institutions*, trans. Magnus Verbrugge (La Jolla, Calif.: Herman Dooyeweerd Foundation, 1986), 11–30.

89. Much ink has been spilled on the number of aspects (fourteen? fifteen?).

tion by Jesus Christ as the incarnate Word of God, in the communion of the Holy Spirit. This basic motive is the central spiritual motive power of every Christian thought worthy of its name" (ITWT, 30).

The whole of creation, then, is to be investigated by special sciences—rooted in the biblical ground-motive—that consider the different aspects of creatures *as* created. Philosophy, however, is unique insofar as it does not investigate a particular aspect but rather considers the relationship between aspects and serves the other disciplines by reflecting on basic questions of ontology and epistemology (ITWT, 9). However, this does not mean that philosophy is an autonomous discipline. Rather, like all modes of being-in-the-world (not just theorizing), and like all the special sciences, even philosophy is rooted in a particular religious ground-motive: either the radical biblical ground-motive or one of any number of "apostate" ground-motives.[90] Therefore, the picture of theoretical activity, and hence a picture of the university, on Dooyeweerd's register looks something like the following.

Table 1. Religion, Philosophy, and the Special Sciences

Mathematics *Numeric aspect*	Other special sciences *Other aspects*	Law/Legal Studies *Jural aspect*	Ethics *Moral aspect*	Theology *Pistic aspect*
Methodology: the philosophy *of* mathematics	Methodology: the philosophy *of* other sciences	Methodology: the philosophy *of* law	Methodology: the philosophy *of* ethics	Methodology: the philosophy *of* theology
Philosophy: ontology, epistemology, relation between totality of aspects				
Ground-Motive (Fundamental Religious Commitments)[91]				

While all theoretical thought is rooted in fundamental religious commitments, this does not entail that all theoretical thought is ultimately Christian. Rather, the *structure* of religious commitment is ineradicable, but the *direction* of such religious commitment can take an apostate direction. So even purportedly secular philosophy or social science is ultimately founded on (apostate) religious commitments (cf. TST, 3).

Now, one will note an important aspect of this table vis-à-vis the discussion above: Theology is not found at the root or foundation of the picture but rather is a distinct, and relatively demarcated and circum-

90. Dooyeweerd tends to suggest that in the West there has been, in addition to the biblical ground-motive, three others, all of which are apostate: the ancient form-matter motive, the medieval nature-grace motive, and the modern nature-freedom motive (ITWT, 29–35; cf. also Herman Dooyeweerd, *Roots of Western Culture: Pagan, Secular, and Christian Options* [Toronto: Wedge, 1979]).

91. This is sometimes referred to as a "worldview" or "world-and-life view" (Kuyper).

scribed, special science. This entails two things: First, in this picture, theology is not queen of the sciences or the fount of all disciplinary reflection; second, theology is a theoretical science and therefore a second-order mode of analysis and reflection.[92] According to Dooyeweerd, we must not confuse theology as a second-order discipline of theoretical reflection with the biblical ground-motive or religious commitment, which is pre-theoretical (or supra-theoretical). Insofar as theology is understood as the special science of the pistic aspect, RO's project of positioning all other sciences in relation to theology would, in fact, amount to absolutizing one of the aspects of creation over the others—resulting in making theology (and/or the pistic aspect) an idol. The result would be a kind of theological reductionism akin to a naturalistic reductionism that reduces all the other aspects to the biotic.[93] In that sense, RO's conception of theology as queen of the sciences sounds, ironically, idolatrous to Reformed ears. Of course, this does not delegitimate RO's project as such; it only suggests that a radically Christian account of economics, for instance, does not require subsuming economics under theology. What such a radically Christian economics requires is economic analysis undergirded by a distinctly Christian philosophy and rooted in the biblical ground-motive, which is itself a response to God's Word-revelation.[94] Dooyeweerd and the Reformed tradition, therefore, would call for, not a theological resituating of the disciplines but rather a confessional framework for all the disciplines. This would produce not "theological economics" or "theological sociology" but confessional economics and confessional

92. Cf. George Lindbeck, *The Nature of Doctrine* (Philadelphia: Westminster, 1984), 10; and Edward Farley, *Ecclesial Reflection: An Anatomy of Theological Method* (Philadelphia: Fortress, 1982), 178–83.

93. On top of this formal concern, Dooyeweerd consistently expresses reservations about the precarious conclusions of theological science and worries about "canonizing" them (ITWT, 93). However, as I suggest below, this betrays a lingering hint of Gnosticism in Dooyeweerd that is not properly confident in human *poiesis* as participating in the divine (to use Milbank's words).

94. That is, the "heart" is properly directed when it is oriented by God's self-revelation. "Thus the central theme of the Holy Scriptures . . . effects the true knowledge of God and ourselves, if our heart is fully opened by the Holy Spirit so that it finds itself in the grip of God's Word and has become the captive of Jesus Christ. So long as this central meaning of the Word-revelation is at issue, we are beyond the scientific problems both of theology and philosophy. Its acceptance or rejection is a matter of life or death to us, and not a question of theoretical reflection" (ITWT, 86). However, this should also be tempered by Kuyper's claim that perhaps no human heart is ever "fully" open to the Holy Spirit, insofar as the line of antithesis runs through every human heart. For a lucid discussion, see Jacob Klapwijk, "Antithesis and Common Grace," in *Bringing into Captivity Every Thought*, ed. J. Klapwijk, S. Griffioen, and G. Groenewoud (Lanham, Md.: University Press of America, 1991), 169–90.

sociology rooted in God's self-revelation and the radical biblical motive of creation, fall, and redemption.[95] While the shift may seem semantic, it is more than that and addresses several of the questions posed above. In the end, this is perhaps what RO is really after: an account of the multiple aspects of being-in-the-world that is rooted in God's self-revelation in Christ. As Ward notes, what he means by theological communities or discourses are those that proceed by "arguing and acting from an explicit confessional standpoint" (TR, 134).[96] One can see Ward doing precisely this, for example, in his radically reconceived ontology of matter that begins from the "ontological scandal" announced in the upper room. "If," he asks, "from the specific standpoint of Christian theology, orderings and accounts of the world proceed from that which has been revealed; and if, therefore, this Eucharistic and Christic body informs all other understandings of 'body' for Christian teaching," then our ontology of matter and bodies should be reconfigured on the basis of the claim that "this is my body" (CG, 83). But not all accounts that "proceed from that which has been revealed" should be described as theology proper.

However, it is also at this juncture that there ought to be a reciprocal corrective. RO's project should push us to reconsider Dooyeweerd's suspicion regarding theology. It is important to note Dooyeweerd's persistent relativization of theology here, especially insofar as this has spawned a trajectory within the Reformed tradition. While Dooyeweerd—along with RO—calls for a radically Christian account of every sphere of existence and a distinctly Christian philosophy, he also refuses any identification of the biblical ground-motive with theology or the church. As he puts it, the radical biblical ground-motive "should not be confused with the ecclesiastical articles of faith, which refer to this motive, and which can be made into the object of a dogmatic theological reflection in the theoretical attitude of thought. As the core of the divine Word-revelation, it is independent of any human theology. Its radical sense can only be explained by the Holy Spirit, operating in the heart, or the religious center of our consciousness, within the communion of the invisible Catholic church" (ITWT, 30–31). It is not without warrant, then, that some have suggested that Dooyeweerd's thought is marked by a deep

95. This is also why Dooyeweerd, unlike Milbank (see "Only Theology Overcomes Metaphysics"; and "Knowledge: The Theological Critique of Philosophy in Hamann and Jacobi," in RONT), can advocate a distinctly *Christian* philosophy. Unlike Milbank, Dooyeweerd does not confuse the apostate (secular) *direction* of philosophy with the *structure* of philosophy as a creational mode of reflection. What is required, however, is a rooting of philosophy in the biblical ground-motive or revelation.

96. Stephen Long also speaks of such a project in terms of incorporating "more specific confessional themes" (*Divine Economy*, 5).

mysticism.[97] In particular, he seems to eschew the mediation of revelation via language and tradition, thus allowing him to suggest that the revelation of the biblical motive can be communicated "directly" to consciousness. Therefore, he faults the tradition for consistently "confusing theoretical Christian theology with the true knowledge of God and true self-knowledge" (ITWT, 80–81). But how could one describe the biblical basic motive as "the radical and central biblical theme of creation, fall into sin and redemption by Jesus Christ as the incarnate Word of God, in the communion of the Holy Spirit" and not consider the content of such a confession theological? Even if Dooyeweerd wants to relativize dogmatic theology vis-à-vis confession or "true knowledge of God and self," is there not a fundamental relationship between the two? Dooyeweerd almost seems to cordon off theology from revelation in any significant sense (ITWT, 94).

But it seems that Dooyeweerd's attempts to de-theologize the biblical ground-motive or Christian worldview is problematic on two fronts: First, the elements of such a worldview are substantive and contentful, culled from revelation, and articulated in the creeds of the church; therefore, there must be some sense in which they are theological. Indeed, if the biblical ground-motive is not going to be thinned out to a mere affirmation of "the goodness of creation," then the worldview that funds confessional scholarship must reflect the robustness of the church's confession, articulated in response to revelation. The fact that this "religious presupposition" (ITWT, 87) is not propositional (as Dooyeweerd rightly emphasizes) does not mean that it is not contentful or substantive.[98] The content of this confession—as embodied, for instance, in the Apostles' Creed or Nicene Creed—has traditionally been understood as theological in some sense.[99] Second, the very desire to

---

97. For suggestions along this line, see John Glenn Friesen, "The Mystical Dooyeweerd," *Ars Disputandi* 3 (2003), www.ArsDisputandi.org.

98. The very ability to articulate "creation-fall-redemption" confirms this: The biblical ground-motive is not so mystical that it cannot be articulated.

99. Let me take a stab at this in Dooyeweerdian terms: Theology as a *theoretical* science is characterized by the general shape of theory, in which a particular aspect is placed "over against" the logical aspect (see Hendrik Hart, "Dooyeweerd's *Gegenstand* Theory of Theory," in *The Legacy of Herman Dooyeweerd*, ed. C. T. McIntire [Lanham, Md.: University Press of America, 1985], 143–66). This is what Dooyeweerd describes as the "antithetical structure of the theoretical attitude" (ITWT, 10). "This theoretical antithesis," he argues, "originates only in our intention to conceive the non-logical aspects of our experience by means of an analytical dissociation whereby they are set apart. In this way we oppose them to the logical aspect of our thought and to each other in order to conceive them in a logical concept" (ITWT, 10). In "scientific theology," the pistic aspect is subjected to analysis over against the logical aspect (ITWT, 99). Therefore, what makes theology "scientific" or "theoretical" is its *attitude* (*gegenstandlisch*), not its content per se. How-

de-theologize the biblical ground-motive seems to indicate a latent Gnosticism and disturbingly Protestant disavowal of the concrete catholic
church in Dooyeweerd's thought. His conception of revelation seems
to indicate an allergy to particularity and concreteness (contra other
aspects of his thought).[100] Granted, Dooyeweerd's concern is that we
not confuse Scripture with theology (ITWT, 93), but he also seems to
be concerned that we not equate revelation (the Word-revelation) with
the particularities of Scripture because Scripture is a manifestation
within the temporal order, whereas the Word-revelation is supra-temporal and supra-theoretical (ITWT, 86–87). Thus, "the actual Christian
faith in its true sense can only originate from the operation of God's
Word, as a central spiritual power, in the heart, i.e., the religious center
of our existence" (ITWT, 94–95). The sense is that the inbreaking of
revelation, because it is a supra-temporal matter, cannot be intrinsi-
cally linked to the concretion of Scripture. Moreover, the individualism
of this picture also explains why the role of the church is completely
absent from Dooyeweerd's picture here. An heir to Kuyper's flattened,
unsacramental theology (unlike that of Calvin), Dooyeweerd's account
of religious faith has inklings of Gnosticism insofar as he devalues the
scandal of particularity in Scripture as well as the role of the believing
community in the church.[101]

In response to these problems, and growing out of dialogue with
RO, I want to suggest a slight reconfiguration of the picture offered
above concerning the relationship between confession, theology, and
disciplinary research.[102]

---

ever, there is also a sense in which my confession that "Jesus is Lord," or that "I believe
in God the Father Almighty," is substantive and contentful, but in a pre-theoretical (or
supra-theoretical) mode. But it also *makes claims* about God and his creation (not all
claims need to be construed as propositions). As I address below, there is some sense in
which these confessions, and even the Scriptures themselves, are the *fruit of* theology
in Dooyeweerd's more technical sense. Therefore, we need to consider the relationship
between these more carefully.

100. As such, Dooyeweerd exhibits what Tillich describes as the "Protestant principle,"
which protests against any identification of divinity with finite mediations (as opposed to
the "Catholic substance," which claims that finitude can embody divinity). See Paul Tillich,
Systematic Theology, vol. 3 (Chicago: University of Chicago Press, 1963), 243–45.

101. Dooyeweerd here represents the left wing of the Kuyperian heritage, which is
interested in de-theologizing worldview, thereby "thinning" it out into a simple affirmation of the goodness of creation. This "thinning" of the fundamental confession enables
the left Kuyperian tradition to (over)emphasize commonality and a bastardized notion of
common grace. A more robust, theological account of our fundamental confession tends
to emphasize antithesis.

102. My thanks to Matt Bonzo and John Monda for conversations that helped me
clarify these issues.

Table 2. Confession, Theology, and the Disciplines Revisited

Mathematics *Numeric aspect*	Other special sciences *Other aspects*	Law/Legal Studies *Jural aspect*	Ethics *Moral aspect*	Theology² *Pistic aspect*
Methodology: the philosophy *of* mathematics	Methodology: the philosophy *of* other sciences	Methodology: the philosophy *of* law	Methodology: the philosophy *of* ethics	Methodology: the philosophy *of* theology
Philosophy: ontology, epistemology, relation between totality of aspects				
Ground-Motive (Fundamental Religious Commitments): Theology¹				

The change here involves two things: first, taking seriously the robustness of Christian confession that undergirds theoretical reflection on our being in the world, and second, taking seriously the degree of interaction between theology in its theoretical mode and the church's pre-theoretical confession. I agree with Dooyeweerd's overall picture that all theoretical investigation of the world is ultimately funded by fundamental religious commitments (a worldview or ground-motive), though this structure can take an apostate direction. I also agree with him that we must relativize, to a degree, the work and findings of theoretical theology—I do not think, for instance, that the particular theological theses and investigations of Milbank or Ward are binding for either Christian discipleship or Christian theoretical reflection across the disciplines. Theology as a theoretical discipline should not be erected as queen of the sciences, as RO sometimes suggests. However, when RO calls for a theological account of economics or social theory, what it really means is a confessional account of economics that begins from a Christian worldview. But unlike Dooyeweerd, it wants that Christian worldview to reflect the fullness of Christian reflection—not just the goodness of creation but also the central themes of incarnation, Trinity, and sacramentality.

We can distinguish between theoretical theology (in terms of the theoretical attitude) and theological confession with a simple notation: Theology¹ refers to the fundamental Christian confession affirmed by the church, embodied in Scripture, and articulated in the confessions and creeds; theology² refers to the ongoing work of specifically theoretical, second-order reflection on the church's confession. The latter is undertaken in the theoretical attitude and is not binding in the sense Dooyeweerd suggests; the former is a pre- and supra-theoretical confession and places constraints on the shape of practice, including theoretical practice.[103]

---

103. This should be qualified to indicate that both theology¹ and theology² could also be Islamic, or Jewish, or Buddhist, etc. The structure can take different (and for Dooyeweerd, apostate) directions.

But what is the relationship between theology[1] and theology[2]? And what is the relationship between these theologies and other disciplines? What are we to make, for instance, of Milbank's claim that theology should "position" other discourses and disciplines? The way to understand this—and this is what Milbank is after—is that theology[1] should position all theoretical reflection, including philosophy. To put this slightly differently, theology[1] should function as queen of the sciences but is not itself a science (as is theology[2]). What, then, is the relationship between theology[1] and theology[2]? Dooyeweerd fails to appreciate the degree to which the biblical ground-motive and Christian confession are informed by theology[2], even if the biblical ground-motive is not itself theology[2]. The creeds and confessions of the church—take uncontroversial examples such as the Apostles' or Nicene creeds—are pistically qualified claims of pre- and supra-theoretical confession and practice, but they are the fruit of theological[1] reflection that has been appropriated and "ratified" by the church as articulating its fundamental confession. Theology[2], therefore, ought to be undertaken in the service of the church, and when it is fruitful, it will inform the church's confession articulated in theology[1].[104] It is then theology[1] that functions as the root of Christian theoretical reflection across the disciplines. So when RO, for example, calls for theological economics, it is really calling for theological[1] economics, or what in the Reformational tradition would be described as confessional economics or simply Christian economics. But because RO—and the revised picture suggested here—takes seriously the interplay and interaction between theology[1] and theology[2], its sense of what is included in the church's confession is more robust and substantive, providing a richer fund to support Christian theoretical reflection across the disciplines. In addition, it takes seriously the work of the church as a community—both globally and historically—as the only proper site in which Scripture can be understood and confession properly articulated. As a result, it rejects the latent Gnosticism in Dooyeweerd by embracing the concrete particularity of both Scripture and the church's confessions—as opposed to Dooyeweerd's flight to the mystical as the basis for an invisible ecumenism.[105] The rich confession of the church's faith—rooted in God's revelation in the Word—consti-

104. Here Martin Heidegger's account of philosophy and theology, which bears important similarities to that of Dooyeweerd, is in fact more attentive to the church-oriented nature of theology as a "practical science" that is "'innately' homiletical" (Martin Heidegger, "Phenomenology and Theology," trans. James G. Hart and John C. Maraldo, in *Pathmarks*, ed. William McNeill [Cambridge: Cambridge University Press, 1998], 45–50).

105. See ITWT, 101: "This spiritual basic motive is elevated above all theological controversies and is not in need of theological exegesis, since its radical meaning is exclusively explained by the Holy Spirit operating in our opened hearts, in the communion of

tutes the theology[1] that should shape Christian theoretical investigation of the world, including theology[2].[106] Alternatively, contrary to Milbank, philosophy can be Christian insofar as it is undergirded by theology[1].

The End of Apologetics

If, as both RO and the Reformed tradition claim, knowledge—and even perception—is conditioned by faith (and hence revelation), then "truth claims" cannot be a matter of neutral adjudication. What may appear to be a biblical confidence that the "invisible attributes of God" are clearly seen in creation actually rests on an insufficiently radical hamartiology, for, in fact, the Pauline witness itself indicates that this revelatory structure of creation cannot be recognized by all because sin has marred humanity's natural perceptual abilities (Rom. 1:21–31). As Dooyeweerd summarizes:

> From the very beginning this revelation of God in all the works of his hands was not open to a would-be autonomous human understanding. This *phanerosis*, as it is called in the first chapter of the Epistle to the Romans (1:19), was elucidated and interpreted by the Word of God that addressed itself to the heart of man by mediation of the temporal function of faith. So long as the human heart was open to the Word of God, man was capable of understanding the sense of God's general *phanerosis* by means of his innate function of faith. But as soon as this heart closed itself and turned away from the Word of God as a result of its apostasy, the faith-aspect of the temporal human experience was also closed. It was no longer the window of our temporal experience, open to the light of eternity, but it became the instrument of the spirit of apostasy. Likewise the innate religious impulsion of the human heart to transcend itself in order to find rest in its divine origin began to unfold itself in an idolatrous direction. It is exclusively by the operation of the Holy Spirit which regenerates the heart that the faith aspect of our temporal experience can be re-opened to the Word of God, so that its negative direction is changed into a positive one. (ITWT, 95–96)[107]

---

this Spirit. This is the only really ecumenical basis of the Church of Christ, which in its institutional temporal appearance is otherwise hopelessly divided." One can see how the church plays little role in Dooyeweerd's thought since, if one followed the logic here, not even preaching is really essential.

106. Theology[2] would be "scholastic" or "accomodationist" insofar as it appropriated a philosophical framework rooted in a non-Christian worldview (or theology[1]).

107. Embedded here are the seeds for a critique of Alvin Plantinga's reading of Calvin's notion of the *sensus divinitatis* in *Warranted Christian Belief* (Oxford: Oxford University Press, 2000). Plantinga rightly observes that this is a kind of faculty or "cognitive mechanism" possessed by all (172). But he goes on to suggest that this mechanism "is a disposition

This is why the message of the cross—which is the culmination of the logic of redemption—is a message of foolishness to the Greeks, such that Paul can celebrate Christ as the "foolishness of God" (1 Cor. 1:18–25). Thus, Paul advocates a mode of public engagement that rests not on demonstration but on proclamation, not on a neutral universal *logos* but on a particular, scandalous *kerygma* (1 Cor. 2:1–5). The neutral, autonomous reason that would have to underwrite a project of demonstration has been forfeited by the fall. An important consequence follows: The project of apologetics[108]—especially "classical apologetics"—must be seen as an illegitimate project, illegitimate not because of its goal of witness or proclamation but because of its mode. Even if one suggests that only the "preambles of faith" (such as the existence of God, the necessity of objective moral standards, etc.) can be demonstrated by appeal to a universal, autonomous reason, one has failed to grasp the scope and ubiquity of the fall. One is unwittingly guarding a sphere of creation that is untouched by sin.

RO recognizes that its critique of the autonomy of reason spells the end of apologetics.[109] As Milbank puts it, persuasion cannot be equated with demonstration, since at the level of competing religious commitments (or *mythoi*), demonstration—which requires a common, universal reason—is not possible.[110] "If my Christian perspective is persuasive," he remarks, "then this should be a persuasion intrinsic to the Christian *logos* itself, not the apologetic mediation of a universal human reason" (TST,

---

or set of dispositions to form theistic beliefs in various circumstances, in response to the sorts of conditions or stimuli that trigger the working of this sense of divinity" (173)—in short, that it can produce "in us beliefs about God" (172). As such, Plantinga still seems to construe Calvin's *sensus divinitatis* as if it were a kind of natural knowledge of God, but with merely muffled and distorted deliverances (215). In fact, he suggests that "perhaps in some people at some times, the *sensus divinitatis* doesn't work at all" (215). This indicates a misunderstanding of Calvin. What Calvin points to is a *sensus* divinitatis, not a *sensus* Dei. In other words, there is a structural human propensity to worship a divinity, not to have *some* knowledge of the Creator God. This is precisely why it could never not be operative; it is a structural propensity. If it is not directed toward the Triune Creator, it is misdirected toward an idol.

108. And its analogues, "natural theology" and "fundamental theology."

109. In this discussion, I generally identify "apologetics" with "classical apologetics." One could certainly argue that the "negative apologetics" of both nonfoundationalist Reformed epistemology and the critique of antinomies in Dooyeweerd remain viable after this critique of secular, autonomous reason. Thus, the end of apologetics does not mean the end of "giving reasons" nor the end of critique of other worldviews. I discussed these themes in more detail in *Who's Afraid of Postmodernism? A Radical Orthodoxy for the Emerging Church* (forthcoming).

110. Milbank is asserting a certain incommensurability of language games here. Not surprisingly, Richard Rorty asserted the basic similarity in strategy between his own project and that of Milbank at a session of the AAR in Atlanta, November 2003.

1). By taking us to the level of ground-motive or *mythos*, RO takes us to the site of incommensurability, where the rules of the game differ from *mythos* to *mythos*. Thus, the strategy cannot be one of demonstration but rather one of narration—or, more specifically, *out*-narration. If one is going to oppose the *mythos* of nihilism and original violence, "One's only resort at this juncture, other than mystical despair, is to return to the demonstration that nihilism, as an ontology, is also no more than a *mythos*. To counter it, one cannot resuscitate liberal humanism, but one can try to put forward an alternative *mythos*, equally unfounded, but nonetheless embodying an 'ontology of peace'" (TST, 279).[111]

The first move in this engagement is a leveling of the playing field in which nihilism's secular ontology is unveiled as a *mythos* and thus equal in epistemic status to the Christian *mythos*. The second move is to so narrate this alternative *mythos* as to persuade.[112] Unlike Alasdair Mac-Intyre, who Milbank suggests wants to *argue* against nihilism, Milbank makes the case that nihilism "is only a *mythos*, and therefore cannot be refuted, but only out-narrated, if we can *persuade* people—for reasons of 'literary taste'—that Christianity offers a much better story" (TST, 330). The mode of cultural engagement in the marketplace of ideas, then, is not syllogistic demonstration but narrative persuasion—telling stories.[113] This narrative persuasion, as a "new apologetic,"[114] begins by pointing to the mythical status of competing ontologies and narratives and offers a counter-narrative from the Christian story that is embodied in practice (TST, 388, 398). The church does not *have* an apologetic; it *is* an apologetic.[115]

However, this does not negate the possibility of critique. The focus of critique is on demonstrating the internal antinomies of secular reason (TST, 362–75). Milbank describes this as an immanent critique (TST,

111. This informs Milbank's critique of Alasdair MacIntyre at this stage: "Against Mac-Intyre," he notes, "I simply do not believe that there *are* any arguments against nihilism of this general kind. . . . I do not find him *sufficiently* relativistic or historicist" (TST, 327). In fact, he suggests that one finds in MacIntyre "an apologetic" (328–29). I wonder, however, whether the more recent Milbank (of BR) is not closer to this old MacIntyre.

112. Cf. 1 Cor. 2:1–5.

113. Ward discusses this reality in terms of Michel de Certeau's account of society as a "recited society," defined by the telling and retelling of stories. See Graham Ward, ed., *The Certeau Reader* (Oxford: Blackwell, 2000), 6–7. See also Certeau's essay, "Believing and Making People Believe," 119–28.

114. Robert Webber, *The Younger Evangelicals* (Grand Rapids: Baker, 2002), chap. 6.

115. Webber points out that this "new" apologetic is, in fact, *ancient*: "Tertullian, a church father of the late second century, declared that the pagans were astonished by how Christians related to each other and those outside of their community. In a pagan world where every person 'lives for himself,' the pagans don't cry, 'Look at the power of their rational arguments' but 'See how they love one another!'" (ibid., 95).

389). The point is that because secular accounts do not properly recognize the status of the world as creation, their framework is plagued with tensions and contradictions that can be demonstrated *ad absurdium*. Here Milbank's account remarkably parallels the accounts of "new apologists" in the Reformed tradition, such as Dooyeweerd (who analyzed the inner antinomies of apostate ground-motives), Cornelius Van Til, and Francis Schaeffer.[116]

It is its refusal of apologetics that allows RO to get beyond the methodological fixation (that characterizes so much of contemporary theology) to actual witness and proclamation—to the articulation of unapologetic Christian theory and practice. As Ward concludes, by providing an account of the mythological grounding of even secular discourse, RO shows that "theological discourse here is in no worse a predicament than any other cultural activity. In fact, what theological discourse is able to do is construct a theological argument for why this must be so" (CG, 74). Thus, in Ward's constructive theological work, "a certain story is being told, a certain act of persuasion is underway, employing the grammar of the Christian faith, expounding the theologic which relates anthropology to the body of Christ, the Eucharistic body to the civic and social bodies" (CG, 74). The result is an ontology and politics that are unapologetically Christian.

Inverting the Emperor's Tale: Political Spaces for Confessional Voices

Modernity, particularly in its liberal polity and secularizing tendencies, is characterized by a deep denuding of our social embodiment and practices. If we take the model sketched by John Rawls as an example, entry into public discourse and practice requires a high price of admission, for this public space is found only behind the veil of ignorance. To pass through this curtain, one must disrobe himself or herself, leaving behind the particularities of his or her vision of the good, deep moral commitments, and theological confession. Once denuded, that person is able to pass through the veil and into the "naked public square" of the original position, governed only by rationality.[117] As Ward observes, in moder-

116. See, for example, Francis Schaeffer, "The Question of Apologetics," in *Trilogy* (Wheaton: Crossway, 1990), 175–87. Schaeffer echoes the claim that the church *is* an apologetic in section VI of *The God Who Is There*, in *Trilogy*, 163–74.

117. See John Rawls, *A Theory of Justice* (Cambridge: Harvard University Press, 1971), 136–39, 399–407. For discussion, see John Neuhaus, *Naked Public Square* (Grand Rapids: Eerdmans, 1984); Richard J. Mouw and Sander Griffioen, *Pluralism and Horizons: An*

nity, even religion itself is denuded of concretion and particularity (TR, 76–81)—which is why proposals for a supposedly postmodern "religion without religion" do nothing to subvert the modern logic of secularity.

But it is precisely here that the preceding discussion bears public or political fruit. The *telos* of the discussion in this chapter is not merely dogmatic or internal to the ecclesial community; rather, the implication is political: If all voices are at root confessional or theological[1], then even the mode of discourse that parades itself as public or secular or rational is, in fact, confessional. The story, therefore, is a kind of inversion of the emperor's tale: What we get in the supposedly "naked public square" is, in fact, a number of skin-colored costumes. The Reformed and RO critiques of secular reason are akin to the child in the earlier tale, but now the child unabashedly observes, "Look, the secularist *has* clothes on!" Thus, when Milbank poses the question, "Is it not outrageous for a political discourse to appeal directly to the theological (which for many people simply represents the fantastic and unbelievable)?" his immediate response is, "No, because it has already been seen how the secular sustains a certain equally 'irrational' and yet nihilistic variant of the theological" (BR, 171). If the secular project has sought to marginalize confessional voices because they are theological—and therefore *not* rational—then the unveiling of secular reason's own theological[1] commitments undercuts the very project of the secular.[118] This should level the playing field in such a way that distinctly confessional voices are no longer muted, because if that were the case, *all* voices would be muted.

However, while this epistemological critique of the secular means that confessional voices must be admitted into the public square, we should not immediately conclude that this is just another way to underwrite the culture wars. In other words, the unveiling of the fact that the emperor of the supposedly naked public square has clothes on should not be seen, according to RO, as an occasion for trying to costume the emperor in Christian vestments. To understand this, we revisit the question of politics in terms of the *ecclesia* in chapter 7.

Essay in Christian Public Philosophy (Grand Rapids: Eerdmans, 1993); and Stephen L. Carter, *The Culture of Disbelief: How American Law and Politics Trivialize Religious Devotion* (New York: Basic Books, 1993).

118. I do not mean to argue for a specific version of the "secularization thesis" currently contested in sociology. For two recent defenses of nuanced versions of secularization theory in sociology, see Christian Smith, ed., *The Secular Revolution: Power, Interests, and Conflict in the Secularization of American Public Life* (Berkeley: University of California Press, 2003), 1–32; and Steve Bruce, *God Is Dead: Secularization in the West* (Oxford: Blackwell, 2002). Gianno Vattimo argues that secularization is, in fact, the *telos* of biblical revelation unveiled by a "spiritualization of the biblical message" (*After Christianity*, trans. Luca D'Isanto [New York: Columbia University Press, 2002], 45–48).

6

Participation and Incarnation

Materiality, Liturgy, and Sacramentality

Related Reading

Milbank, John. "Materialism and Transcendence." In *Theology and the Political*, edited by Creston Davis, John Milbank, and Slavoj Žižek. Durham, N.C.: Duke University Press, 2004.

———, and Catherine Pickstock. "Truth and Vision." Chap. 2 in *Truth in Aquinas*. London: Routledge, 2001.

Pickstock, Catherine. "Socrates Goes Outside the City." Chap. 1 in *After Writing: On the Liturgical Consummation of Philosophy*. Oxford: Blackwell, 1998.

Ward, Graham. "Transcorporeality: The Ontological Scandal." Chap. 3 in *Cities of God*. London: Routledge, 2000.

Radical Orthodoxy articulates a radical (i.e., root-targeted) critique of secular modernity (chap. 4) by calling into question its attendant epistemology (chap. 5). But ultimately, for RO, the unwarranted epistemology of secular modernity is generated by an ontological framework that must be called into question, an ontology grounded in the univocity of being that grants an autonomy to things such that it is supposed that the world can be properly understood in itself—that is, without reference to its transcendent origin, the Creator. (A secular reason, which closes off transcendence, is thought to be able to grasp reality without needing to make reference beyond the closed system of "the world." The root of both RO's critique of secular modernity and the articulation of its alternative theological[1] vision are found at the level of ontology. In opposition to the ontology of immanence produced by the shift to the univocity of being, RO proposes a *participatory* ontology that understands transcendence as an essential feature of material reality.

This chapter first explores RO's articulation of this participatory ontology and then considers some Reformational reservations with such a project. It concludes by briefly considering two important implications of this participatory ontology: its (re)affirmation of a liturgical, sacramental worldview and its attendant affirmation of the aesthetic aspect of creation and hence the arts.

Suspending the Material: On Participation

One of the most refreshing aspects of RO is its unabashed and shameless affirmation of the project of metaphysics, despite all the supposedly postmodern talk of "the end of metaphysics" in the wake of Nietzsche, Heidegger, and Derrida.[1] While RO is suspicious of what Heidegger describes as the totalizing project of "onto-theo-logy," adherents do not conclude that this means abandoning the project of ontology altogether (WMS, 44–45).[2] Indeed, how could we ever theorize without a metaphysics—an understanding of the nature of being and reality?[3] Moreover, RO takes seriously the notion that ideas have legs and that the contemporary cultural milieu is very much the product of ontological shifts that have taken place in modernity.[4] Thus, if we are to counter secular modernity's politics and epistemology, we must begin with a *counter*-ontology (TST, 422–32).

As shown in chapter 3, RO offers a genealogy that provides an account of the way in which the world has been flattened to a sheer immanence (and thus unhooked from its dependence on a transcen-

1. For an account that sees Heidegger continuing the project of classical metaphysics in different form, see Matthew Halteman, *The Problem of Transcendence in Heidegger and Derrida* (Ph.D. diss., University of Notre Dame, 2003), chaps. 2–3.

2. In the midst of Milbank's polemics regarding the "overcoming of metaphysics" (WMS) or the evacuation of philosophy, he qualifies this by noting that "the 'object' of Philosophy—being—is not denied; rather it is argued, after Jacobi, that a philosophical treatment of being on its own, or the search simply to know being by reason, will reach aporetic and nihilistic conclusions" (RONT, 37n49). As noted above, Milbank here (unjustifiably) equates philosophy with autonomy, confusing structure and direction.

3. Here it is curious that (biblicist) Open theists such as John Sanders and Gregory Boyd also speak in terms that suggest we need to construct theology *without* metaphysics—where metaphysics is understood to be inherently Greek. But that is to confuse a particular *direction* metaphysics has taken with the *structure* of metaphysical reflection as such. As RO suggests, one can generate a *biblical* metaphysics, whereas Open theists tend to oppose Scripture and metaphysics.

4. One can find a similar analysis in Jean-Luc Marion, *The Crossing of the Visible*, trans. James K. A. Smith (Stanford: Stanford University Press, 2004), chap. 3, where Marion traces the current status of the "self-as-image" to a nihilist ontology.

dent Creator) or "closed" as an autonomous system (and thus closed off to the transcendent). According to this genealogy, this flattening or closure was the result of an ontological shift (which RO sees in Scotus) whereby created reality was seen as having a mode of being in itself such that it could be understood without reference to the transcendent Creator—without theology[1] (WMS, 44). The result was an "autonomous 'metaphysics,' later to become 'ontology,' which claims to be able fully to define the conditions of finite knowability, or to arrive at possible being as something 'in itself'" (WMS, 44). In other words, modernity assumes that it can properly understand the world without the theological[1] lens of revelation;[5] moreover, when the world is thus understood "neutrally," it is taken to be a flattened reality without reference or index to the transcendent. This results in what Catherine Pickstock describes as the "spatialization" of the world, whereby the world is reduced to a geometrical *mathesis* in Ramus and Descartes (AW, 52). Modernity, then, is a kind of new sophistry characterized by an expanded "immanentism"[6] that rejects the liturgical and doxological character of the world and is characterized by "an increasing denial of genuine transcendence, understood as doxological reliance upon a donating source which one cannot command" (AW, 49). This spatialization is the result of an "absolutization" (to use Herman Dooyeweerd's term) of space and time (AW, 49); thus, the "Cartesian city" is "entirely predictable because [it is] immunized against new arrivals in time" and "totalized in order to be defensible. This double circumstance amounts to spatialization, since time is neutralized, and all is ordered and surveyable without remainder, within absolute borders" (AW, 60). This absolutization, therefore, takes an aspect of creation and erects it as if it were uncreated, objectifying being as something in itself. Thus, "Descartes transforms the determinations of reality into purely spatial classifications, as the 'given' rather than the gift of a donor through which the transcendent is mediated" (AW, 62). By means of "an ontology prised away from theology," Descartes "consummates a movement which separates being from its donating source by taking Being to be, first

5. Milbank (WMS, 44; RONT, 23) and Pickstock (AW, 64) both claim that this results from Scotus's separation of ontology from theology such that ontology becomes an autonomous discipline "without reference to God." What they mean by this is that Scotus's account of the univocity of Being suggests that one can understand "being" and "the world" without reference to revelation (or theology[1]). They would be equally critical of "theistic ontologies," which suggest that there is a kind of neutral reference to a "theistic" origin in ontology. Here it becomes clear that theology[1] is robust enough to be distinctly Christian and trinitarian and therefore is dependent on special revelation.

6. Cf. Dooyeweerd on "immanence philosophy" (NC, I:12–21).

of all, not the divine gift of participation in a plenitude of infinite actuality, but rather the mere inert *given* of a contentless 'notion' of existence univocally common to the finite and the infinite" (AW, 64). Now construed as merely "given," reality is left without depth. But it is precisely here that Pickstock locates modernity's nihilism: "In spite of this gesture to secure the object, there is, after all, something nihilistic about the Cartesian 'given' which at once contradicts and fulfills the project of the universal mathematics, for, as I shall show, it is above all 'nothing' which fulfills the criteria of clarity and distinctness" (AW, 64). All that we are left with are anticipations of Gilles Deleuze, with an "epistemological virtual reality" (AW, 64) in which reality is reduced to an image without depth and thus merely a flattened world of simulacra.

As a result of this ontology of immanence (which also understands the differences within this immanent plane as only oppositionally related), modernity generates anthropologies of immanence that no longer see humanity as ek-statically constituted, desiring and bound to pursue a transcendent *telos*. Rather, human beings are mere bundles of empirical memories (David Hume) or the nexus of immanent forces at play (Deleuze). As a result, notions of human community reduce intersubjective relations to flattened, immanent relations of power, a picture already presaged in Thomas Hobbes and Benedict Spinoza but culminating in the accounts of Deleuze and Foucault (TST, 313–21). But here we also see all three levels of RO's *countering strategy:* RO counters secular modernity's account of the essential war-of-all-with-all nature of social relationships and its flattened notion of human nature by getting to the root of both: the ontology of immanence that closes down the ecstatic and dependent nature of created reality in its relationship to the transcendent.

In the face of the ontology of immanence and its attendant anthropology and sociology, RO proposes an ontology of participation that is attended by an ek-static, transcendence-oriented anthropology and an account of social relationships that begins with peace. The concern here is threefold: (1) to articulate an ontology of depth that recognizes the dependence of the creation on the Creator and affirms immanence as such; (2) to develop an anthropology that grows out of this ontology that both recognizes the supernatural *telos* of human be-ing and affirms our essential embodiment; and (3) to provide an account of sociality and intersubjective relationships that is oriented around charity, not power. One important way that RO has articulated this counter-ontology is in terms of "the suspension of the material" (RONT, 1–5). While the language of suspension may suggest a certain extrinsic relationship between the transcendent and the immanent,[7] this is not RO's intention. Rather, it contends that "only transcendence, which 'suspends' things in the sense of interrupting them, 'suspends' them also in the other sense of upholding their relative worth over-against the void" (RONT, 3). The targets or effects of such an affirmation are twofold: On the one hand, it refuses the secular and nihilism because it sees *all* as participating in the divine and thus only properly understood and inhabited in light of that participation; on the other hand, it also "reenvisions" a "Christianity which *never* sufficiently valued the mediating participatory sphere which can alone lead us to God" (RONT, 3). A participatory ontology, then, is the antidote to both nihilism and fundamentalist dualism. This is because these phenomena are, ontologically, mirror images of each other. In other words, the supposed affirmation of materialism that characterizes ontologies of immanence (Nietzsche, Deleuze) actually ends up devaluing the material by means of another dualism: "It is immanence that is dualistic and tends to remove the mysterious diversity of matter in assuming that appearances do not exceed themselves" (RONT, 4). No longer appearances *of* a transcendent original or prototype, they are no longer "appearances" at all. By contrast:

> The theological perspective of participation actually saves the appearances by exceeding them. It recognizes that materialism and spiritualism are false alternatives, since if there is only finite matter there is not even that, and that for phenomena really to be there they must be more than there. . . . This is to say that all there is *only* is because it is more than it is. (RONT, 4)

A participatory ontology, then, actually engenders a "theological materialism."[8] The following unpacks this counter-ontology in two modes: first, in its affirmation of materiality, and second, in its unique account of difference.

Counter-Ontology 1: Materialism and Transcendence

A recent rearticulation of this participatory framework reminds us that, in a sense, the *telos* of these ontological investigations is political. In "Mate-

---

7. "Suspension" could convey a pendulum-like picture whereby the created order "hangs" from the Creator in a somewhat distant relationship. RO, in contrast, is concerned to provide an account of the way in which the immanent *participates* in transcendence (and vice versa). As such, there is a certain sense of "inherence" rather than extrinsic relation. However, RO employs the term *suspension* also to emphasize a sense of *interruption*. My thanks to Terence Cuneo for discussions on this point.

8. Cf. Graham Ward, "Theological Materialism," in *God and Reality: Essays on Christian Non-realism*, ed. Colin Crowder (London: Mowbray, 1997), 144–59.

rialism and Transcendence," Milbank begins by asserting that every politics presupposes (and needs) an ontology.[9] Nihilist ontologies (whether idealist or materialist) suffice for capitalism, but socialism, Milbank contends, needs something else: a nonreductive materialism[10]—materialist because it is concerned with embodied, material reality and distributions; nonreductive because only transcendence can make immanence to be immanence as such. In other words, only when immanence is "suspended" from transcendence does it make sense to speak about freedom and liberation, subjectivity and meaning. The context here is important. Milbank's essay was written in the wake of Michael Hardt and Antonio Negri's *Empire*, a call for a new Deleuzian socialism that received a great deal of attention. Milbank agrees that we should work for a socialist construction of the political but argues that Hardt and Negri[11] cannot have what they want unless they adopt a more robust ontology—or, more specifically, a theology (theology[1]). Why? Because only theology can provide a nonreductive materialist ontology rooted in the doctrine of creation (and incarnation). Materialisms currently on offer—whether Marxist, Deleuzean, or neo-Darwinian—end up reductionistic (as do all ontologies of immanence) because in them "matter is totally etherealized and idealized" such that these materialisms actually create a new idealism[12] in which "real material processes become epiphenomena of logical processes, or else the magical outcome of pure willing." "If this is reality, then it is capitalism that gets nearest to acknowledging it without ever quite doing so, since it reduces the meaningful goal to an *agon* round an empty fetish."[13] If all we have is "pagan immanence" and all that characterizes immanence is a play of forces, then the socialist call for justice or the regulation of forces runs counter to the very ontology that contemporary Marxists adopt. Hence, Milbank states, "An ontology that legitimated socialism would have to discover a way of locating ideality in matter without idealizing matter away, nor finally canceling ideality."[14] Only Christian theology, Milbank argues, can offer such an ontology: "The

9. John Milbank, "Materialism and Transcendence," in *Theology and the Political*, ed. Creston Davis, John Milbank, and Slavoj Žižek (Durham, N.C.: Duke University Press, forthcoming). (I will be citing an unpublished manuscript version of Milbank's essay.)

10. Or, in other words, "Marxism, and indeed every socialism, requires an account of human nature" (ibid., 1).

11. Michael Hardt and Antonio Negri, *Empire* (Cambridge: Harvard University Press, 2001).

12. This is also why, according to Milbank, "recent secular attempts to develop a materialist ontology which will undergird socialist aspirations have had recourse to appeal to theology: to notions of the *via negativa*, of the absolutely other, of grace, hope, and *agape*" (Milbank, "Materialism and Transcendence," 2). Milbank has in mind figures such as Jacques Derrida, Slavoj Žižek, and Alain Badiou.

13. Ibid., 3.

14. Ibid.

theological appeal to transcendence alone sustains a non-reductive materiality and is the very reverse of any notion of idealism."[15] Milbank's strategy constitutes something of a negative apologetic: While he ultimately wants to articulate a participatory ontology because it is the picture given by revelation, in his dialogue with post-Marxist socialism, he tries to show the way in which thought that wants to be secular and immanentist actually needs theology[1] to achieve what it wants.[16]

The shape of this theological[1] or participatory ontology is nonreductive and incarnational: On the one hand, it affirms that matter as created exceeds itself and "is" only insofar as it participates in or is suspended from the transcendent Creator; on the other hand, it affirms that there is a significant sense in which the transcendent inheres in immanence.[17] This is why, as we saw in chapter 3, RO understands this basically as a Platonic ontology, particularly as mediated through the tradition of theurgical Neoplatonism (Iamblichus, Proclus) and later Cambridge Platonism—though it ultimately wants to affirm that this is a biblical model.[18] Things, then—and the created order in general—do not have any kind of sheer or autonomous existence, as if possessing some kind of inalienable right to be. Rather, being is a gift from the transcendent Creator such that things exist only insofar as they participate in the being of the Creator—whose being is goodness. Within this framework, the vocation of things is both imitation and reference[19]—"the paradox

15. Ibid., 4. In TA, this framework is described as a "theontology" (TA, 35, 44, 47, 51).

16. Cf. RONT, 4: "In a bizarre way, it seems that modernity does not really want which it thinks it wants; but, on the other hand, in order to have what it thinks it wants, it would have to recover the theological."

17. Insofar as this is predicated upon a robust theology of creation *ex nihilo,* this cannot be criticized as a panentheism; rather, it would seem to have the same ambiguities that attend Jonathan Edwards's orthodox (though quite Platonic) ontology. My thanks to John Bolt for conversations on this point. Robert W. Jensen also rejects the label of panentheist for Edwards because Edwards rejects the in/out distinction of panentheism and replaces it "with a biblical way of conceiving our otherness from God. God wills to know a world, and this world rather than some other; thus the world is willed reality and God is reality that does not need to be willed" (*On Thinking the Human* [Grand Rapids: Eerdmans, 2003], 50–52).

18. These assertions of the biblical filiation of participation have been more recent. For example, Pickstock claims that "participation is not merely a 'Greek' thesis alien to the Biblical legacy; it is a framework perfectly compatible with free creation *ex nihilo*" ("Modernity and Scholasticism: A Critique of Recent Invocations of Univocity," *Antonianum* 78 [2003]: 22, citing 2 Pet. 1:4, where we are said to be "sharers in the divine nature"). So also Milbank asserts that "*methexis* is logically more Biblical than Hellenic" (BR, 115) and suggests that "St Paul with self-conscious irony proclaimed *methexis* to the Athenians (Acts 17)" (BR, 114).

19. On the latter point, the centrality of typology and semiotics in Jonathan Edwards's theology is an important point of parallel between RO and the Reformed tradition (Jona-

of the natural orientation to the supernatural" (BR, 115). As Milbank and Pickstock summarize with respect to Aquinas:

> Aquinas seems to suggest that when one knows a thing, one does not know that thing as it is by itself, but only insofar as one meaningfully grasps it as imitating God. How very odd this seems, for one would normally regard imitation as a secondary and therefore less authentic operation of life, but here it becomes the highest form of authenticity attainable for material things. However, the placing of imitation ahead of autonomy suggests that, for Aquinas, borrowing is the highest authenticity which can be attained. One must copy in order to be, and one continues only as a copy, never in one's own right. (TA, 10)[20]

Within a Christian theological framework—as distinguished from a merely Platonic notion of *methexis*—this relationship of dependence of the creation on the Creator could be described in terms of a grace or giftedness: "One could interpret this to mean that, for Aquinas (and here we press perhaps beyond the *nouvelle théologie*), all creatures subsist by grace *in the sense that* they only subsist in their constant 'return' to full divine self-presence" (TA, 37–38). "Everything is therefore 'engraced'" (BR, 115). In this way, a participatory ontology is, at root, an affirmation of the goodness of creation (TA, 41).

Just as only transcendence can properly retain the depth of immanence, so also only transcendence can properly value embodiment. Therefore, despite postmodern philosophy's talk about the body, Milbank criticizes it (in Derrida, Deleuze, Alain Badiou, and Slavoj Žižek) for being ultimately Gnostic.[21] In Deleuze's and Guattari's celebration of the plane of immanence alone, we have "a 'reduced' matter once more," for "to lose the human is here to lose the body"—in the sense that a body is only properly a body when animated by a soul; otherwise it is a corpse.[22] Therefore, "it is also not surprising that Deleuze and Guattari celebrate machines, albeit 'abstract ones,' reduced to 'matter

---

than Edwards, *Typological Writings*, ed. Wallace E. Anderson and Mason I. Lowance Jr. [New Haven: Yale University Press, 1993]). See also Stephen H. Daniel, *The Philosophy of Jonathan Edwards: Divine Semiotics* (Indianapolis: Indiana University Press, 1994) for an interesting discussion on Edwards's semiotics. My thanks to Jerry Stutzman for his work on these matters.

20. One can already discern an ethical and political trajectory here: Rather than valuing the autonomy and freedom of liberal invention, this ontology privileges imitation and formation according to a *telos* determined by the Creator (cf. Stanley Hauerwas).

21. Milbank, "Materialism and Transcendence," 11, 28.

22. Ibid., 13. Cf. John Milbank, "Beauty and the Soul," in John Milbank, Graham Ward, and Edith Wyschogrod, *Theological Perspectives on God and Beauty* (Harrisburg, Pa.: Trinity Press International, 2003).

and function' so avidly, for the abstraction does not render the machine less purely material: to the contrary, as in the case of the Cartesian reduction of physical space to geometrical space, the ordinary physical machine without a unifying *eidos* or directive *telos* is already an abstract machine for just this reason."[23] Without an ek-static *telos,* and thus without transcendence, these human bodies are not even bodies. Invoking the tradition of Cambridge Platonism, Pickstock appeals to Ralph Cudworth, who "re-invoked the Platonic participation of the material in the psuchic [*sic*] which alone sustains its full materiality. Now, as in the seventeenth century, it needs to be affirmed that the problem with any mere materialism or functionalism is that it always reduces matter, and leaves it as less than it intuitively appears to be."[24] Thus, RO suggests that only a participatory ontology—nourished by the theological[1] doctrines of creation and resurrection—can properly nourish the affirmation of embodiment that postmodernism so often pretends to assert, for only orthodox Christian theology is able to resist the Gnosticism that plagues both fundamentalism and postmodernism.

The most radical way to articulate this participation is in RO's persistent assertion that "'in itself' matter is nothing"[25]—echoing Augustine's assertion that "matter participates in something belonging to the ideal world, otherwise it would not be matter."[26] This is most consistently developed in Graham Ward's account of materiality and embodiment. Because of the "nothingness" of creation (in itself), as Ward puts it, "nature cannot be natural without the spiritual informing it at every point" (CG, 88).[27] Thus, only the suspension of the material from the ideal or transcendent is able to guard the material from nothingness, from dissolving into the *nihil*. In other words, if one really wants to value immanence, it must be suspended from the transcendent; if one wants to valorize appearances, one can do so only by exceeding them. But if one does this, then materiality loses its autonomy and the *stasis*

23. Milbank, "Materialism and Transcendence," 13.

24. Catherine Pickstock, "The Soul in Plato," in *Explorations in Contemporary Continental Philosophy of Religion,* ed. Deane-Peter Baker and Patrick Maxwell (New York: Rodopi, 2003), 125. For further discussion of Ralph Cudworth on these matters, see Edmund Newey, "The Form of Reason: Participation in the Work of Richard Hooker, Benjamin Whichcote, Ralph Cudworth, and Jeremy Taylor," *Modern Theology* 18 (2002): 1–26.

25. Milbank, "Materialism and Transcendence," 21. This is also what underwrites Conor Cunningham's claim in *Genealogy of Nihilism* (London: Routledge, 2002) that, ironically, nihilism is a kind of preamble to orthodox Christian theology (chap. 10).

26. Augustine, *De vera religione* 11.21, cited by Michael Hanby, *Augustine and Modernity,* Radical Orthodoxy (London: Routledge, 2003), 87. Hanby later glosses Augustine's claim by arguing that "apart from participation in this gift, there is finally nothing" (90).

27. I hope to explain below why such a participatory ontology can slide toward an occasionalism (Malebranche) versus the integrity of creation (Leibniz).

that is often accorded to it. For Ward, the material is subject to a kind of semiotic ordering: "Since none of us has access to bodies *as* such, only to bodies that are mediated through the giving and receiving of signs, the series of displacements or assumptions of Jesus's body" entails a revised ontology. This is what Ward describes as "the ontological scandal" of the Words of Institution, "this is my body"—"the scandal of that 'is'" (CG, 82). Ward's ontology is radically orthodox because it seeks to provide an ontological account of the world "from that which has been revealed" (CG, 83). "What does that ontological scandal in that upper room announce about bodies? What kind of bodies occupy what kind of spaces and in what kind of relationships to other such bodies" (CG, 83)?[28]

As illustrated in the Eucharistic pronouncement, for Ward, "bodies here are frangible, permeable; not autonomous and self-defining, but sharing and being shared. . . . This is the ontological scandal announced by the Eucharistic phase—bodies are never simply there (or here)" (CG, 91).[29] In this model, he draws on Gregory of Nyssa, who, in *The Life of Moses*, asserts that "none of those things which are apprehended by sense perception and contemplated by the understanding really subsists, but only the transcendent cause of the universe, on which everything depends. For even if the understanding looks upon any other existing things (*ousin*), reason observes in absolutely none of them the self-sufficiency by which they could exist without the participation in true being" (CG, 90). If one begins with a radical sense of creation's dependence or gift-character, then the autonomous *stasis* of materiality must be revised in such a way that this ontological scandal of the Eucharistic pronouncement can be absorbed—just as the doctrines of Christ's bodily resurrection and ascension must entail a distinctly Christian ontology of materiality (CG, 91–93). Hence, "there is only one radical critique of modernity—the critique that denies the existence of the secular as self-subsisting, that immanent self-ordering of the world which ultimately had no need for God. . . . The Christian doctrines of incarnation and creation stand opposed to closed, immanentalist systems" (CG, 94). Thus, to counter the politics and epistemology of secular modernity, one must subject its ontology to critique (and unveil its status as a *mythos*), then

28. If this seems too fanciful to some, perhaps it would be helpful to put it this way: Ward wants to generate an ontology of materiality that can do justice to the Eucharistic claim that "this is my body." If our ontology—our account of "being"—cannot do justice to this "is" and "body," then we are working with an ontology that is not radically Christian.

29. Ward assumes a transubstantionist model of the Eucharist here and explicitly criticizes Calvin on this score (CG, 161–67), but he interprets Calvin as if he were a nominalist and a Zwinglian. I would argue that Calvin's doctrine of (a kind of) real presence sustains something close to the picture Ward offers here.

articulate the only counter-ontology that can do justice to materiality and embodiment as such.

Counter-Ontology 2: Difference and Peace

In addition to RO's theontological grounding of the affirmation of materiality and embodiment, its counter-ontology has one other important feature: a way of thinking and evaluating *difference* not open to secularity. This is particularly important given all the celebration of difference that apparently motivates postmodern thought from Derrida and Levinas to Deleuze and Foucault. But here again, RO's critique is subversive and refuses to accept the claims of postmodernism, for according to RO's account, what we get in postmodern philosophies of difference are, in fact, philosophies of sameness that either are not able to think difference (because they are locked within a plane of immanence and are thus ultimately a monism) or are forced to conceive of differences as only oppositionally related because they have only the resources of a flattened monism on which to draw—even if it is a "dualism-within-monism," as Conor Cunningham suggests.[30] As such, the plane of immanence can only be a realm of essential violence.

This aspect of RO's ontology—and ontological critique of (post)modernity—goes back to Milbank's early analysis in TST. In Derrida, Deleuze, and Foucault—stemming from Nietzsche—Milbank locates what could be described as a "differential ontology" or even an "ontology of violence." Within an ontology of immanence, differences are construed as competing and thus ultimately oppositional: Being reduces to war. Without recourse to a notion of analogical relation, immanentist ontologies conceive of difference in terms of opposition and thus assume a kind of primordial violence in the order of being. Reality is seen as inherently "conflictual" (TST, 296), and thus all relationships are but war by another means (TST, 282). By subscribing to an original or transcendental violence, these ontologies of immanence end up ontologizing the fall as a structural feature of finite existence (TST, 302).

But here Milbank argues that this "differential ontology is but one more *mythos*. . . . To counter it, one cannot resuscitate liberal humanism, but one can try to put forward an alternative *mythos,* equally unfounded, but nonetheless embodying an 'ontology of peace,' which conceives differences as analogically related, rather than equivocally at variance" (TST, 279). Thus, one can legitimately protest and call into question the supposed rationality of the secular paradigm. As Milbank

---

30. Cunningham, *Genealogy of Nihilism,* 236.

asks, "Does one need to interpret every disturbance, every event, as an event of war? Only, I would argue, if one has transcendentally understood all differences as negatively related. . . . If one makes no such presupposition, then it would be possible to understand the act of affirmative difference, in its passing over to the other, as an invitation to the other to embrace this difference because of its objective desirability" (TST, 289). Such "an 'analogical relation' is *as possible* a transcendental conception as the positing of an *a priori* warfare" (TST, 289). In other words, the ontological claims regarding both univocity and original violence are theological[1] claims that can be rejected in favor of a different theology[1] that—though "equally unfounded" (in the sense of a universal, rational demonstration)—may be better able to do justice to the arena of our experience and avoid the "antinomies" of secular reason (TST, 362ff.).[31] "By exposing the critical non-necessity of the reading of reality as conflictual, and the hopelessly metaphysical nature of even *this* ontology, an alternative possibility of reading reality as itself peaceful is gradually opened to view" (TST, 296).

Rather than beginning from an assumption regarding original violence, a Christian ontology—rooted in theology[1]—begins from the confession of an original peace that understands difference as analogically related. Thus, one finds in Christianity the "precise opposite of nihilism—a creed which rigorously excludes all violence from its picture of the original, intended, and final state of the cosmos" (TST, 288). This stems first from the doctrine of the Trinity, the *arche* in which we confess "a multiple which is not set dialectically over against the one, but itself manifests unity" (TST, 376).[32] Christian revelation of the Trinity, then, enables an utterly singular account of difference not available to secular modernity or nihilism. But this peaceable account of difference as harmoniously related is also affirmed in the doctrine of creation, where an order of multiplicity and difference is pronounced "good" (Gen. 1:31). Violence and oppositional relations are not inscribed into the structure of creation but rather befell creation with the fall.[33]

---

31. The point is that, though Milbank's account is nonfoundationalist, it is not without warrant.

32. See also Milbank, "The Second Difference," in WMS. In my own *Speech and Theology: Language and the Logic of Incarnation*, Radical Orthodoxy (London: Routledge, 2002), I argue that the incarnation is also a site where we see the distinctly Christian articulation of an analogical account of difference (chap. 5).

33. The difference between these competing ontologies is illustrated in the conclusion of the film *The Mission*. After a horrific slaughter of natives sanctioned by church and government, the cardinal is moved to tears by sorrow. The Portuguese governor attempts to assuage his despair by reminding him, "We live in the world; the world is thus." "No, Señor Hantab," the cardinal replies, "thus have we *made* the world. Thus have *I* made it."

Following Augustine, we must read war "as an absolute intrusion, an ontological anomaly" (TST, 294) and not reify or ontologize such in our ontologies.[34] If violence is ontologized, then, in fact, it cannot be resisted or eradicated—only minimized. But a specifically Christian onto-logic affirms both a peaceful origin and a peaceful eschaton.

A Reformed Caveat: The Goodness of Creation and Plato Revisited

RO's participatory ontology finds deep resonance with the Reformed tradition's affirmation of the goodness of creation and its long-standing critique of fundamentalist dualism. However, the tradition does have two reservations or sets of questions related to this central ontological piece of the RO picture.

As noted above (and in chap. 3), one of the central themes of RO is the articulation of a participatory ontology (and theology) that is at once "more incarnate" and "more Platonic" (RONT, 3). To Reformed ears, those two things sound mutually exclusive. The first criticism, therefore, addresses the Reformed allergy to Platonism to elicit the response of Radical Orthodoxy and to generate a dialogue on this question.

Without wanting to slip into theological autobiography, I must confess that my own "Reformed" critique of Platonism stems from a strange alchemy, the product of a kind of chemical reaction whose reagents are Protestant fundamentalism and Nietzsche. The Protestant fundamentalism of my early Christian formation[35] was characterized by what I would come to describe—following in the wake of Kuyper and Dooyeweerd—as dualism.[36] While dualism can refer to an oppositional bifurcation between

---

34. Critics have been confused by Milbank's claim regarding the priority of an "ontology of peace" and its link to Augustine (e.g., Dodaro). Augustine did not exactly advocate peace when it came to the Donatists, these critics retort. But this is to miss the point: Milbank's ontology of peace does not deny the reality of violence nor even the *justification* of violence. Unlike Hauerwas, Milbank is not a pacifist and certainly is not claiming that Augustine was. See John Milbank, "Violence: Double Passivity," in *Must Christianity Be Violent?* ed. Kenneth R. Chase and Alan Jacobs (Grand Rapids: Brazos, 2003), 183–200 (now BR, chap. 2), along with the exchange between Milbank and Hauerwas (207–23).

35. Below I note that this different horizon—and hence different "enemy"—explains the difference of emphasis between RO and aspects of the Reformed tradition. If one is battling Gnostic escapism, then Plato still seems infected with the worst of diseases. If, however, one is battling naturalistic materialism, then Plato can seem a powerful antidote and ally.

36. For representative discussions of dualism, see Brian J. Walsh and J. Richard Middleton, *The Transforming Vision: Shaping a Christian Worldview* (Downers Grove, Ill.: InterVarsity, 1984), 91–116; Albert M. Wolters, *Creation Regained: Biblical Basics for a*

sacred and secular, I have been particularly concerned with a (related) more docetic dualism that erects a hierarchical and oppositional bifurcation between the immaterial and the material, the soul and the body, the invisible and the visible. In broad segments of the evangelical tradition, this Gnostic dualism has translated into a denigration of modes of creaturely life linked to embodiment and finitude, such as sexuality or the arts. Fundamentalism is a kind of transcendent(al)ism.[37] As such, it parallels the Platonism that Nietzsche criticizes in *The Twilight of the Idols:* Both Christianity and Platonism, for Nietzsche, take "the same negative stance toward life"; both are characterized by a decadence that seeks escape from the world of bodies and smells, instincts and passions.[38] Both evangelical Christianity and Nietzsche's Platonism cry out, "And above all, away with the *body!*"[39]

One of the central themes of the continental Reformed tradition is a holistic affirmation of the goodness of creation and materiality, which thus also affirms those spheres and modes of life associated with creaturely embodiment (the arts, sociopolitical engagement, etc.). As a result, the Reformed tradition has articulated a persistent critique of the dualism of much of Protestant, especially evangelical, Christianity. Against the horizon of the Reformed affirmation of the goodness of creation, both evangelical dualism and Platonic ascent seem to be characterized by an anti-life, anti-body, anti-materiality stance. Insofar as fundamentalist dualism is something to be overcome, so also is Platonism.[40]

Because of this reading of Platonism, characterized by the denigration of the goodness of creation, I continue to be confused by RO's central claim that Plato's ontology—and, in particular, Plato's doctrine of participation (*methexis*)—offers a (necessary?)[41] framework for articulating Christian theology. Graham Ward has recently asserted that this is a

---

Reformational Worldview (Grand Rapids: Eerdmans, 1985), 41–43; and Cornelius Plantinga Jr., *Engaging God's World: A Reformed Vision of Faith, Learning, and Living* (Grand Rapids: Eerdmans, 2002), chap. 2.

37. My work is concerned with contesting this transcendent(al)ism. I have come to appreciate that RO is more concerned with contesting its opposite: materialism (nihilism). This partially explains our difference in sympathies for a Platonic ontology.

38. Friedrich Nietzsche, *The Twilight of the Idols,* trans. Richard Polt (Indianapolis: Hackett, 1997), 13–15.

39. Ibid., 18.

40. For a representative discussion, see Michael Horton, *Covenant and Eschatology: The Divine Drama* (Louisville: Westminster John Knox, 2002), 20–45.

41. This question needs to be asked: Just why does RO invest so much in demonstrating the amenity of Christian theology to a Platonic ontology? Can we do Christian theology without a Platonic ontology? Does Platonism constitute the *preambula fidei* of Christian theology?

fundamental theme of RO and the key to understanding common elements of RO, though he goes on to define this theme as the "Christian doctrine of participation."[42]

The central question is this: Is there really an overlap between the Platonic doctrine of participation (and a Platonic ontology in general) and a distinctly Christian incarnational or sacramental ontology? Or is there in fact a deep antithesis—even incommensurability—between *methexis* and incarnation?[43] If the latter is the case, then building a Christian theology on the framework of a Platonic philosophy would constitute a scholastic move par excellence.[44] I do not mean to invoke here a simplistic Hellenization thesis; rather, I want to take seriously the integrity of a biblically (i.e., revelationally) informed ontology and its uniqueness vis-à-vis the ultimately pagan ontology of Plato. Recalling Catherine Pickstock's reading of Plato's ontology (sketched in chap. 3), I now want to return to Pickstock's reading of Plato to indicate two problems: (1) its ability to account for aspects of the Platonic corpus, and (2) its failure to discern some fundamental differences between Platonic and Christian understandings of materiality.

At this juncture, there is an interesting overlap with the picture of participation offered by Milbank and Pickstock in TA. Here the more constructive aspect of this Platonic ontology comes to the fore.[45] As they note, Aquinas's criticisms of Plato are often motivated by Aquinas's affirmation of the goodness of creation (TA, 41). Aquinas rejects any notion of either an inherently fallen world or an autonomous nature; rather, his theontology reveals "a cosmos in a sense already graced" (TA, 44).[46] But

---

42. Graham Ward, "In the Economy of the Divine: A Response to James K. A. Smith," *PNEUMA: Journal of the Society for Pentecostal Studies* 25 (2003): 118–19.

43. Pickstock is explicit that she is trying to undo the standard contrast between the Socratic and the Christian articulated in Kierkegaard's *Philosophical Fragments:* "As I have argued in chapter 1, Plato's implicit account in the *Phaedrus* of the erotic mediation of the good in the beauty of the physical world suggests that it is possible to overstate this contrast between Platonic retrospective recollection and Kierkegaardian prospective repetition" (AW, 268).

44. "Scholastic" in the sense discussed in chapter 5, following Dooyeweerd.

45. Cf. Jan Aertsen, *Medieval Philosophy and the Transcendentals: The Case of Thomas Aquinas* (New York: E. J. Brill, 1996); and idem, "Thomas Aquinas," in *Bringing into Captivity Every Thought*, ed. J. Klapwijk, S. Griffioen, and G. Groenewoud (Lanham, Md.: University Press of America, 1991), 95–121, where he discusses Thomas's "transformation" of the Neoplatonic circulation motif (105–8).

46. Later they remark that "the leading characteristic of this ontology is a grasp of creation in the light of grace, as itself graced or supplemented, and so as a preparation for human deification" (AW, 51).

since elative individual self-subsistence, always open to the super-essential addition of second act, is now itself radically participatory, Platonism trumps Aristotelianism in Aquinas, in such a way that instead of the most general and abstract being removed from material things, it is rather individual material things which are paradoxically removed from themselves—referred beyond themselves in order to be recognized as themselves (and this may well be the real Plato, as Aquinas could not have known). (TA, 41–42)

Aquinas is a Platonist because of (not in spite of) his affirmation regarding the goodness of creation.

However, when we turn from creation to eschaton, there is some slippage regarding the goodness of creation. Recall Pickstock's suggestion that the necessary condition of physical mediation is "perpetual." This she linked to the hermeneutical character of the philosophic life. In TA, Milbank and Pickstock express a correlate hermeneutical aspect when they recognize the necessarily discursive aspect of (human) thought. For Aquinas, knowledge is a "never completed project" because of the "essential mediation of signs" (TA, 15). In fact, *ratio* (reason) itself is discursive: "No pure scientific cognition is ever exercised by us without discursive mediation: no cognitive 'sight' without cognitive 'language'" (TA, 22–23). But when we consider this situation of discursivity eschatalogically, it seems that Milbank and Pickstock posit a certain diminishing of the hermeneutic mediation insofar as they suggest that discursivity is not perpetual. Indeed, the picture seems to be closer to the "traditional" Plato: an overcoming of the conditions of mediation and discursivity on the way to an immediate, nondiscursive intuition. The progression of intensity in given light signals a passage "from the relatively discursive to the relatively intuitive, as we more nearly approach the pure divine insight" (TA, 28). Thus, they seem to suggest that discursivity "is necessary on account of the innate deficiency of human reason, which cannot, short of the final vision of glory, grasp what is in itself most intelligible" (TA, 27). "Once freed from our bodily carapace," they continue, "the contrast between object seen and medium-seen-by disappears . . . , and we see only what we see by, the uncreated light, though we receive it still only in part, and also as created" (TA, 37). Both of these claims seem to suggest that the beatific vision—and the *theosis* that is the *telos* of participation—is an event of nondiscursive immediacy; the need for material mediation, they conclude, is something that we shall "outgrow" (TA, 124n76). That, however, does not sound like the new or real Plato they have introduced to us. Rather, it sounds like the traditional Plato who has been the object of the Reformed critique.

We now turn to a rearticulation of that critique in light of the RO Plato just outlined. The criticisms here are both historical and constructive. On the one hand, there are questions regarding the viability of the RO Plato as an interpretation of the Platonic corpus. On the other hand, there are questions regarding the constructive ontology itself, quite irrespective of its historical provenance. Let's think about this ontology in terms of creation and eschaton.

The Goodness of Creation

The positive account of physicality seen by Pickstock in *Phaedrus* attributes, at best, an instrumental goodness to the physical. There is a certain "sacramentality" in *Phaedrus'* account of the physical. But despite Pickstock's claim to the contrary, it is difficult not to see Plato suggesting that the body and time are indeed ladders that are kicked away once the ascent has been completed (particularly in other dialogues, such as the *Phaedo*). If the physical has a positive role (AW, 14) to play in Plato—and it does—its role seems to be remedial at best. That is, given our current embodied situation, theurgical mediation is the only way out. One does not need a ladder to walk to school, but if one finds oneself in a deep pit, a ladder becomes both a good and a necessary thing for attaining school attendance.

But this raises an additional question: How did one get in the hole? More specifically, what occasions the embodiment of the soul for Plato? Accounts in the *Phaedrus*, *Phaedo*, and *Timaeus* make it difficult to conclude that embodiment is a good. The body is variously described as an "evil" (*Phaed.* 66b), a "contamination" or "pollution" of the soul (67a), and a "prison" for the soul (81d). Of course, Pickstock and Milbank have read these passages. I simply have not yet heard an account of how their reading of Plato would deal with such passages, which seem to convey a negative, not a positive, view of physicality. If one wanted to somehow bypass the embarrassing case of the *Phaedo*, there are other passages in the Platonic corpus, even in *Phaedrus*, that clearly communicate that the soul was detached from the body. Moreover, the erotic desire of the soul is to effect this detachment once again, since reembodiment is clearly seen as a punishment (*Phaedr.* 246–247; *Phaed.*). This *telos* of the Platonic soul points to the second theme.

Eschatology

The Christian affirmation of the goodness of creation entails the affirmation of the inherent goodness of materiality and the body in a way that makes embodiment an original, essential, creational aspect of being human. The very origin of materiality and embodiment, therefore, is affirmed as a good. This seems to stand in contrast to Platonic accounts of the body that grant it, at best, an instrumental, remedial goodness.

The same antithesis holds when we consider the future. I will take it as a given that the *telos* of an immortal, disembodied soul has nothing to do with the Christian hope for resurrection, and no one speaks more eloquently about the goodness of materiality than Ward, Milbank, and Pickstock. The hope for a resurrected eschatological existence remains a hope for a material, embodied existence. Thus, the aspects of herme-neutical mediation that characterize our current situation of finitude must persist in the eschaton.[47] But here we find a curious tension in RO, both historical and constructive. On the one hand, Pickstock seems to claim that for Plato, the necessary condition of physical and temporal mediation is "perpetual." As a constructive claim, that is correct, but as a historical or exegetical claim of Plato scholarship, it has serious prob-lems insofar as Plato regularly articulates the *telos* of the soul as one of disembodiment. Pickstock, however, wants to claim that in Plato—and in the *Phaedo* no less—"there may be many more elements of a kind of figural anticipation of the resurrection of the body than one might at first imagine."[48] But her argument is confusing and seems to proceed as follows:

P$_1$ The themes of sacrifice and return are intrinsic to the Christian doctrine of resurrection.

P$_2$ Both themes of sacrifice and return are explicitly formulated in the *Phaedo*.

C Therefore, there is a fundamental continuity between Plato and the Christian doctrine of resurrection.[49]

Granted, as with the discussion of *Phaedrus* in chapter 3, one can find certain instrumental affirmations of materiality and embodiment in Plato. It is fair, therefore, for Pickstock to claim that "Socrates' meta-physical convictions [i.e., *methexis*] allow him to see inexhaustible value as continuously *manifest* in the physical realm" and that "the body *need not* preclude us from living psuchically [*sic*] even now."[50] We can

47. I unpacked this in more detail in James K. A. Smith, *The Fall of Interpretation: Philosophical Foundations for a Creational Hermeneutic* (Downers Grove, Ill.: InterVarsity, 2000).

48. Pickstock, "Soul in Plato," 117.

49. Ibid.

50. Ibid., 121.

grant a certain theurgical relation between the soul and the body,[51] but Pickstock seems to ignore the temporal qualifiers for such claims. All of these claims in Plato are made with respect to what we might call a postlapsarian/pre-eschatological state—a time between fall and consummation when materiality is granted a certain remedially redemptive role. "The contemplation of the Forms and the concomitant gathering of the soul to itself require an engagement with the body, not its eschewal,"[52] but there is a crucial qualifier here that even Pickstock includes: This scenario holds only in this life, that is, in this postlapsarian material existence. But the overwhelming *telos* of such embodied souls is the employment of the body and matter in order to *escape* them.[53] In this respect, Pickstock's avoidance of prison and contamination language in the *Phaedo* serves only to shore up suspicions about the degree to which this attempt to make Plato proto-Christian is deeply flawed.

So in the end, P_1 is too weak to say anything substantial about the Christian theological[1] affirmation of the resurrection of the body. And the legitimate claims that materiality *can* doxologically lead us to the transcendent hardly secures the distinctly Christian affirmation that such a situation is an eradicable aspect of our creational goodness and eschatological condition. Plato's eschaton is not liturgical or doxological; is RO's?

Here we come to the "other hand" of the tension noted above. The eschatological *telos* of the beatific vision in TA seems to posit a more "traditional" Platonic suggestion that our end is to somehow escape embodiment (TA, 37) and thus outgrow both the conditions and the necessity for discursive mediation (TA, 124n76, 43). In other words, the model of the beatific vision as immediate intuition seems to require a negation of the embodiment of those who would experience such a vision. Insofar as discursivity is linked to physicality, a suggestion of an immediate, nondiscursive intuition for human beings must entail the assertion of a disembodied existence.[54] This seems to suggest that embodiment is

---

51. Ibid., 122.

52. Ibid., 124.

53. In moments of remarkable speculation, Pickstock claims that in Plato "the notion of the immortality of the soul allows a certain positive return to the body" (ibid.) and that "the *Phaedo* concludes with the myth of a higher realm within the cosmos itself, a higher material sphere which is almost like a sphere of purified (one is tempted to say 'resurrected') bodies" (125). I do not think many would be tempted to make such a claim given the overwhelming trajectory of Plato's account of the soul's disembodied *telos*.

54. Some would in this context appeal to the Pauline anticipation of one day seeing "face to face" (1 Cor. 13:12). But as I argued in *Fall of Interpretation*, face-to-face encounter is *not* immediate or directly intuitive: Even the face-to-face encounter is a mediated, hermeneutical meeting that happens "semiotically"—and this is precisely because faces have

accidental to human creatures, whereas the Reformed tradition asserts the essential—and essentially good—character of embodiment that persists in the eschaton (even if the conditions of materiality are modified). While I want to affirm the broadly participatory ontology articulated by RO, I remain unconvinced and concerned by the attempt to ascribe this distinctly Christian framework to Plato's pagan ontology.

The Integrity of Creation and the Specter of Occasionalism

There is a second area of criticism or reservation with regard to this participatory ontology: Does the suspension of the material (CG, 91, 117) negate the integrity of a good creation (CG, 88–89, 166)? The picture of the nothing-in-itself-ness of creation and created things in this framework gives a sense that God must continually and constantly reach into creation for it to *be* creation. As Ward puts it, things "are continually in a state of being gifted to us, animated for us, by God himself" (CG, 89). The potential of things "is not contained within the material but 'in and around it'" (CG, 88). So there is a sense in which the being of things seems to be extrinsic to them rather than inhering in them. As a result, RO's participatory ontology can slide toward an occasionalism that requires the incessant activity of the Creator to uphold what would seem to be a deficient creation—a tendency to emphasize the creature's participation in the divine to the extent that it seems the divine does everything. While seeking to undo the regnant secular concept of an autonomous nature, does RO's participatory framework risk sliding toward an alternative model that does not grant any independence to the creation? How can we affirm both the radical dependence of the creation on the Creator and also the goodness of creation as created?

Here the constructive and historical elements of the ontological project coalesce, for we need to revisit where we would expect to find the resources for a creational ontology: in Plato's affirmation of transcendence or in Deleuze's affirmation of immanence? The ontological question that is really at stake is an evaluative one: How will we understand the being of material reality? Is it something to be affirmed as positive, even glorified? This question, drawing on the language of the players involved, reminds us that ontology is a descriptive project, concerned with both the investigation of the structures of reality and the evaluation of such. And those evaluations are informed by a fundamental set of beliefs and values. In other words, every ontology has a deep well of beliefs from

---

bodies. Our face-to-face encounter remains governed by the hermeneutical conditions of creaturehood. For further discussion, see *Fall of Interpretation*, chaps. 2 and 5.

which it draws its evaluations—a theology[1]. One of the primary tasks of philosophical investigation within the Christian tradition is to discern where that well is located.

In the contemporary revival or overturning of Platonism (depending on whom one talks to), much is at stake for Christian philosophy in the contemporary ontological milieu, particularly for a creational ontology. At issue in an ontology of creation is how to evaluate or glorify the being of materiality and how to conceive its relation to its origin—how to understand the relationship between creature and Creator. I have argued elsewhere (and above) that a traditional Platonic ontology, by devaluing the material order of immanence, is fundamentally opposed to an ontology that begins with a commitment to the goodness of creation and its reaffirmation in the incarnation.[55] Following the lead of Deleuze and Badiou, therefore, we can formulate the parameters of this contemporary debate in terms of what will (or ought to) be glorified: Does a Christian understanding of the world as creation demand a certain devaluing of creation to glorify the Creator, as we so often encounter in evangelicalism? That is, to guard against idolatry, is it necessary to revert to a version of Platonism as traditionally understood? (And is that not just what we so often encounter under the rubric of Christian philosophy—just more Platonism?)[56] On the other hand, does the Deleuzian affirmation of the univocity of being and the glorification of the world as simulacrum represent a certain idolatry, a substitution of immanence for transcendence (Rom. 1:21–23)? Or could we perhaps find in the Deleuzian model a more radically creational ontology that glorifies the Creator by glorifying creation? Could it be that the most radical affirmation of transcendence is accomplished in the affirmation of immanence? And in that case, would not Deleuze be an important ally in the development of a creational ontology?

What follows offers a critical refinement of RO's participatory ontology by sketching the lineaments of a creational ontology, or what Hanby

55. See Smith, *Speech and Theology*, chap. 5; and idem, "A Principle of Incarnation in Derrida's *(Theologische?) Jugendschriften*," *Modern Theology* 18 (2002): 217–30.

56. In the end, this is a question that must be put to even Jean-Luc Marion's "iconic" ontology, which, it seems, wants to get *through* or *past* the material or the visible to the invisible. This is why there is an important difference between his "iconic" ontology and what I describe as an "incarnational" ontology. While the latter also begins from the affirmation that Christ is the "image of the invisible God" (Col. 1:15), this must be coupled with the even more fundamental affirmation of materiality in the claim that "anyone who has seen me has seen the Father" (John 14:9). There is, we could say, a "real presence" in creation that does not require a negation or "going beyond." This is discussed below in terms of the "integrity" of creation. I discussed Marion's iconic ontology in James K. A. Smith, "Picturing Revelation: The Aesthetic in Marion and Rosenzweig" (forthcoming).

describes as Augustine's "doxological ontology."[57] This is offered as a refinement in the direction of avoiding the specter of occasionalism raised above. But insofar as it appropriates key aspects of RO's participatory ontology, the creational ontology counters the kind of static autonomy to which other Reformed ontologies can tend. Further, rather than seeking a Platonic filiation, this creational ontology seeks a more positive appropriation of Deleuze while resisting his commitment to the univocity of being. Ultimately, this creational ontology is offered as a way forward that both avoids the univocity of being (by affirmation of incarnational inherence) and also guards against the tendency toward occasionalism (by affirmation of the integrity of creation).

A Case Study: Leibniz-Deleuze[58] and the Integrity of Creation

As a start to pursuing these questions, the following case study provides indications of why these resources are important and helpful for the development of an integrally Christian philosophy and, in particular, a creational ontology.[59]

Drawing on the brief study that follows, I want to argue that it is because of an affirmation of the transcendence of the Creator that we affirm the immanence of creation—and affirm it in such a way that it has a certain integrity (which cannot be equated with autonomy). More specifically, (1) as RO's account of suspension has already suggested, a creational (or incarnational) ontology must provide an account of materiality and immanence that counters the overwhelming current of traditional Platonism in Christian thought, and (2) the seeds for such an alternative ontology can be seen in the work of Leibniz, particularly as read through Deleuze's own ontological project. What we find in

57. Michael Hanby, *Augustine and Modernity*, Radical Orthodoxy (London: Routledge, 2003).

58. Alain Badiou employs this hyphenated reference in discussing Gilles Deleuze, *The Fold: Leibniz and the Baroque*, trans. Tom Conley (Minneapolis: University of Minnesota Press, 1993), indicating the difficulty of sorting out the voices in this text, so far from being a "commentary" and yet speaking so eloquently for Leibniz. See Alain Badiou, "Gilles Deleuze, *The Fold: Leibniz and the Baroque*," trans. T. Sowley, in *Gilles Deleuze and the Theater of Philosophy*, ed. Constantin V. Boundas and Dorothy Olkowski (New York: Routledge, 1994), 51–69.

59. This should be understood in (at least) two senses. By a "creational ontology" I mean an ontology (i.e., philosophy of the nature of reality) that begins with the commitment that the reality or world with which we are grappling is to be understood fundamentally as creation and hence as a gift of the Creator; in this sense, it is an ontology *of* creation, and as such, it must be a task rooted in the pretheoretical commitments of Christian faith. But I also understand it to refer to the fact that ontology—the reflexive project of "understanding our world"—is a good, creational task for humans being-in-the-world and that by such reflexive pursuits we discover something about the Creator.

Leibniz and Deleuze are the resources for countering a Platonic and modern disenchantment of the world via the reenchantment of nature, emphasizing the creational character of reality by an affirmation of the integrity of immanence. The integrity of creation is seen as a third way between autonomy and occasionalism.

It may seem odd to return to Leibniz—described by Dooyeweerd, for instance, as the quintessential instantiation of "immanence philosophy" and its "humanistic secularization of the Christian religion" (NC, I:227). And it would appear even more odd to engage one who has only pushed that to a further extreme—the philosopher of immanence par excellence, Gilles Deleuze.[60] However, in the spirit of the Reformational principle of common grace, I want to return to these two philosophers of immanence with a slightly different horizon, namely, the notion of the folds of creation or a theory of interlacements or *enkapsis*. A creational ontology will find surprising alliances with such philosophies of immanence. In this sense, this project may be following lines already suggested by Conor Cunningham, who argues that nihilism provides a kind of propaedeutic to a radically creational theology.[61]

Planes of Immanence: Deleuze's Leibniz and a "Hymn to Creation"[62]

Deleuze's ontology is the production of a confluence of two related trajectories: the Nietzschean project of "overturning Platonism"[63] and the "one ontological proposition" that "being is univocal," as inherited from Scotus. In fact, Deleuze concluded early on, "There has only ever been one ontological proposition: Being is univocal. There has only ever been one ontology, that of Duns Scotus, which gave being a single voice. . . . From Parmenides to Heidegger it is the same voice which is taken up, in an echo which itself forms the whole deployment of the univocal. A single voice raises the clamor of being."[64] The common ground of these

---

60. Granted, there is some equivocation between what Dooyeweerd describes as "immanence philosophy" (which posits the autonomy of philosophical thought) and what Deleuze means by a "philosophy of immanence." However, there is an important relation: For Deleuze, this is a question of *reference*, so that what is at stake is "the being of creation" as *meaning*. We return to these questions in more detail below.

61. Cunningham, *Genealogy of Nihilism*, chap. 10.

62. "The affirmation that the virtual is the real becomes, in its turn . . . a hymn to creation" (Alain Badiou, *Deleuze: The Clamor of Being* [Minneapolis: University of Minnesota Press, 2000], 49).

63. See Gilles Deleuze, *Difference and Repetition*, trans. Paul Patton (New York: Columbia University Press, 1994), 66–67. For one of Nietzsche's most lucid accounts of this project, see *Twilight of the Idols*, esp. "How the 'True World' Finally Became a Fiction."

64. Deleuze, *Difference and Repetition*, 35. He goes on to suggest that "the essential in univocity is not that Being is said in a single and same sense, but that it is said, in a single

two projects is their rejection of a Platonic dualism or "scale of being" that devalues the being of materiality in the name of intelligibility or seeks to escape this "plane of immanence" to ascend to an unencumbered transcendence. The test case for such Platonic ontologies is in accounts of the body. The Platonic philosopher, as a lover of reason, eschews the living force of becoming in favor of "conceptual mummies." "And above all," the Platonist cries, "away with the *body!*"[65] According to Deleuze, this is yet another symptom of the "reactive" character of such a metaphysics.[66] Thus, the opening line of Deleuze's ontology is a line from Nietzsche: "The 'apparent' world is the only world: the 'true world' is just *added to it by a lie.*"[67]

As a means of subverting Platonism—rather than simply reversing it—Deleuze constructs an ontology of the virtual or simulacrum that affirms that which *is*—indeed, as all that there is. "The simulacrum is not a degraded copy," he concludes. "It harbors a positive power which denies *the original and the copy, the model and the reproduction.*"[68] This fundamental affirmation of the virtual or simulacrum is also described as an affirmation of the plane of immanence, which entails for Deleuze the rejection of transcendence in the Platonic sense of an ideal realm of universals. As he later reflects, "Setting out a plane of immanence, tracing out a field of immanence, is something that all the authors I've worked on have done. . . . Abstractions explain nothing, they themselves have to be explained: there are no such things as universals, there's nothing transcendent."[69] Thus, more than just

---

and same sense, *of* all its individuating differences or intrinsic modalities. Being is the same for all these modalities, but these modalities are not the same" (35). This calls out for comparative and critical analysis with Dooyeweerd's affirmation that (1) "*meaning* is the *being* of all that has been *created*" (a claim that could only be understood phenomenologically) (NC, I:4) and (2) "*Being* is only to be ascribed to God, whereas creation has only *meaning*, the dependent mode of reality or existence. A true concept of being is impossible. The *word* being has no unity of meaning" (NC, I:73n1). It appears that Dooyeweerd is affirming something like the *equivocity* of being, but a phenomenological analysis would prove otherwise; on Dooyeweerd's own terms, we ought to reconsider his rejection of analogicity (see his important "unless," NC, I:73).

65. Nietzsche, *Twilight of the Idols*, 18.

66. Gilles Deleuze, *Nietzsche and Philosophy*, trans. Hugh Tomlinson (New York: Columbia University Press, 1983), 39–44.

67. Nietzsche, *Twilight of the Idols*, 19.

68. Gilles Deleuze, *The Logic of Sense*, trans. Mark Lester and Charles Stivale (New York: Columbia University Press, 1990), 262. See also *Difference and Repetition*, 208, emphasis in original: "*The virtual is fully real in so far as it is virtual.*"

69. Gilles Deleuze, "On Philosophy," in *Negotiations*, trans. Martin Joughin (New York: Columbia University Press, 1995), 145–46. We should note, however, that Badiou questions whether there isn't a covert operation of transcendence at work in Deleuze (Badiou, *Deleuze*, 46).

"sounding out idols,"[70] Deleuze's project is the "overturning of icons"[71] insofar as icons are intended to be windows that take us "beyond" immanence. According to Deleuze, this iconic desire itself harbors a devaluation of immanence. In contrast, Deleuze's virtual ontology urges us to stay with what appears, to celebrate immanence. As Badiou observes, "The affirmation that the virtual is real becomes, in its turn—with Deleuze writing here under the influence of Bergson—a hymn to creation."[72]

If the impetus of this project is found in Scotus and Nietzsche, its *telos* is found in Leibniz.[73] "We are all still Leibnizian," Deleuze concludes. "We are discovering new ways of folding, akin to new envelopments, but we all remain Leibnizian because what always matters is folding, unfolding, refolding."[74] What was it that he found in Leibniz? A fellow philosopher of immanence. And what is important is that it is precisely the notion of creation that nourishes Leibniz's affirmation of immanence.

What Deleuze sees Leibniz doing is overturning Platonism—while at the same time rejecting nominalism[75]—by means of subverting dualism (though there certainly remain dualities in Leibniz). "The question of reality," Deleuze notes, "is posited in respect to bodies."[76] Thus, what Deleuze finds in Leibniz is a certain reenchantment of the material whereby nature is invested with a dynamism and a plenitude.[77] The sensible or material world is no longer a veil of shadows but rather the site of "what's happening," no longer a space of detention or exile to be escaped but the "theater of matter"[78] where the real is actualized. This is why, in Leibniz, "Neo-Platonic emanations give way to a large zone of immanence, even if the rights of a transcendent God or an even

70. Nietzsche, *Twilight of the Idols*, 3. My thanks to Bruce Benson for his *Graven Ideologies: Nietzsche, Derrida, and Marion on Modern Idolatry* (Downers Grove, Ill.: InterVarsity, 2002), in which he so carefully elucidates this as Nietzsche's methodology.

71. Badiou, *Deleuze*, 44. This bears directly on the concern above regarding Marion's "iconic" ontology.

72. Ibid., 49.

73. However, these sorts of questions are contested, particularly because it is impossible to distinguish Deleuze from the "histories" of philosophy he has written (e.g., on Hume, Nietzsche, Kant, Bergson, Leibniz, and Foucault). These are not simple histories: "All the authors I dealt with had for me something in common" ("On Philosophy," 135). There he suggests that we must factor Leibniz into "the great Nietzsche-Spinoza equation."

74. Deleuze, *Fold*, 137.

75. Ibid., 100.

76. Ibid., 105.

77. "If the world is infinitely cavernous, if worlds exist in the tiniest bodies, it is because everywhere there can be found 'a spirit in matter'" (ibid., 7).

78. Ibid., 37.

higher Unity are formally respected."[79] Thus, Deleuze finds in Leibniz a cartographer who has mapped this zone of immanence, a developer who has constructed its space, and something of a real estate agent who sings its praises. The glorification of the zone of immanence indicates Leibniz's subversion of a Platonic ontology.

For Deleuze, this subversion of Platonic dualism is seen in the persistent motif of folding in Leibniz's corpus. Rather than a break or a line of separation, the fold (*le pli*) indicates a duality without disjunction, a difference within a unitary structure.[80] Thus, Deleuze likens Leibniz's philosophy to a Baroque architecture—particularly a Baroque chapel—"where a crushing light comes from openings invisible to their very inhabitants."[81] What characterizes the Baroque building is a distinction of two[82] floors that are nevertheless inseparable and, to a degree, indistinguishable. "For Leibniz, the two floors are and will remain inseparable; they are really distinct and yet inseparable by dint of a presence of the upper in the lower. The upper floor is folded over the lower floor" in the way that the Baroque chapel separates the upper sacristy from the common areas only by the draping folds of a canvas.[83] Keeping in mind the ontological stakes in this metaphor, Deleuze asks in conclusion, "Is it not in this zone, in this depth or this material fabric between two levels, that the upper is folded over the lower, such that we can no longer tell where one ends and the other begins, or where the sensible ends and the intelligible begins?"[84]

---

79. Ibid., 24. I argue below that it is precisely *because* of this "respect" for transcendence that Leibniz revalues this "zone of immanence."

80. Deleuze later remarks that "only similar things can differ, and only different things can be similar. One proposition says similarity's primary, the other says things themselves differ, and differ above all from themselves. Straight lines are all alike, but folds vary, and all folding proceeds by differentiation. . . . Folds are in this sense everywhere, without the fold being a universal. It's a 'differentiator,' a 'differential'" (Deleuze, "On Leibniz," in *Negotiations*, 156).

81. Deleuze, *Fold*, 28. Thus, "the architectural ideal is a room in black marble, in which light enters only through orifices so well bent that nothing on the outside can be seen through them" (ibid.). In this sense, Deleuze holds up Le Corbusier's Abbey of La Tourrette as a Baroque model.

82. It is this distinction of *only* two floors that distinguishes Leibniz's Baroque from what would be a Neoplatonic architecture with "an infinite number of floors, with a stairway that descends and ascends" (ibid., 29). But rejecting "the universe as a stairwell," Leibniz represents an early modern rejection of Neoplatonism *in favor of* an Augustinian imperative that there be no mediator between human and divine except the "one Mediator" (see, for instance, *Nature Itself*, in G. W. Leibniz, *Philosophical Texts*, ed. R. S. Woolhouse and Richard Francks [Oxford: Oxford University Press, 1998], §6). He shares this in common with Malebranche. My thanks to Wayne Hankey and Robert Dodaro for their insights on the Augustinian influences in early modern thought.

83. Deleuze, *Fold*, 119, 29, 5.

84. Ibid., 119.

As suggested above, the test case for any such ontology is the microcosm of the human person. Deleuze contends that in Leibniz there is a communication between "the pleats of matter and the folds in the soul."[85] The two levels of body and soul are distinguished but inseparable, related by a fold: "The great equation, the world thus has two levels, two moments, or two halves, one by which it is enveloped or folded in the monads, and the other, set or creased in matter."[86] In this sense, the early modern question of the union of body and soul is approached by Leibniz in terms that are decidedly un-Cartesian and hence un-Platonic: "There exists only one and the same world, conveyed on the one hand by the souls that actualize it and, on the other, by the bodies that realize it; this world does not itself exist outside of its expressants. We are dealing with two cities, a celestial Jerusalem and an earthly one, but with the rooftops and foundations of a [sic] same city, and the two floors of a same house."[87] But for Leibniz, this appurtenance is characteristic not only of the human person but of matter in general, both organic and inorganic. "The unit of matter, the smallest element of the labyrinth, is the fold."[88] Thus, what he finds in Leibniz, as a philosopher of the fold, is a philosopher who revalues this zone of immanence in itself, without a Platonic move of suspending the material from the intelligible. The following section considers the way in which Leibniz's affirmation of immanence stems directly from a creational imperative.

Giving the Creator His Due: Leibniz on Nature and Creation

Leibniz was once subjected to a curious charge: According to Pierre Bayle, Leibniz ascribed too much to God by ascribing too much to creation. His theory of nature, Bayle thought, "raises the power and intelligence of divine art far beyond anything that we can understand."[89] Leibniz took the critique as a compliment: "Only this theory," he concluded, "shows up the greatness of God in an appropriate way."[90] This concern for the greatness or worthiness of God was a persistent concern and motivation for Leibniz, precisely in his development of a metaphysical account of nature or creation. As in our brief consideration of Deleuze

85. Ibid., 4.

86. Ibid., 102.

87. Ibid., 119. We return to Deleuze's interest in Leibniz's theory of "expression" below.

88. Ibid., 6.

89. Pierre Bayle, in Note L to the "Rorarius" article in his *Dictionarre historique et critique*, 2nd ed. (Rotterdam, 1702), reprinted in G. W. Leibniz, *Philosophical Texts*, ed. R. S. Woolhouse and Richard Francks (New York: Oxford, 1998), 225 (§3). Unless otherwise noted, all citations from Leibniz refer to this edition.

90. Leibniz, *Monadology*, in *Philosophical Texts*, §59.

and Badiou, at stake here is a question of glorification: the glory of the Creator in relation to the glorification of creation.[91] For Leibniz, doing justice to the worthiness of the Creator demands that one affirm the integrity[92] of creation, in particular, the materiality of creation.

Leibniz carried out this project in two debates: first, in challenging the occasionalism of Malebranche, and second, in rejecting the mechanistic view of nature offered by Robert Boyle. The following considers Leibniz's motivation and strategy in each of these debates.

Creation as Miracle: The Critique of Occasionalism

As heir to a classical framework, Leibniz grappled with the question of the relationship between soul and body as a microcosmic example of larger ontological questions about the relationship between the material and the immaterial or immanence and transcendence.[93] Rejecting Cartesian interactionism—which suggested that the material body somehow influenced the immaterial soul—both Malebranche and Leibniz were pressed to find another solution. Our interest here is not the particularities of their different solutions but rather the motivation behind Leibniz's critique of Malebranche and what this reveals about his understanding of the ontological structure of creation.

91. Here a "creational" perspective opens up Leibniz in ways that contemporary scholarship has ignored; the notion of "creation" (and Creator/creature distinction) in Leibniz—so central to this thought—has been (systematically?) ignored by contemporary Leibniz scholarship. This is all the more curious since historical studies have demonstrated that "throughout his life, many of Leibniz's most important metaphysical projects are motivated by theological questions, and he frequently criticizes other philosophers for not having the proper concern for such theological matters" (Christina Mercer and R. C. Sleigh Jr., "Metaphysics: The Early Period to the *Discourse on Metaphysics*," in *The Cambridge Companion to Leibniz*, ed. Nicholas Jolley [Cambridge: Cambridge University Press, 1995], 68–69). Important for Leibniz's ontology was the notion of not only creation but also incarnation. See his early *On the Incarnation of God or Hypostatic Union*, where he first grapples with questions of materiality. And his most important later discussions of materiality occur in his correspondence with Des Bosses regarding the metaphysics of transubstantiation.

92. By the "integrity" of creation, or an individual thing, I mean to denote its (relative) independence and ability to function discretely. The term is akin to Hendrik Hart's notion of *functors* as "relatively complete and independent units" (*Understanding Our World: An Integral Ontology* [Lanham, Md.: University Press of America, 1984], 100). The *relativity* of this "independence" is important for both Hart and, as we will see, Leibniz, precisely because they are providing a *creational* account. Leibniz would also share Hart's tendency to describe functors (or "monads") as "action centers" or "concentrations of energy," since, for Leibniz, the essence of what he calls substance is actually *force* (*New System*, in *Philosophical Texts*, §3; *Nature Itself*, §11).

93. In contemporary analytic philosophy, as for Leibniz, such questions regarding "philosophy of mind" fall under the broader canopy of metaphysics.

Malebranche's solution would come to be known as occasionalism, attributing all activity of both body and soul to a direct, supernatural intervention by God. As Leibniz summarizes, according to occasionalism, "we are aware of the property of bodies because God produces thoughts in the soul on the occasion of the motions of matter; and when in its turn our soul wishes to move the body, they said that it is God who moves the body for it" (*New System*, §12). For example, since there cannot be a direct interaction between the material body and the immaterial soul, when a person stubs his or her toe on a table, God produces in the soul the sensation of pain. Or when someone wants to wave his or her hand at a passing motorist, God intervenes to move the body in such a way. In contrast to this demand for constant divine intervention for creation to operate, Leibniz offers a theory of preestablished harmony that emphasizes the relative self-sufficiency of nature as ordered by the Creator.

He draws out the contrast between these two positions with the helpful analogy of two clocks: Imagine two clocks that always tell exactly the same time. This could be accomplished in a couple of ways: One way "of making two clocks (even poor ones) always tell the same time would be to have them constantly looked after by a skilled workman, who adjusts them from moment to moment."[94] This requires a perpetual caretaker, a "man who is employed constantly to synchronize two *inferior* clocks that cannot keep the same time by themselves."[95] Another way "would be to make these two clocks, from the beginning, with such skill and accuracy that we could be sure that they would always afterwards keep time together" (§4). The two clocks represent body and soul, and the first method is that posited by occasionalism, while the second is Leibniz's "way of pre-established agreement."

Leibniz's critique of occasionalism is twofold: First, he notes that this system requires a "perpetual miracle" (*New System*, §13; *Letter*, §7), a constant intervention of God into the order (or lack thereof) of nature. By miracle, Leibniz does not mean an event that is rare or even one that violates natural laws (contra Hume) but "something which exceeds the power of created things" (*Letter*, §7). In this sense, occasionalism posits perpetual miracles, since it cannot account for these relations within the structure of creation itself. This is the basis for the second part of Leibniz's critique: The occasionalist account of nature or creation provides a deficient creation—an inferior clock, as it were. For Leibniz, such

94. Leibniz, *Third Explanation of the New System*, §3, in *Philosophical Texts*.
95. Leibniz, *A Letter from M. Leibniz to the Editor, Containing an Explanation of the Difficulties Which M. Bayle Found with the New System* (1698), §7, emphasis added, henceforth cited as *Letter* in text.

an understanding of the structures of creation as deficient reflects back upon the deficiency of the Creator, just as a poorly made clock reflects the incompetence of its maker. While we may think that the occasionalist emphasis on the dependence of creation on the Creator would prevent an idolization of creation, Leibniz's analysis points out that occasionalism posits this dependence in such a way that it denigrates the Creator by making creation's dependence the result of an original deficiency. This is why he believes that "the doctrine of occasional causes which some defend can lead to dangerous consequences": "Far from increasing the glory of God by removing the idol of nature, this doctrine seems, with Spinoza, to make God into the very nature itself of things, and to reduce created things to mere modifications of a single substance" (*Nature Itself*, §15). For Leibniz, therefore, at stake in this understanding of creation is an understanding of the Creator. Thus, he concludes that his theory of preestablished harmony—which is "just as possible as that of the [perpetual] caretaker"—is "more *worthy* of the creator of these substances, clocks, or machines" (*Letter*, §7). To do justice to the Creator, we need to construct an account of the structure of creation that affirms its integrity as a reflection of the goodness and power of the Creator. In other words, to provide an account of creational, material structures that is worthy of the Creator, Leibniz radically affirms the self-sufficiency of creation as created—what he describes as the "God-given nature of things" (*Letter*, §7). The result, however, is an account of creational structures that, at first sight, seems to construct a plane of immanence without reference to the Creator—an almost deistic account of nature operating autonomously. If we look closely, however, we see that this is not the case.

In his constructive proposal, Leibniz argues forcefully for the sufficiency of nature *as created*. Rather than lacking something, and thus needing perpetual divine intervention, creation is front-loaded, so to speak, with all that it requires to function. "God first created the soul," he emphasizes, "or any other real unity, in such a way that everything in it arises from its own nature" (*New System*, §14). The emphasis here is on an original goodness or sufficiency: God grants integrity "at the outset" (§15), at the moment of creation. In terms of the metaphor above, the wise, good, powerful clock maker creates a system that is able to work properly "from the beginning" (*Third Explanation of the New System*, §4), and so the system of creation is "set up by a contrivance of divine foreknowledge, which formed each of these substances *from the outset* in so perfect, so regular, and so exact a manner, that merely by following out its own laws, which were given to it *when it was brought into being*, each substance is nevertheless in harmony with the other" (§5, emphasis added). In the *Letter*, Leibniz describes this as the "God-given nature of things" (§7). The "glory" of the Creator—which is what is at stake here for Leibniz—demands that one affirm the (almost absolute) integrity of the order of creation, almost to the point of creating what might seem an "idol of nature," as when he concludes that "every mind is like a world apart, sufficient to itself, independent of every other created thing, involves the infinite, and expresses the universe, and so it is as lasting, as continuous in its existence, and as absolute as the universe of created things itself" (*New System*, §16). But it is Leibniz's opposition to the "idol of nature"—namely, the autonomy of the other early moderns—that can be seen in his critique of mechanistic understandings of nature. As we turn from his critique of occasionalism to his critique of mechanism, we will understand why Leibniz's affirmation of the integrity of creation should not be confused with an idolatrous or deistic absolutization of nature.

Against the Idol of Nature

In *Nature Itself* (1698),[96] Leibniz enters into a debate concerning not the relation of soul and body but rather an account of nature and materiality itself. At stake in this debate is what we might describe as Boyle's disenchantment of nature and Leibniz's reenchantment of such. Again, in a way analogous to the critique of occasionalism, it is the worthiness (§8) of the Creator that is at stake in the metaphysics of the creation. Boyle's view of nature, according to Leibniz, makes created material reality a kind of lifeless collection of aggregates—to which Boyle opposed the vulgar conception of nature, a pagan divinization of nature by special forces. But Leibniz saw Boyle's theory as a kind of "gutting" of nature, making it less than it was and thus denigrating the worthiness of the Creator; it represented a "detriment to piety" (§3). This is why Leibniz thought that Boyle was making an idol of nature (§8).

Leibniz sets himself up between Boyle and Spinoza, and his critique revolves around just what is in matter or nature. He argues that there is (and must be) an active, creative force inherent in things (§2). Thus, what distinguishes his theory from Boyle's is that, for Boyle,

---

96. As with almost everything Leibniz wrote, this piece is an occasional one, and it is important to know something about the occasion. In 1682, Robert Boyle published his *Free Inquiry into the Vulgarly Received Notion of Nature*, and in 1688, *On Nature Itself*. In both he defended a purely mechanistic understanding of nature (the "corpuscular theory of matter") consistent with a Cartesian theory of extension. This was taken up and defended by J. C. Sturm in *The Idol of Nature* (1692). The position was criticized by G. C. Schelhammer in his *Vindication of Nature* (1697). Sturm, in turn, defended his (and Boyle's) view in his "Defense," appended to his *Elective Physics* (1698). In *Nature Itself*, Leibniz is responding to Sturm's 1698 "Defense" and taking up a position more closely allied with Schelhammer.

the "divine law" that governs nature is external to nature rather than inherent to the structures of nature (§5). This is why he draws a parallel between Boyle and Malebranche: Both posit a nature that is defective and in need of a constant caretaker, which means that God's initial will was ineffective (§6). In contrast, Leibniz emphasizes an ordering that is inherent to nature: "For since this earlier command does not now exist, it cannot now do anything unless it left behind some continuing effect which still endures and operates" (§6). Theories of nature that require a perpetual governance by God are, according to Leibniz, denigrations of the Creator, for what would we think of a clock maker who needed to constantly turn the hands of the clock manually? So the test of the effectiveness of the divine ordering of nature is the extent to which the initial ordering is effective and does not require perpetual attention. This ordering leaves a kind of trace that inheres in the structure of nature itself (§6), whereas in Boyle's theory, the ordering "had no lasting effect." In contrast, "if things have been formed by the command in such a way that they are capable of fulfilling the meaning of the command—then it must be admitted that things have been given a certain ability, a form or force from which the series of phenomena follows in accordance with the dictates of the original command" (§6). It is precisely Leibniz's desire to do justice to the glory of the Creator that leads him to so emphasize the self-sufficiency or integrity of creation as a structure of immanence.[97]

This is why this emphasis on the integrity of creation is a structural valuing of materiality per se. The basic units that Leibniz describes as monads are composed of force and matter and cannot be separated from matter (*Nature Itself,* §11). In fact, for Leibniz, the immaterial aspect of the monad is identified with force,[98] and this force "is itself an inherent law imprinted by divine decree" on materiality (§12). In this sense, what is compressed or folded into the monad is simply order that inheres in matter. The temporal structure of materiality permits the unfolding of this original order folded into the organism. As Deleuze comments, "The first fly contains the seeds of all flies to come, each being called in its turn to unfold its own parts at the right time."[99] This is because the ordering command is compressed or folded into materiality from the beginning, granting a certain independence and

97. On the relation between inherence and immanence, see *Nature Itself,* §10.

98. See, for example, *Reflections on the Advancement of True Metaphysics and Particularly on the Nature of Substance Explained by Force,* §4, in *Philosophical Texts;* and *New System,* §3.

99. Deleuze, *Fold,* 8.

integrity. Thus again, undoing Platonism, Leibniz concludes that "souls never leave behind their whole body" (*Nature and Grace*, §6); "there are also no *souls* which are completely *detached* from matter, and no *spirits* without bodies. Only God is completely removed from matter" (*Monadology*, §72).[100] Leibniz's affirmation of materiality in his ontology stems from early reflections on the incarnation, so there is a sense in which the creation is a collection of hypostatic unions.[101] Therefore, not only is the plane of immanence imprinted with a divine order from the beginning, but it is only in this materiality that the original fold of the command can be unfolded; matter,[102] or the body, is the theater of unfolding *ad infinitum*.

From the account above, we can see why Leibniz's emphasis on the integrity of creation (as a relative independence that entails discrete functioning) should not be conflated with a notion of autonomy. For Leibniz, there is a sense in which self-sufficiency and independence are the results of a fundamental dependence on the Creator. For instance, consider the important qualifications that he makes regarding created monads: These simple substances are described as *entelechies* "because they have within them a certain perfection; there is a kind of self-sufficiency which makes them sources of their own internal actions, or incorporeal automata, as it were" (*Monadology*, §18). Even in early correspondence with Arnauld, Leibniz emphasizes that "all its [a substance's] actions come from its own depths, except for its dependence on God" (§2.13). And so in this encounter with Boyle, Leibniz rejects Boyle's mechanism because "that mechanism itself has its origin not merely in a material principle or in mathematical reasons, but in some higher and, so to speak, metaphysical source" (*Nature Itself*, §211). Emphasizing the integrity of creation guards against an ontology that views the structures of creation as somehow incomplete or deficient, which in turn reflects a deficiency in the Creator. So just as with the critique of the occasionalists, it is

---

100. Thus, with respect to matters of personal identity after death, Leibniz emphasizes the resurrection of the body rather than the simple immortality of the soul. For a discussion, see George Mavrodes, "The Life Everlasting and the Bodily Criterion of Identity," in *Contemporary Philosophy of Religion* (Oxford: Oxford University Press, 1982), 199–210; and Peter Van Inwagen, "The Possibility of Resurrection," *International Journal for Philosophy of Religion* 9 (1978): 114–21.

101. For a helpful discussion of this point, see Mercer and Sleigh, "Metaphysics," 78–84.

102. There is not a hard-and-fast line between "bodies" of living organisms and "inert" matter for Leibniz. "Every portion of matter can be thought of as a garden full of plants, or as a pond full of fish. . . . Thus there is no uncultivated ground in the universe; nothing barren, nothing dead" (*Monadology*, §§67, 69). For a discussion, see Deleuze, *Fold*, 115–18.

to glorify the Creator that Leibniz glorifies the structures of nature/creation as characterized by a completeness that indicates a relative self-sufficiency.

In fact, the relativity of this independence is what undergirds a theory of expression at work in Leibniz's metaphysics. To put this another way, the integrity of creation is the integrity *of creation* (not just nature), which thus has a referential structure that points to or reflects its *Creator*. Thus, Leibniz constantly emphasizes the reflective or expressive activity of the universe in general and the (rational) monad in particular. A monad "is representative in its nature," and it is "the body by means of which the universe is represented in the soul" (*Monadology*, §§60, 63). Each individual is a "living mirror" of the universe, which as a whole is a mirror of the Creator (§56).[103] Therefore, the key to understanding Leibniz's theory of expression or reflection—a key that Deleuze misses—is the notion of the *imago Dei*, transferred now to the universe as a whole (*Nature and Grace*, §14). The multiplication of beings, then, is a multiplication of mirrors, which, in turn, multiplies the reflections of the Creator. Hence, for Leibniz, the Creator's injunction to "multiply" represents both the Creator's desire for fullness and plenitude and the opportunity for the glory of God to abound, and it is the zone of immanence that is the "theater of his glory."[104]

Integrity, Immanence, and the Folds of Creation: Implications for a Creational Ontology

We can draw some programmatic conclusions regarding the engagement, critique, and possible appropriation of Leibniz-Deleuze from the standpoint of a Christian philosophy that seeks to elaborate a creational ontology vis-à-vis RO's participatory ontology. These are programmatic insofar as they stand less as conclusions and more as trajectories for further work that needs to be done. In particular, there are three important themes.

---

103. However, each monad represents the universe only from its own point of view or "perspective" (*Monadology*, §§56–57). No monad has a "God's-eye-view"—"otherwise, every monad would be divine" (§60). This gives birth to what Deleuze describes as Leibniz's "perspectivalism," which, in some ways, anticipates Nietzsche. See Deleuze, *Fold*, 23–26.

104. I am playing here with Calvin's notion as developed by Susan Schreiner, *The Theater of His Glory: Nature and the Natural Order in the Thought of John Calvin* (Durham, N.C.: Labyrinth, 1991). For a helpful discussion of this theme in Leibniz, see Mercer and Sleigh, "Metaphysics," 91–115.

Affirming Immanence in a Creational Ontology

In the contemporary milieu, one of the primary objectives in the construction of an ontology from a Christian perspective is the rejection of a persistent temptation: Platonism.[105] The first prayer of a creational ontology should be, "Lead us not into dualism, but deliver us from Platonism." The analysis above indicated that in our rejection of dualism in ontology,[106] we find surprising allies in philosophers of immanence such as Leibniz and Deleuze. This is precisely because the celebration of the richness of immanence is, as Leibniz demonstrates, a celebration of the richness of its Creator; emphasizing the integrity of creation is a mode of doxology, which indicates the worthiness of the Creator. Conversely, the devaluing of materiality—the zone of immanence—correlates with a denigration of the Creator. It is by affirming the integrity of creation as a relatively independent structure that we do justice to the Creator. For Leibniz, this entails the rejection of both Malebranche's occasionalism and Boyle's mechanism, because both posit an incompleteness to creation that indicates a deficiency of the Creator. Both of these positions do so by an appeal to some kind of supernatural maintenance or intervention. Instead, Leibniz emphasizes the wonder of creation itself as unfolding that which was enfolded from the beginning.

In this sense, he is close to the classic statement of Johann Diemer in *Nature and Miracle:* "To say that the beginning of a new phylum is grounded in creation means in no way that God created in a supernatural way by intervening in independent natural events. Anyone who thinks it does begins with an autonomous natural process wherein he then allows God to introduce something new from the outside. This way of thinking is not in line with Scripture."[107] In other words, the occasionalists and mechanists posit an autonomy of nature at the same time that they posit its insufficiency. In contrast, Diemer asserts (and Leibniz would agree) that "the new structural principles are not immaterial, metaphysical forms that come from outside of nature to direct material events. Rather, they are principles of structures which were worked out in the divine creation act and *enclosed* in the religious root of nature."[108]

105. The other challenge in contemporary philosophy of mind is a reductionary materialism, which should also be rejected. In this sense, Leibniz still occupies an interesting site—between a Cartesian dualism and a Hobbesian materialism.

106. Dualism in philosophical anthropology is always a "case" of such an ontology; this is why issues of philosophy of mind and personal identity fall under the canopy of metaphysics.

107. Johann H. Diemer, *Nature and Miracle*, trans. Wilma Bouma (Toronto: Wedge, 1977), 5.

108. Ibid., 9.

Because of this concept of the integrity of creation, one need not refer "outside" these structures of immanence; rather, one does justice to the Creator by affirming the zone of immanence or region of materiality as the theater of his glory. Thus, with Deleuze, a creational ontology seeks to overturn not only idols (i.e., Platonism) but also icons that would still have us turn our eyes from or through immanence to transcendence in a way that devalues materiality.[109] Thus, Deleuze's affirmation of the simulacrum as real, of what appears, is a sign, Badiou remarks, of his "unwavering love for the world," which gives birth to "a hymn to creation."[110] Certainly, a creational ontology should be characterized by this love for the world and hence must work from a fundamental affirmation of immanence and materiality.

Meaning, Expression, and Transcendence

However, a creational ontology must also affirm transcendence in some important sense insofar as it maintains the Creator/creature distinction and thus that God is other than the world. As indicated above, this does not necessitate a denigration of immanence but the affirmation of immanence as the integrity of creation. In this way, transcendence is affirmed in immanence, or what we might describe as "enfolded transcendence" as a creational given.[111] In other words, this ontology emphasizes the referential structure of creational immanence—that "*meaning* is the *being* of all that has been *created*" (NC, I.4). The question of transcendence, then, is not a matter of an immaterial "substance" inhering in matter but rather a structure of "referring and expressing" that points to an origin. The only way in which this can avoid becoming a Platonic, or even an iconic, dualism is if we understand "meaning" in a phenomenological sense of intention that is not substantial. Even the affirmation of the integrity of creation ultimately points to "its dependent non-self-sufficient nature" (NC, I.4), the same move we saw in Leibniz. Thus, the zone of immanence is invested with transcendence, not as a kind of container for an ethereal substance but rather as a structure of phenomenological reference to an origin that is not itself subject to temporal conditions (or even "being").[112]

Therefore, the affirmation of the integrity of creation (or the goodness of materiality) contains within itself an affirmation of transcendence, not

109. I have in mind Jean-Luc Marion's "iconic" ontology as unpacked in *The Crossing of the Visible*, trans. James K. A. Smith (Stanford: Stanford University Press, 2004), chap. 3.

110. Badiou, *Deleuze*, 44, 49.

111. My thanks to Hans Boersma for this formulation.

112. On this point, see NC, III:107–8.

as another intelligible world (hence, we agree with Deleuze's critique of Platonism) but rather as that which inheres in the structure of creation insofar as it points to a Creator. In this way, Deleuze's and Leibniz's emphasis on "expression" in the plane of immanence is a fruitful point of contact for conceptualizing the referential structure of creation without canceling the affirmation of immanence.

Foldings and *Enkapsis:* Dooyeweerd, Deleuze, and Leibniz

Finally, the notion of folding—opened by Leibniz and appropriated by Deleuze—is a rich concept for understanding the integrity of creation as created. In Leibniz more than in Deleuze, we find the centrality of creation as an orienting hub that accounts for the unfolding that characterizes the differentiation and development of the material world. This insight requires us to reevaluate Dooyeweerd's critique of Leibniz for positing what he describes as the "self-sufficient individuality of the monads" (NC, I:231), or what he calls the "autarchy" of the monad (NC, I:231n1, 235–36). By this charge, Dooyeweerd argues that Leibniz is assigning an (absolute) autonomy to nature. "Even the sensory perceptions in the human soul-monad," he concludes, "are produced in absolute autarchy, entirely from the inside" (NC, I:237). But based on the analysis above, we must conclude that Dooyeweerd has confused integrity with autonomy because he has missed the central role of creation in Leibniz's ontology. While it is true that the monad "has no windows" (NC, I:239; *Monadology*, §7)—and that this would require that we critically evaluate his notion of relations among created structures—Leibniz is here emphasizing the relative autonomy of monads vis-à-vis other created things. Monads have no windows, but we might say that, for Leibniz, God can walk through walls. Therefore, this is not at all an affirmation of an absolute autonomy.[113]

In fact, with this Leibnizian-Deleuzian concept of the fold as integral to immanence, do we not find a structure of *enkapsis*—that enfolded into each whole are folds of modes or aspects? That wholes can be en-

---

113. Dooyeweerd later hints at this: "It is extremely interesting to notice the ground on which Leibniz rejects the conception of ancient philosophy which sought the origin of evil in 'matter.' The ground for this rejection is that the ancients viewed matter as uncreated and independent of God" (NC, I:257)—entailing that Leibniz emphasized that matter is created and dependent on God. However, Dooyeweerd is right to point out that we would need to effect a certain deconstruction of Leibniz on this score, since he does elsewhere point to an "original imperfection of created things" (*Monadology*, §42). But here he simply repeats elements in Augustine's ontology. I attempted to deconstruct the latter in James K. A. Smith, "Time of Language: The Fall to Interpretation in Early Augustine," *American Catholic Philosophical Quarterly*, Supplement: Annual ACPA Proceedings 72 (1998): 185–99.

folded into larger wholes?[114] And that folded into the origin of creation are those multiple folds that are unfolded in a process of differentiation and development? Again, Diemer reminds us that it is precisely this conception of an original enfolding that guards the integrity of creation: "The appearance of something new is not the result of a power above and beyond nature bringing into it what was not there before. Rather, what is already there is disclosed through the subjective activity of individual creatures *within* created constant structures."[115] The enfolding is an original enclosing that grants a relative autonomy to the created order that now unfolds itself, disclosing the folds in the "root."[116] The affirmation of the integrity of materiality entails a rich account, in both Leibniz and Deleuze, of the "interlacements" within the zone of immanence that occasion the unfolding of that which was enfolded at the origin (cf. NC, III:92–93, 627–44).

A creational ontology, in contrast to the varieties of traditional Christian-Platonic ontologies, is a philosophy of immanence that affirms the materiality of creation at the same time that it affirms the Creator. Thus, Hanby shows the way in which Augustine's "doxological ontology" is governed by a "proto-Chalcedonion logic," affirming an ontology (and an attendant anthropology that can account for "a movement which fully belongs to creatures precisely insofar as it belongs to God")—"at once ours *and* a gift of the Holy Spirit."[117] We find a similar "ontological compatibilism" in Leibniz. Such an ontology must begin from the integrity of creation as the theater of the Creator's glory without the Platonic desire to peek behind the curtain, for this Platonic desire assumes that what appears on stage is a farce, a deceptive melodrama distracting us from the real story behind the scenes. But neither should we fall prey to the nihilistic conclusion that the stage is merely a simulacrum—an image without an original or a zone of immanence without reference to transcendence. In contrast to both of these, a creational ontology affirms that "all the world is a stage." There is no pristine, immediate access behind the scenes; rather, the invisible is seen *in* the visible, such

114. On this score, Leibniz might offer a unique conception. For Hart, "Wholes that function as parts, or apparently function as parts, will be said to be functioning in enkapsis. Parts functioning as wholes . . . do not really exist" (*Understanding Our World*, 217). For Leibniz, "wholes" go all the way down, or, in Hart's terms, "functors" go all the way down (cf. 220).

115. Diemer, *Nature and Miracle*, 5, emphasis added.

116. Diemer speaks of a "primordial organism" in which "the potencies of all types—that is, all phyla, classes, orders, families—would be enclosed" (8).

117. Hanby, *Augustine and Modernity*, 89. The immediate context here is the Pelagian controversy and the "mechanics of grace," but the ontological intentions are broader than that.

that seeing the visible is to see more than the visible. This zone of immanence is where transcendence plays itself out, unfolding itself in a way that is staged by the Creator.[118]

The Beauty of God: Liturgy and Aesthetics

Two related implications flow out of RO's participatory ontology, or what I have refined as a creational ontology: the reaffirmation of liturgical sacramentality and the affirmation of the aesthetic. If secular modernity is characterized by a nonliturgical flattening of the world (AW, 45–48), then RO's ontology rehabilitates what Pickstock variously describes as a liturgical or doxological understanding of the created order as a plane that is ordered to praise (AW, xiii). While it is true that, for RO, the Eucharist (particularly in its transubstantionist model) is central for rethinking other zones such as language (AW)[119] and materiality (CG), the point is much broader: All the world is a sacrament, we might say, such that RO emphasizes "the primacy of the doxological and liturgical within every realm of culture" (AW, xiv).[120] This generates a sacramental revaluing of the material and thus an affirmation not just of sacred art but of the arts in general.[121]

A radically orthodox account of the arts, drawing on the wells of Augustine's doxological ontology, is part of a broader Christian aesthetic

118. My thanks to Steve Long for helping me revise this metaphor in a more orthodox direction.

119. As Pickstock summarizes her position: "The event of transubstantiation in the Eucharist is the condition of possibility of all human meaning" (AW, xv).

120. I have not explicitly engaged in questions of Eucharist here. In this respect, I would have two central concerns: first, to demonstrate that Calvin's doctrine of "real presence" is not the Zwinglian picture that RO tends to suggest but is, in fact, quite close to the ontological concerns expressed in RO. For further discussion of these matters, see the essays by Vandervelde and Smit in *Creation, Covenant, and Participation: Radical Orthodoxy and the Reformed Tradition*, ed. James K. A. Smith and James H. Olthuis (Grand Rapids: Baker Academic, forthcoming). Second, it seems to me that for Ward and Pickstock, the Eucharist is more a site of ontological speculation than a means of grace and sanctification. In other words, the Eucharist in these models means more for ontology than for discipleship.

121. I cannot do justice here to the extent of RO's engagement with the arts. For discussions, see Graham Ward, "The Beauty of God," in *Theological Perspectives on God and Beauty;* Phillip Blond, "The Primacy of Theology and the Question of Perception," in *Religion, Modernity, and Postmodernity,* ed. Paul Heelas (Oxford: Blackwell, 1998), 285–313; and Blond's contribution to RONT, "Perception: From Modern Painting to the Vision in Christ" (220–41). For further analysis, see Adrienne Dengerink Chaplin, "The Invisible and the Sublime: From Participation to Reconciliation," in *Creation, Covenant, and Participation.*

grounded in three key dogmatic themes: the goodness of creation, the enfleshing of God in the incarnate (and crucified) One, and the eternal affirmation of embodiment in the doctrine of the resurrection. As a result, this affirmation of the arts is underwritten by both an ontology and a distinct (and related) anthropology. A creational or incarnational account of *aisthesis* in general understands the mode of affectivity as a means of knowing that is more fundamental—and perhaps more primordial—than the cognitive. Rather than a Platonic subordination of affective and imaginative *aisthesis* to intellectual *noesis* (*Resp.* 509d–11e), a Christian epistemology in the Augustinian and Pascalian tradition affirms the priority of "reasons of the heart of which reason knows nothing."[122] This epistemological and anthropological claim challenges not only rationalism but also traditional aesthetics informed by rationalism. Conversely, a Christian aesthetic is part of a Christian epistemology and ontology that, epistemologically, challenge the hegemony of cognitive knowing that dominates the Western tradition and, thus, ontologically, question the devaluation of images. Of interest from a Christian perspective is the way in which art is an embodied, incarnate means by which truth is communicated. Given a Christian anthropology that affirms the integrity of the embodied self (in contrast to a Platonic privileging of the soul), a Christian epistemology must resist the Western temptation to reduce knowing to only one of its modes—the cognitive—and rather appreciate the multiple modes of knowing (affective, tactile, sensible, etc.).[123] Or to put it in terms of classic discussions of the faculties, rather than privileging the intellect, a Christian epistemology accords equal status, if not primacy, to the senses and imagination.[124] So rather than making an aesthetic that is subservient to a rationalist epistemology, a Christian

122. Elsewhere, I have argued that the early Heidegger placed the same emphasis on affectivity because of his debts to Augustine and Pascal. See James K. A. Smith, "Taking Husserl at His Word: Towards a 'New' Phenomenology with the Young Heidegger," *Symposium: Journal of the Canadian Society for Hermeneutics and Postmodern Thought* 4 (2000): 103–7. One could also point to the role of sensibility and affectivity in Levinas. See Emmanuel Levinas, *Totality and Infinity*, trans. Alphonso Lingis (Pittsburgh: Duquesne University Press, 1969), 187–93.

123. For full development, see NC, vol. 2; and Calvin Seerveld, "Dooyeweerd's Legacy for Aesthetics: Modal Law Theory," in *The Legacy of Herman Dooyeweerd*, ed. C. T. McIntire (Lanham, Md.: University Press of America, 1985), 41–79.

124. I have in mind a basically Johannine account that affirms the importance of the tactile and the sensuous. See, for instance, the opening of 1 John, which emphasizes that God spoke in Christ a sensible and sensuous Word: "What was from the beginning, what we have *heard*, what we have *seen with our eyes*, what we beheld and *our hands touched*, concerning the Word of Life— . . . what we have seen and heard we proclaim to you also" (1 John 1:1, 3 NASB, emphasis added). This is the correlate of the Johannine emphasis on the incarnation and the enfleshing of God (John 1:14).

account of *aisthesis* in general (as a component of an anthropology) grounds both an epistemology and an aesthetic. The result is the revaluing of images and aesthetic media as perhaps the most fundamental and effective means for the communication of truth. Thus, theater, for instance, is seen as an arena of images and a feast for the senses[125] that can play a positive role in Christian formation.[126]

As noted earlier, a Christian account of *aisthesis* and an aesthetic developed from such is grounded in three key dogmatic themes. This Christian aesthetic in general, and a revisioning of theater in particular, claims an Augustinian heritage insofar as the motifs of the goodness of creation, the centrality of the incarnation, and the affirmation of the resurrection are central elements of Augustine's thought that constitute a unique contribution to the tradition, even if they are also elements that undermine his own explicit critique of theater.[127] Let's unpack each of these three themes to determine their Augustinian birthright and how they inform a Christian aesthetic.

First is the goodness of creation (Gen. 1:31), which constitutes a primordial affirmation of embodiment and finitude not as lack but as gift. In other words, the soul does not fall into embodiment from which it then seeks escape. To be embodied and finite is not to be construed as lacking in any sense.[128] While there are tensions in Augustine's account

125. As Max Harris notes, the theater engages senses that film does not (e.g., smell and even touch); and by means of simultaneity (multiple scenes occurring on stage at once), theater can play with space and time in ways in which film cannot because of the hegemony of the camera's perspective. See Max Harris, *Theater and Incarnation* (New York: St. Martin's, 1990), 29–34, 65–66.

126. I am struck by the way in which contemporary currents in evangelical and charismatic churches, which employ drama as part of both worship and evangelism, unwittingly affirm just this point—while nevertheless retaining a largely dualist anthropology.

127. I have taken this up in more detail in James K. A. Smith, "Staging the Incarnation: Revisioning Augustine's Critique of Theatre," *Literature and Theology* 15 (2001): 123–39.

128. The burden of my argument in *Fall of Interpretation* is to provide an account of finitude as creational and therefore fundamentally good—against a (fundamentalist) ontology that devalues the material as always already fallen. In particular, see the derivation of this from a deconstruction of Augustine's diverse accounts of creation and materiality and their resulting tension (*Fall of Interpretation*, 133–48). In the book, I argue that given the goodness of creation, we ought to resist describing finitude as "limited" or "lacking" in any sense, since this would imply a standard that exceeds finitude. I argued something similar, against Marion, in James K. A. Smith, "Respect and Donation: A Critique of Marion's Critique of Husserl," *American Catholic Philosophical Quarterly* 71 (1997): 523–38. This is why I prefer the Thomistic account of the distinction between Creator and creature (the creature being that being for whom its existence is a gift) rather than the Augustinian, which on a Platonic scale of being and nothingness construes the creature as always "lacking" being in some sense. The Augustinian affirmation of the goodness of materiality needs to be—and can be—unhitched from this Platonic scale of being.

of this—in the commentaries on Genesis, for instance, he considers this original goodness of creation as referring to a spiritual or intelligible creation[129]—his most un-Platonic moment is located in his affirmation of the goodness of materiality based on a logic of creation rather than emanation (*Conf.* 4.15.24; 7.5.7; 13.2.2–13.4.5).[130]

Second, this affirmation of materiality and embodiment is reaffirmed (and perfected) in the incarnation as a movement of condescension wherein the transcendent inhabits the immanent without loss. This final qualification—without loss—is that which distinguishes a Christian incarnational ontology from a specifically Platonic ontology.[131] While the Platonic doctrine of *methexis* (participation) grants a role for the material in recollection (e.g., Phaedrus' beautiful, sensible face as a catalyst for the recollection of Beauty itself), this is only because the soul has, regrettably, fallen into a body, and therefore, materiality is necessary as a kind of remedial propadeutic.[132] Thus, Augustine remarks that what was missing from "the books of the Platonists" was the radical notion that "the Word was made flesh and dwelt among us" (*Conf.* 7.9.13). The "putting on" of flesh was not a temporary cloak for an earthly pilgrimage but rather the assumption of materiality for eternity (Phil. 2:5–11)—a notion that runs counter to the Platonic ideal of immateriality and thus undermines the Platonic ontology that grounds the critique of theater.

Third, this consistent valuation of materiality and embodiment is affirmed as an eternal state of affairs in the eschatological hope of resurrection. Unlike in a Platonic framework, embodiment is not a temporary, postlapsarian state of affairs but rather is integral to human identity, demanding the resurrection of the body in the eschaton.[133] Augustine affirms just this point, against the Platonists, in *De civitate Dei* 22.11–20, arguing that the body is essential to the identity of the self and thus requires resurrection.

But what does all this mean for a Christian aesthetic? What are the implications of these three dogmatic themes for a Christian under-

129. For an exposition and critique, with special attention to the Genesis commentaries (including *Conf.* 11–13), see Smith, "Time of Language."

130. For earliest indications, see *Soliloquies* 1.1.2 and *De vera religione* 11.21.

131. Here I mean to distinguish a classically Platonic ontology from RO's theurgical, Neoplatonic participatory ontology.

132. This is why I believe that Pickstock overstates the case for *methexis* as sacramental in AW, 11–20. On a radically incarnational register, the material does not play simply a "remedial" role in a postlapsarian state of affairs but rather as integral and essential for creatures *as* created. The eschaton will not be without sacraments.

133. For a Thomistic argument that deduces the necessity of resurrection from the integrity of body and soul, see Montague Brown, "Aquinas on the Resurrection of the Body," *Thomist* 56 (1992): 165–207.

standing of the arts? Creation, incarnation, and resurrection are three fundamental moments of the Christian affirmation and sanctification of the material that counter the persistent docetic tendencies of Christian thought. Of particular interest here is the way in which this docetic tendency is evidenced, for example, in the "anti-theatrical prejudice"[134] (seen even in Augustine),[135] which is critical of theater because of its materiality and embodiment—that is, because it is sensible and stirs the passions. But if to be embodied (and thus to be both sensible and sensuous) is constitutive of being a creature, and creation is fundamentally good (though also corrupted by the fall), then being embodied and passionate must be structural aspects of being human and affirmed in their goodness. As a result, the critique of theater is undermined and the possibility for the affirmation of drama is opened—and an affirmation of the arts in general. However, this would not mean a blanket sanction of all manifestations of the arts.

Here it is helpful to distinguish between the structure of embodiment and the passions and the direction that they might take. In other words, it is part of the essential structure of the human person as created to be embodied, to "know" via images, and to be passionate, but that structure can take a direction (or *intentio*) that denies the Creator and thus constitutes a twisting or perversion of that structure. To invoke an Augustinian theme that grounds this distinction, the structure is being used in ways not intended by the Creator. As a result, rather than functioning as a means to enjoying God, the structure is enjoyed as an end in itself and constituted as a substitute for God—that is, an idol. For instance, that the embodied self knows via images means that images can have an iconic function, but if that structure is distorted, the images become idols. Further, passion is a structural aspect of a good creation that finds its completion in a passion for God, but if passionate desires are distorted and directed to false ends, the passions become

134. As described by Harris, following Jonas Barish, in *Theater and Incarnation*, 65–68. In earlier aspects of the tradition, the anti-theatrical prejudice stems from a Platonic privileging of the intelligible over the sensible (as seen in Augustine); later in the tradition, particularly in the Protestant Reformation and Puritan writings, the critique of art stems from a privileging of the Word over the image—what we might describe as a kind of logocentrism. Even Dürer believed that his images needed to be supplemented by "the word" to protect their function and complete their intention. For discussion of these matters, see Jonas Barish, *The Anti-theatrical Prejudice* (Berkeley: University of California Press, 1981); and Margaret Miles, *Image as Insight: Visual Understanding in Western Christianity and Secular Culture* (Boston: Beacon, 1985), 95–126. At stake in this later Protestant critique is an entire logic of language and supplementarity that invites critique (in the vein of Derrida's *Of Grammatology*), but which I cannot perform here due to space limitations.

135. *Conf.* book III.

idolatrous.[136] What tended to happen in Augustine's critique of theater was a collapsing of structure and direction. In other words, in criticizing the direction that pagan theater took, Augustine failed to discern the possibility of redeeming the structure and seeing the powerful possibility of Christian theater as an aspect of a Christian "public theology."

We are now in a place to see how we can have an affirmative Christian and Augustinian account of the arts without giving up the possibility for criticism. In other words, we can constitute the aesthetic otherwise, envisioning alternate ends and different intentions. Art, as an affective medium of images that moves and stirs the passions, can function in such a way as to move the soul toward God to find its ultimate enjoyment. Therefore, a Christian incarnational ontology rejects the devaluing of images in two respects: First, the sensible world is to function as a sacrament or image that points us to God. Thus, images have a positive, iconic role to play as an essential aspect of their structure. This is consummated in the incarnation: the enfleshing of the Son as the "image [*eikon*] of the invisible God" (Col. 1:15).[137] The icon is not a mere copy but rather contains the "real presence" of the divine. Thus, the iconic image is not a mere propadeutic to be discarded (as in Plotinus) but that which points to the transcendent and in which the transcendent inheres. As a result, a creational ontology not only subverts a Plotinian devaluing of the material but also subverts the immanentism (RONT, 221) of nihilist and materialist accounts of the image as simulacrum—as an image without original.[138] Thus, Phillip Blond emphasizes the way in which a radically orthodox ontology must affect our sense of the work of art and "the relation between the ideal and the real":

> For if indeed, as Christianity suggests, this material reality we inhabit is a God-given participation by us in him and his ideality, then we can never be equal to the gifts we are given, not least because we are not God and cannot engender the ideal out of ourselves and so provide our own foundation. Theology, then, re-describes the created world, not as nothing, nor indeed as a self-sufficient something, but as the real testimony and loving expression of God who donates the ideal to the real in order to make it so. (RONT, 221)

---

136. In chapter 7, we consider this same point in terms of the Augustinian notion of desire.

137. This is a central text in the Eastern tradition. For a discussion, see Gregory of Nazianus, *The Theological Orations* 4.20. Cf. also Marion, *Crossing of the Visible*, chap. 3.

138. Blond considers modern art to be the realization of "autonomy" in the realm of aesthetics (RONT, 223–25).

Blond, echoing both Ward and Marion, goes on to describe the way in which "Christ binds together in his own body the invisible and the visible, and as a result he incarnates the transcendent in the flesh and prevents any subsequent account of human materiality divorcing itself from theology" (RONT, 239). The result is the "re-consecration" of our world and hence those features of embodied worldliness, such as the arts (RONT, 239–41).

Second, given the embodied structure of the human person, images (and imagination) play an essential role in human knowing and thus contribute to knowledge rather than deceive us. If images can be icons, and the imagination is a structural aspect of creaturehood, then the passions—as structural—can also be affirmed as fundamentally good, even if their direction can be distorted. This even Augustine appreciates, for the *Confessions* themselves are written to stir up and arouse (*excitant*) the hearts and emotions of readers to move them toward God (*Conf.* 10.3.4). But this activation of passion is redeemed by its end, or *telos*—the "good results" that come from the confession (10.3.4), namely, that people are moved toward God. In this sense, Augustine's own life is a drama that engages the audience in a way that follows the *ordo amoris:* His story in the *Confessions* is intended to be enjoyed not as an end in itself but rather as a means by which the reader's heart is affectively moved to seek God (cf. *Retract.* 2.32.1).

But if the literary work of the *Confessions* can be redeemed by arousing passion to an alternative end (*fruitio Dei*), could we not see the same possibility for theater, film, and painting? Might we not envision a drama that stirs the heart and lifts the affections toward God, that forms and transforms passion so that we desire that alone in which we ought to delight—the Triune God? And could this redeemed theater be an integral aspect of a Christian public theology, particularly in a culture that is so centrally directed by the image? Thus, rather than a reactionary critique of an image-saturated culture,[139] might not our time be the "fullness of time" for staging the incarnation? RO's doxological ontology undergirds an incarnational aesthetic, revaluing aesthetic being-in-the-world and reaffirming a sacramental worldview.

139. Miles's analysis in *Image as Insight* is suggestive for considering the primacy of the image in pretextual culture such that the late modern or postmodern primacy of the image might actually constitute a *retrieval* and revaluation of the sensible vis-à-vis the intelligible.

7

Cities of God

Cultural Critique and Social Transformation

Related Reading

Bell, Daniel M., Jr. "Infinite Undulations of the Snake" and " The Church of the Poor." Chaps. 1–2 in *Liberation Theology after the End of History: The Refusal to Cease Suffering*. Radical Orthodoxy. London: Routledge, 2001.

Cavanaugh, William T. "The City: Beyond Secular Parodies." In *Radical Orthodoxy: A New Theology*, edited by John Milbank, Catherine Pickstock, and Graham Ward, 182–200. London: Routledge, 1999.

Milbank, John. "The Other City: Theology as a Social Science." Chap. 12 in *Theology and Social Theory: Beyond Secular Reason*. Oxford: Blackwell, 1990.

Ward, Graham. "Cities of the Good." Chap. 9 in *Cities of God*. London: Routledge, 2000.

While the intricacies of the preceding discussion of ontology may suggest a trajectory aimed at abstraction and speculation, in fact, the *telos* of RO's participatory ontology is practice. As Graham Ward puts it, RO is engaged in "reading the signs of the times" and should be understood as a mode of "Christian *Kulturkritik*," which is itself part of "the constructive, therapeutic project of disseminating the Gospel."[1] In addition to other dualisms that RO decon-

1. Graham Ward, "Radical Orthodoxy and/as Cultural Politics," in *Radical Orthodoxy? A Catholic Enquiry*, ed. Laurence Paul Hemming (Burlington, Vt.: Ashgate, 2000), 104. Here Ward explicitly links RO's project to the tradition of *Kulturkritik* generated by the Frankfurt School of Walter Benjamin and Habermas, also fostered by a commitment to socialism. But here he suggests that RO offers something unique: "In the collapse of socialism as a secular political force I see Radical Orthodoxy as offering one means whereby socialism can be returned to its Christian roots" (103). As John Milbank argued

231

structs, it also calls into question the dualism of theory and practice, aspects that are too often formulated as mutually exclusive—as when some suggest that we need to stop being so concerned with theology and just get down to the work of doing justice or proclaiming the gospel or that theoretical reflection is an inherently bourgeois abstraction that distracts us from practice.[2] For RO, there is a symbiotic, reciprocal, and necessary relationship between the two. Here again, this sentiment echoes Herman Dooyeweerd's understanding of the relationship between theory and practice, or what we could describe as the "theoretical attitude" and the "everyday or natural attitude" (ITWT, 13–17). Theory, in this respect, is diaconal and is itself a practice. This is why ideas matter, or, to put it differently, ontologies make a difference.

The effect of an ontology of immanence rooted in the univocity of being is a kind of ontological atomism (and here Gilles Deleuze is the culmination of Scotist ontology, as Deleuze himself affirms). This ontological atomism translates into a social atomism that is intensified by the advent of virtual reality and cyberspace (CG, 248–49). In contrast, RO's participatory ontology undoes the ontological atomism of ontologies of immanence; as such, it also counters the social atomism of secular modernity by generating an alternative account of sociality rooted in participation. "Humankind was created for communion" (RONT, 182), and the goal of redemption is the renewal and restoration of community. For RO, the primary site of this renewed sociality is the *ecclesia*—the body of Christ (RONT, 184). But as already mentioned, the relationship between theory and practice is reciprocal: The possibilities of a participatory or creational ontology and its attendant account of sociality are unfolded in and by the formation of the liturgy and practice of being the community of God. As John Milbank emphasizes, "There can only be a distinguishable Christian social theory because there is also a distinguishable Christian mode of action, a definite practice. The theory explicates this practice. . . . The theory, therefore, is first and foremost an *ecclesiology*" (TST, 380).

This chapter unpacks this core claim regarding the church as it has unfolded in Radical Orthodoxy and briefly articulates its implications for both theory and practice—including realms of practice that

---

above, *only* theology could properly ground socialism (John Milbank, "Materialism and Transcendence," in *Theology and the Political*, ed. Creston Davis, John Milbank, and Slavoj Žižek [Durham, N.C.: Duke University Press, forthcoming]).

2. This kind of attitude plagues not only pragmatic evangelicalism but also the more recent "emerging church," which, for all its talk of "postmodernism," too often forestalls careful theoretical analysis of the issues. I have tried to address this lacuna in James K. A. Smith, *Who's Afraid of Postmodernism? A Radical Orthodoxy for the Emerging Church*, Critical Theory for the Postmodern Church (Baker Academic, forthcoming).

are traditionally discussed under the rubrics of ethics, politics, and economics. In addition, it continues the dialogue with the Reformed tradition by both articulating Reformed reservations with this claim and also showing RO's ecclesiology poses a welcome challenge to the Kuyperian tradition.[3]

The Church as Social Theory

A Christian Sociology

As Stanley Hauerwas has claimed, "The church does not *have* a social ethic; the church *is* a social ethic."[4] Milbank's claim echoes this sentiment: The church does not *have* a social theory; it *is* a social theory (TST, 380).[5] To put this otherwise, Christian social theory is "first and foremost an *ecclesiology*, and only an account of other human societies to the extent that the Church defines itself, in its practice, as in continuity and discontinuity with these [other] societies" (TST, 380).[6] To understand these claims, we need to get a handle on what

3. More than others, this chapter is transitional—a programmatic sketch of the next phase of my research, which will focus on political theology and confessional politics, with a particular interest in a renewed dialogue between the Reformed and Anabaptist traditions. As I note in this chapter, while there are important differences, there are also deep similarities between the RO project and recent theological and ethical proposals in the vein of John Howard Yoder and Stanley Hauerwas, particularly in the work of William Cavanaugh and D. Stephen Long.

4. Stanley Hauerwas, *The Peaceable Kingdom: A Primer in Christian Ethics* (Notre Dame: University of Notre Dame Press, 1983), 99. The question of the relationship between Hauerwas and Radical Orthodoxy is an important one. As we saw in chapter 2, when Ward or Pickstock discusses theologians who are operating within the same "sensibility," Hauerwas is always on the list. In addition, some of the authors in the RO series were students of Hauerwas (Daniel Bell, Michael Hanby, D. Stephen Long), and we will find their voices prevalent in this chapter. On the other hand, of late, Milbank has been quite critical of Hauerwas, particularly on the matter of universalism versus Hauerwas's supposed sectarianism (see Milbank, "Materiality and Transcendence"). But in TST, Milbank is very close to Hauerwas.

5. And correlatively, "*all* theology has to reconceive itself as a kind of 'Christian sociology': that is to say, as the explication of a socio-linguistic practice" (TST, 381). This bears affinity to George Lindbeck's "postliberal" account of theology in *The Nature of Doctrine* (Philadelphia: Westminster, 1984).

6. This, of course, raises an important question: If a Christian sociology is really an *ecclesiology*, then what does a Christian social theory have to say about *other* societies? As Milbank says here, the church's account of society—that is, of authentic human community—is "only an account of other human societies to the extent that the Church defines itself, in its practice, as in continuity and discontinuity with these societies" (TST, 380). But if one responds that, as a result, a Christian sociology cannot give "a universal 'ratio-

Milbank means by a sociology or a social theory. Clearly, it is not merely an empirical description of a social organization; rather (somewhat in the vein of Karl Marx and the Frankfurt school),[7] what is being offered is a normative or a priori account of human relationality within communities. In fact, as shown above, Milbank's radical critique of social theory calls into question the dominant empiricist paradigm in sociology that purports merely to describe society and the construction of human relationships. Such descriptions, Milbank has argued, are theory laden such that every sociology always already presumes a social theory. What is needed for a normative social theory, however, is a normative account of human nature and the nature of human relationships—what we might call a "philosophical anthropology."[8] Here Milbank's critique of secular sociology echoes the critique of social science that Dooyeweerd articulated a generation earlier. Dooyeweerd also emphasized that the descriptions of social structures offered by social science must presuppose a "theoretical view of the totality of human social relationships"; moreover, such descriptions and theories must be normed by an account of social norms: "We can never discuss [so-called] factual social relations in human society without discussing real social norms, even when these violate the norms. . . . If we try to make a consistent attempt to eliminate normative criteria, we shall

---

nal' account of the 'social' character of all societies," Milbank's response is simple: This is because no such sociology is possible on any grounds (380–81). While it is true that no "universally rational" account is possible (on the epistemological side, we might say), it does not seem to follow that one cannot provide an account of other societies or social structures, albeit from a determinate Christian perspective. Here Dooyeweerd seems to offer a better framework insofar as he recognizes perduring structures of sociality in all societies and institutions that can be subject to analysis in light of the *norms* for these social structures (*A Christian Theory of Social Institutions*, trans. Magnus Verbrugge, ed. John Witte Jr. [La Jolla, Calif.: Herman Dooyeweerd Foundation, 1986], 64–69). In light of these norms, a Christian sociological analysis can point out the *misdirection* of these structures. And insofar as all secular structures fail to be ordered to the Creator, they are all fundamentally characterized by misdirection—contra a rosy Kuyperianism, which, in the name of a bastardized "common grace," wants to assert the perduring "goodness" of these social structures and institutions. In other words, such a Christian sociology could describe "society in general" but always in the mode of critique. The model I am trying to suggest here, as an amalgam of Milbank and Dooyeweerd, can offer an account of social structures in general—quite apart from any "continuity or discontinuity" with the church—but also retain the antithesis between properly ordered human community and the misdirected structures of all secular or pagan instantiations of them.

7. See Rolf Wiggershaus, *The Frankfurt School* (Cambridge, Mass.: MIT, 1994), for a discussion of their self-understanding regarding the normative or prescriptive nature of social theory.

8. Sociologist Christian Smith has unapologetically taken up such a project in his recent work, *Moral, Believing Animals: Human Personhood and Culture* (Oxford: Oxford University Press, 2003).

discover that we end up with no real *human* facts."[9] Like Milbank, Dooyeweerd argued that such a theory is always rooted in theological[1] commitments. Thus, every social theory is, at root, confessional.[10] RO begins by putting that on the table: A Christian social theory begins from a sense of the normative vocation of the human community and the way in which that (creational) vocation is renewed in the life and practice of the church.[11]

Redeeming Community: The Church as Polis

RO offers a story about human society and community in terms of creation, fall, and redemption (RONT, 182). As William Cavanaugh re-counts it, "Humankind was created for communion" (RONT, 182). In other words, with creation came a "natural unity"[12] of the human race grounded in the *imago Dei,* which grounds humanity's participation in both God and one another (RONT, 184).[13] The disruption of this unity and communion was occasioned by the fall, beginning with Adam's attempt to blame Eve for sin and spilling over into the murderous narratives of Genesis 3–11 (RONT, 184). Contrary to the modern secular narratives of Hobbes and Machiavelli, therefore, humanity was not originally at war as part of a kind of natural opposition between individuals; rather, this is a postlapsarian condition. In fact, Cavanaugh suggests, "The effect of sin is the very creation of individuals as such, that is, the creation of an ontological distinction between individual and group" (RONT, 184). Redemption of sociality, then, means the restoration of original unity or communion. This happens "through participation in Christ's Body" (RONT) and *only* in Christ's body,[14] for it is in Christ Jesus that peace and reconciliation are effected (Eph. 2:13–18). The *ecclesia* is the site

9. Dooyeweerd, *Christian Theory of Social Institutions,* 33, 38.

10. Ibid., 45–58.

11. As we note below, on the latter aspect of RO's account—the identification of the *ecclesia* with authentic human community—Dooyeweerd demurs.

12. The notion of unity gives some pause (particularly for those inspired by Derrida and Levinas), seeming to suggest a kind of hegemony or totalizing imposition of "same-ness." But this is not the case: The unity here is one of communal difference—recalling that the "analogical worldview" (Ward) is the only one really able to conceive of differ-ences in non-oppositional relation. The unity is one of *koinonia,* which is the community of those who are different.

13. William Cavanaugh cites Henri De Lubac, who sums up patristic anthropology: "For the divine image does not differ from one individual to another: in all it is the same image. The same mysterious participation in God which causes the soul to exist effects at one and the same time the unity of spirits among themselves" (RONT, 183).

14. As we will see below, then, the question will be, *Where* do we find or participate in Christ's body? Ward's account of the diffusion of Christ's body, as well as Milbank's most

of renewed creational community but is itself only an "anticipation of the eschatological gathering of all the nations to Israel"—an eschatological gathering that is "neither an entirely worldly nor an entirely otherworldly event" but rather the advent of a new heaven and earth "which are already partially present" (RONT, 185). This eschatological proviso is an important reminder regarding the provisional character of the church. Framing it in Augustinian terms, Ward cautions against the identification of the church with the heavenly city:

> The Church is also a human and earthly institution. Insofar as it is ordered towards the worship and love of God, and participates in the triune operation of that God . . . , then it is the heavenly city. But Augustine is also aware that those who make up the ecclesial community are subject to the same desires and temptations of those espoused to the *civitas terrena*. (CG, 229)[15]

Nevertheless, the true commonwealth—and hence communion—is located not in the empire but in the *ecclesia* (RONT, 185). And here is one of the reasons why Ward and Catherine Pickstock suggest a substantial constructive agreement between RO and the theological project of Stanley Hauerwas. While there are points of disagreement, it is both justified and helpful to see Hauerwas's project allied with RO's account of the church as *polis*—and to see both as a constructive way forward for Christian thought and practice.

As shown in chapter 4, this account of human community undergirds RO's critique of secular modernity and the state in particular. In other words, the fall was the advent of social atomism and individualism, and the modern state, working with a pseudo-soteriology, attempts to effect peace but ends up with only a parody of the *ecclesia* insofar as it attempts to construct a community without calling into question the supposed naturalness of individualistic opposition and without the redemption effected in Christ. The modern state[16] attempts to effect

---

recent comments on the church, seems to make Christ's body coextensive with humanity. Cavanaugh hints in that direction as well: "The salvation of individuals is only through Christ's salvation of the whole of humanity" (RONT, 184). Below I suggest that a more persistent Augustinian picture links the body of Christ to election. (For all my reservations with Kuyper's ecclesiology, he is more of an Augustinian in this respect than RO.)

15. Ward makes much of what he describes as Augustine's theology of the *permixtum* or "commingling" (CG, 227), which "blurs" the distinction between the two cities. From this, coupled with his account of the "expansion" or "diffusion" of the body of Christ, Ward seems to conclude that we cannot draw boundaries for the church or boundaries between the church and the world (CG, 257). I return to this below.

16. Though it would seem that this is not the case for *just* the modern state. As Peter Leithart comments, "Aristotle's *Politics* begins with the claim that 'every state is an association

peace, now understood negatively as merely the absence of conflict or the undoing of the *bellum omnis contra omnem* (war of all with all). By contrast, the new Adam who will save us is not the Son but Leviathan (RONT, 188).[17] It is in this sense that RO sees the state as a quasi- or pseudo-*ecclesia* and sees the *ecclesia* as the only authentic *polis*. Here RO clearly echoes the Hauerwasian understanding of the church as an alternative polity and a "holy nation." As Hauerwas puts it, "The church therefore is a polity like any other, but it is also *unlike* any other insofar as it is formed by a people who have no reason to fear the truth." Because the church is called as its own *polis* and nation, Christians "are at home in no nation."[18] The church, then, is not an organization that can fit within the civil society of the nation-state or regnant *polis* because it is an alternative *polis* that calls into question the aims of the state—whether ancient or modern. "The church," Hauerwas remarks, "does not exist to provide an ethos for democracy or any other form of social organization, but stands as a political alternative to every nation, witnessing to the kind of social life possible for those that have been formed by the story of Christ."[19] The church as a community—both a *polis* and *koinonia*—is constituted differently because it is animated by the Holy Spirit and has as its *telos* and aim friendship with God and neighbor. Authentic relations of charity and love are possible within this community because it alone is the community in which "the love of God is shed abroad in our hearts through the Holy Spirit which is given to us" (Rom. 5:5 NASB). What distinguishes the community that is the body of Christ is not only its redirection to humanity's proper *telos* but also the regeneration of the heart that makes redirection toward and pursuit of this *telos* possible.

(*koinonia*)'" and that "the city (*polis*) is the highest kind of *koinonia*, a political *koinonia*" (Peter J. Leithart, *Against Christianity* [Moscow, Idaho: Canon Press, 2003], 25). He goes on to note the way in which the church forms an alternative *koinonia* (Acts 2): "Paul did not attempt to find a place for the Church in the nooks and crannies of the Greco-Roman *polis*. The Church was not an addition, but an alternative to, the *koinonia* of the *polis*" (26–27). The difference between ancient and modern is the difference between city-state and nation-state. But both, it seems, have the characteristic of quasi-ecclesiality (in which the ultimate *telos* of humanity and human community is immanentized).

17. The results of such a salvation are minimal: "Beginning with an anthropology of formally equal individuals guided by no common ends, the best the state can hope to do is to keep these individuals from interfering with each other's rights" (RONT, 193).

18. Hauerwas, *Peaceable Kingdom*, 102.

19. Stanley Hauerwas, "Reforming Christian Social Ethics: Ten Theses," in *The Hauerwas Reader*, ed. John Berkman and Michael Cartwright (Durham, N.C.: Duke University Press, 2001), 114–15. For an oblique justification of my overlapping of Hauerwas and RO on these points, see William Cavanaugh, "Stan the Man: A Thoroughly Biased Account of a Completely Unobjective Person," in *Hauerwas Reader*, 17–32.

This is why the church is a *sacramental* community. This redirection is a question not only of salvation but also of sanctification. It is not an event but the fruit of discipleship. Worship is political because it forms us otherwise, renewing our creational vocation.[20] The Eucharist, for instance, is both a political (i.e., *polis*-related) reality that "undercuts the primacy of contract and exchange in modern social relations" (RONT, 195) and a means of grace that nourishes the community (and individuals within the community) to pursue its proper *telos* and enact authentic sociality.[21] The Eucharist also "transgresses national boundaries and redefines who our fellow-citizens are" (RONT, 194), reminding us that we are primarily citizens of a global *polis* who pledge allegiance to Christ, not to the nation-state we currently inhabit.[22] The central point is that the constitution of this community in which authentic sociality is renewed is not the mere product of "Christian"[23] thinking or principles but the embodied practice of the church, where Word and sacrament are means of grace for the alternative formation that is the necessary condition for this community of love to take shape as a colony of the "heavenly commonwealth [*politeuma*]"[24] whose Lord is not Caesar but Christ (Phil. 3:20). The liturgy is political and that which nourishes the

20. For Augustine, a true "commonwealth," or *res publica*, is possible only where there is true worship (see *City of God* 19.11–28). My thanks to Robert Dodaro for discussions on this point.

21. From a Reformed perspective, this would require that we abandon Kuyper's flattened, unsacramental ecclesiology and recover instead Calvin's robust, sacramental ecclesiology, including his doctrine of (a kind of) real presence. For an account that attempts to restore a certain co-centrality to the Lord's Table in Reformed worship, see Keith A. Mathison, *Given for You: Reclaiming Calvin's Doctrine of the Lord's Supper* (Phillipsburg, N.J.: Presbyterian & Reformed, 2002).

22. This undergirds one of Hauerwas's basic arguments for Christian pacifism: If my fundamental allegiance is to Christ, and my fundamental citizenship is as a member of his body, then how can I participate in actions that—in the service of the interests of the nation-state—would require me to kill a brother or sister in Christ who currently inhabits a different nation-state?

23. Leithart well articulates all the problems with the abstraction of "Christianity" apart from the concrete, incarnate embodiment of the church (*Against Christianity*, 13–40).

24. See N. T. Wright, "Paul's Gospel and Caesar's Empire," in *Paul and Politics: Essays in Honor of Krister Stendahl*, ed. Richard A. Horsley (Harrisburg, Pa.: Trinity Press International, 2000), 173–81. As Leithart points out, many English translations fail to convey the political nature of Paul's call to the Philippians to live as a community of friends who are citizens of a different empire. In particular, Paul's exhortation to conduct themselves as citizens (*politeuo*, Phil. 1:27) is often unrendered, thus missing the link with Philippians 3:20 and the general sense in which Paul is calling them to constitute an alternative *polis:* "The Philippians, so proud of being Roman citizens and so protective of Roman custom, needed to learn to live as citizens of a different commonwealth that placed new demands on its citizens" (Leithart, *Against Christianity*, 28). The translation to a context of American empire seems clear enough.

possibility of an authentic *polis* energized by charity: "These rites, baptism and eucharist, are not just 'religious things' that Christian people do," Hauerwas comments. "They are the essential rituals of our politics. Through them we learn who we are. Instead of being motives or causes for effective social work on the part of Christian people, these liturgies *are* our effective social work."[25]

In particular, the shape of the *ecclesia* as authentic community and sociality is centered around *agape,* a love that undoes the power-centered false *ecclesia* of the state (TST, 390).[26] To put this another way, the church is a community of peace, an authentic, positive peace of harmony, not the merely negative peace of stilled conflict.[27] It is a community in which harmony is possible because it undoes the swirling eddy of self-love (and corresponding self-appointed *teloi*) by orienting the community toward a common *telos* that engenders charity.[28] "True society," Milbank observes, "implies absolute consensus, agreement in desire, and entire harmony amongst its members, and this is exactly (as Augustine reiterates again and again) what the church provides, and that in which salvation, the restoration of being, consists" (TST, 402). Given our postlapsarian context, this must translate into a community of forgiveness: "Without 'mutual forgiveness' and social peace, says Augustine, 'no-one will be able to see God.' The pagans were for Augustine unjust, because they did not give priority to peace and forgiveness" (TST, 409).[29] The Christian community, then, is a unique *polis* that is demarcated by (1) a distinct narrative that is recounted in distinct practices; (2) a different *telos* that transcends the contemporary order; and (3) the common presence of the Spirit at work among its members through Word and sacrament. As such, it stands in contrast to every other *polis* insofar as no other shares its narrative (the Scriptures) or is the site for the Spirit's regenerative, sacramental, and sanctifying presence.

25. Hauerwas, *Peaceable Kingdom,* 108.

26. As we will see below, the real concern is not so much the state but the globalized market that the state serves.

27. Here Milbank recalls Augustine's critique of the so-called "peace of Rome" as only an "apparent" peace—a semblance—"because it is but an arbitrary limitation of a preceding state of anarchic conflict" and could be seen only as the effect of "the exercise of *dominium*" (TST, 390).

28. In other words, ecclesial formation must counter liberal conceptions of freedom and "the idol of 'liberty,' which we are supposed to worship" (John Milbank, "Sovereignty, Empire, Capital, and Terror," in *Dissent from the Homeland: Essays after September 11,* ed. Stanley Hauerwas and Frank Lentricchia [Durham, N.C.: Duke University Press, 2003], 64).

29. For an extended analysis of the place of forgiveness within the *ecclesia,* see Daniel M. Bell Jr., *Liberation Theology after the End of History: The Refusal to Cease Suffering,* Radical Orthodoxy (London: Routledge, 2001), chap. 4.

Against Ethics: Christian Morality and the Antithesis

By construing the church as a *polis*, RO—like Hauerwas—unveils something not only about the church but also about the shape of the *polis* as we experience it in the modern state, especially the modern liberal state that is currently globalized by the American empire. In particular, RO calls into question the naive assumption regarding the state's "neutrality" and highlights the antithesis between the kinds of people the state wants to create and the kind of persons the Spirit forms through the church. This antithesis is considered more carefully below.

First, however, we need to address another important area of antithesis in the arena of ethics. Because of the framework of antithesis assumed by both RO and Hauerwas, any notion of a "common" morality or universal ethics must be jettisoned, along with any project of deriving morality from a perduring "natural law" that holds for all communities (because nature has been obfuscated by sin such that there is no perduring "humanity").[30] Rather, as Hauerwas puts it, "Ethics always requires an adjective or qualifier." An ethic is tied to a particular *ethos* and thus must always be a qualified ethic (whether Jewish, Christian, pagan, liberal, etc.).[31] This view appropriates and radicalizes the insights of Alasdair MacIntyre, on which both Milbank and Hauerwas draw. The point they share is this: Formally speaking, the norms of human social life, and therefore the norms for ethical action, are determined by the *telos* of a community; this *telos* is both revealed and unfolded in a particular story that sustains and orients this community. As such, the norms for communal life are story-relative and therefore distinct to that community. More specifically, for the Christian community, the norms for social life and ethical action are specified by a distinct *telos*, communion with God and neighbor, which is itself specified only in the distinct Christian story embodied in God's revelation in Scripture.

For both Milbank and Hauerwas, then, ethics must be distinctly narrative in its framework and foundation and distinctly Christian in its shape. Following George Lindbeck, Milbank agrees that "these stories are not situated within the world: instead, for the Christian, the world is situated within these stories. They define for us what reality is, and

---

30. Hauerwas's critique of natural law ethics is insightful here: "Emphasis on the distinctiveness of Christian ethics does not deny that there are points of contact between Christian ethics and other forms of the moral life. While such points frequently exist, they are not sufficient to provide a basis of a 'universal' ethic grounded in human nature per se. Attempts to secure such an ethic inevitably result in a minimalistic ethic and often one which gives support to forms of cultural imperialism," which can then be taken to underwrite coercion (Hauerwas, *Peaceable Kingdom*, 60–61).

31. Ibid., 1.

they function as a 'metanarrative,' not in the sense of a story based on, or unfolding foundational reason (Lyotard's sense) but in the sense of a story privileged by faith, and seen as the key to the interpretation and regulation of all other stories" (TST, 385–86).[32] This is because, for Milbank, Christian knowledge—as all knowledge—is ultimately "narrative knowledge" (TST, 263): "Claims for objective truth, goodness and happiness can only be made by identification with a particular form of life that is claimed to participate in them. . . . Christianity can be seen as representing such a form of life." However, it is not "merely one more perspective. It is also *uniquely* different" (TST, 262).[33] The uniqueness of the Christian story (and revelation) entails the uniqueness of a Christian ethic and its antithesis vis-à-vis other "qualified" ethics. "Christian ethics," then, "must serve and be formed by the Christian community, a community whose interest lies in the formation of character and whose perduring history provides the continuity we need to act in conformity with that character."[34]

Therefore, when Milbank asks, "Can morality be Christian?" the answer is quick and blunt: No (WMS, 219). "Christian morality is a thing *so* strange, that it must be declared immoral or amoral according to all other human norms and codes of morality" (WMS, 219). There is not a tidy continuity between what the Christian narrative describes as "good" and what modern liberals consider "good" practices; rather, there is a deep antithesis that brokers no overlapping consensus.[35] This emphasis on the unique and antithetical nature of a distinctly Christian

32. There is a sense in which stories are both an environment to be inhabited and a lens through which to see. On the latter point, cf. Hauerwas: "We do not come to see merely by looking, but must develop disciplined skills through initiation into that community that attempts to live faithful to the story of God. Furthermore, we cannot see the world rightly unless we are changed, for as sinners we do not desire to see truthfully. Therefore Christian ethics must assert that by learning to be faithful disciples, we are more able to see the world as it is, namely God's creation" (ibid., 29–30; cf. TA, 23).

33. Like Dooyeweerd, Milbank claims that the Christian *mythos* is not plagued by the antinomies that characterize non-Christian *mythoi*.

34. Hauerwas, *Peaceable Kingdom*, 33.

35. Milbank's essay, "Can Morality Be Christian?" in WMS, 219–32 (to which I cannot do justice here) is a brilliant analysis of the deep commonality between seemingly disparate ethical frameworks, plotting Nietzsche and Levinas along a continuum that makes them the same in kind. What this one "morality" shares in common is a fundamentally reactive notion of virtue, a concomitant valorization of sacrifice, a complicity with death, all operating under a logic of scarcity that breeds agonism, and a myth of generality or universality. To this Milbank opposes the distinctly Christian themes of gift, end of sacrifice, resurrection, plentitude, and confidence or hope. More recently, Milbank has argued that Levinas and Derrida, though they claim to escape a "sacrificial economy," in fact take it to its logical (and immoral) extreme and fail to see the way in which *only* the Christian economy of gift exchange can subvert the sacrificial economy (BR, 138–61).

ethics generates a critique not only of natural law ethics or deontological notions of a universal human morality but also of virtue theory, which itself criticizes these other objectivist accounts. Given that what constitutes a virtue is determined by the narrative of a particular community, the virtues of the Christian community must be unique to the Christian community and not simply translatable from or into Greek or Hellenic notions. This is the burden of Milbank's critique of McIntyre: Rather than make an appeal to virtue or tradition in general in the face of modernity, Milbank appeals to the specificities of "Christian virtue in particular" (TST, 331). He goes on to assert a fundamental antithesis between Greek conceptions of virtue that begin with the valorization of the "heroic" (and therefore participate in the "morality" criticized above) and the "new Christian 'non-heroic' virtue," which is "almost a contradiction in terms" (TST, 331). In particular, the Christian reordering of the virtues to *charity* occasions "a disturbance of the entire Aristotelian conceptual equipment" (TST, 362). This is because the Greek conception of virtue—like the modern—presupposes an ontology of violence such that virtue is understood within the model of war.[36] As a result, there is a deep complicity between antique and modern reason on just this point (undermining McIntyre's project of retrieving the antique *contra* the modern). Here again we see a link between ontology and *praxis:*

> Considerations concerning ontology, peace and conflict (the prime concern already of the pre-Socratics) have therefore, as Augustine realized, a power to unsettle one's whole conception of virtue, or of what morality is at all. And the main consideration here is that antiquity failed really to arrive at the ontological priority of peace to conflict and therefore failed—from a Christian point of view, and *even* from that of the aspirations of Plato and Aristotle—to break with a heroic conception of virtue, and arrive at a genuinely ethical "good." (TST, 364)

Not only is there no common deontological code for humanity, but there is also no universal human virtue. Rather, in a situation of postlapsarian pluralism, there are only concrete, determinate, story-constituted communities that narrate a particular *telos* and form the habits (i.e., virtues) necessary for pursuing that *telos.* According to the Christian narrative, there is only one authentic *telos:* "You have made us for yourself, and our

---

36. Cf. Hauerwas's similar analysis of the very different paragons of courage in Aristotle and Aquinas (the soldier vs. the martyr) in "Courage Exemplified," with Charles Pinches, in *Hauerwas Reader,* 287–306. They formulate the antithesis as follows: "The world of the courageous Christian is different from the world of the courageous pagan. This is so because of their differing visions of the good that exceeds the good of life itself" (299–300).

hearts are restless until they rest in You."[37] Therefore, the only authentic ethic is that informed by the story of God's revelation in Christ, and the only authentic practice is that nourished by the community of the Spirit.[38]

Erotic Subjects: A Postmodern Augustinianism

The Augustinian axiom noted above points to a central theme in RO's understanding of community and human nature: Against rationalist reductions of the self to a rational animal, and against rule-oriented ethical accounts of the self as an autonomous subject, RO recaptures the Augustinian vision of the creature as a desiring agent. As creatures who are defined by love, we are fundamentally characterized by a desire, an erotic pull toward the Creator, and because this desire can find its proper target only in the Creator, its misdirection toward anything else (such as a mere aspect of creation) generates anxiety and restlessness.[39] Selfhood, then, is intentional: "The creature's 'nature' is not primarily an indeterminate self-positing given, subsisting behind its intentions, but

37. Augustine, *Conf.* 1.1.1.

38. This, of course, raises a question about whether non-Christians can be good or moral. Kuyper's supposition that his non-Christian friends and neighbors were good and moral led him to invoke (invent?) a notion of common grace to account for their goodness, which, given his doctrine of total depravity, he expected not to observe (Abraham Kuyper, *Calvinism: Six Stone Foundation Lectures* [Grand Rapids: Eerdmans, 1943], 121–22). (In the tradition, this has come to function basically like the Catholic notion of a preserved nature.) But, of course, if one concluded that non-Christians were *not* truly good and moral, then one would not need to invent this notion of common grace. Partly because of the problems with Kuyper's notion of common grace (and the way it has been appropriated), and partly because of the biblical witness (Rom. 3:10–19), I am inclined toward this latter conclusion: Morality or authentic virtue is possible only for the community of the redeemed—which should not, of course, issue in self-congratulations since even this is a gift. What appear to be instances of mercy or compassion or justice outside the body of Christ are merely semblances of virtue. For a discussion of "semblance" in this respect, see Hauerwas and Pinches, "Courage Exemplified," 291–302. This is just another way of trying to think through the logic of Aquinas's claim that all the virtues are ordered by charity. If love is a gift, and shed abroad in our hearts only by the Spirit (Rom. 5:5), and if the Spirit indwells only the ecclesial community (Rom. 8; 12), then love—and hence true virtue—is possible only within and for the ecclesial community (cf. similar hints in ITWT, 125–26). I see something similar at least suggested (without the Reformed baggage) in D. Stephen Long, *The Goodness of God: Theology, the Church, and Social Order* (Grand Rapids: Brazos, 2001).

39. This is the focus of Augustine's narrative from books II–V of the *Confessions*, where he seeks to illustrate the frustrations of a misdirected desire—or, better, an idolatrous desire that substitutes alternatives to the Creator. I have analyzed this in more detail in James K. A. Smith, "Confessions of an Existentialist: Reading Augustine after Heidegger," *New Blackfriars* 82 (2001): 273–82, 335–47; and idem, *Speech and Theology: Language and the Logic of Incarnation*, Radical Orthodoxy (London: Routledge, 2002), chap. 4.

rather is finally determined through its intentions by the company she keeps and the objects of her worship, expressed through the descriptions she gives of herself and the world" (RONT, 115). The primary intentional relation of the self to its world is not theoretical reflection (Husserl) or pragmatic concern (Martin Heidegger) but rather love (Augustine). As ek-static, the self is defined by its love, its *eros*. Thus, RO's conception of the self calls into question the reductionist accounts of the self offered by rationalism, liberalism, and capitalism.[40] Describing this desire structure as "the doxological self," Michael Hanby rightly describes it as one that the self "cannot escape, but can only pervert" (RONT, 115).[41] Dooyeweerd picks up and radicalizes this Augustinian theme by arguing that, as ek-static, the self only "is" in relation: "The mystery of the human *I* is that it is, indeed, nothing *in itself;* that is to say, it is nothing as long as we try to conceive it apart from the three central relations [God, human community, temporal world] which alone give it meaning" (ITWT, 124). If the self is constituted and defined by its relations, and these relations are constituted by a mode of intentionality that is desire or love, then "love is who we are."[42]

Daniel Bell expounds the way in which Bernard of Clairvaux developed this account of the human person as a desiring subject who "thirsts" for God (Ps. 63:1). For Bernard, desire is a basic movement of being human and therefore should not be construed in negative terms (as it was by the Stoics or even Buddhism); rather, desire is a gift of God engendered by God's own desire: "Human desire is nothing less than a mirror of the positive, creative desire of God."[43] As such, human desire is not the result of a lack or privation but rather plentitude and excess—a positive movement toward God. Desire, then, is not the negative craving for a lack but the positive passion characteristic of love: "As an expression of charity, desire is not so much an acquisitive drive, characteristic of a lack, but a generosity and donation expressed in the many forms of charity." Because such desire is constitutive of creaturehood in its original goodness, "Bernard speaks of human desire continuing in heaven."[44] Therefore, despite historical tendencies to equate desire with sin and fallenness, for Bernard "human being is constituted

40. I have further explored this Augustinian account of the self in *Speech and Theology*, chap. 4. For a more systematic philosophical anthropology ordered around this center of love, see James H. Olthuis, *The Beautiful Risk* (Grand Rapids: Zondervan, 2001).

41. In *Augustine and Modernity* ([London: Routledge, 2003], 93–94), Hanby shows the way in which Augustine's conception of the self in terms of desire informs his critique of Stoicism (which he takes to be proto-modern).

42. Olthuis, *Beautiful Risk*, 68–71.

43. Bell, *Liberation Theology after the End of History*, 90.

44. Ibid.

by a positive movement of desire. Such was humanity and its desire in the pristine condition of Creation." However, this does not prevent Bernard from giving an account of fallen desire. Invoking a framework analogous to Augustine's *ordo amoris*, Bernard describes corrupted desire as the misdirection of this good creational structure.[45] Bernard articulates this by distinguishing between the "image" of God and the "likeness" of God: "The 'image' was deemed a reference to a fundamental ontological reality, in Bernard's case, desire. The 'likeness,' in turn, was equated with an ethical orientation, with the direction of this desire in harmony with God. Hence, when Bernard asserts that humanity lost its likeness, he is saying that human desire is no longer in harmony with the desire from whence it came."[46] The fall was not the occasion for the advent of desire but rather the distortion and misdirection of the creational structure of desire. Or as Bell puts it, the problem is ethical, not ontological: "Desire remains positive, productive. Only now it finds joy in the wrong productions; it takes pleasure in the wrong goods."[47] Redemption, then, is the reordering of desire to its creational aim by the Word, who came to heal desire.

As Ward points out, however, this creational desire is an *eros* that has not yet been reduced to a libidinal economy, as it will be in late modernity. In other words, while Ward wants to subvert the erroneous notion (inherited from Anders Nygren) that places *agape* in opposition to *eros*, he does not mean to reduce *agape* to *eros*, nor does he reduce the erotic to the libidinal. In this respect, he refuses the dualisms of the tradition on the one hand and the monism of modernity on the other. "Having undone the knot that tied eros to sexuality," Ward suggests, "and hopefully rescued the idea that Christians are also governed by desire, that desire is fundamental to our nature as human beings as God created us, theology will have to show how Christian desire operates in a way that does not accord with the operation of desire in secular culture, the culture of seduction" (CG, 76). A Christian account of desire, in addition to refusing its equation with the libidinal or the sexual, also refuses secularity's reduction of desire to an economy of lack (CG, 172–73). It is because of this link between desire and lack that "desire in secular culture can never be satisfied—that is fundamental" (CG, 76). But this cannot be the understanding of desire in the Christian tradition for two reasons.

45. This echoes the Reformational framework of structure/direction articulated in Albert M. Wolters, *Creation Regained: Biblical Basics for a Reformational Worldview* (Grand Rapids: Eerdmans, 1985). Cf. also ITWT, 129–30.
46. Bell, *Liberation Theology after the End of History*, 90–91.
47. Ibid., 91.

First, desire is located in God, and God cannot be characterized by lack or privation but only by plenitude. "God does not love us because God needs us to complete God's own desire"—and yet God does love us (CG, 77). A Christian theological[1] account of desire "begins with God's desire for me (a prerequisite for any doctrine of election and hence redemption)" (TST, 187). Therefore, God's desire does not operate according to a logic of privation. Second, if our desire for God operated according to a logic of privation, then two problematic scenarios would follow: Either the desire could never be satisfied, in which case we could never achieve peace and rest, or the desire would be satisfied, in which case eternity would shut down (contra Gregory of Nyssa's picture in his commentary on *Song of Songs*). "There is a profound difference between participating in God and a need for God. In the Christian tradition," Ward notes, "God is not there to fulfill human demands. For that is to treat God as we might treat any other commodity in the market-place" (CG, 77). Here we see a marked difference between a properly Christian account of desire and the erotic paradigm adopted by contemporary evangelical worship, which operates according to a logic of privation and construes God as yet another commodity to satisfy a lack.

As Ward concludes, "We are, then, persons of desire. This is the image of God in whom we were created and we are constituted as persons through the operations of this desire (as Hegel saw). Our desire for God is constituted by God's desire for us such that redemption, which is our being transformed into the image of God, is an economy of desire" (CG, 172). It is, in fact, an entrée into trinitarian life such that "in Christ" we participate in the economy of love that characterizes the Trinity itself and the desire within the Godhead (CG, 174). In this sense, then, authentic (and properly directed) *eros* is also communal: "As with the Prodigal Son, the coming to oneself is also a movement towards the others one has separated oneself from in one's voluptuous greed for the world's 'goods'" (CG, 174). Dooyeweerd observes the same communal structure and overflow of desire:

> As the central seat of the image of God, the human selfhood was endowed with the innate religious impulse to concentrate its whole temporal life and the whole temporal world upon the service of love to God. And since the love for God implies the love for his image in man, the whole diversity of God's temporal ordinances is related to the central, religious commandment of love, namely, "thou shalt love the Lord, thy God, with all thy heart, soul and mind, and thy neighbor as thyself" (Mark 12:30–31). (ITWT, 129)

Christian desire, then, is never a private, Kierkegaardian-like love affair with the absolute but always an embodied desiring for the Creator that, as in the Trinity, always involves a third: the Other. Thus, Ward reconfigures the *ecclesia* as an "erotic community" (CG, 152–81).

The burden of this postmodern Augustinian understanding of the self in terms of desire is to unveil the radically different ways in which desire is formed in modernity and postmodernity—and the function of the church as the site of a proper and counter-formation. In other words, the erotic structure of the creature can take different directions, and these different *intentios* are the products of the formation of desire by particular stories narrated by particular communities and enacted by particular disciplines. RO is concerned to analyze the specific forms of desire produced by different communities and to articulate the antithesis between these and the church as the site for authentic *eros*. It is to these analyses that we now turn.

Technologies of Desire: Church, State, Market

While trumpeting the end of history and the triumph of liberal, free-market democracy, Francis Fukuyama conceded the Augustinian axiom above insofar as he suggested that the globalization of liberal democracy and the free market confirmed the conjoining of the two as the regime that best "satisfies the most basic human longings."[48] By assuming that humans have basic or fundamental desires, Fukuyama also confirmed that capitalism and liberal democracy are not just instrumental goods. Rather, they have set themselves up as ultimate goods—as systems and institutions that would purport to satisfy humanity's most basic desires. But of course, if one begins with Augustine and the assumption that humanity's most basic desire is for God, then any regime that pretends to fulfill such a desire can only be an idol—not merely an economic theory or a political framework subservient to God but a rival god. As a result, the relationship between Christianity (or, better, the body of Christ) and these politico-economic regimes cannot be one of simply rapprochement or accommodation. Insofar as these regimes ultimately seek to satisfy the most basic human longings, they set themselves up in contest with the God of Jesus Christ, who also claims to and offers to satisfy these most basic human desires. The Christian, therefore, must critically consider whether it is possible to serve both.

Daniel Bell's brilliant analysis refines this contestation even further, along two levels. First, he forces us to reconsider, today, what is the most

48. Francis Fukuyama, "Reflections on *The End of History,* Five Years Later," in *After History? Francis Fukuyama and His Critics,* ed. Timothy Burns (Lanham, Md.: Rowman & Littlefield, 1994), 241, as cited in Bell, *Liberation Theology after the End of History,* 1.

important competitor of Christ and his body, the church. From the first
century and into modernity, if the church has been aware of competing
allegiances, it has been especially suspicious of the state—particularly in
its imperial form—as that which most threatens the authentic *polis*, the
church. Thus, the early *ecclesia* unfolded in the shadow of a politically
constituted empire, and both the church and the empire recognized
that the gospel of Christ subverts the empire's claims to monopolize
allegiance (cf. Acts 16).[49] Through modernity, this political regime crystallized in the form of the nation-state but still demanded the same kind
of total, or at least ultimate, allegiance that trumped others (RONT,
183). (Anything like a Patriot Act can broach no compromise.) In this
respect, one could see John Howard Yoder's and Hauerwas's analyses
largely working within a paradigm in which the state is the looming
idol that the church is most tempted to worship. But Bell suggests
that this is a dated and therefore somewhat impotent mode of analysis
and critique, for in a globalized world it is no longer states that wield
imperialist power but rather capitalism and the market.[50] While there
is obviously a link between this globalized market and North Atlantic
nation states, especially the United States, the new empire is capitalism
as a global, transnational phenomenon—an empire of which states are
only colonies.[51] This is also why he criticizes liberation theology for
continuing to think that "statecraft"[52] is the means for securing peace
and justice. What can states really do in the face of the transnational
phenomenon of the market—particularly when states are servants of
this market?

Following Deleuze and Guattari, Bell considers the way in which
capitalism has unleashed a "deterritorializing" power that now exceeds

49. Cf. Wright, "Paul's Gospel and Caesar's Empire," 173–81.

50. Bell's consideration of this new empire echoes the analyses in Michael Hardt and
Antonio Negri, *Empire* (Cambridge: Harvard University Press, 2001).

51. This contention regarding the trumping of the state by the market does not mitigate
the critiques of Yoder, Hauerwas, and others insofar as states *serve* capitalism and remain
a primary mode of formation. The reason for this deep coalescence is due to the fundamental link between liberalism and capitalism (see D. Stephen Long, *Divine Economy:
Theology and the Market*, Radical Orthodoxy [London: Routledge, 2000], 10–12); therefore,
Hauerwas's critique still holds insofar as liberalism is now a worldview that is imbedded
in transnational capitalism, not just in nation-states.

52. Bell defines "statecraft" as that (modern) conception of politics "that holds that
the realm where persons come together in a polity, in a politics, is rightly overseen by and
finds its highest expression in the state; it is the investiture of the state with sovereign
authority over the socius and, consequently, privileging the state as the fulcrum of social
and political change" (*Liberation Theology after the End of History*, 13). Milbank takes this
notion of sovereignty to be central to the modern nation-state and that which was most
threatened by the attacks of 9/11/01 (Milbank, "Sovereignty," 63–69).

that of the state and overwhelms it—as a kind of invention that Dr. Frankenstein can no longer control. Thus, the state can no longer play the regulative role it once did: "The modern nation-state is the state-form completely subsumed by the capitalist axiomatic. Capitalism is 'an independent, worldwide axiomatic that is like a single City, megapolis, or "megamachine" of which the States are parts or neighborhoods.'"[53] Because "economy escapes the state"—and eventually "returns to capture its former master"—the economic aspect is absolutized in its capitalist mode,[54] with the result that every mode of life becomes construed in terms of the economic. "Neoliberal government aggressively encourages and advocates the extension of economic reason into every fiber and cell of human life. Economic or market rationale controls all conduct. Capitalism has enveloped society, absorbing all the conditions of production and reproduction. It is as if the walls of the factory had come crumbling down and the logics that previously functioned in that enclosure had been generalized across the entire space-time continuum."[55] Every aspect of society—schools, athletics, even the church[56]—must insert itself in the capitalist machine. Capitalism, then, is the new empire the gospel must oppose because it demands an allegiance that rivals allegiance to Christ.

Second, Bell refines the analysis by considering this tension and clash in terms of desire or, more specifically, what he calls, in Foucauldian terms, "technologies of desire."[57] By this he indicates the fairly classical notion that selfhood (and community) is the product of formation, and formation is the product of a regime of disciplines and practices. Disciplines are aimed at forming certain kinds of persons whose aim

---

53. Bell, *Liberation Theology after the End of History,* 17 (citing Gilles Deleuze, *Thousand Plateaus,* 434–35).

54. Because the "economic" has become so closely identified with its "capitalist" manifestation, there is often a tendency to collapse the two, concluding that the "economic" simply means "capitalism." But Kuyper and Dooyeweerd's framework enables us to recognize exchange and commerce as a creational *structure* and to see capitalism as a particular *direction* (better, misdirection) that this creational structure has taken. As such, it also permits us to envision a different, noncapitalist manifestation of the economic aspect.

55. Bell, *Liberation Theology after the End of History,* 31. This notion of a "generalization" of a disciplinary practice across society echoes Foucault's account of the "generalization of punishment" in *Discipline in Punish,* trans. Alan Sheridan (New York: Vintage, 1977). I discussed this in more detail in Smith, *Who's Afraid of Postmodernism?* chap. 4.

56. For further discussion of this point, see Philip Kenneson and James Street, *Selling Out the Church: The Dangers of Church Marketing* (Nashville: Abingdon, 1997); and Michael Budde and Robert Brimlow, *Christianity Incorporated: How Big Business Is Buying the Church* (Grand Rapids: Brazos, 2002).

57. For my own critical appropriation of Foucault for thinking about Christian discipleship, see my *Who's Afraid of Postmodernism?* chap. 4.

or *intentio* is a particular *telos*[58] (or "vision of the Good").[59] Cashing this out in the Augustinian terms above, discipline is aimed at the formation of desire, and desire constitutes the heart of the self. It is in these terms that we are able to understand that "the conflict between capitalism and Christianity is nothing less than a clash of opposing technologies of desire,"[60] for each is trying to form very different people for very different ends. In particular, capitalism is a technology of desire that deforms creational desire, misdirecting it to an idolatrous *telos* (namely, consumption, accumulation, and the disposal of material goods as the primary mode for securing happiness).[61] Thus, Bell describes capitalism as that "discipline of desire" that is "a form of sin, a way of life that captures and distorts human desire in accord with the golden rule of production for the market."[62] The fundamental logic of capitalist discipline "is a logic of acquisition and consumption." However, this does not mean that capitalism forms everyone as a consumer: "On the contrary, capitalism covers a broad spectrum of subject positions: from the hyper-acquisitive

58. On this score, the case of the state is ambiguous. On the one hand, the modern liberal state is too vacuous to offer a substantive vision of the Good. As Milbank suggests, "The modern secular state rests on no substantive values. It lacks full legitimacy even of the sort that Saint Paul ascribed to the 'powers that be,' because it exists mainly to uphold the market system, which is an ordering of a substantively anarchic (and therefore not divinely appointed in Saint Paul's sense) competition between wills to power" ("Sovereignty," 64). On the other hand, its very liberalism *is* a particular vision of the Good, which it holds exclusively. It is in this sense that we must appreciate the way that liberalism is a worldview and therefore fundamentally religious (or theological[1])—and therefore a gospel competing with the gospel of Christ. John Owen is helpfully forthright in describing liberalism in these terms: "Liberalism is first a worldview, a set of fundamental categories through which individuals understand themselves and the world. It thus shapes individuals' conceptions of their identities and interests by telling them of what human nature and the good consist" (John Owen IV, *Liberal Peace, Liberal War* [Ithaca, N.Y.: Cornell University Press, 1997], 19).

59. In this respect, Bell's neologism "technologies of desire" describes the notion of disciplinary formation at the heart of both Foucault's and Hauerwas's ethics.

60. Bell, *Liberation Theology after the End of History*, 2.

61. Long is particularly interested to deconstruct the way economics undertakes this project under the guise of a neutral, scientific account of "the facts" (accepting Weber's fact/value distinction). But Long does not buy it: "While it appears to give us merely the facts, it gives us much more. It invites us to construe our lives, primarily our lives as family members, in terms of the activities of producers and consumers" (Long, *Divine Economy*, 4).

62. Bell, *Liberation Theology after the End of History*, 2. He later specifies this: "Capitalism is sin because it fractures the friendship of humanity with God. It disrupts the original, peaceable flow of desire that is charity; it ruptures the sociality of desire, which by nature seeks out new relations in the joyous conviviality that is love. Capitalism is sin because it harnesses the productive power of desire in its original mode, which is donation or giving, to the market. In so doing it corrupts it, rendering it proprietary" (151).

Trumps and Reagans (the latter a trope for the collective subjectivity of empire), to the bulk of humanity, the two-thirds world who although hardly partaking of the fruits of the capitalist order are nevertheless subject to and disciplined by it. In other words, capitalist discipline celebrates consumption, but does not form all of its subjects as consumers."[63] With the generalization of capitalist technologies of desire across the *socium*, almost every sphere of cultural and public engagement—government, schools, entertainment, even religious life—are directed toward consumption, all under the politicized banner of "freedom."[64] This is why appeals to civil society—recently adopted by liberation theology—are insufficient for resisting the "infinite undulations of the snake":

> In this era of global capitalism, when Coca-Cola and Nike find their way into every nook and cranny of the earth well ahead of clean water, roads, and life-sustaining diets, far from furthering the cause of liberation and life, civil society can only be a means of discipline, an instrument of the regnant capitalist order for overcoming resistance and forming desire in its own image.[65]

When even the church has become co-opted by the regnant capitalist technologies of desire—as its consumerization of religious fetishes confirms—what possibilities remain for the healing of desire?

By considering capitalism as a (globalized) technology of desire, Bell unveils its theological[1] (albeit idolatrous) freight. Far from being merely a "neutral" mode for economic distribution, capitalism is a particular religious (and imperial) vision of "basic human longings" (Fukuyama) or desires. Capitalism, then, is not merely an instrument or tool that can be put to work as a servant of other substantive construals of the Good; rather, it proposes its own account of the *telos* to which human desire ought to be aimed (consumption and accumulation). This alternative *telos* can only be seen as a rival god and therefore an idol that must be resisted by those who follow Christ. On top of this, Bell considers the horrible injustices that have been (and must be) the fruit of globalized capitalism. Not only does capitalism deform the creational structure of desire, but it also lays waste to God's creatures and creation.[66]

---

63. Ibid., 7n6.

64. Bell considers the way in which the market model of relations—viz., competition—both reflects and feeds anthropology of secular modernity (a "war of all with all"), which is in turn rooted in an ontology of violence (ibid., 33–35). Thus, "capitalist discipline distorts desire into a competitive force" (35).

65. Ibid., 70.

66. Here we must note an important qualification: Some might hear this radical, trenchant critique of capitalism as a rather naive and very *un*-Reformed banishment of

Why, then, has the church failed to resist capitalist discipline—or even worse, how did the church come to serve capitalist discipline? The church and individual Christians have bought secular economics' myth of religious neutrality. In other words, the church believed economists when they pronounced the facts of economic reality that confirmed capitalism's picture of the world. By granting the very notion of a secular, autonomous temporal realm, the church left it to supposedly secular reason to describe the realities of economic organization. But what was being purveyed under the banner of science and facts was, in fact, an idolatrous theology. Admitting the Trojan horse of secular economic theory into the church was at the same time an admission of a false religion that seductively offered an account of the *telos* of human desire that was deeply antithetical to the message of the cross.

Having unveiled the ultimately theological[1] or confessional nature of capitalism and thus pointing to the dangers of its secular liturgies and modes of discipline (in advertising, for instance), Bell considers the way in which Christianity offers a different technology of desire—a technology that actually heals desire and offers a "therapy" for distorted desire. In this sense, Christianity is "a therapy, a way of life that releases desire from its bondage, that cures the madness so that desire may once again flow as it was created to do."[67] Given the transnational "megapolis" of capitalism—and hence its deterritorialized means of discipline in which states are merely municipalities for administration of its technology of desire—the only way in which capitalist technologies of desire can be resisted is by an alternative *polis*, itself transnational, that is not simply another subsector of the state or "civil society" (which is itself a subsector of capitalism).[68] This alternative *polis*, for Bell, is located in the

---

economics as inherently sinful. But this is not the case at all. In fact, such a response naively and unimaginatively assumes that economic distribution could *only* be capitalist. Within a Reformed rubric, however, I would affirm that the sphere of commerce, exchange, and distribution of goods is indeed a good structure of creation. But capitalism is a particular *direction* in which that good structure has been taken—and more specifically, it is a *mis*direction of creational norms for commerce, exchange, and distribution. To reject capitalism as basically idolatrous is not to naively reject the realm of economic and commercial vocation. But it does require *re*directing our practices in this sphere (as seen in the early church's mode of distribution and exchange). My thanks to Bill Dyrness for pushing me on this point.

67. Ibid., 3.

68. This is one reason why Miroslav Volf's critique of Bell is somewhat mistargeted on this score. Volf takes Bell to task for proposing the church as "an alternative to the state" (Miroslav Volf, "*Liberation Theology after the End of History*: An Exchange," *Modern Theology* 19 [2003]: 263). But this is not really Bell's claim. The problem here is capitalism, which is transnational; entities operating at the level of the state are insufficient to resist its deterritorialization.

ecclesia, the universal and catholic body of Christ. Hence, "if Christians are to resist capitalism, if Christianity is to heal desire, the modern differentiation of life, with its separation of politics and religion, must be refused."[69] In other words, if we accept the modern compartmentalization of life into sacred and secular realms (which map onto the private and public distinction), and if we concede the shape of economics and politics to the secular, public realm, then we are, in fact, serving other gods, either without knowing it or without sensing a tension between doing so and our confession of faith in Christ. We will end up spending our workweek making cakes for the queen of heaven and spending our weekends with Yahweh (Jer. 7:16–19)—without seeing the way in which our service to the queen of heaven is forming us into queen-of-heaven kinds of people.

Thus, Bell calls into question not only the sacred/secular, private/public distinctions of modernity but also the apolitical understandings of the church that have dominated modern theology and practice. Like Hauerwas, Bell asserts that the church does not *have* a politics; it *is* a politics. The means for securing justice and resisting capitalist discipline, then, is not statecraft but rather being the church as the site for an alternative (creational and therefore proper) technology of desire. This requires "Christianity's reassertion in the material realm as the true politics. Christianity is the true politics, the true polity, over against the agony of capitalist discipline, in the Augustinian sense that the church embodies the true form of human social, political, and economic organization because its order is one of liturgy, or worship of the triune God."[70] Therefore, "the Christian *mythos* finds its political correlate, not in the state—even one ordered toward the common good—but in the church as the exemplary form of human community."[71] The only technology of desire that can properly resist capitalist discipline is one that is directed to the creational *telos* of humanity: the Triune God. Insofar as such a redirection of desire requires regeneration of the desiring heart and the continued sanctification of the desiring agent, and insofar as the site for such regeneration and sanctification of desire is the sacramental worship community, then resistance to capitalist discipline can happen only in the *ecclesia.*[72] It is the very material practices of baptism, Eu-

69. Bell, *Liberation Theology after the End of History,* 71.

70. Ibid., 4.

71. Ibid., 72.

72. This is where Volf lodges one of his major complaints with Bell's argument. Volf criticizes "the absence—or rather insufficient presence—of the Holy Spirit in Bell's technology of desire. In other words, the church with its practices has absorbed the Holy Spirit" (Volf, "Exchange," 265). As he reiterates it in his response to Bell's response, Volf's

charist, prayer, and catechesis that transform the self and heal desire.[73]
Sacramental worship is the primary site for the reformation of human
desire, which, in a capitalist world, can only be a subversive, counter-
cultural gesture.[74]

RO's Church: Questions and Reservations

A Creational Church? Questions about the State as Ecclesia and the Church as Polis

From a Reformed perspective, particularly in the heritage of Kuyper
and Dooyeweerd (less so in the sacerdotal tradition of Calvin's Geneva),
one of the most disconcerting aspects of RO's account of cultural engagement is its attribution of this work of cultural redemption to
the church as such and its suggestion that the state and church are,
fundamentally, competitors—one *polis* versus another.[75] If Leviathan
swallowed the church, the Reformed tradition would worry that Bell's
"more substantive ecclesiology" signals a church that threatens to in-
gest the state. In the orthodox Kuyperian picture of social institutions,

"free church" line comes to the fore when he emphasizes "the *internal* work of the Spirit,"
which is not necessarily connected to the church: "It is *God* who opens the hearts to the
Gospel, *God* who kills the old self and makes alive the new, *God* who comes to dwell in the
soul—and all the self-binding of God to the means of grace notwithstanding, God does all
this when and where God wants, with no strict correlation between external means of grace
('technologies') and their internal effect" (Miroslav Volf, "Against a Pretentious Church:
A Rejoinder to Bell's Response," *Modern Theology* 19 [2003]: 283). But this just seems to
be a reiteration of a "Protestant principle" that feeds into the minimalist ecclesiologies of
evangelicalism—as well as that of Kuyper. I would affirm, with Calvin, the correlation of
the means of grace with the advent of grace, even while agreeing with Volf regarding the
necessity of "subjective appropriation" (Volf, "Exchange," 266).

73. Bell, *Liberation Theology after the End of History*, 85–86.

74. Bell's project raises a nexus of important questions that I cannot sufficiently address here. In particular, further reflection is needed on the relationship between change
in agents and change in structures—or, in other words, the role of the Great Commission
with respect to the cultural mandate. Having been extricated from a fundamentalist and
revivalist fixation on "evangelism" as the only agent of social change, evangelical theology
has finally come to appreciate the necessary requirements of *structural* change. However,
there is a tendency within the Reformed tradition to think structural change is a necessary
and sufficient condition for the advent of justice. But are we perhaps in a place where we
can once again, tentatively, think about the role of the conversion of individual agents as
a necessary condition? In other words, have we made sin *only* structural? Bell seems to
keep both aspects in helpful tension (ibid., 177–78). I think the same is true in Miroslav
Volf, *Exclusion and Embrace* (Nashville: Abingdon, 1996).

75. Here in particular the programmatic nature of my reflections comes to the surface.
This final section should be read as a series of questions for further research.

the state and the church are distinct spheres—and for Dooyeweerd, at least, these spheres are constitutive of creation as created.[76] If the state is creational, and the church is creational, then their distinction must be essential (even if their differentiation is only unfolded in history). In that case, where RO tends to see a relationship of competition between the church and the state (competing for the task of specifying the *telos* of human community), the Reformational tradition sees two legitimately distinct spheres of social organization and community. Is there a way to account for the difference?

There are a couple of points to consider. First, there is a tendency in RO to conflate and confuse a particular direction of the state with the structure of the state as such. As we saw in Bell's discussion of desire, it is important to distinguish between the creational structure and the postlapsarian direction that structure can take and has taken. In this respect, the Reformational tradition would affirm RO's critique of the state as a quasi-*ecclesia* and pseudo-soteriological institution by seeing such a version of the state as a disordering of creational structures, where the state has assumed the role of the church and thus both confused distinct aspects of creation and falsely specified the end to which humanity is called. But unlike RO, the Reformational tradition—because it recognizes this distinction between creation structure and postlapsarian direction—points to the possibility of constituting the state otherwise. The state, *as state*, can be properly ordered toward the Creator without the state becoming the *ecclesia*. However, in the picture given so far, it seems that the church is a remedial site for the renewal of authentic community, and as such, after the eschaton and securing of this renewal, it will wither away and we will have a universal human community—a *polis*?—properly oriented to God (a "holy nation"). This then raises questions about Dooyeweerd's contention that the church and the state are essential creational spheres, for if that is the case, how do they persist in the eschaton? In this respect, Kuyper's account of the state as a postlapsarian phenomenon[77] seems to require an eschatological correlate in which the "need" for the state is erased

---

76. There is a tendency within the tradition, stemming from Kuyper, to see the advent of the state with the fall, such that the "restraining" work of the state is needed only *after* the advent of sin, which disorders creation (see Kuyper, *Calvinism*, 79–81). In this sense, Kuyper's framework might be more amenable to something such as Cavanaugh's or Bell's claims. For Dooyeweerd, however, the state is a natural or creational social institution, as is the church (see *Christian Theory of Social Institutions*, 86–93). Here he simply echoes the Augustinian and Reformed tradition that sees the church as instituted with Adam.

77. It almost seems that, for Kuyper, the state is a kind of quasi-redemptive structure, even though it is not a creational structure included in the pronouncement of goodness in Gen. 1:31.

in the eschaton and only the church perdures. The link of the state to the fall, in Kuyper, resonates with the picture painted by Cavanaugh and Bell. Where they differ, however, is with respect to the pre-eschatological relationships between the two institutions. One could take a Kuyperian—though not Dooyeweerdian—logic concerning the state, recognizing a kind of essential fallenness about the state. But even this requires a revision of Kuyper's positive posture toward the state as an institution. A third way may be found in a new appropriation of the work of Klaas Schilder.[78]

Second, RO's account of the church as the only true *polis* is persuasive because it begins, in a way, with a more robust account of the fall and the way in which alternative social communities are fundamentally misdirected and operate on the basis of a fundamentally flawed anthropology (and ontology). In this sense, RO could be an occasion for the Reformed tradition to reconsider and reappropriate its sense of antithesis[79] and to more consistently think through its theology of election and regeneration. If authentic community is possible only where there is love, and love is only properly shed abroad in our hearts by the Spirit's indwelling presence (Rom. 5:5), and the Spirit indwells only the redeemed (i.e., the elect), then authentic community is possible only in the company of the redeemed[80]—the renewed *polis* that is the

---

78. This is a direction for future research, spurred by Richard Mouw's suggestions in "Klaas Schilder as Public Theologian," *Calvin Theological Journal* 38 (2003): 281–98. Mouw suggests a certain overlap between Schilder's Reformed version and the Anabaptist vision of Hauerwas, with some important differences. For instance, while Schilder advocated a kind of "abstinence" with respect to sociopolitical engagement, "it is not because he is convinced that a larger cultural program is illegitimate as such, but rather it is because of his gloomy assessment of the historical circumstances in which he finds himself" (292). This might be a way of saying that I disagree with RO's conflation of structure and direction with respect to the state, but given the current configuration of the state, I think we should perhaps posture ourselves *as if* the structure itself were flawed.

79. Of course, this requires rethinking the notion of common grace as bequeathed to us by Kuyper and appropriated in quite disturbing ways in contemporary Reformed thought. In this sense, in my future research, I hope to take up the line of thought suggested by Klaas Schilder, *Christ and Culture*, trans. G. van Rongen and W. Helder (Winnipeg, Man.: Premier Printing, 1977), perhaps answering Richard Mouw's call for an "American 'translator-interpreter'" of Schilder's thought for the contemporary context" (Mouw, "Klaas Schilder," 288). (Hopefully a Canadian can fit the bill.)

80. One can find evidence for this logic in Dooyeweerd when, speaking of the possibility of authentic communion between fellow human beings, he claims, "A real inner meeting presupposes real self-knowledge and can only occur in the central religious sphere of our relation with our fellow-man" (ITWT, 125–26). If, as Dooyeweerd goes on to argue, "real self-knowledge" is possible only on the basis of "the Word-revelation of God operating in the heart, in the religious center of our existence by the power of the Holy Spirit" (ITWT, 126), then it would seem that authentic sociality is possible only in the community of the Spirit (the church).

church. If that is the case, then Reformed confidence in the possibilities of just communities or social structures must be revisited in light of the Reformed tradition's own Augustinian theology. In this respect, the Reformed account should be revised in the direction of RO.

A Church without Boundaries?

A second reservation with RO's account of the church is the most recent accounts of the *ecclesia* offered by Milbank and Ward. They stem from their new Thomism, which, in calling into question the traditional nature/grace distinction, seems to preclude any distinction between being human and being redeemed. In other words, the human community and the community that constitutes the *ecclesia* would be coextensive. One already sees this suggested in Ward's *Cities of God*, where his emphasis on the "blurring" of the heavenly and the earthly city makes it impossible to draw boundaries around either.[81] Invoking Augustine's account of the "interwoven" (*permixtum*) relation of the two cities, Ward concludes to "a necessary agnosticism" (CG, 228–29). Therefore, not only does he resist identifying the church with the heavenly city—as Augustine rightly counseled against (CG, 229)—but he is also reticent to identify boundaries of this earthly human institution (CG, 257–58). This seems to stem from his ontology: Taking Christ's body as the paradigm for all bodies, Ward understands the Eucharistic "fracturing" of Christ's body

---

81. This is one place where a significant difference between Ward and Milbank can be seen. Ward is very much still within a post-Kantian ("anti-realist") framework (rather than Milbank and Pickstock's more confident, robust "realism"). Thus, in the name of hermeneutic humility, Ward seems to concede the Cartesian paradigm of epistemic certainty as the ideal of knowledge. And since that is not possible, he must end with a certain skepticism—with "not knowing." "We may speak of two kingdoms or two cities, as Augustine and later Luther did," he says, "but none of us can know the extent to which one is independent of the other. None of us have that true knowledge of where we are at any given moment, or where anyone else is. . . . There is faith, hope and charity which operates by seeing through a glass darkly" (CG, 226). This skepticism hits full stride in the conclusion, where he asserts—because he needs to—"I can and do remain a Christian" (CG, 257), but one is not really sure *why*, since "we do not know what we say when we say 'Abba,' 'Lord,' 'Christ,' 'salvation,' 'God'" (CG, 259). In this respect, Ward is still quite close to John Caputo and Derrida in their Kantian inheritance, whereas Milbank and Pickstock seem to resist the Kantian paradigm. Here I should confess that my own work in the past has been characterized by elements of this skeptical tradition (see James K. A. Smith, *The Fall of Interpretation: Philosophical Foundations for a Creational Hermeneutic* [Downers Grove, Ill.: InterVarsity, 2000], 175–78; and *Speech and Theology*, 96–102). In the past, I have been infected by the "Protestant principle." Most notably lacking in my earlier work was a robust role for the church. Thus, in criticizing Ward on this matter, I am happy to concede that this critique might also apply to some aspects of my own work, which I would now want to revise.

to be something that spills over onto all bodies. Thinking through the logic not only of resurrection but also of ascension, Ward suggests that the Eucharistic fracture of the body of Christ entails both a displacement and an expansion of the body of Christ, which Ward describes as "transcorporeality" (CG, 93). "In Christ's ascension his body is expanded" (CG, 94) so that "through the brokenness of the transcorporeal body God's grace operates through his creation" (CG, 95–96). But this seems to entail that the body of Christ—the church (CG, 94)—is coextensive with the order of creation. This is later confirmed, albeit obliquely, when he equates God's founding of society with the *ecclesia* (CG, 117) and when he asserts that "*all* human bodies participate in this one body and this participation and belonging constitutes the ecclesial body, the Church" (CG, 225, emphasis added).

A similar expansion of the ecclesial body is found in Milbank's most recent work (not, I would contend, in TST). In *Being Reconciled*, Milbank's theology of nature as always already graced tends toward a similar blurring of the orders of creation and redemption and therefore the group that constitutes humanity and the community that constitutes the *ecclesia*. Because the gift of grace seems to be immediately "lost and renewed" (BR, 27) by God's "immediate correction" (BR, 42)—and because this seems to be a universal gift and renewal (BR, 169)—there seems to be a sense in which none of this "is exactly 'outside' the Church" (BR, 121).[82] This conflation of humanity *en toto* with the community that constitutes the *ecclesia* is confirmed in several ways: by the hasty equation of human talents with spiritual gifts[83] (BR, 106), by the suggestion that the Holy Spirit is operative "throughout the social body" (BR, 183), and that "education into virtue" is possible within the strictures of the state (BR, 186).

But wasn't it Milbank, in *Theology and Social Theory*, who asserted the fundamental antithesis of the *ecclesia* vis-à-vis other configurations of the *polis*—and asserted that the church alone was the site for renewed communion and sociality? It seems that this requires a twofold emphasis and corrective. First, Ward's skeptical stance with respect to boundaries

---

82. Thus, Milbank poses the question: "How is the peace of the Church mediated to and established in the entire human community? I still believe that the answer is 'socialism'" (BR, 162). But what if the question begins from a mistaken assumption? We should first ask not *how* the peace of the church is universally mediated but *whether* it is. I do not think a reader of TST in the early 1990s would have come to the conclusion that this question in BR presupposes.

83. Of course, there is a sense in which even human talents, possessed by all humans, are gifts of the Creator. But it seems from Rom. 12 and 1 Cor. 12 (as well as Eph. 4 and 1 Pet. 4) that "spiritual gifts" *(pneumatikon, charismata)* are empowerments that attend the indwelling of the Holy Spirit, which is true only of those who are "born of the Spirit."

should be jettisoned for a post-critically dogmatic stance that asserts the necessity of boundaries as the condition for community. As Reinhard Hütter has argued, there can be no "public" without borders: "An unlimited, altogether open space does not constitute a public. Openness in all directions actually destroys any public."[84]

Second, the conception of the church as counter-*polis* must be deeply pneumatological. As Hütter suggests, improvising on Kant, "Pneumatology without ecclesiology is empty; ecclesiology without pneumatology is blind."[85] The assertion of an ecclesial antithesis requires a more persistent Augustinianism that resists the tendencies to make the human community coextensive with the *ecclesia* by recovering the centrality of the Spirit's operation in the work of regeneration (and sanctification) and risking the scandalous affirmation of the utter particularity of that work in the community of the elect, while still constructing the community as one of welcome and hospitality. Such a pneumatological ecclesiology, particularly with an emphasis on regeneration, can be found in both Kuyper and Calvin. In other words, an ecclesiology that construes the church as *polis* requires a robust pneumatology and a recovery of the doctrine of election, providing the shape of an ecclesiology that is Reformed, catholic, and charismatic.[86] In this respect, RO stands in need of reform.

84. Reinhard Hütter, "The Church as Public: Dogma, Practice, and the Holy Spirit," *Pro Ecclesia* 3 (1994): 347.

85. Ibid., 358.

86. We find this in Hütter's proposal, which—eschewing the "Protestant principle" and in contradistinction to Volf's critique of Bell—unabashedly links the work of the Spirit with the dogmas of the church. He concludes that "while the church clearly cannot lay claim to the Holy Spirit as if the church's dogma and practices would 'manage' the Spirit (in this sense the Spirit always remains Lord over against the church) nevertheless, the church's dogma and practices are far from being irrelevant for the Spirit's own publicity and activity. To put it another way: the Spirit can do a 'new thing,' guide the church into all the truth (John 16:13) only if there is a binding set of dogmas and practices in the church" (ibid., 359).

Conclusion

Taking Radical Orthodoxy to Church

To fully appreciate a symphony, one needs acoustics that do it justice. There is a sense in which the sketch of Radical Orthodoxy provided here is a score that demands performance, and the only fitting place for the symphony of Radical Orthodoxy is within the reverberating acoustics of the cathedral—like the Reformed yet catholic churches of Saenredam. Or to use the cartographer metaphor, the point of maps is to navigate travel—launching treks on difficult trails and dirty streets. Thus, the ultimate *telos* of this introduction to Radical Orthodoxy should be the worship of the church and its task of discipleship. I hope that the trajectory of such a performance or journey has been sketched here, but it remains for those laboring in the church to perform it for themselves.

If the composer could provide a few interpretive hints regarding the score, I would suggest that the core themes of RO translate into some concrete proposals for worship and discipleship:[1]

- If we are desiring creatures, then our worship and discipleship should be directed toward forming and directing that desire to find

1. I explore more concrete implications for worship and discipleship in my *Who's Afraid of Postmodernism? A Radical Orthodoxy for the Emerging Church,* Critical Theory for the Postmodern Church (Baker Academic, forthcoming).

261

its *telos* in God, countering the malformations of desire effected by the state and the market.

- If the claims of secular modernity and its institutions are in fact theological and antithetical to the claims of the gospel, then we must develop in the saints, through effective modes of Christian formation, a critical awareness of the pseudo-theologies lurking behind seemingly neutral phenomena.
- If we are working from a participatory or creational ontology, then our worship should reflect the rich sacramental and aesthetic heritage of the church, affirming that God meets the whole person in a full-bodied revelation.
- If the church is a unique *polis*, then the saints should be formed in such a way that relativizes their allegiances to the state, market, or any other antithetical *polis* that seeks their ultimate allegiance.

These are only hints of where Radical Orthodoxy should push us to reconsider our faith and practice in a post-secular world. My goal here has been to provide a map for such a task; its enactment requires ecclesial travelers willing to launch excursions into this post-secular territory.

Bibliography

This bibliography was first compiled with the assistance of Shannon Schutt Nason, includes contributions from Kristen Deede Johnson, and has been significantly updated and organized by Jerry Stutzman. An electronic version of this bibliography, with updates, is found at www.radicalorthodoxy.org. Works include both proponents and critics. Reviews for the RO series appear in parentheses after the listing. For other reviews of listed books, see below under "Articles and Reviews."

Books

Radical Orthodoxy Series (Routledge)

Bell, Daniel M., Jr. *Liberation Theology after the End of History: The Refusal to Cease Suffering*. London: Routledge, 2001.

Cunningham, Conor. *Genealogy of Nihilism*. London: Routledge, 2002.

Hanby, Michael. *Augustine and Modernity*. London: Routledge, 2003.

Long, D. Stephen. *Divine Economy: Theology and the Market*. London: Routledge, 2000. (John Atherton, *Theology* 104 [2001]; M. Douglas Meeks, *Journal of the American Academy of Religion* 70 [2002]; Paul Oslington, *Markets and Morality* 4 [2001]; and Jonathan Rothchild, *Journal of Religion* 82 [2002].)

Milbank, John. *Being Reconciled: Ontology and Pardon*. London: Routledge, 2003.

———, and Catherine Pickstock. *Truth in Aquinas*. London: Routledge, 2001. (David B. Burrell, "Recent Scholarship on Aquinas," *Modern Theology* 18 [2002]; Christine Helmer, *International Journal of Systematic Theology* 5 [2003]; Mark D. Jordan, *Journal of Religion* 83 [2003]; Anthony Kenny, *Times Literary Supplement* 5140 [2001]; Bruce D. Marshall, *Thomist* 66 [2002]; Aidan Nichols, *Theology* 104 [2001]; and Thomas Weinandy, *Expository Times* 113 [2001].)

————, Catherine Pickstock, and Graham Ward, eds. *Radical Orthodoxy: A New Theology*. London: Routledge, 1999. (Deane Baker, *Journal of Theology for Southern Africa* 109 [2001]; Jeffrey L. Bullock, *Theology Today* 57 [2000]; David Cloutier, *Pro Ecclesia* 9 [2000]; David S. Cunningham, *Christian Century* 116 [1999]; Douglas Farrow, *Neue Zeitschrift für Systematische Theologie und Religionsphilosophie* 42 [2000]; Douglas Hedley, *Journal of Theological Studies* 51 [2000]; Paul Helm, *Scottish Bulletin of Evangelical Theology* 19 [2001]; Ron Highfield, *Restoration Quarterly* 42 [2000]; Gavin Hyman, *New Blackfriars* 80 [1999]; David Jasper, *Literature and Theology* 13 [1999]; Gareth Jones, *Times Literary Supplement* 5009 [1999]; Paul O'Grady, *Religious Studies* 36 [2000]; John Reader, *Expository Times* 111 [1999]; Russell R. Reno, *Modern Theology* 15 [1999]; Vaughan S. Roberts, *Modern Believing* 40 [1999]; C. Schnekloth, *Word & World* 21 [2001]; and Henry W. Spaulding, *Wesleyan Theological Journal* 35 [2000].)

Miner, Robert C. *Truth in the Making: Knowledge and Creation in Modern Philosophy and Theology*. London: Routledge, 2003.

Rowland, Tracy. *Culture and the Thomist Tradition: After Vatican II*. London: Routledge, 2003.

Smith, James K. A. *Speech and Theology: Language and Logic of Incarnation*. London: Routledge, 2002. (*Reviews in Religion and Theology* 10 [2003]; Sue Patterson, *International Journal of Systematic Theology* 6 [2004]; L. Renwort, *Nouvelle Revue Théologique* 125 [2003]; Merold Westphal, *Modern Theology* 20 [2004]; and William D. Wood, *Sophia* 42 [2003]).

Ward, Graham. *Cities of God*. London: Routledge, 2000. (M. J. Bullimore, *New Blackfriars* 82 [2001]; Stephen Carr, *Theology* 104 [2001]; William T. Cavanaugh, *Modern Theology* 18 [2002]; Mark D. Chapman, *Expository Times* 112 [2001]; Timothy J. Gorringe, *Scottish Journal of Theology* 55 [2002]; David Jasper, *Literature and Theology* 16 [2002]; and William W. Young, *Journal of Religion* 82 [2002].)

Radical Orthodoxy

Blond, Phillip, ed. *Post-secular Philosophy: Between Philosophy and Theology*. London: Routledge, 1998.

Cavanaugh, William T. *Torture and Eucharist: Theology, Politics, and the Body of Christ*. Oxford: Blackwell, 1998.

Long, D. Stephen. *The Goodness of God: Theology, Church, and the Social Order*. Grand Rapids: Brazos, 2001.

Loughlin, Gerard. *Telling God's Story: Bible, Church, and Narrative Theology*. Cambridge: Cambridge University Press, 1996.

Milbank, John. *The Religious Dimensions in the Thought of Giambattista Vico, 1668–1744. Part 1. The Early Metaphysics*. Lewiston, N.Y.: Mellen, 1991.

————. *The Religious Dimensions in the Thought of Giambattista Vico, 1668–1744. Part 2. Language, Law, and History*. Lewiston, N.Y.: Mellen, 1992.

————. *Theology and Social Theory: Beyond Secular Reason*. Oxford: Blackwell, 1990.

————. *The Word Made Strange: Theology, Language, Culture*. Oxford: Blackwell, 1997.

———, Graham Ward, and Edith Wyschogrod. *Theological Perspectives on God and Beauty.* Harrisburg, Pa.: Trinity Press International, 2003.

Pickstock, Catherine. *After Writing: On the Liturgical Consummation of Philosophy.* Oxford: Blackwell, 1998.

———. *Ascending Numbers.* Oxford: Westview, 2001.

———. *A Short Guide to Plato.* Oxford: Oxford University Press, forthcoming.

Ward, Graham. *Barth, Derrida, and the Language of Theology.* Cambridge: Cambridge University Press, 1995.

———. *The Postmodern God: A Theological Reader.* Oxford: Blackwell, 1997.

———. *Theology and Contemporary Critical Theory: Creating Transcendent Worship Today.* 2nd ed. New York: St. Martin's Press, 1999.

———. *True Religion.* Blackwell Manifestos. Oxford: Blackwell, 2003.

Extensive Responses to Radical Orthodoxy

Clayton, Crockett. *A Theology of the Sublime.* London: Routledge, 2001.

Hankey, William J., and Douglas Hedley. *Radical Orthodoxy: Rhetoric or Truth, an Introduction to Reading Philosophical Theology.* Forthcoming.

Hemming, Laurence Paul, ed. *Radical Orthodoxy? A Catholic Enquiry.* Burlington, Vt.: Ashgate, 2000.

Hyman, Gavin. *The Predicament of Postmodern Theology: Radical Orthodoxy or Nihilist Textualism?* Louisville: Westminster John Knox, 2001.

Smith, James K. A., and James H. Olthuis, eds. *Creation, Covenant, and Participation: Radical Orthodoxy and the Reformed Tradition.* Grand Rapids: Baker Academic, forthcoming.

Limited Responses to Radical Orthodoxy

Cunningham, David S. *These Three Are One: The Practice of Trinitarian Theology.* Oxford: Basil Blackwell, 1998.

Hauerwas, Stanley. *Wilderness Wanderings: Probing Twentieth-Century Theology and Philosophy.* Boulder: Westview, 1997.

Insole, Christopher. *The Politics of Human Frailty: A Theological Defense of Political Liberalism.* South Bend: SCM/Notre Dame Press, forthcoming.

Jones, L. Gregory. *Embodying Forgiveness: A Theological Analysis.* Grand Rapids: Eerdmans, 1995.

McGrath, Alister E. *A Scientific Theology.* Vol. 2, *Reality.* Grand Rapids: Eerdmans, 2002.

Rose, Gillian. *The Broken Middle: Out of Our Ancient Society.* Oxford: Blackwell, 1992.

———. *Judaism and Modernity: Philosophical Essays.* Oxford: Blackwell, 1993.

Toole, David. *Waiting for Godot in Sarajevo: Theological Reflections on Nihilism, Tragedy, and Apocalypse.* Boulder: Westview, 1998.

Webber, Robert E. *The Younger Evangelicals.* Grand Rapids: Baker, 2002.

Articles

Andonegui, Javier. "Escoto en el punto de mira." *Antonianum* 76 (2001): 145–91.
Baker, Anthony D. "Theology and the Crisis of Darwinism." *Modern Theology* 18 (2002): 183–215.
Balcomb, Anthony O. "Is God in South Africa or Are We Still Clearing Our Throats?" *Journal of Theology for Southern Africa* 111 (2001): 57–65.
Barrett, Alastair. "'Find a Space': Theodramatic Hermeneutics in Church and World." *Modern Believing* 43 (2002): 32–39.
Bauerschmidt, Frederick C. "Aesthetics: The Theological Sublime." In *Radical Orthodoxy: A New Theology*, edited by John Milbank, Catherine Pickstock, and Graham Ward, 201–19. London: Routledge, 1999.
———. "The Politics of Disenchantment." *New Blackfriars* 82 (2001): 313–34.
———. "The Word Made Speculative? John Milbank's Christological Poetics." *Modern Theology* 15 (1999): 417–32.
Bell, Daniel. "'Men of Stone and Children of Struggle': Latin American Liberationists at the End of History." *Modern Theology* 14 (1998): 113–41.
———. "The Insurrectional Reserve: Latin American Liberationists, Eschatology, and the Catholic Moment." *Communio* 27 (2000): 643–75.
———. "Sacrifice and Suffering: Beyond Justice, Human Rights, and Capitalism." *Modern Theology* 18 (2002): 333–59.
———. "What Gift Is Given? A Response to Volf." *Modern Theology* 19 (2003): 271–80.
Blond, Phillip. "Perception: From Modern Painting to the Vision of Christ." In *Radical Orthodoxy: A New Theology*, edited by John Milbank, Catherine Pickstock, and Graham Ward, 220–42. London: Routledge, 1999.
———. "The Primacy of Theology and the Question of Perception." In *Religion, Modernity, and Postmodernity*, edited by Paul Heelas and David Martin, 285–313. Oxford: Blackwell, 1998.
———. "Prolegomena to an Ethics of the Eye." *Studies in Christian Ethics* 16 (2003): 44–60.
———. "Review Essay: The Absolute and the Arbitrary." *Modern Theology* 18 (2002): 277–85.
———. "Theology and Perception." *Modern Theology* 14 (1998): 523–34.
Boer, Roland. "Deutero-Isaiah: Historical Materialism and Biblical Theology." *Biblical Interpretation* 6 (1998): 181–204.
Bowlin, John R. "Augustine on Justifying Coercion." *Annual of the Society of Christian Ethics* 17 (1997): 49–70.
Brown, Frank Burch. "Radical Orthodoxy and the Religion of Others." *Encounter* 63 (2002): 45–53.
Bullimore, Matthew, and John Hughes. "Notes and Commentary: What Is Radical Orthodoxy?" *Telos* 123 (2002): 183–89.
Bullock, Jeffrey L. "A Conversation with Robert Wuthnow and John Milbank." *Theology Today* 57 (2000): 239–52.
Burrell, David B. "An Introduction to *Theology and Social Theory*." *Modern Theology* 8 (1992): 319–29.

Caputo, John D. "What Do I Love When I Love My God? Deconstruction and Radical Orthodoxy." In *Questioning God*, edited by John D. Caputo, Michael Scanlon, and Mark Dooley, 291–317. Bloomington: Indiana University Press, 2001.

Cavanaugh, William T. "The City: Beyond Secular Parodies." In *Radical Orthodoxy: A New Theology*, edited by John Milbank, Catherine Pickstock, and Graham Ward, 182–200. London: Routledge, 1999.

———. "Coercion in Augustine and Disney." *New Blackfriars* 80 (1999): 283–90.

———. "'A Fire Strong Enough to Consume the House': The Wars of Religion and the Rise of the State." *Modern Theology* 11 (1995): 397–420.

———. "A Joint Declaration? Justification as Theosis in Aquinas and Luther." *Heythrop Journal* 41 (2000): 265–80.

———. "The World in a Wafer: A Geography of the Eucharist as Resistance to Globalization." *Modern Theology* 15 (1999): 181–96.

Coles, Romand. "Storied Others and Possibilities of Caritas: Milbank and Neo-Nietzschean Ethics." *Modern Theology* 8 (1992): 331–51.

———. "Thinking the Impossible: Derrida and the Divine." *Literature and Theology* 14 (2000): 313–34.

Collins, Guy. "Defending Derrida: A Response to Milbank and Pickstock." *Scottish Journal of Theology* 54 (2001): 344–65.

Cross, Richard. "'Where Angels Fear to Tread': Duns Scotus and Radical Orthodoxy." *Antonianum* 76 (2001): 7–41.

Cunningham, Conor. "The Difference of Theology and Some Philosophies of Nothing." *Modern Theology* 17 (2001): 289–312.

———. "Jacques Lacan, Philosophy's Difference, and Creation from No-One." *American Catholic Philosophical Quarterly* (forthcoming).

———. "Language: Wittgenstein after Theology." In *Radical Orthodoxy: A New Theology*, edited by John Milbank, Catherine Pickstock, and Graham Ward, 64–90. London: Routledge, 1999.

Cunningham, David S. "The New Orthodoxy?" *Christian Century* (November 1999): 1127–29.

Daniels, John. "Not the Whole Story: Another Response to John Milbank's *Theology and Social Theory*." *New Blackfriars* 82 (2001): 188–96.

———. "Not the Whole Story: Another Response to John Milbank's *Theology and Social Theory*, Part 2." *New Blackfriars* 82 (2001): 224–40.

D'Costa, Gavin. "Seeking after Theological Vision." *Reviews in Religion and Theology* 6 (1999): 354–60.

Desmond, William. "Review of *After Writing*." *Modern Theology* 15 (1999): 99–101.

Dixon, Thomas. "Theology, Anti-Theology, and Atheology: From Christian Passions to Secular Emotions." *Modern Theology* 15 (1999): 297–330.

Dodaro, Robert. "Augustine's Secular City." In *Augustine and His Critics*, edited by Robert Dodaro and George Lawless, 231–59. London: Routledge, 2001.

———. "Loose Canons: Augustine and Derrida on Their Selves." In *God, the Gift, and Postmodernism*, edited by John D. Caputo and Michael J. Scanlon, 79–111. Bloomington: Indiana University Press, 1999.

Doerkson, Paul G. "For and against Milbank: A Critical Discussion of John Milbank's Construal of Ontological Peace." *Conrad Grebel Review* 18 (2000): 48–59.

Dooley, Mark. "The Catastrophe of Memory: Derrida, Milbank and the (Im)possibility of Forgiveness." In *Questioning God*, edited by John D. Caputo, Michael Scanlon, and Mark Dooley, 129–49. Bloomington: Indiana University Press, 2001.

Douglas, Mary. "The Eucharist: Its Continuity with the Bread Sacrifice of Leviticus." *Modern Theology* 15 (1999): 209–24.

Finn, Daniel Rush. "Catholic Social Thought and Contemporary Economic Thinking." Paper, Commonweal Spring 2002 Colloquium, New York, April 19–21, 2002.

Flanagan, Kieran. "A Sociological Critique of Milbank." In *Theology and Sociology: A Reader*, edited by Robin Gill, 451–60. 2nd ed. New York, Cassell, 1996.

Ford, David F. "British Theology: Movements and Churches." *Christian Century* 117 (April 2000): 467–73.

———. "Radical Orthodoxy and the Future of British Theology." *Scottish Journal of Theology* 54 (2001): 385–404.

———. "A Response to Catherine Pickstock." *Scottish Journal of Theology* 54 (2001): 423–25.

———. "Theological Wisdom, British Style." *Christian Century* 117 (2000): 388–91.

Geroux, Robert J. "A New Theology? Radical Orthodoxy, Modernity, and Tragedy." In *The European Legacy*. Forthcoming.

Godzieba, Anthony J. "Fear and Loathing in Modernity: The Voyages of Captain John Milbank." *Philosophy and Theology* 9 (1996): 419–33.

———. "Prolegomena to a Catholic Theology of God between Heidegger and Postmodernity." *Heythrop Journal* 40 (1999): 319–39.

Gunton, Colin. "Editorial: Orthodoxy." *International Journal of Systematic Theology* 1 (1999): 113–18.

Guretzki, David. "Barth, Derrida, and Difference: Is There a Difference?" *Didaskalia* 13 (2002): 50–71.

Hanby, Michael. "Desire: Augustine beyond Western Subjectivity." In *Radical Orthodoxy: A New Theology*, edited by John Milbank, Catherine Pickstock, and Graham Ward, 109–26. London: Routledge, 1999.

Hankey, Wayne. "Between and beyond Augustine and Descartes: More Than a Source of the Self." *Augustinian Studies* 32 (2001): 65–88.

———. "Theoria Versus Poesis: Neoplatonism and Trinitarian Difference in Aquinas, John Milbank, Jean-Luc Marion, and John Zizioulas." *Modern Theology* 15 (1999): 387–415.

———. "Why Philosophy Abides for Aquinas." *Heythorp Journal* 42 (2001): 329–48.

Hart, Kevin. *Mystery Today, Orthodoxy Today*. Edinburgh: T & T Clark, forthcoming.

———. "Response to Graham Ward." In *Sacramental Presence in a Postmodern Context*, edited by Lieven Boeve and Lamber Leijssen, 205–11. Leuven: Peeters Publishing, 2001.

Hauerwas, Stanley. "Explaining Christian Nonviolence: Notes for a Conversation with John Milbank." In *Must Christianity Be Violent? Reflections on History, Practice, and Theology*, edited by Kenneth R. Chase and Alan Jacobs, 172–82. Grand Rapids: Brazos, 2003.

———. "On Being 'Placed' by John Milbank: A Response." In *Christ, Ethics, and Tragedy*, edited by Kenneth Surin, 197–201. Cambridge: Cambridge University Press, 1989.

Hawkins, Alex. "Beyond Narrative Theology: John Milbank and Gerhard Loughlin as the Non-Identical Repetition of Hans Frei." *Koinonia* 10 (1998): 61–87.

Hedley, Douglas. "Should Divinity Overcome Metaphysics? Reflections on John Milbank's 'Theology beyond Secular Reason' and 'Confessions of a Cambridge Platonist.'" *Journal of Religion* 80 (2000): 271–98.

Heilke, Thomas. "On Being Ethical without Moral Sadism: Two Readings of Augustine and the Beginnings of the Anabaptist Revolution." *Political Theory* 24 (1996): 493–517.

Hemming, Laurence Paul. "Heidegger's God." *Thomist* 62 (1998): 373–418.

———. "More Than Just a Ticklish Subject: History, Postmodernity, and God." *Heythrop Journal* 42 (2001): 192–204.

———. "Nihilism: Heidegger and the Grounds of Redemption." In *Radical Orthodoxy: A New Theology*, edited by John Milbank, Catherine Pickstock, and Graham Ward, 91–108. London: Routledge, 1999.

———. "Speaking out of Turn: Martin Heidegger and 'die Kehre.'" *International Journal of Philosophical Studies* 6 (1998): 393–423.

———. "Who Is Heidegger's Zarathustra?" *Literature and Theology* 12 (1998): 268–93.

Herbert, David. "Christian Ethics, Community, and Modernity." *Modern Believing* 39 (1998): 44–52.

———. "Getting by in Babylon: MacIntyre, Milbank, and a Christian Response to Religious Diversity in the Public Arena." *Studies in Christian Doctrine* 10 (1997): 61–81.

Hollerich, Michael J. "John Milbank, Augustine, and the Secular." *Augustinian Studies* 30 (1999): 311–26.

Huculak, Benedykt. "De Mature Augustiniano Opere Joannis Duns Scoti." *Antonianum* 76 (2001): 429–78.

Huebner, Chris K. "Can a Gift Be Commanded? Theological Ethics without Theory, by Way of Barth, Milbank, and Yoder." *Scottish Journal of Theology* 53 (2000): 472–89.

Hughes, Kevin L. "The 'Fourfold Sense': De Lubac, Blondel, and Contemporary Theology." *Heythrop Journal* 42 (2001): 451–62.

Hütter, Reinhard. "The Church's Peace beyond the 'Secular': A Postmodern Augustinian's Deconstruction of Secular Modernity and Postmodernity." *Pro Ecclesia* 2 (Winter 1993): 106–16.

Hyman, Gavin. "John Milbank and Nihilism: A Metaphysical (Mis)Reading?" *Literature and Theology* 14 (2000): 430–43.

Irwin, Kevin W. "Critiquing Recent Liturgical Critics." *Worship* 74 (2000): 2–19.

Joas, Hans. "Social Theory and the Sacred: A Response to John Milbank." *Ethical Perspectives* 7 (2001): 233–43.

Jobling, J'annine. "On the Liberal Consummation of Theology: A Dialogue with Catherine Pickstock." In *Theological Liberalism*, edited by J'annine Jobling and Ian Markham, 15–30. London: SPCK, 2000.

Jones, Irwin. "Deconstructing God: Defending Derrida against Radical Orthodoxy."
    In *Explorations in Contemporary Continental Philosophy of Religion*, edited by
    Deane-Peter Baker and Patrick Maxwell, 35–48. New York: Rodopi, 2003.
Kaye, Bruce N. "Social Context and Theological Practice: Radical Orthodoxy and
    Richard Hooker." *Sewanee Theological Review* 45 (2002): 385–98.
Kerr, Fergus. "Rescuing Girard's Argument?" *Modern Theology* 8 (1992): 385–99.
———. "Reviews: *Word Made Strange; The Liturgical Consummation of Philosophy;
    Post-secular Philosophy*." *New Blackfriars* 79 (1998): 352–58.
———. "Transubstantiation after Wittgenstein." *Modern Theology* 15 (1999):
    115–30.
Kevern, Peter. "My Beloved Is Mine and I Am His: Non-commensurable-giving as
    a Metaphor for the Divine-Human Relationship." *New Blackfriars* 83 (2002):
    574–83.
Lakeland, Paul. "Mysticism and Politics: The Work of John Milbank." *Philosophy
    and Theology* 13 (1996): 455–59.
Large, Will. "Inverted Kantianism and Interiority: A Critical Comment on Milbank's
    Theology." In *Explorations in Contemporary Continental Philosophy of Religion*,
    edited by Deane-Peter Baker and Patrick Maxwell, 23–34. New York: Rodopi,
    2003.
Lash, Nicholas. "Not Exactly Politics or Power?" *Modern Theology* 8 (1992): 353–
    64.
———. "Where Does Holy Teaching Leave Philosophy? Questions on Milbank's
    Aquinas." *Modern Theology* 15 (1999): 433–45.
Leithart, Peter J. "Can Radicals Be Orthodox?" *Weekly Standard* (November 15,
    1999): 36–39.
———. "Making and Mis-Making: Poiesis in Exodus 25–40." *International Journal
    of Systematic Theology* 2 (2000): 307–18.
———. "Review of *After Writing*." *Westminster Theological Journal* 61 (1999):
    303–7.
———. "Review of *The Word Made Strange*." *Westminster Theological Journal* 60
    (1998): 175–78.
Long, D. Stephen. "Bernard Dempsey's Theological Economics: Usury, Profit, and
    Human Fulfillment." *Theological Studies* 57 (1996): 690–706.
———. "Called to Take Up Arms? The Service of the Other." *Word & World* 15 (1995):
    483–85.
———. "Charity and Justice: Christian Economy and the Just Ordering of the Com-
    mandments." *Communio* 25 (1998): 14–28.
———. "A Global Market—A Catholic Church: The New Political (Ir)Realism."
    Theology Today 52 (1995): 356–65.
———. "Making Theology Moral." *Scottish Journal of Theology* 52 (1999): 306–27.
———. "Pledging Allegiance." *Regeneration Quarterly* 1 (1995): 32.
———. "Radical Orthodoxy." In *The Cambridge Companion to Postmodern Theology*,
    edited by Kevin J. Vanhoozer, 65–85. Cambridge: Cambridge University Press,
    2003.
———. "Radical Orthodoxy and Methodism." *Quarterly Review* 23 (2003).
Loughlin, Gerard. "Christianity at the End of the Story or the Return of the Master-
    Narrative." *Modern Theology* 8 (1992): 365–84.

———. "Erotics: God's Sex." In *Radical Orthodoxy: A New Theology*, edited by John Milbank, Catherine Pickstock, and Graham Ward, 143–62. London: Routledge, 1999.

———. "Living in Christ: Story, Resurrection, and Salvation." In *Resurrection Considered*, 118–34. Oxford: One World, 1996.

Macquarrie, John. "Postmodernism in Philosophy of Religion and Theology." *International Journal for Philosophy of Religion* 50 (2001): 9–27.

Malcolm, Lois. "Recovering Theology's Voice: Radical, Orthodox." *Christian Century* 117 (2000): 1074–79.

Martin, David. "The Stripping of Words: Conflict over the Eucharist in the Episcopal Church." *Modern Theology* 15 (1999): 247–61.

Mattes, Mark C. "A Lutheran Assessment of Radical Orthodoxy." *Lutheran Quarterly* 15 (2001): 354–67.

McCabe, Herbert O. P. "The Eucharist as Language." *Modern Theology* 15 (1999): 131–41.

Milbank, John. "Against the Resignations of the Age: Social Space and Time in Socialism, Catholic Social Thought." In *Things Old and New: Catholic Social Teaching Revisited*, edited by Francis P. McHugh and Samuel M. Natale, 1–39. Lanham, Md.: University Press of America, 1993.

———. "Between Purgation and Illumination: A Critique of the Theology of Right." In *Christ, Ethics, and Tragedy*, edited by Kenneth Surin, 161–96. Cambridge: Cambridge University Press, 1989.

———. "The Body of Love Possessed: Christianity and Late Capitalism in Britain." *Modern Theology* 3 (1986): 35–65.

———. "Can a Gift Be Given? Prolegomena to a Future Trinitarian Metaphysics." In *Rethinking Metaphysics*, edited by Gregory L. Jones, 119–61. Cambridge: Blackwell, 1995.

———. "Can Morality Be Christian?" *Studies in Christian Ethics* 8 (1995): 45–59.

———. "Christ the Exception." *New Blackfriars* 82 (2001): 541–56.

———. "Enclaves, or Where Is the Church?" *New Blackfriars* 73 (1992): 341–52.

———. "The End of Dialogue." In *Christian Uniqueness Reconsidered: The Myth of a Pluralistic Theology of Religions*, edited by Gavin D'Costa, 174–91. Maryknoll, N.Y.: Orbis, 1990.

———. "The End of Enlightenment: Post-modern or Post-secular?" In *The Debate on Modernity*, edited by Claude Geffrè and Jean Pierre Jossua, 39–48. London: SCM, 1992.

———. "An Essay against Secular Order." *Journal of Religious Ethics* 15 (1987): 199–224.

———. "The Ethics of Self-Sacrifice." *First Things* 91 (1999): 33–38.

———. "Forgiveness and Incarnation." In *Questioning God*, edited by John D. Caputo, Michael Scanlon, and Mark Dooley, 92–128. Bloomington: Indiana University Press, 2001.

———. "Gregory of Nyssa: The Force of Identity." In *Studies in Christian Origins*, edited by L. Ayres and G. Jones, 94–116. London: Routledge, 1998.

———. "Intensities." *Modern Theology* 15 (1999): 445–97.

———. "'I Will Gasp and Pant': Deutero-Isaiah and the Birth of the Suffering Subject." *Semeia* 59 (1992): 59–71.

———. "Knowledge: The Theological Critique of Philosophy in Hamann and Jacobi." In *Radical Orthodoxy: A New Theology*, edited by John Milbank, Catherine Pickstock, and Graham Ward, 21–37. London: Routledge, 1999.

———. "Man as Creative and Historical Being in the Theology of Nicholas of Cusa." *Downside Review* 97 (1979): 245–57.

———. "Materialism and Transcendence." In *Theology and the Political*, edited by Creston Davis, John Milbank, and Slavoj Žižek. Durham, N.C.: Duke University Press, forthcoming.

———. "The Name of Jesus: Incarnation, Atonement, Ecclesiology." *Modern Theology* 7 (1991): 311–33.

———. "Only Theology Overcomes Metaphysics." *New Blackfriars* 76 (1995): 325–42.

———. "Out of the Greenhouse." *New Blackfriars* 74 (1993): 4–14.

———. "Postmodernité." In *Dictionnare Critique de Théologie*, edited by J. Y. Lacoste, 916–17. Paris: Cerf, 1998.

———. "Problematizing the Secular: The Post-Postmodern Agenda." In *Shadow of Spirit*, edited by Philippa Berry, 30–44. New York: Routledge, 1992.

———. "The Programme of Radical Orthodoxy." In *Radical Orthodoxy? A Catholic Enquiry*, edited by Laurence Paul Hemming, 33–45. Burlington, Vt.: Ashgate, 2000.

———. "Radical Orthodoxy: Participation, Political, and Metaphysical." In *Liberal Democracy and Religion*. Forthcoming.

———. "Sacred Triads: Augustine and the Indo-European Soul." *Modern Theology* 13 (1997): 451–74.

———. "The Second Difference: For a Trinitarianism without Reserve." *Modern Theology* 2 (1986): 213–34.

———. "A Socialist Economic Order." *Theology* 91 (1988): 412–15.

———. "The Soul of Reciprocity, Part 1: Reciprocity Refused." *Modern Theology* 17 (2001): 335–91.

———. "The Soul of Reciprocity, Part 2: Reciprocity Granted." *Modern Theology* 17 (2001): 485–507.

———. "Spaemann, Glueck, and Wohlwollen." *Studies in Christian Ethics* 8 (1995): 84–92.

———. "Stories of Sacrifice." *Modern Theology* 12 (1996): 27–56.

———. "The Sublime in Kierkegaard." *Heythrop Journal* 37 (1996): 298–321.

———. "Sublimity: The Modern Transcendent." In *Religion, Modernity, and Postmodernity*, edited by Paul Heelas, 258–84. Oxford: Blackwell, 1998.

———. "Theology without Substance: Christianity, Signs, Origins," part 1. *Literature and Theology* 2 (1998): 1–17.

———. "Theology without Substance: Christianity, Signs, Origins," part 2. *Literature and Theology* 2 (1998): 131–52.

———. "Towards a Christological Poetics." *Downside Review* 100 (1982): 1–21.

———. "Violence: Double Passivity." In *Must Christianity Be Violent? Reflections on History, Practice, and Theology*, edited by Kenneth R. Chase and Alan Jacobs, 201–6. Grand Rapids: Brazos, 2003.

———. "William Warburton: An Eighteenth-Century Bishop Fallen among the Post-Structuralists." *New Blackfriars* 64 (1983): 315–24.

———, and Stanley Hauerwas. "Christian Peace: A Conversation between Stanley Hauerwas and John Milbank." In *Must Christianity Be Violent? Reflections on History, Practice, and Theology,* edited by Kenneth R. Chase and Alan Jacobs, 207–23. Grand Rapids: Brazos, 2003.

———, and Paul Morris, eds. "The Sacred Word: Religious Theories of Language." *Literature and Theology* 3 (1989): 138–250.

Minney, Penelope. "Dostoevsky's Dialogic Imagination and the British School of Radical Orthodoxy." *Dostoevsky Journal* 2 (2001).

Montag, John. "Revelation: The False Legacy of Suárez." In *Radical Orthodoxy: A New Theology,* edited by John Milbank, Catherine Pickstock, and Graham Ward, 38–63. London: Routledge, 1999.

Moss, David. "Difference—the Immaculate Concept? The Laws of Sexual Difference in the Theology of Hans Urs von Balthasar." *Modern Theology* 14 (1998): 377–401.

———. "Friendship." In *Christian Spirituality: An Introduction,* edited by Alister McGrath, 31–46. London: SPCK, 1999.

———. "Friendship: St. Anselm, *theoria,* and the Convolution of the State." In *Radical Orthodoxy: A New Theology,* edited by John Milbank, Catherine Pickstock, and Graham Ward, 127–42. London: Routledge, 1999.

Murphy, Debra Dean. "Power, Politics, and Difference: A Feminist Response to John Milbank." *Modern Theology* 10 (1994): 131–42.

Murray, David. "Baptizing Postmodernism." *Crisis* (February 2000): 42–44.

Newey, Edmund. "The Form of Reason: Participation in the Work of Richard Hooker, Benjamin Whichcote, Ralph Cudworth, and Jeremy Taylor." *Modern Theology* 18 (2002): 1–26.

Nichols, Aidan. "Hymns Ancient and Postmodern: Catherine Pickstock's *After Writing.*" *Communio: International Catholic Review* 26 (1999): 429–45.

O'Grady, Paul. "Anti-Foundationalism and Radical Orthodoxy." *New Blackfriars* 81 (2000): 160–76.

———. "Review of *Radical Orthodoxy: A New Theology.*" *Religious Studies* 36 (2000): 227–31.

Ormerod, Neil. "'It Is Easy to See': The Footnotes of John Milbank." *Philosophy and Theology* 11 (1999): 257–64.

———. "System, History, and a Theology of Ministry." *Theological Studies* 61 (2000): 432–46.

Oviedo, Lluis. "Il Dibattito Contemporaneo su Scoto e la Sua Eredità." *Antonianum* 76 (2001): 3–196.

———. "La teologia de J Milbank y la 'Radical Orthodoxy.'" *Antonianum* 74 (1999): 545–53.

Pabst, Adrian. "De la Chrétien à la Modernite? Lecture-critique des Theses de Radical Orthodoxy sûr la Rupture Scotiste et Ockamienne et le Renouveau de la Théologie de Saint Thomas d'Aquin." *Revue des sciences Philosophiques et Théologiques* 86 (2002): 561–99.

Pickstock, Catherine. "Ascending Numbers: Augustine's *De Musica* and the Western Tradition." In *Studies in Christian Origins,* edited by L. Ayres and G. Jones, 185–215. London: Routledge, 1998.

———. "Asyndeton: Syntax and Insanity: A Study of the Revision of the Nicene Creed." *Modern Theology* 10 (1994): 321–40.

————. "Imitating God: The Truth of Things according to Aquinas." *New Blackfriars* 81 (2000): 308–26.

————. "Justice and Prudence: Principles of Order in the Platonic City." *Heythrop Journal* 42 (2001): 269–82.

————. "Liturgy and Language: The Sacred Polis." In *Liturgy in Dialogue,* edited by Paul Bradshaw and Bryan Spinks, 115–37. London: SPCK, 1993.

————. "Liturgy and Modernity." *Telos* 113 (1998): 19–41.

————. "Liturgy, Art, and Politics." *Modern Theology* 16 (2000): 159–80.

————. "Modernity and Scholasticism: A Critique of Recent Invocations of Univocity." *Antonianum* 78 (2003): 3–47.

————. "Music: Soul, City, and Cosmos after Augustine." In *Radical Orthodoxy: A New Theology,* edited by John Milbank, Catherine Pickstock, and Graham Ward, 243–77. London: Routledge, 1999.

————. "Necrophilia: The Middle of Modernity: A Study of Death, Signs, and the Eucharist." *Modern Theology* 12 (1996): 405–33.

————. "Plato's Deconstruction of Derrida." *Telos* 107 (1996): 9–43.

————. "Postmodern Theology?" *Telos* 110 (1998): 167–80.

————. "The Problem of Reported Speech: Friendship and Philosophy in Plato's Lysis and Symposium." *New Blackfriars* 82 (2001): 525–40.

————. "Reply to David Ford and Guy Collins." *Scottish Journal of Theology* 54 (2001): 405–22.

————. "Rethinking the Self." *Telos* 112 (1998): 161–78.

————. "A Sermon for Saint Cecilia." *Theology* 100 (1996): 411–18.

————. "The Soul in Plato." In *Explorations in Contemporary Continental Philosophy of Religion*, edited by Deane-Peter Baker and Patrick Maxwell, 115–26. New York: Rodopi, 2003.

————. "Thomas Aquinas and the Quest for the Eucharist." *Modern Theology* 15 (1999): 159–81.

Preston, Ronald. "Christian Socialism Becalmed." *Theology* 91 (1988): 24–32.

Rashkover, Randi. "The Semiotics of Embodiment: Radical Orthodoxy and Jewish-Christian Relations." *Journal of Cultural and Religious Theory* 3 (2002), www.jcrt.org.

Rasmussen, Barry G. "Radical Orthodoxy, Luther, and the Challenge of Western Secularization." *Dialog: A Journal of Theology* 41 (2002): 135–48.

Reno, R. R. "The Radical Orthodoxy Project." *First Things* 100 (2000): 37–44.

————. Review of *The Word Made Strange: Theology, Language, Culture*, by John Milbank. *Pro Ecclesia* 8 (1999): 231–38.

Roberts, Richard. "Transcendental Sociology? A Critique of John Milbank's *Theology and Social Theory: Beyond Secular Reason.*" *Scottish Journal of Theology* 46 (1993): 527–35.

Rubin, Miri. "Whose Eucharist? Eucharistic Identity as Historical Subject." *Modern Theology* 15 (1999): 209–24.

Scott, Peter. "'Global Capitalism' vs. 'End of Socialism': Crux Theologica? Engaging Liberation Theology and Theological Postliberalism." *Psychology and Theology* 4 (2001): 36–54.

Shakespeare, Steven. "The New Romantics: A Critique of Radical Orthodoxy." *Theology* 103 (2000): 163–77.

Sharlet, Jeff. "Theologians Seek to Reclaim the World with God and Postmodernism." *Chronicle of Higher Education* (June 23, 2000): A20–22.

Smith, James K. A. "Between Predication and Silence: Augustine on How (Not) to Speak of God." *Heythrop Journal* 41 (2000): 66–86.

———. "Confessions of an Existentialist: Reading Augustine after Heidegger." *New Blackfriars* 82 (2001): 123–39.

———. "Determined Violence: Derrida's Structural Religion." *Journal of Religion* 78 (1998): 197–212.

———. "How (Not) to Tell a Secret: Interiority and the Strategy of 'Confession.'" *American Catholic Philosophical Quarterly* 74 (2000): 135–51.

———. "How to Avoid Not Speaking: Attestations." In *Knowing Other-Wise*, edited by James H. Olthuis, 217–34. New York: Fordham University Press, 1997.

———. "Liberating Religion from Theology: Marion and Heidegger on the Possibility of a Phenomenology of Religion." *International Journal for Philosophy of Religion* 46 (1999): 17–33.

———. "A Little Story about Metanarratives: Lyotard, Religion, and Postmodernism Revisited." *Faith and Philosophy* 18 (2001): 261–76.

———. "A Principle of Incarnation in Derrida's *(Theologische?) Jugendschriften.*" *Modern Theology* 18 (2002): 217–30.

———. "Re-Kanting Postmodernism? Derrida's Religion within the Limits of Reason Alone." *Faith and Philosophy* 17 (2000): 558–71.

———. "Respect and Donation: A Critique of Marion's Critique of Husserl." *American Catholic Philosophical Quarterly* 71 (1997): 523–38.

———. "Review of Gavin Hyman, *The Predicament of Postmodern Theology: Radical Orthodoxy or Nihilist Textualism?*" *New Blackfriars* 83 (2002): 545–47.

———. "Staging the Incarnation: Revisioning Augustine's Critique of Theater." *Literature and Theology* 15 (2001): 129–39.

———. "The Time of Language: The Fall to Interpretation in Early Augustine." *American Catholic Philosophical Quarterly* 72 (1998): 185–99.

Spjuth, Roland. "Gudstro Bortom Modern Metafysik—en Jamforelse Mellan Jean-Luc Marions och John Milbanks Postmoderna Teologier." *Svensk Teologisk Kvartalskrift* 72 (1996): 158–67.

———. "Redemption without Actuality: A Critical Interrelation between Eberhard Jüngel's and John Milbank's Ontological Endeavours." *Modern Theology* 14 (1998): 505–22.

Stevenson, Kenneth. "Review of *After Writing.*" *Journal of Theological Studies* 50 (1999): 452–55.

Taylor, Simon J. "Keep Taking the Medicine: Radical Orthodoxy and the Future of Theology (review)." *Modern Believing* 41 (2000): 34–40.

Thompson, Ross. "Immanence Unknown: Graham Ward and the New-Pagans." *Theology* 95 (1992): 18–26.

———. "Postmodernism and the 'Trinity': How to Be Postmodern and Post-Barthian Too." *New Blackfriars* 83 (2002): 173–87.

Tolson, Jay. "Academia Gets Religion Again." *U.S. News & World Report*, August 28, 2000, 52.

Turner, Denys. "The Darkness of God and the Light of Christ: Negative Theology and Eucharistic Presence." *Modern Theology* 15 (1999): 143–58.

Venard, Olivier-Thomas, O. P. "Radical Orthodoxy: Une Première Impression." *Revue Thomiste* 101 (2001): 409–44.

Volf, Miroslav. "Against a Pretentious Church: A Rejoinder to Bell's Response." *Modern Theology* 19 (2003): 281–85.

———. *"Liberation Theology after the End of History*: An Exchange." *Modern Theology* 19 (2003): 261–69.

Ward, Graham. "Allegoria: Reading as Spiritual Exercise." In *Revelation and Story*, edited by Gerhard Sauter and John Barton, 99–125. Burlington, Vt.: Ashgate, 2000.

———. "Barth, Modernity, and Postmodernity." In *Cambridge Companion to Karl Barth*, edited by John Webster, 274–95. New York: Cambridge University Press, 2000.

———. "Between Postmodernism and Postmodernity: The Theology of Jean-Luc Marion." In *Postmodernity, Sociology, and Religion*, edited by Kieran Flanagan and Peter C. Jupp, 190–205. London: Macmillan, 1996.

———. "Between Virtue and Virtuality." *Theology Today* 59 (2002): 55–70.

———. "Biblical Narrative and the Theology of Metonymy." *Modern Theology* 7 (1991): 335–49.

———. "Bodies: The Displaced Body of Jesus Christ." In *Radical Orthodoxy: A New Theology*, edited by John Milbank, Catherine Pickstock, and Graham Ward, 163–81. London: Routledge, 1999.

———. "Church as the Erotic Community." In *Sacramental Presence in a Postmodern Context*, edited by Lieven Boeve and Lamber Leijssen, 167–204. Leuven: Peeters Publishing, 2001.

———. "Deconstructive Theology." In *The Cambridge Companion to Postmodern Theology*, edited by Kevin J. Vanhoozer, 76–91. Cambridge: Cambridge University Press, 2003.

———. "Divinity and Sexuality: Luce Irigaray and Christology." *Modern Theology* 12 (1996): 221–37.

———. "The Erotics of Redemption: After Karl Barth." *Theology and Sexuality* 8 (1998): 52–72.

———. "The Gendered Body of the Jewish Jesus." In *Religion and Sexuality*, edited by Michael A. Hayes, Wendy Porter, and David Tombs, 170–92. Sheffield: Sheffield Academic Press, 1998.

———. "In the Daylight Forever? Language and Silence." In *Silence and the Word: Negative Theology and Incarnation*, edited by Oliver Davies and Denys Turner, 159–84. Cambridge: Cambridge University Press, 2002.

———. "In the Economy of the Divine: A Response to James K. A. Smith." *PNEUMA: Journal of the Society for Pentecostal Studies* 25 (2003): 115–16.

———. "In the Name of the Father and of the Mother: Luce Irigaray and Inclusive Language." *Literature and Theology* 8 (1994): 311–27.

———. "John Milbank's Divina Commedia." *New Blackfriars* 73 (1992): 311–18.

———. "Kenosis and Naming: Beyond Analogy and Towards *Allegoria* and *Amoris*." In *Religion, Modernity, and Postmodernity*, edited by Paul Heelas, 233–57. Oxford: Blackwell, 1998.

———. "Mimesis: The Measure of Mark's Christology." *Literature and Theology* 8 (1994): 1–29.

———. "A Postmodern Version of Paradise." *Journal for the Study of the Old Testament* 65 (1995): 3–12.

———. "Questioning God." In *Questioning God,* edited by John D. Caputo, Michael Scanlon, and Mark Dooley, 274–90. Bloomington: Indiana University Press, 2001.

———. "Religion in the Transformation of Society: Problem or Potential?" *Journal of Theology for South Africa* 104 (1999): 78–80.

———. "The Revelation of the Holy Other as the Wholly Other: Between Barth's Theology of the Word and Levinas's Philosophy of Saying." *Modern Theology* 9 (1993): 159–80.

———. "Sacramental Presence or Neopaganism?" *Theology* 94 (1991): 279–84.

———. "Speaking Otherwise: Postmodern Analogy." In *Rethinking Philosophy of Religion: Approaches from Continental Philosophy,* edited by Philip Goodchild, 187–211. Bronx: Fordham University Press, 2002.

———. "Suffering and Incarnation." In *Blackwell Companion to Postmodern Theology,* edited by Graham Ward, 192–208. Oxford: Blackwell, 2001.

———. "Theological Materialism." In *God and Reality,* edited by Colin Crowder, 144–59. London: Mowbray, 1997.

———. "Theology and Cultural Sadomasochism." *Svensk Teologisk Kvartalskrift* 78 (2002): 2–10.

———. "Theology and Postmodernism." *Theology* 100 (1997): 435–40.

———. "Theology and the Crisis of Representation." In *Literature and Theology at Century's End,* edited by Gregory Salyer and Robert Detweiler, 131–58. Atlanta: Scholars Press, 1995.

———. "To Be a Reader: Bunyan's Struggle with the Language of Scripture in *Grace Abounding to the Chief of Sinners." Literature and Theology* 4 (1990): 29–49.

———. "Tragedy as Subclause: George Steiner's Dialogue with Donald MacKinnon." *Heythrop Journal* 34 (1993): 274–87.

———. "Transcorporeality: The Ontological Scandal." *Bulletin of the John Rylands University Library of Manchester* 80 (1998): 235–52.

———. "Why Is Derrida Important for Theology?" *Theology* 95 (1992): 263–70.

———. "Why Is the City So Important for Christian Theology?" *Cross Currents* 52 (2003): 462–73.

Webb, Stephen H. "Stateside: A North American Perspective on Radical Orthodoxy." *Reviews in Religion and Theology* 8 (2001): 319–25.

Wells, Samuel. "Stanley Hauerwas's Theological Ethics in Eschatological Perspective." *Scottish Journal of Theology* 53 (2000): 431–48.

Name Index

Subject Index